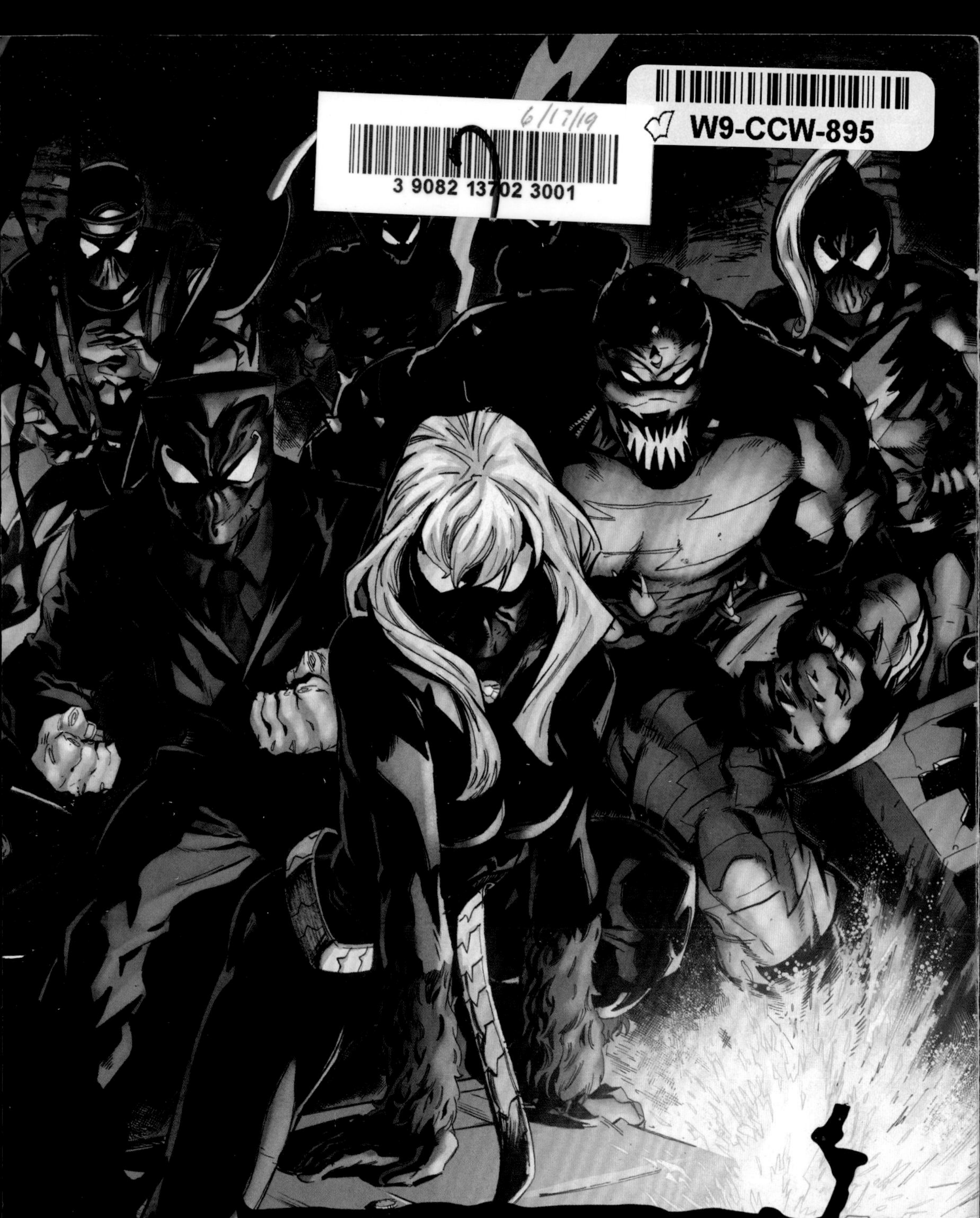

AMAZING SPIDER-MAN:

VENOM INC.

AMAZING SPIDER-MAN: VENOM INC.

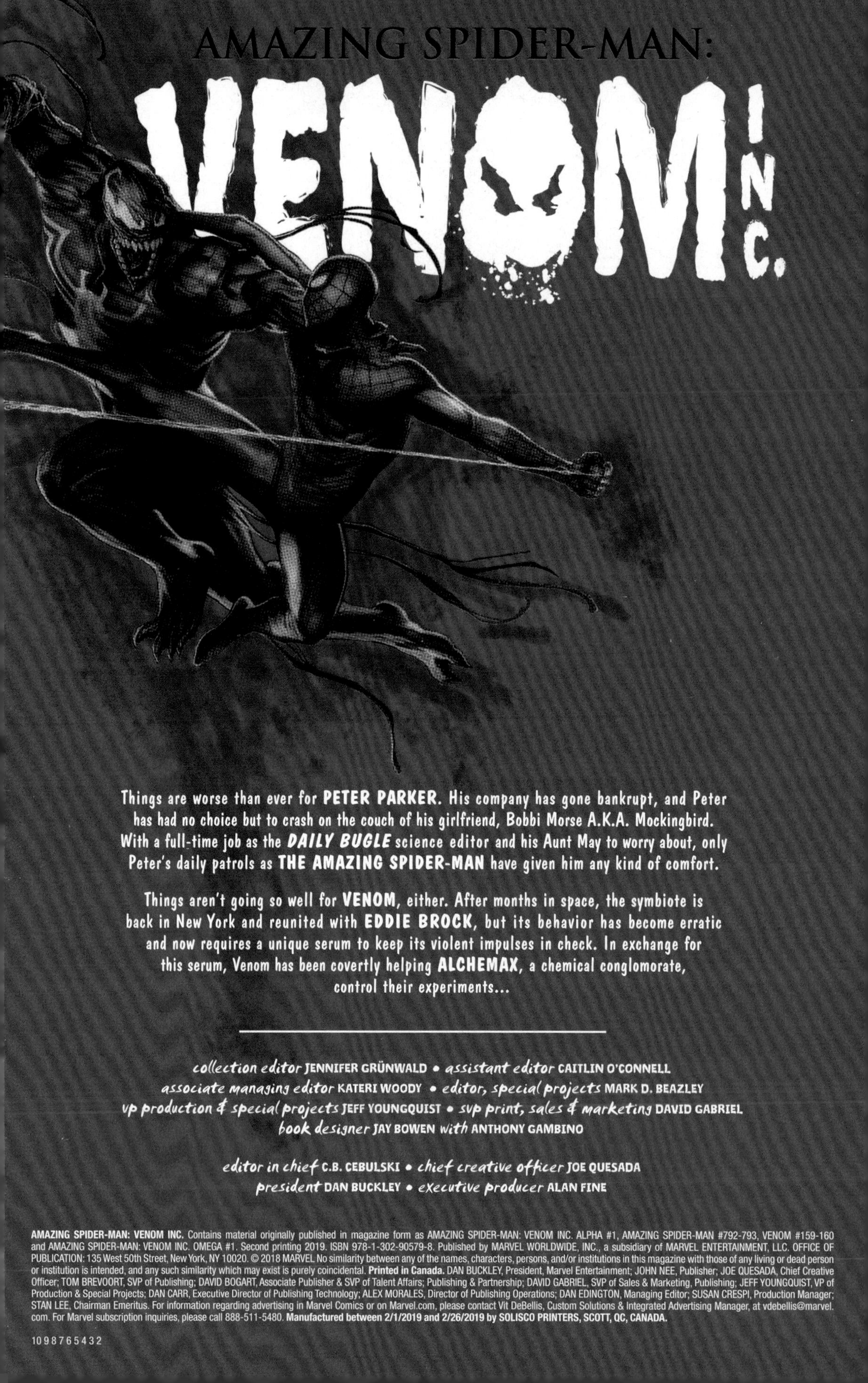

Things are worse than ever for **PETER PARKER**. His company has gone bankrupt, and Peter has had no choice but to crash on the couch of his girlfriend, Bobbi Morse A.K.A. Mockingbird. With a full-time job as the ***DAILY BUGLE*** science editor and his Aunt May to worry about, only Peter's daily patrols as **THE AMAZING SPIDER-MAN** have given him any kind of comfort.

Things aren't going so well for **VENOM**, either. After months in space, the symbiote is back in New York and reunited with **EDDIE BROCK**, but its behavior has become erratic and now requires a unique serum to keep its violent impulses in check. In exchange for this serum, Venom has been covertly helping **ALCHEMAX**, a chemical conglomorate, control their experiments...

---

collection editor JENNIFER GRÜNWALD • *assistant editor* CAITLIN O'CONNELL
associate managing editor KATERI WOODY • *editor, special projects* MARK D. BEAZLEY
vp production & special projects JEFF YOUNGQUIST • *svp print, sales & marketing* DAVID GABRIEL
book designer JAY BOWEN *with* ANTHONY GAMBINO

editor in chief C.B. CEBULSKI • *chief creative officer* JOE QUESADA
president DAN BUCKLEY • *executive producer* ALAN FINE

AMAZING SPIDER-MAN: VENOM INC. Contains material originally published in magazine form as AMAZING SPIDER-MAN: VENOM INC. ALPHA #1, AMAZING SPIDER-MAN #792-793, VENOM #159-160 and AMAZING SPIDER-MAN: VENOM INC. OMEGA #1. Second printing 2019. ISBN 978-1-302-90579-8. Published by MARVEL WORLDWIDE, INC., a subsidiary of MARVEL ENTERTAINMENT, LLC. OFFICE OF PUBLICATION: 135 West 50th Street, New York, NY 10020. © 2018 MARVEL No similarity between any of the names, characters, persons, and/or institutions in this magazine with those of any living or dead person or institution is intended, and any such similarity which may exist is purely coincidental. **Printed in Canada.** DAN BUCKLEY, President, Marvel Entertainment; JOHN NEE, Publisher; JOE QUESADA, Chief Creative Officer; TOM BREVOORT, SVP of Publishing; DAVID BOGART, Associate Publisher & SVP of Talent Affairs; Publishing & Partnership; DAVID GABRIEL, SVP of Sales & Marketing, Publishing; JEFF YOUNGQUIST, VP of Production & Special Projects; DAN CARR, Executive Director of Publishing Technology; ALEX MORALES, Director of Publishing Operations; DAN EDINGTON, Managing Editor; SUSAN CRESPI, Production Manager; STAN LEE, Chairman Emeritus. For information regarding advertising in Marvel Comics or on Marvel.com, please contact Vit DeBellis, Custom Solutions & Integrated Advertising Manager, at vdebellis@marvel.com. For Marvel subscription inquiries, please call 888-511-5480. **Manufactured between 2/1/2019 and 2/26/2019 by SOLISCO PRINTERS, SCOTT, QC, CANADA.**

10 9 8 7 6 5 4 3 2

DAN SLOTT & MIKE COSTA
storytellers

AMAZING SPIDER-MAN: VENOM INC. ALPHA

DAN SLOTT & MIKE COSTA
writers

RYAN STEGMAN
artist

BRIAN REBER
color artist

VC'S JOE **CARAMAGNA**
letterer

RYAN **STEGMAN** & BRIAN **REBER**
cover art

AMAZING SPIDER-MAN 792-793

DAN SLOTT
writer

RYAN STEGMAN
artist

BRIAN REBER
color artist

VC'S JOE **CARAMAGNA**
WITH JOE **SABINO** (#792)
letterer

ALEX **ROSS**
cover art

VENOM 159-160

MIKE COSTA
writer

GERARDO SANDOVAL
artist

DAVID CURIEL
color artist

VC'S CLAYTON **COWLES**
letterer

GERARDO **SANDOVAL**
& DAVID **CURIEL**
cover art

AMAZING SPIDER-MAN: VENOM INC. OMEGA

DAN SLOTT & MIKE COSTA
writers

RYAN **STEGMAN** &
GERARDO **SANDOVAL**
artists

JAY **LEISTEN**
inker

BRIAN **REBER**
color artist

VC'S JOE **CARAMAGNA**
letterer

RYAN **STEGMAN** & BRIAN **REBER**
cover art

assistant .... NEMAN

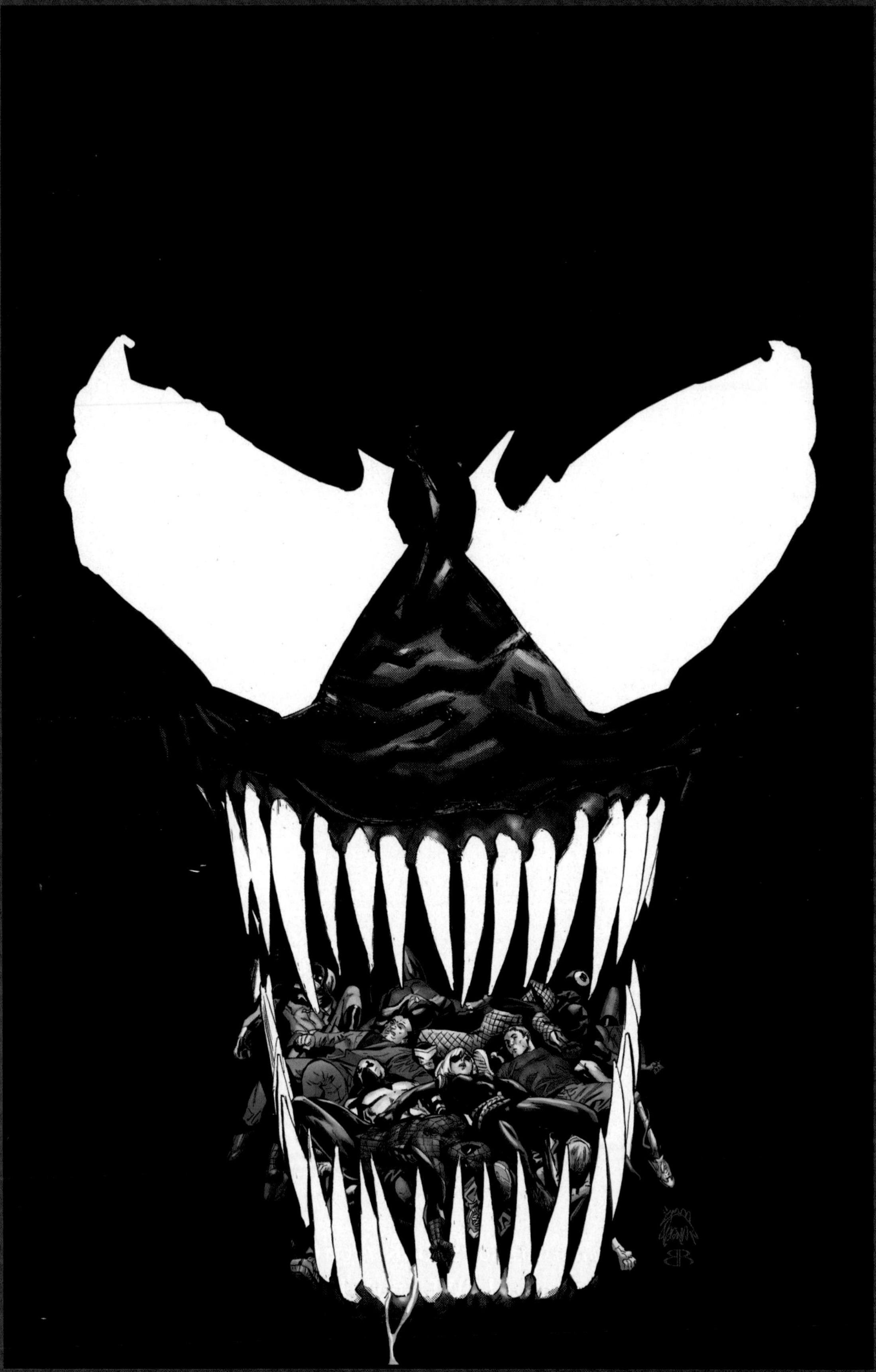

AMAZING SPIDER-MAN: VENOM INC. ALPHA 1

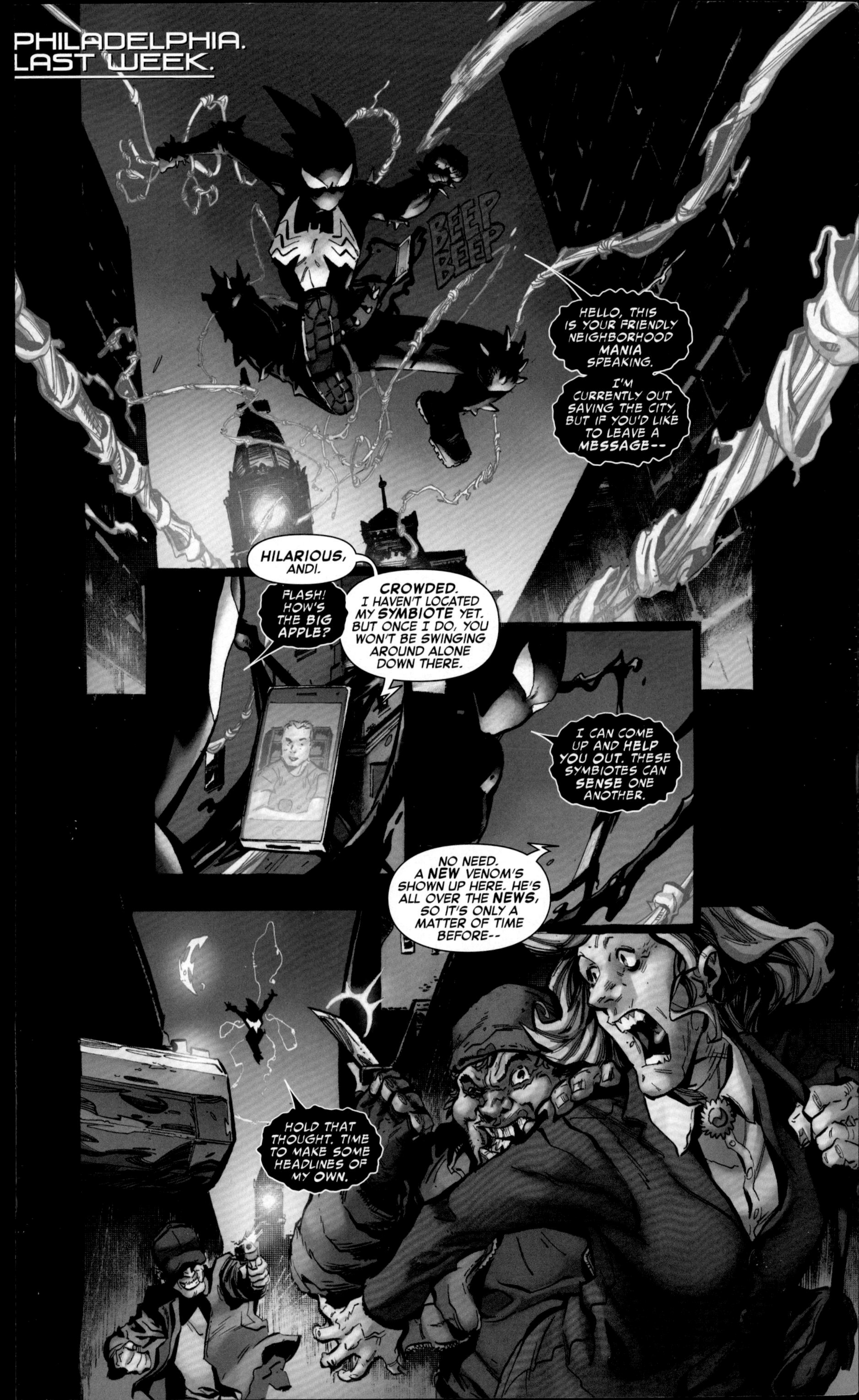
PHILADELPHIA. LAST WEEK.
BEEP BEEP
HELLO, THIS IS YOUR FRIENDLY NEIGHBORHOOD MANIA SPEAKING.
I'M CURRENTLY OUT SAVING THE CITY, BUT IF YOU'D LIKE TO LEAVE A MESSAGE--
HILARIOUS, ANDI.
FLASH! HOW'S THE BIG APPLE?
CROWDED. I HAVEN'T LOCATED MY SYMBIOTE YET. BUT ONCE I DO, YOU WON'T BE SWINGING AROUND ALONE DOWN THERE.
I CAN COME UP AND HELP YOU OUT. THESE SYMBIOTES CAN SENSE ONE ANOTHER.
NO NEED. A NEW VENOM'S SHOWN UP HERE. HE'S ALL OVER THE NEWS, SO IT'S ONLY A MATTER OF TIME BEFORE--
HOLD THAT THOUGHT. TIME TO MAKE SOME HEADLINES OF MY OWN.

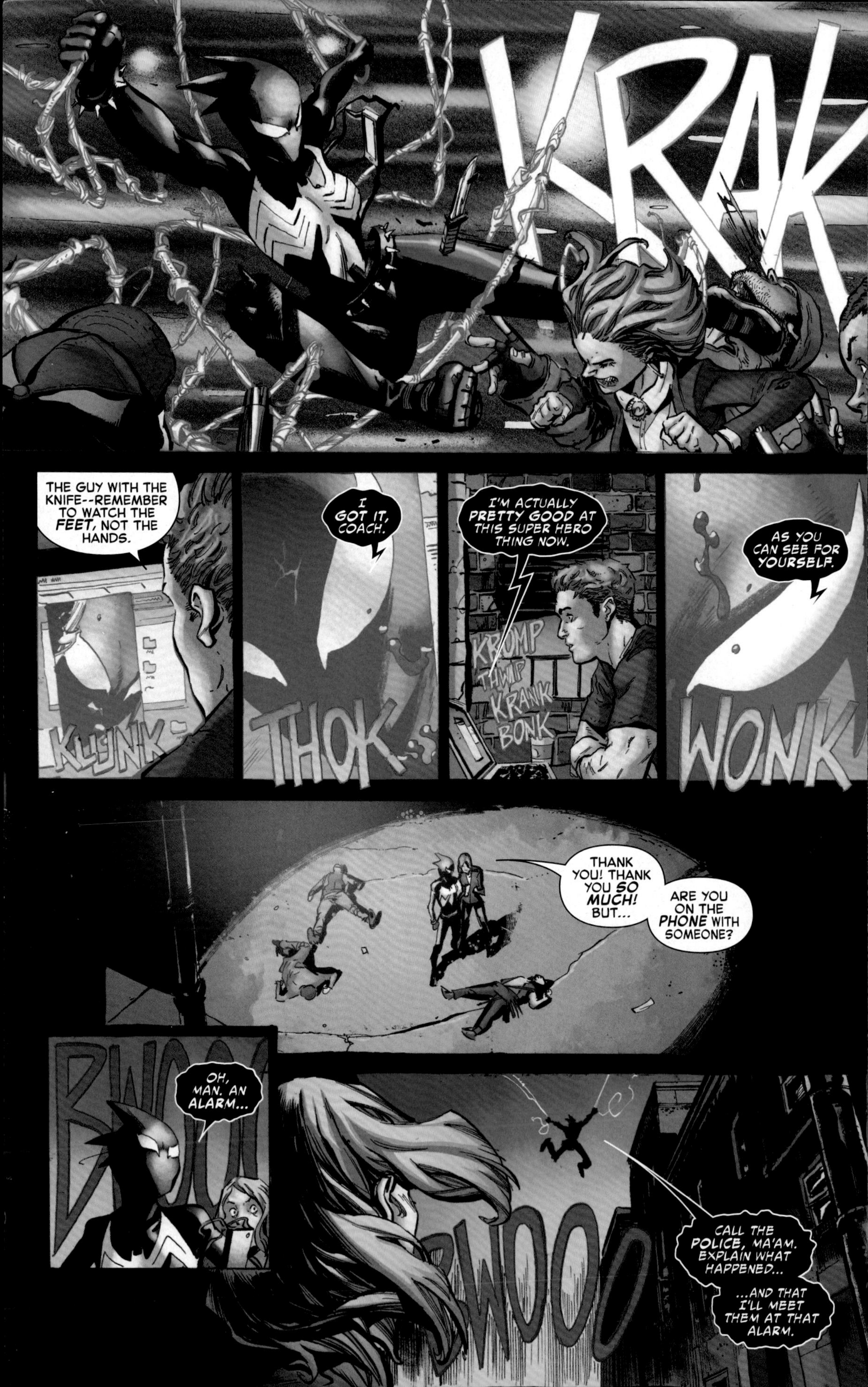

KRAK
THE GUY WITH THE KNIFE--REMEMBER TO WATCH THE FEET, NOT THE HANDS.
KLUNK
I GOT IT, COACH.
THOK
I'M ACTUALLY PRETTY GOOD AT THIS SUPER HERO THING NOW.
KROMP
THWIP
KRANK
BONK
AS YOU CAN SEE FOR YOURSELF.
WONK
THANK YOU! THANK YOU SO MUCH! BUT...
ARE YOU ON THE PHONE WITH SOMEONE?
OH, MAN. AN ALARM...
BWOOOO
CALL THE POLICE, MA'AM. EXPLAIN WHAT HAPPENED...
...AND THAT I'LL MEET THEM AT THAT ALARM.

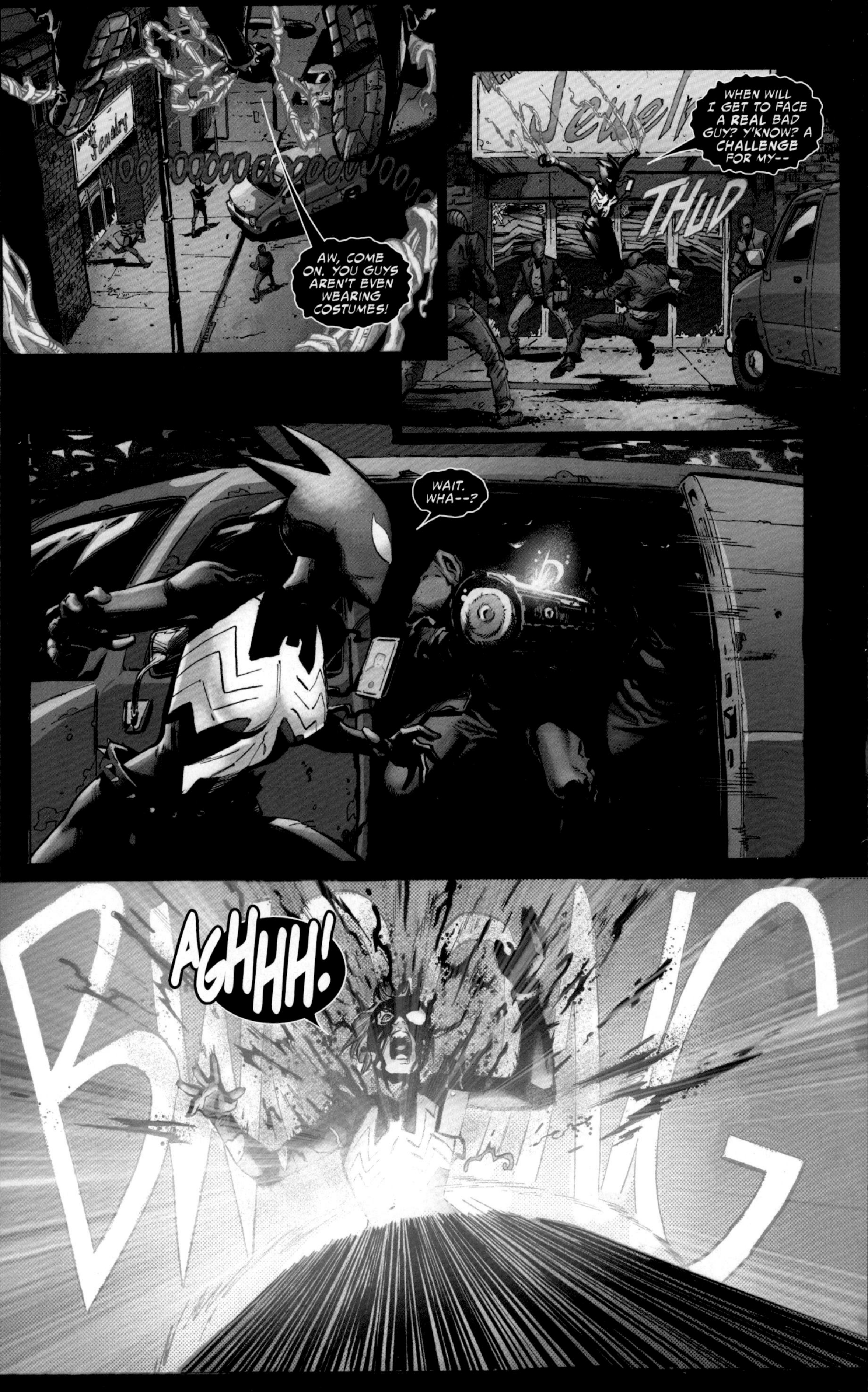
WOOOOOOOOOOOOOOOOOO
AW, COME ON. YOU GUYS AREN'T EVEN WEARING COSTUMES!
WHEN WILL I GET TO FACE A REAL BAD GUY? Y'KNOW? A CHALLENGE FOR MY--
THUD
WAIT. WHA--?
AGHHH!

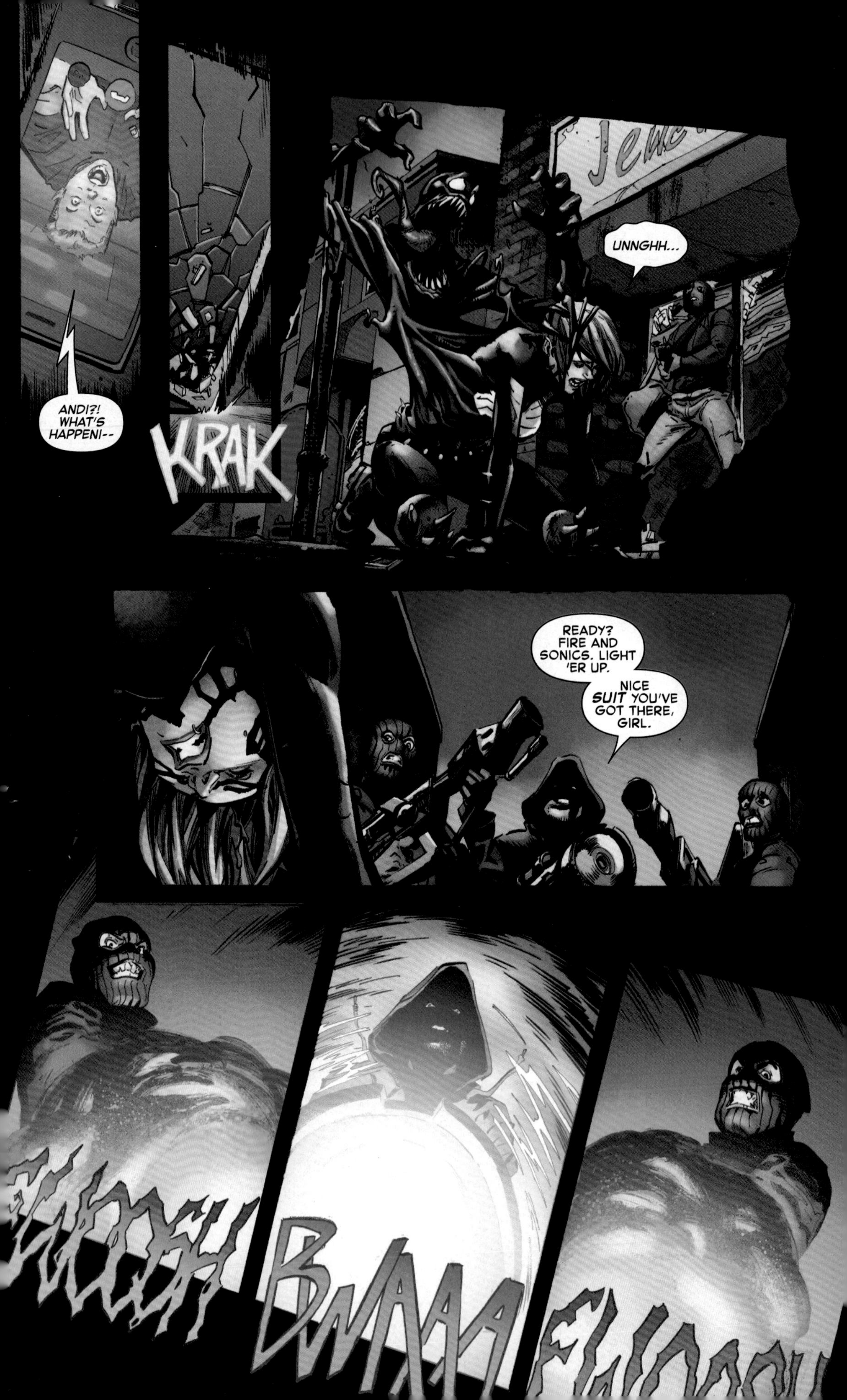
ANDI?! WHAT'S HAPPENI--
KRAK
UNNGHH...
READY? FIRE AND SONICS. LIGHT 'ER UP.
NICE SUIT YOU'VE GOT THERE, GIRL.

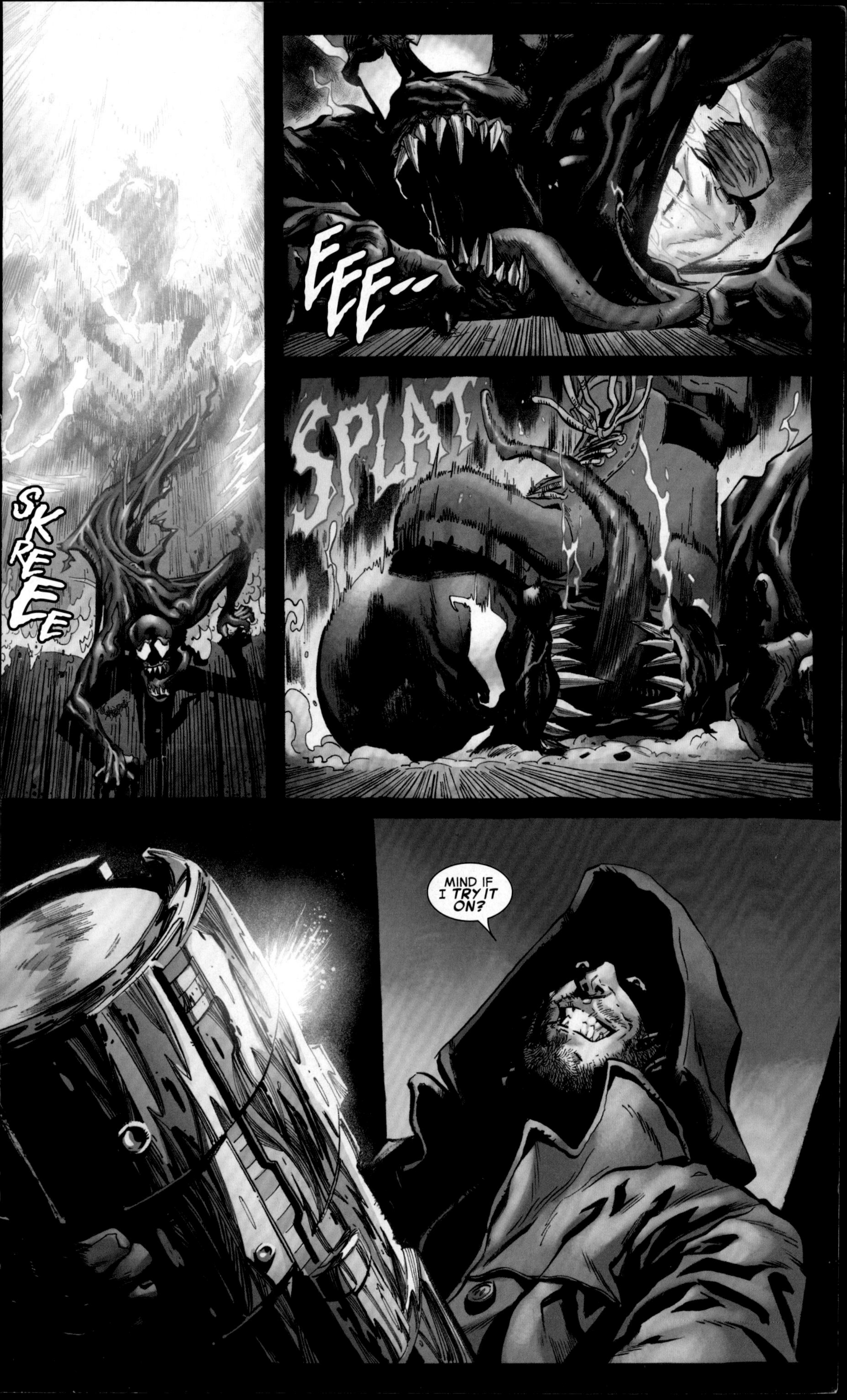
SKREEEE
EEE--
SPLAT
MIND IF I TRY IT ON?

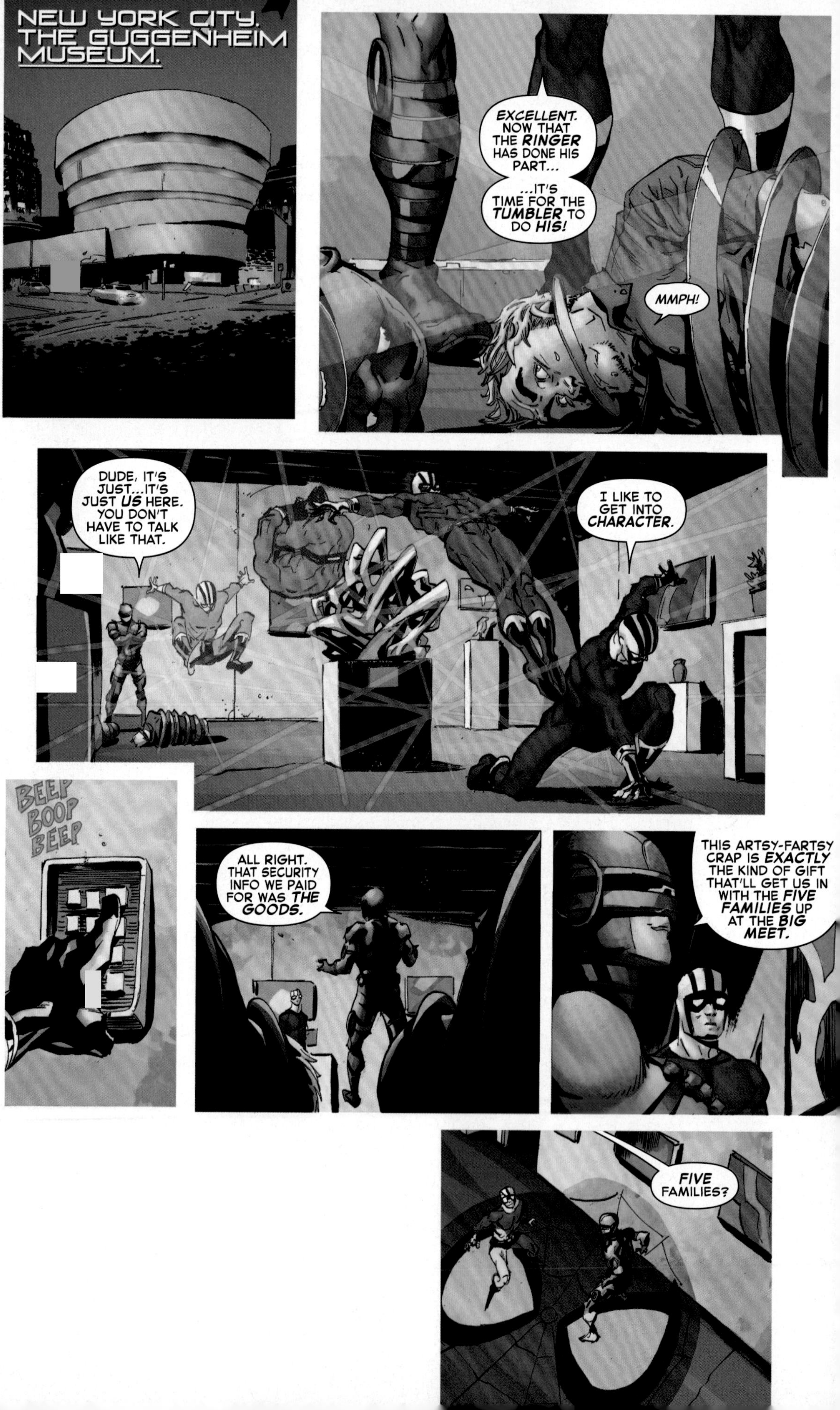
NEW YORK CITY. THE GUGGENHEIM MUSEUM.
EXCELLENT. NOW THAT THE RINGER HAS DONE HIS PART...
...IT'S TIME FOR THE TUMBLER TO DO HIS!
MMPH!
DUDE, IT'S JUST...IT'S JUST US HERE. YOU DON'T HAVE TO TALK LIKE THAT.
I LIKE TO GET INTO CHARACTER.
BEEP BOOP BEEP
ALL RIGHT. THAT SECURITY INFO WE PAID FOR WAS THE GOODS.
THIS ARTSY-FARTSY CRAP IS EXACTLY THE KIND OF GIFT THAT'LL GET US IN WITH THE FIVE FAMILIES UP AT THE BIG MEET.
FIVE FAMILIES?

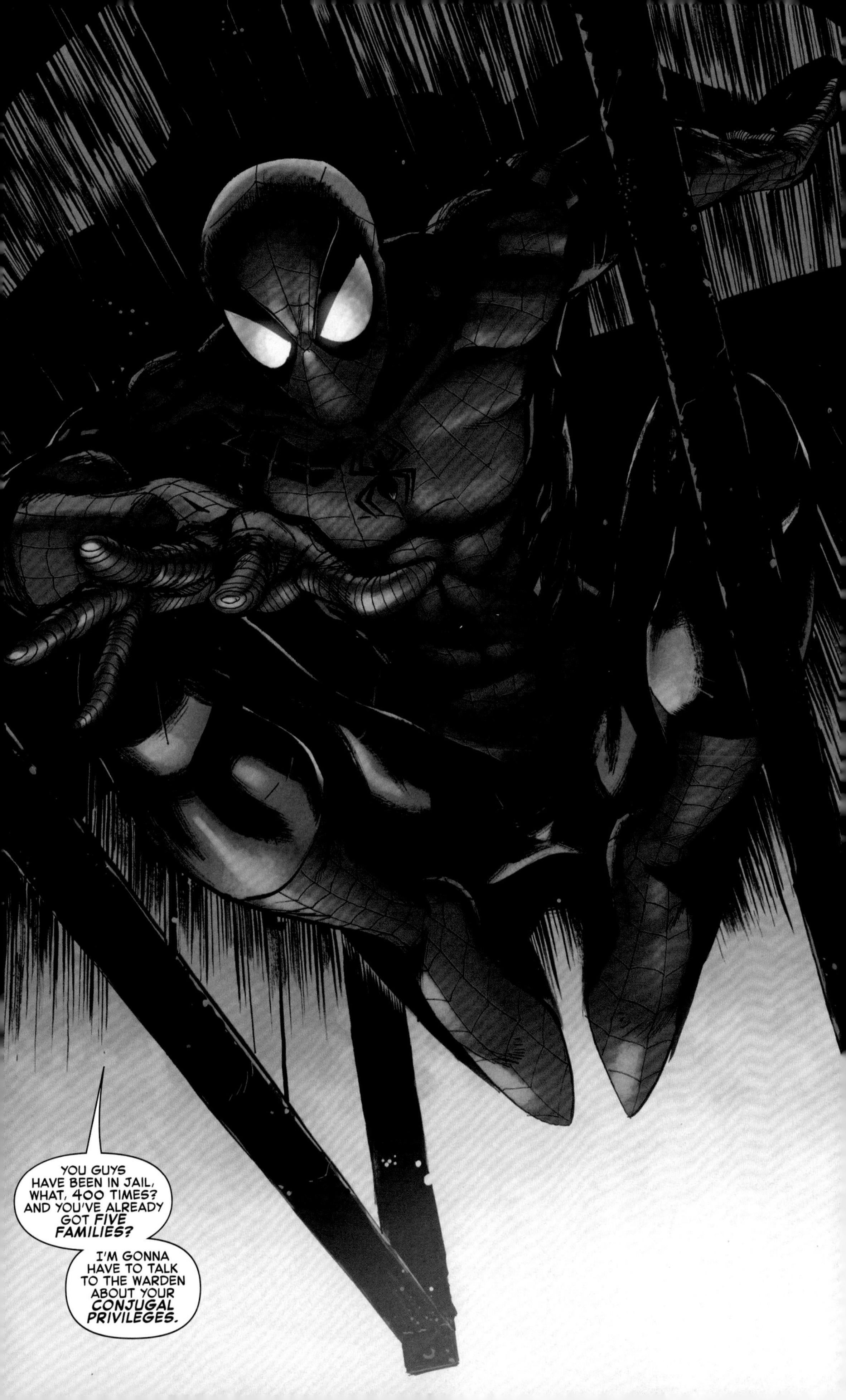
YOU GUYS HAVE BEEN IN JAIL, WHAT, 400 TIMES? AND YOU'VE ALREADY GOT *FIVE FAMILIES?*
I'M GONNA HAVE TO TALK TO THE WARDEN ABOUT YOUR *CONJUGAL PRIVILEGES.*

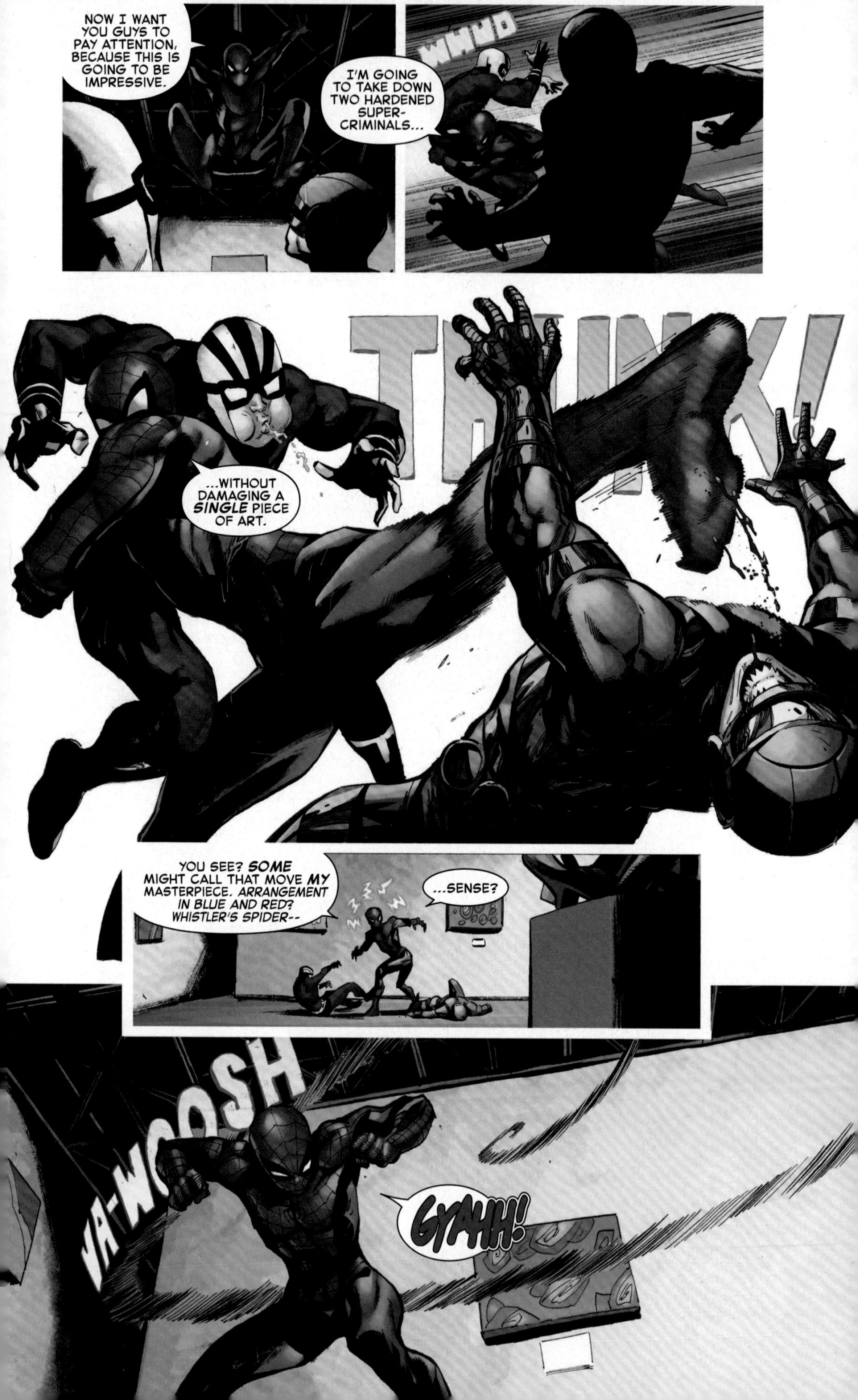
NOW I WANT YOU GUYS TO PAY ATTENTION, BECAUSE THIS IS GOING TO BE IMPRESSIVE.
I'M GOING TO TAKE DOWN TWO HARDENED SUPER-CRIMINALS...
...WITHOUT DAMAGING A *SINGLE* PIECE OF ART.
YOU SEE? *SOME* MIGHT CALL THAT MOVE *MY* MASTERPIECE. *ARRANGEMENT IN BLUE AND RED? WHISTLER'S SPIDER--*
...SENSE?
VA-WOOSH
GYAHH!

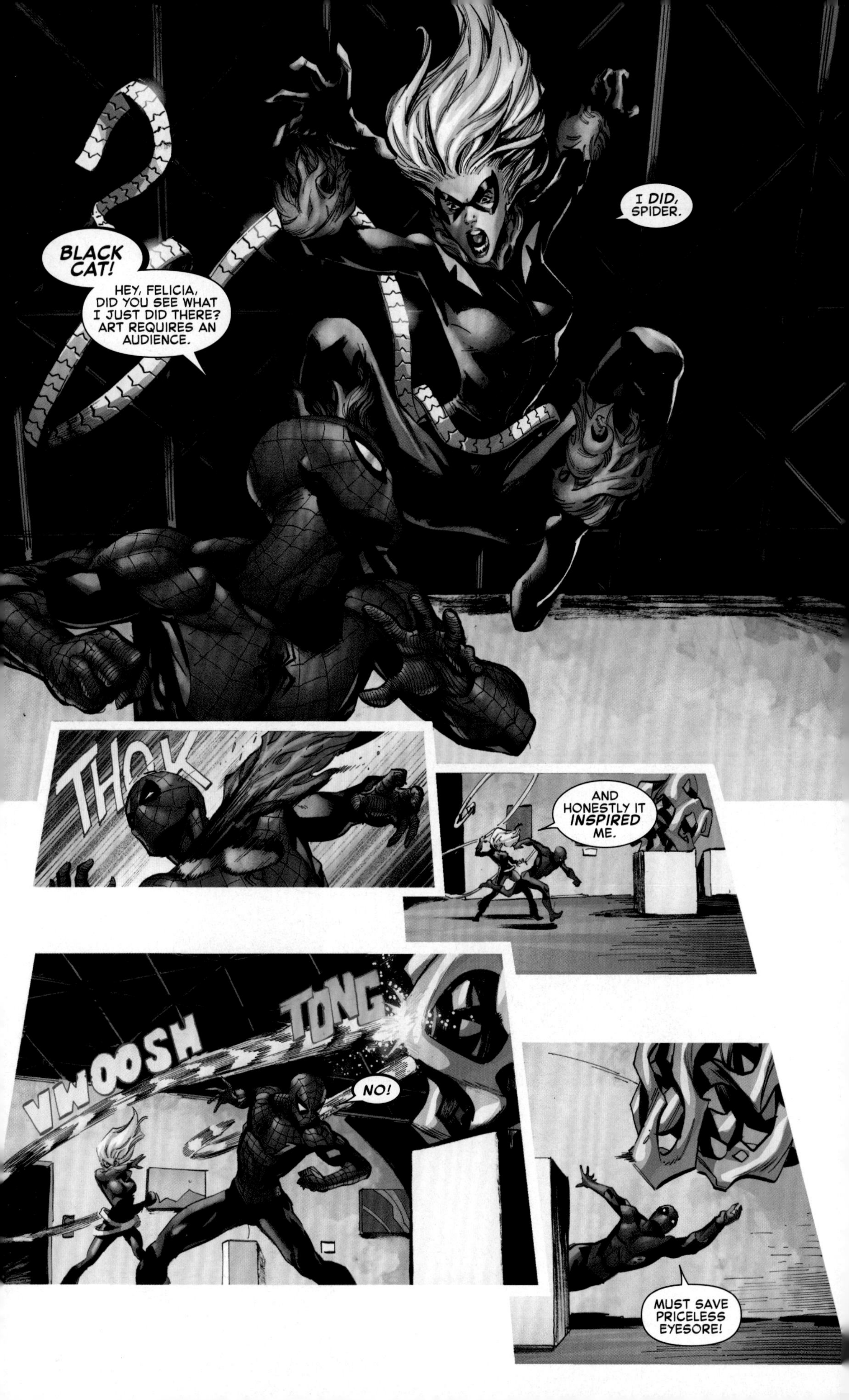
BLACK CAT!
HEY, FELICIA, DID YOU SEE WHAT I JUST DID THERE? ART REQUIRES AN AUDIENCE.
I DID, SPIDER.
THOK
AND HONESTLY IT INSPIRED ME.
VWOOSH
TONG
NO!
MUST SAVE PRICELESS EYESORE!

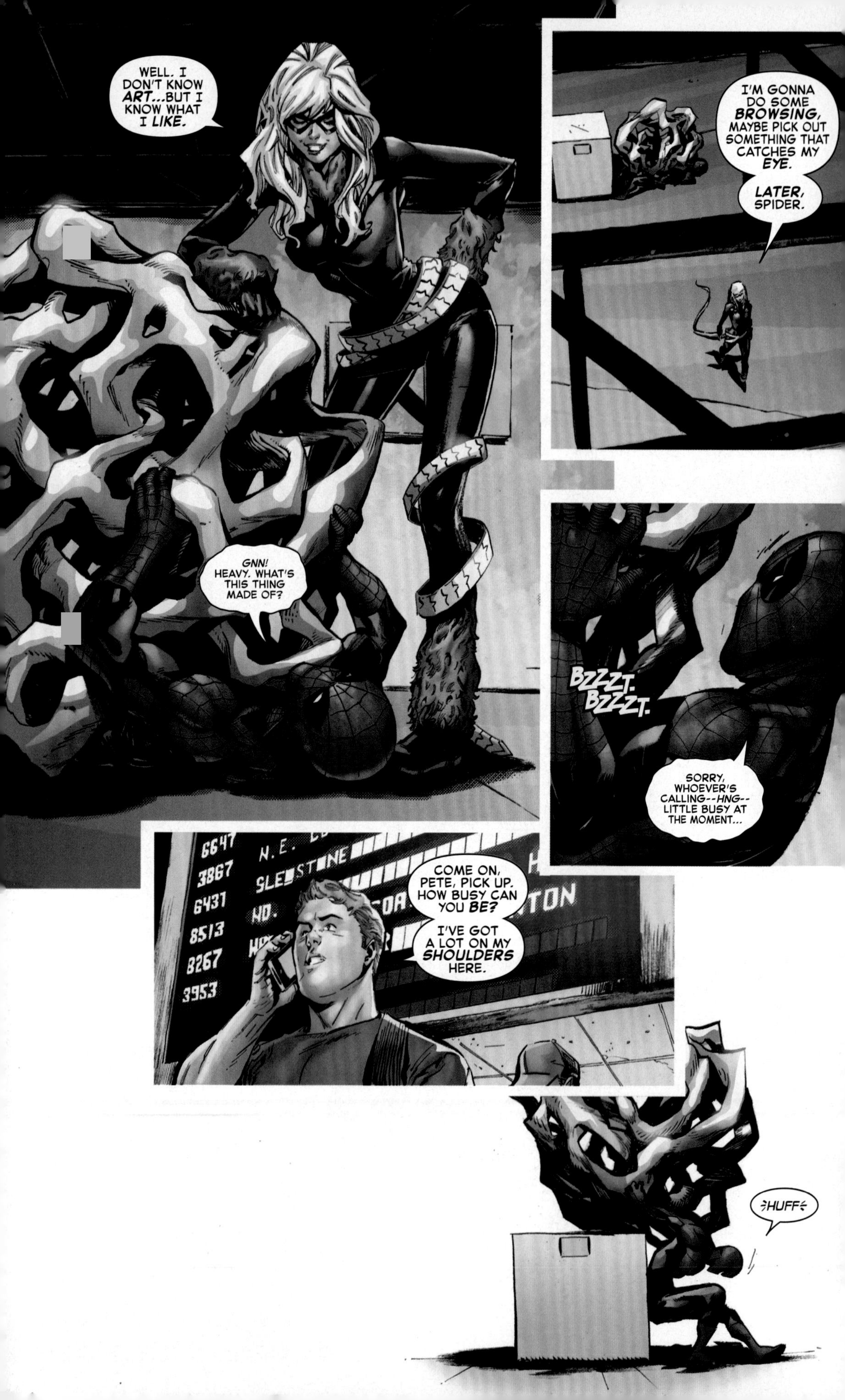
WELL. I DON'T KNOW ART...BUT I KNOW WHAT I LIKE.
GNN! HEAVY. WHAT'S THIS THING MADE OF?
I'M GONNA DO SOME BROWSING, MAYBE PICK OUT SOMETHING THAT CATCHES MY EYE.
LATER, SPIDER.
BZZZT. BZZZT.
SORRY, WHOEVER'S CALLING--HNG--LITTLE BUSY AT THE MOMENT...
COME ON, PETE, PICK UP. HOW BUSY CAN YOU BE?
I'VE GOT A LOT ON MY SHOULDERS HERE.
HUFF

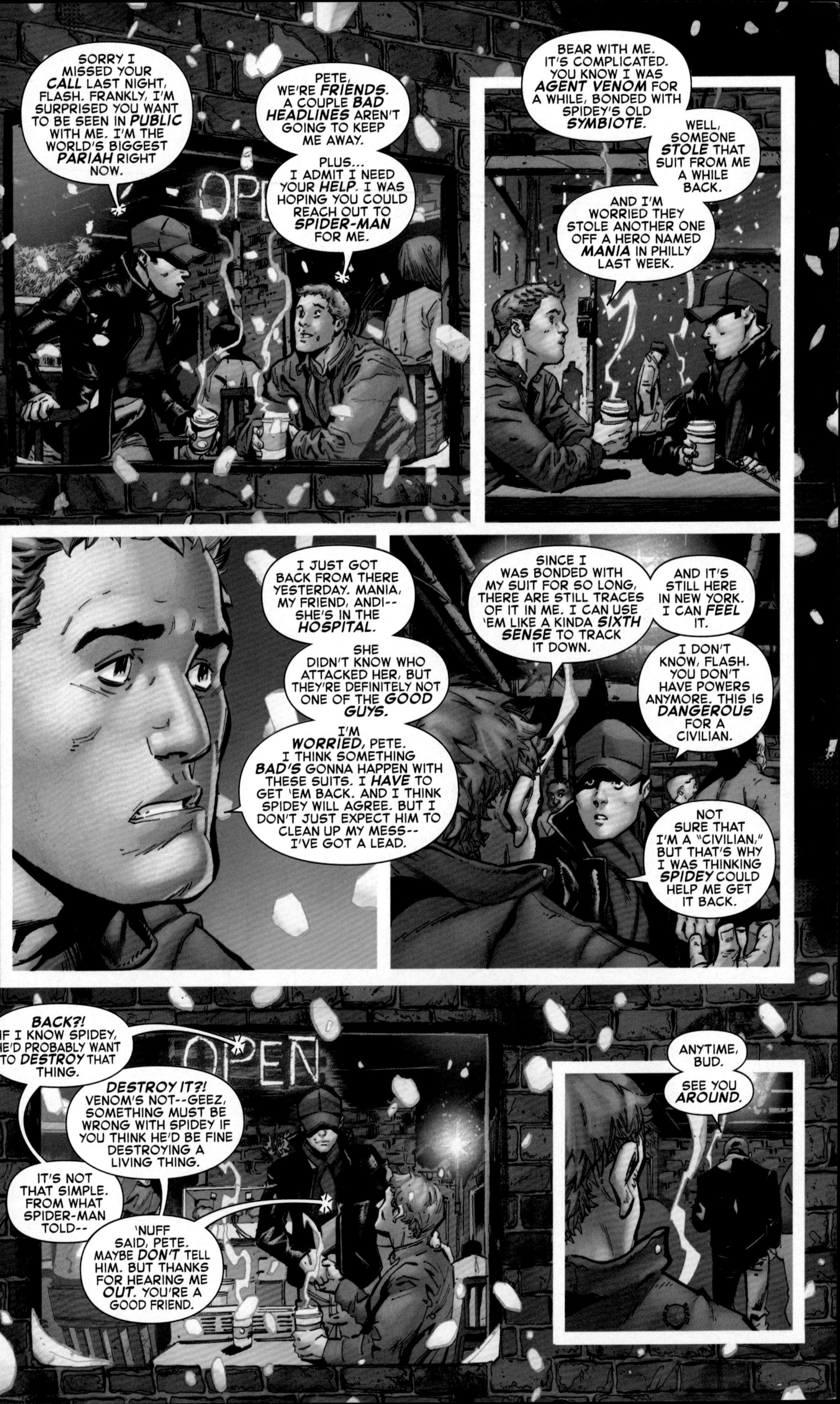
SORRY I MISSED YOUR CALL LAST NIGHT, FLASH. FRANKLY, I'M SURPRISED YOU WANT TO BE SEEN IN PUBLIC WITH ME. I'M THE WORLD'S BIGGEST PARIAH RIGHT NOW.
PETE, WE'RE FRIENDS. A COUPLE BAD HEADLINES AREN'T GOING TO KEEP ME AWAY.
PLUS... I ADMIT I NEED YOUR HELP. I WAS HOPING YOU COULD REACH OUT TO SPIDER-MAN FOR ME.
BEAR WITH ME. IT'S COMPLICATED. YOU KNOW I WAS AGENT VENOM FOR A WHILE, BONDED WITH SPIDEY'S OLD SYMBIOTE.
WELL, SOMEONE STOLE THAT SUIT FROM ME A WHILE BACK.
AND I'M WORRIED THEY STOLE ANOTHER ONE OFF A HERO NAMED MANIA IN PHILLY LAST WEEK.
I JUST GOT BACK FROM THERE YESTERDAY. MANIA, MY FRIEND, ANDI-- SHE'S IN THE HOSPITAL.
SHE DIDN'T KNOW WHO ATTACKED HER, BUT THEY'RE DEFINITELY NOT ONE OF THE GOOD GUYS.
I'M WORRIED, PETE. I THINK SOMETHING BAD'S GONNA HAPPEN WITH THESE SUITS. I HAVE TO GET 'EM BACK. AND I THINK SPIDEY WILL AGREE. BUT I DON'T JUST EXPECT HIM TO CLEAN UP MY MESS-- I'VE GOT A LEAD.
SINCE I WAS BONDED WITH MY SUIT FOR SO LONG, THERE ARE STILL TRACES OF IT IN ME. I CAN USE 'EM LIKE A KINDA SIXTH SENSE TO TRACK IT DOWN.
AND IT'S STILL HERE IN NEW YORK. I CAN FEEL IT.
I DON'T KNOW, FLASH. YOU DON'T HAVE POWERS ANYMORE. THIS IS DANGEROUS FOR A CIVILIAN.
NOT SURE THAT I'M A "CIVILIAN," BUT THAT'S WHY I WAS THINKING SPIDEY COULD HELP ME GET IT BACK.
BACK?! IF I KNOW SPIDEY, HE'D PROBABLY WANT TO DESTROY THAT THING.
DESTROY IT?! VENOM'S NOT--GEEZ, SOMETHING MUST BE WRONG WITH SPIDEY IF YOU THINK HE'D BE FINE DESTROYING A LIVING THING.
IT'S NOT THAT SIMPLE. FROM WHAT SPIDER-MAN TOLD--
'NUFF SAID, PETE. MAYBE DON'T TELL HIM. BUT THANKS FOR HEARING ME OUT. YOU'RE A GOOD FRIEND.
OPEN
ANYTIME, BUD.
SEE YOU AROUND.

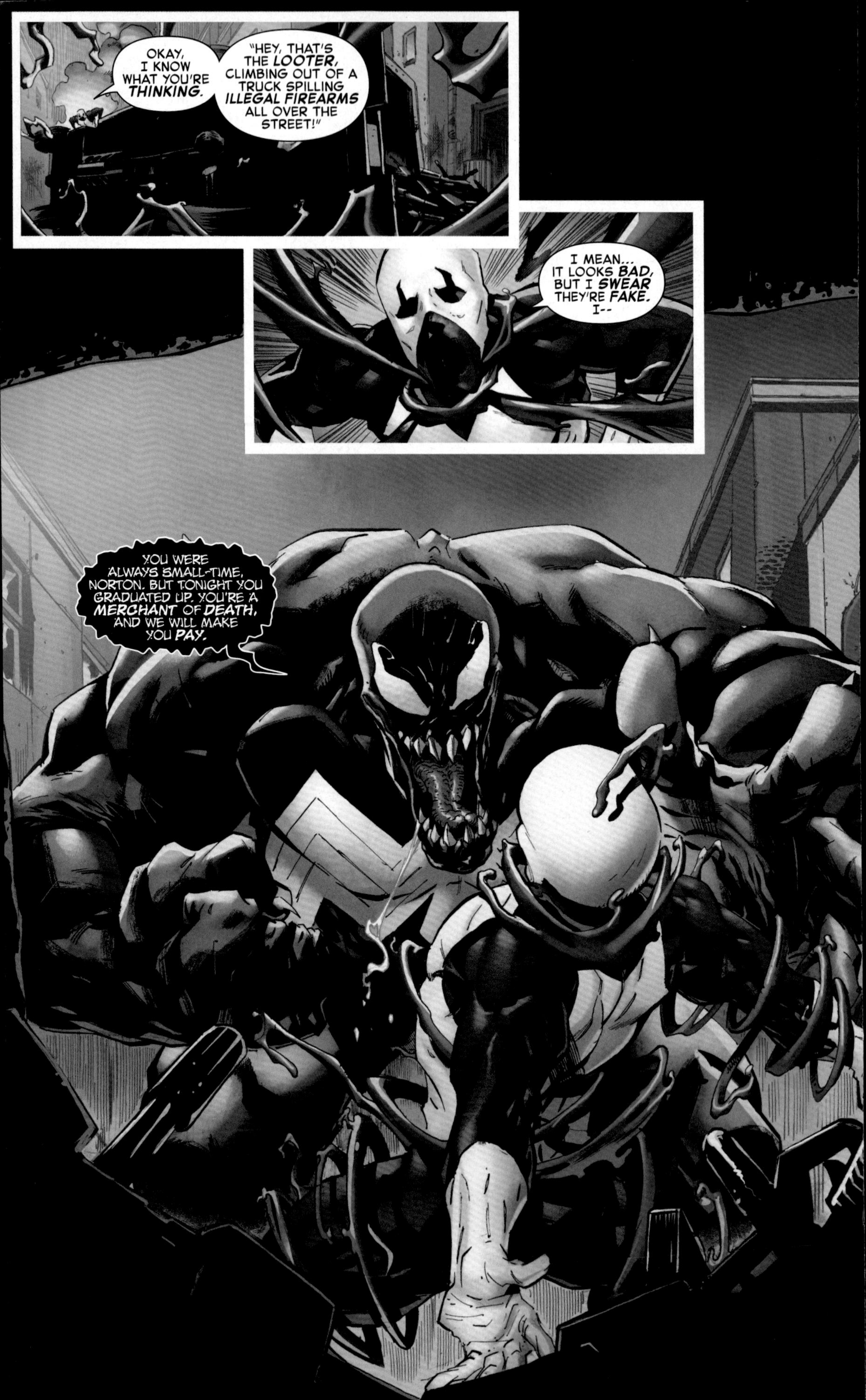
OKAY, I KNOW WHAT YOU'RE THINKING.
"HEY, THAT'S THE LOOTER, CLIMBING OUT OF A TRUCK SPILLING ILLEGAL FIREARMS ALL OVER THE STREET!"
I MEAN... IT LOOKS BAD, BUT I SWEAR THEY'RE FAKE. I--
YOU WERE ALWAYS SMALL-TIME, NORTON. BUT TONIGHT YOU GRADUATED UP. YOU'RE A MERCHANT OF DEATH, AND WE WILL MAKE YOU PAY.

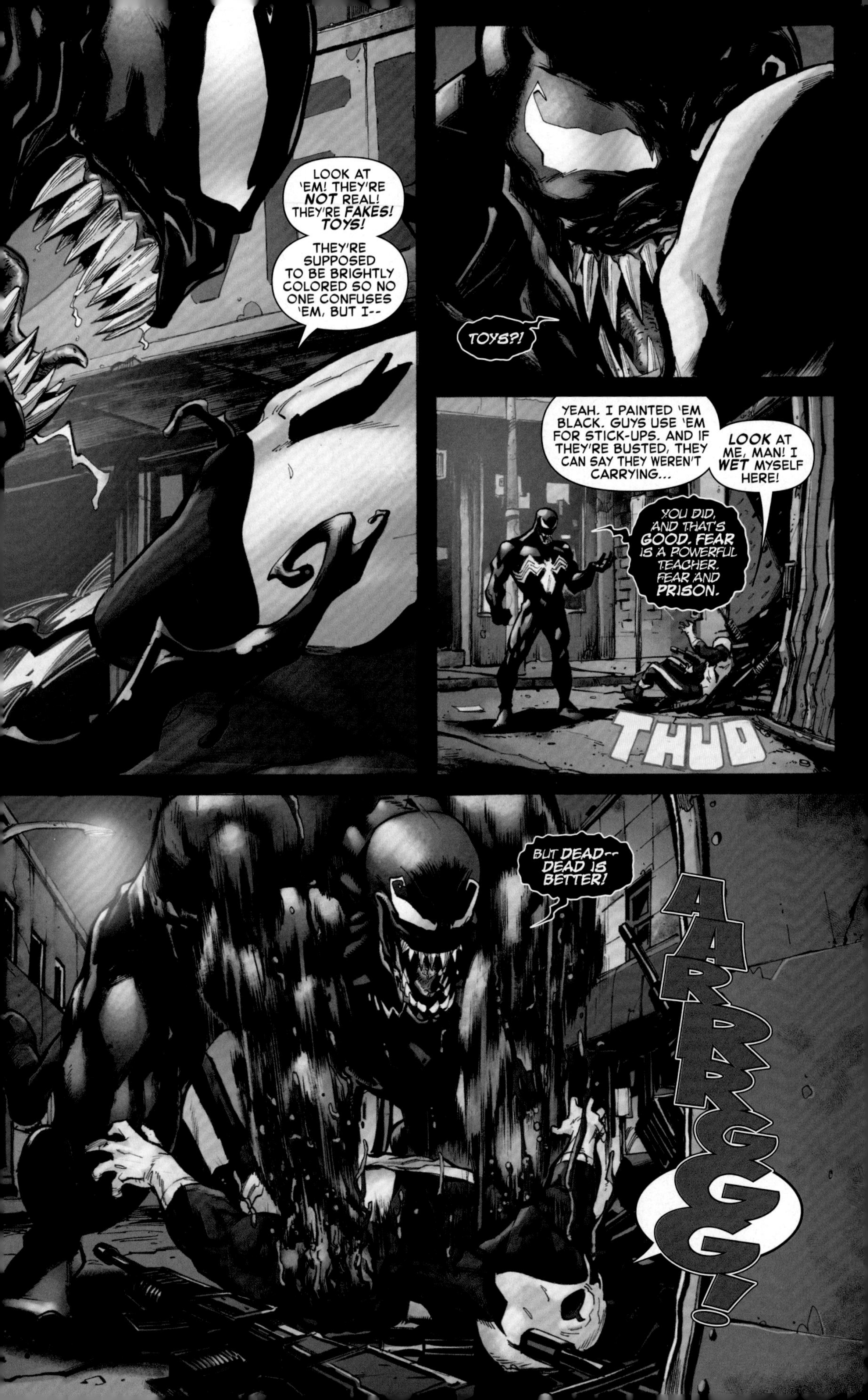
LOOK AT 'EM! THEY'RE NOT REAL! THEY'RE FAKES! TOYS!
THEY'RE SUPPOSED TO BE BRIGHTLY COLORED SO NO ONE CONFUSES 'EM, BUT I--
TOYS?!
YEAH. I PAINTED 'EM BLACK. GUYS USE 'EM FOR STICK-UPS. AND IF THEY'RE BUSTED, THEY CAN SAY THEY WEREN'T CARRYING...
LOOK AT ME, MAN! I WET MYSELF HERE!
YOU DID, AND THAT'S GOOD. FEAR IS A POWERFUL TEACHER. FEAR AND PRISON.
THUD
BUT DEAD-- DEAD IS BETTER!
AARRRGGG!

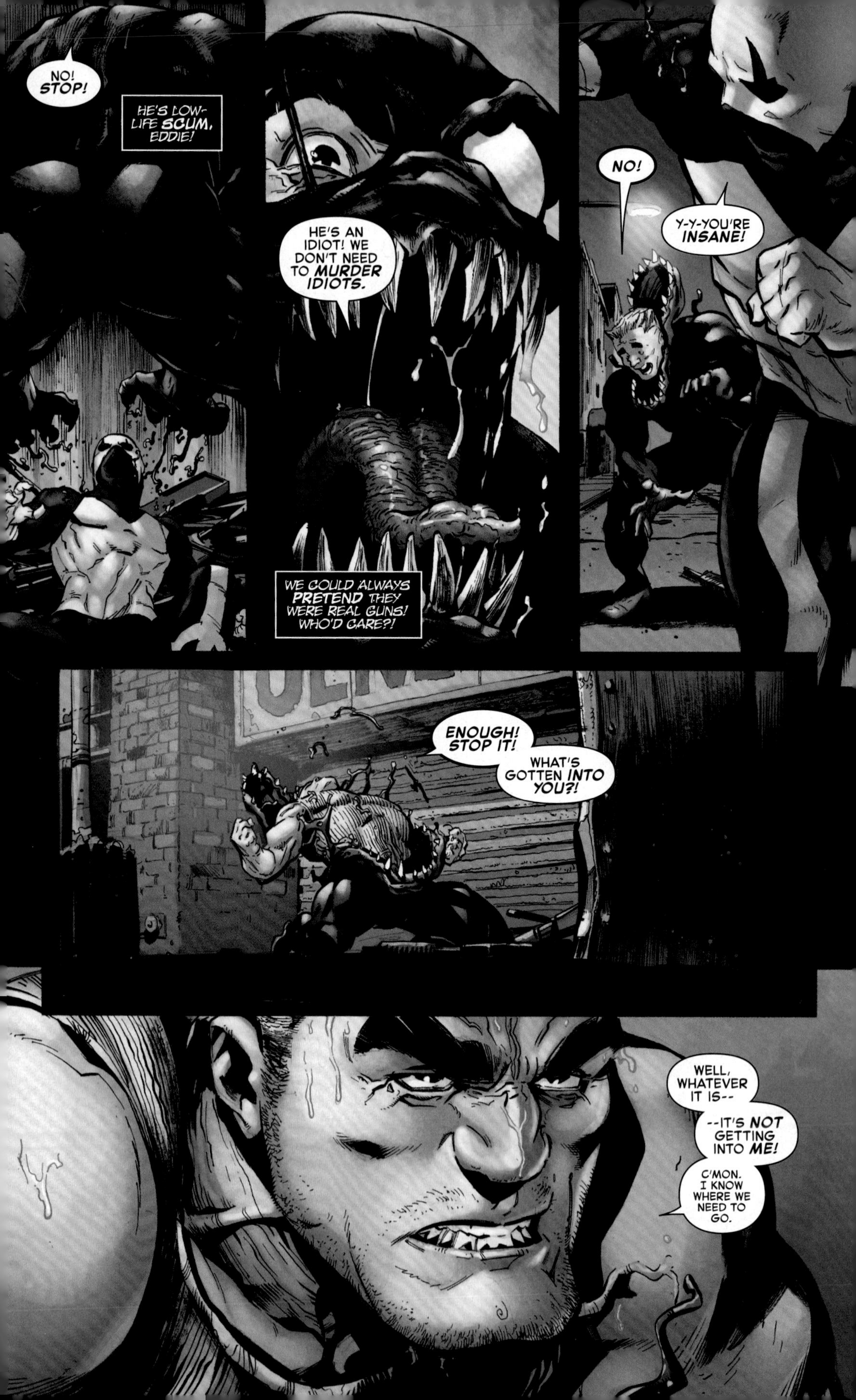
NO! STOP!
HE'S LOW-LIFE SCUM, EDDIE!
HE'S AN IDIOT! WE DON'T NEED TO MURDER IDIOTS.
WE COULD ALWAYS PRETEND THEY WERE REAL GUNS! WHO'D CARE?!
NO!
Y-Y-YOU'RE INSANE!
ENOUGH! STOP IT!
WHAT'S GOTTEN INTO YOU?!
WELL, WHATEVER IT IS--
--IT'S NOT GETTING INTO ME!
C'MON. I KNOW WHERE WE NEED TO GO.

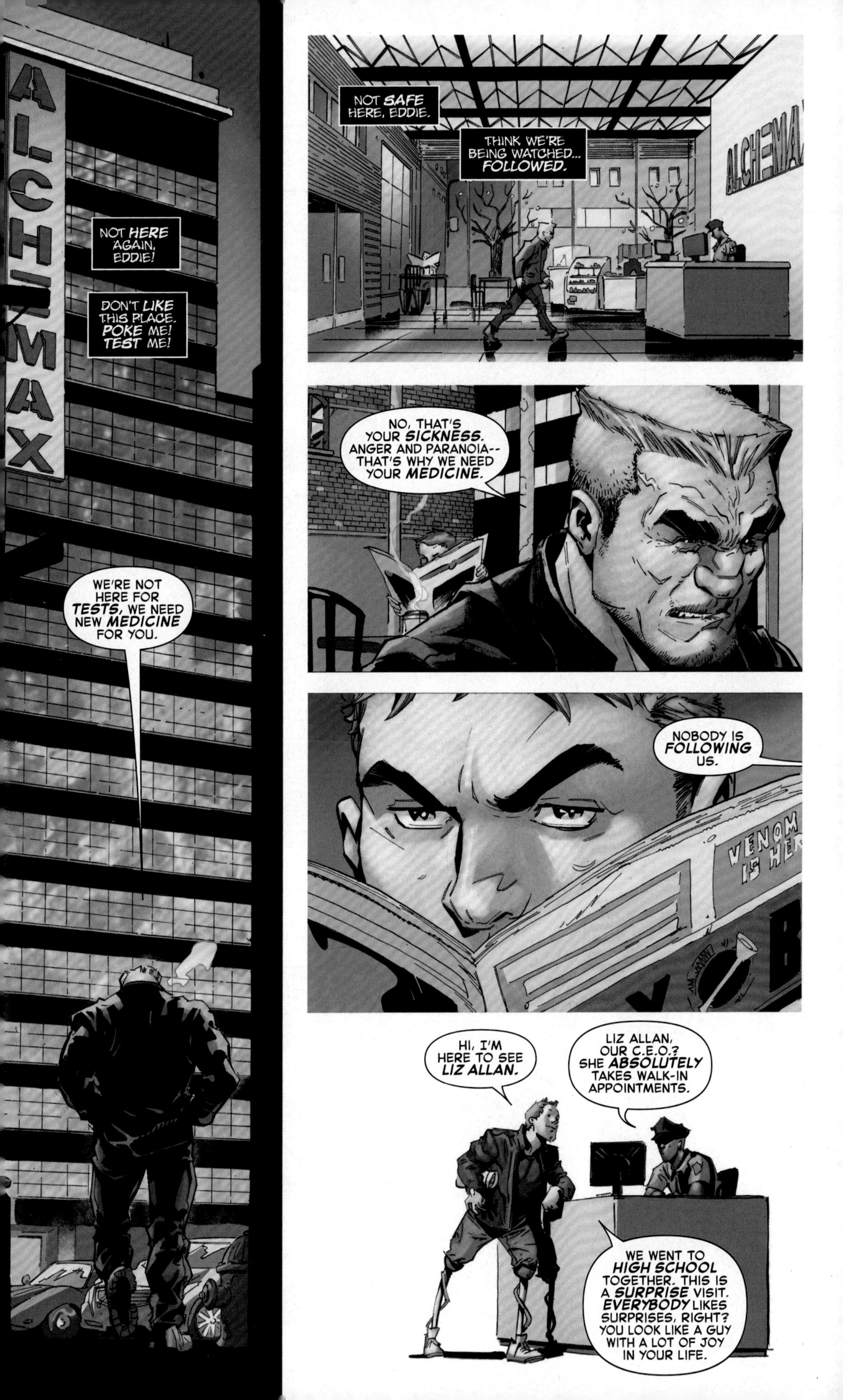
A
L
C
H
E
M
A
X
NOT HERE AGAIN, EDDIE!
DON'T LIKE THIS PLACE. POKE ME! TEST ME!
WE'RE NOT HERE FOR TESTS, WE NEED NEW MEDICINE FOR YOU.
NOT SAFE HERE, EDDIE.
THINK WE'RE BEING WATCHED... FOLLOWED.
ALCHEMAX
NO, THAT'S YOUR SICKNESS. ANGER AND PARANOIA-- THAT'S WHY WE NEED YOUR MEDICINE.
NOBODY IS FOLLOWING US.
VENOM IS HER
HI, I'M HERE TO SEE LIZ ALLAN.
LIZ ALLAN, OUR C.E.O.? SHE ABSOLUTELY TAKES WALK-IN APPOINTMENTS.
WE WENT TO HIGH SCHOOL TOGETHER. THIS IS A SURPRISE VISIT. EVERYBODY LIKES SURPRISES, RIGHT? YOU LOOK LIKE A GUY WITH A LOT OF JOY IN YOUR LIFE.

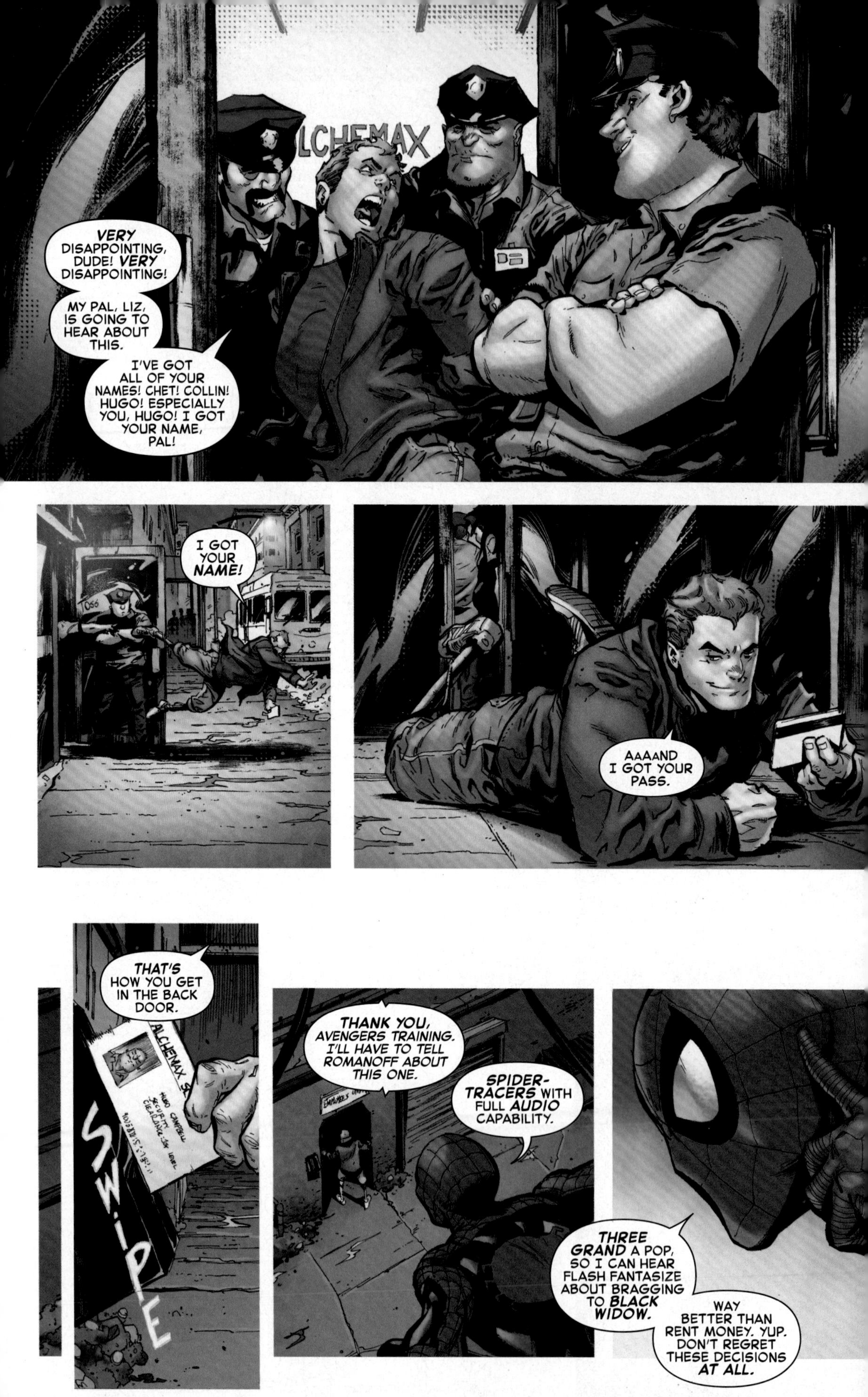

VERY DISAPPOINTING, DUDE! VERY DISAPPOINTING!
MY PAL, LIZ, IS GOING TO HEAR ABOUT THIS.
I'VE GOT ALL OF YOUR NAMES! CHET! COLLIN! HUGO! ESPECIALLY YOU, HUGO! I GOT YOUR NAME, PAL!
I GOT YOUR NAME!
AAAAND I GOT YOUR PASS.
THAT'S HOW YOU GET IN THE BACK DOOR.
SWIPE
THANK YOU, AVENGERS TRAINING. I'LL HAVE TO TELL ROMANOFF ABOUT THIS ONE.
SPIDER-TRACERS WITH FULL AUDIO CAPABILITY.
THREE GRAND A POP, SO I CAN HEAR FLASH FANTASIZE ABOUT BRAGGING TO BLACK WIDOW.
WAY BETTER THAN RENT MONEY. YUP. DON'T REGRET THESE DECISIONS AT ALL.

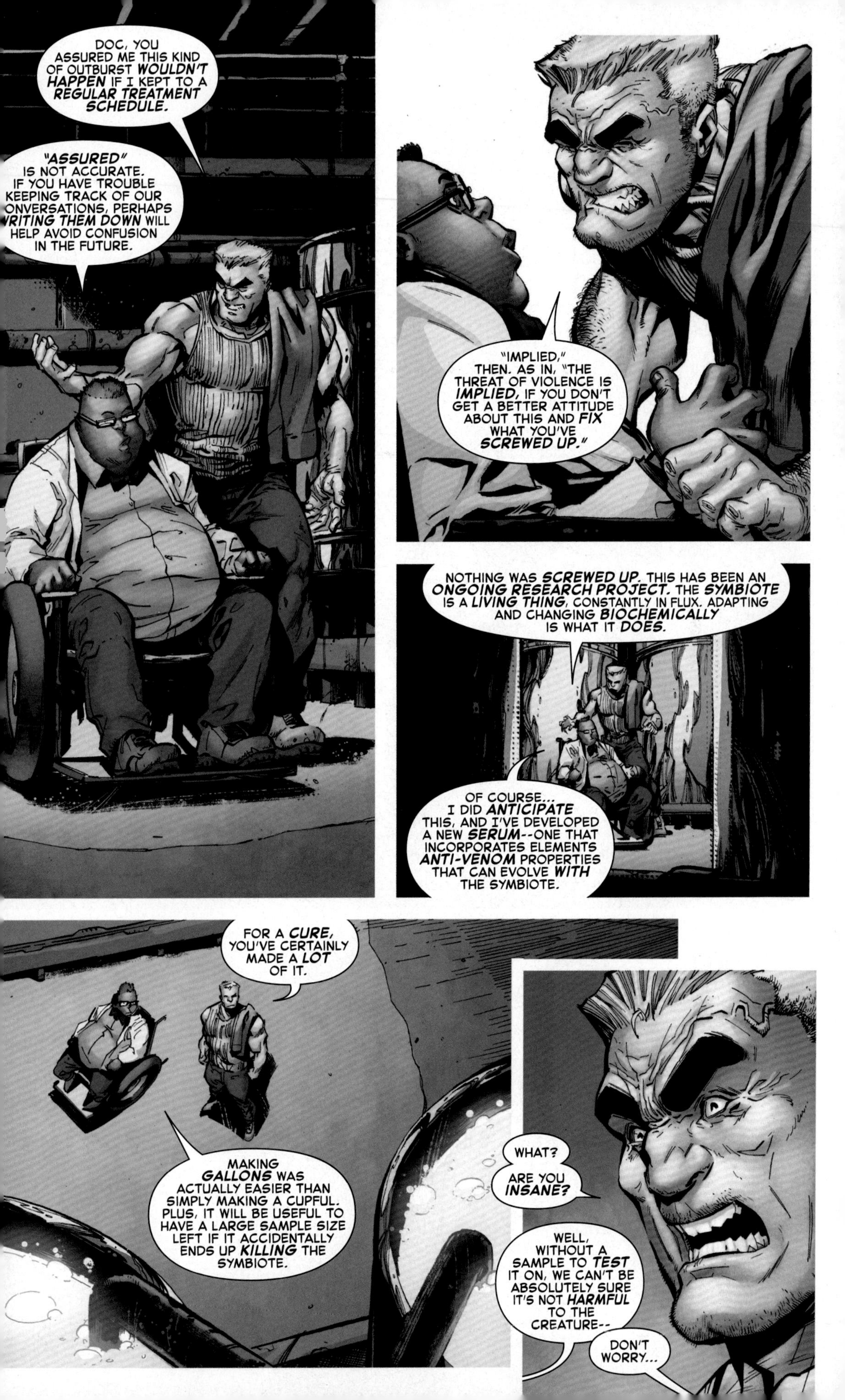

DOC, YOU ASSURED ME THIS KIND OF OUTBURST WOULDN'T HAPPEN IF I KEPT TO A REGULAR TREATMENT SCHEDULE.
"ASSURED" IS NOT ACCURATE. IF YOU HAVE TROUBLE KEEPING TRACK OF OUR ONVERSATIONS, PERHAPS VRITING THEM DOWN WILL HELP AVOID CONFUSION IN THE FUTURE.
"IMPLIED," THEN. AS IN, "THE THREAT OF VIOLENCE IS IMPLIED, IF YOU DON'T GET A BETTER ATTITUDE ABOUT THIS AND FIX WHAT YOU'VE SCREWED UP."
NOTHING WAS SCREWED UP. THIS HAS BEEN AN ONGOING RESEARCH PROJECT. THE SYMBIOTE IS A LIVING THING, CONSTANTLY IN FLUX. ADAPTING AND CHANGING BIOCHEMICALLY IS WHAT IT DOES.
OF COURSE... I DID ANTICIPATE THIS, AND I'VE DEVELOPED A NEW SERUM--ONE THAT INCORPORATES ELEMENTS ANTI-VENOM PROPERTIES THAT CAN EVOLVE WITH THE SYMBIOTE.
FOR A CURE, YOU'VE CERTAINLY MADE A LOT OF IT.
MAKING GALLONS WAS ACTUALLY EASIER THAN SIMPLY MAKING A CUPFUL. PLUS, IT WILL BE USEFUL TO HAVE A LARGE SAMPLE SIZE LEFT IF IT ACCIDENTALLY ENDS UP KILLING THE SYMBIOTE.
WHAT?
ARE YOU INSANE?
WELL, WITHOUT A SAMPLE TO TEST IT ON, WE CAN'T BE ABSOLUTELY SURE IT'S NOT HARMFUL TO THE CREATURE--
DON'T WORRY...

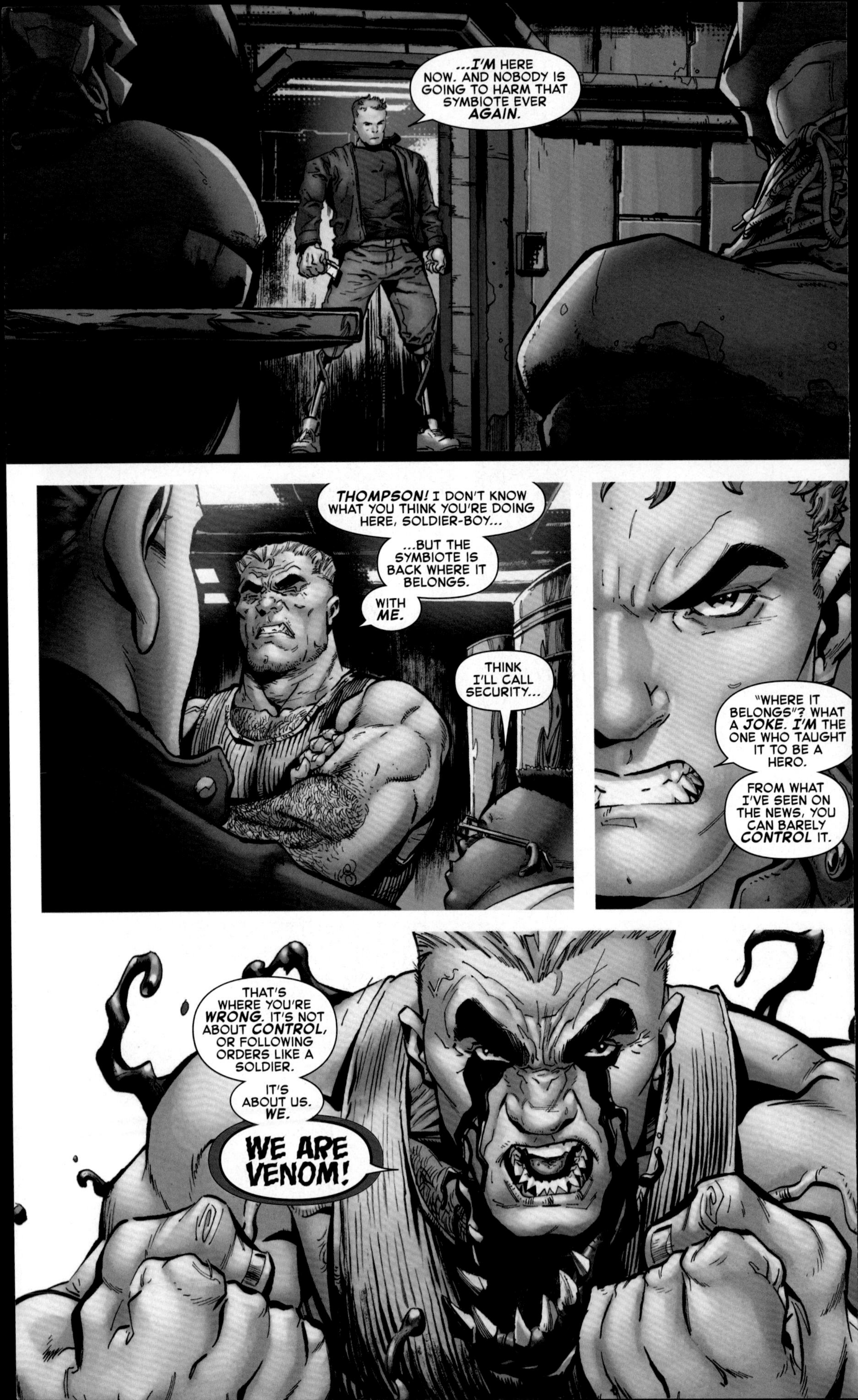
...I'M HERE NOW. AND NOBODY IS GOING TO HARM THAT SYMBIOTE EVER AGAIN.
THOMPSON! I DON'T KNOW WHAT YOU THINK YOU'RE DOING HERE, SOLDIER-BOY...
...BUT THE SYMBIOTE IS BACK WHERE IT BELONGS.
WITH ME.
THINK I'LL CALL SECURITY...
"WHERE IT BELONGS"? WHAT A JOKE. I'M THE ONE WHO TAUGHT IT TO BE A HERO.
FROM WHAT I'VE SEEN ON THE NEWS, YOU CAN BARELY CONTROL IT.
THAT'S WHERE YOU'RE WRONG. IT'S NOT ABOUT CONTROL, OR FOLLOWING ORDERS LIKE A SOLDIER.
IT'S ABOUT US. WE.
WE ARE VENOM!

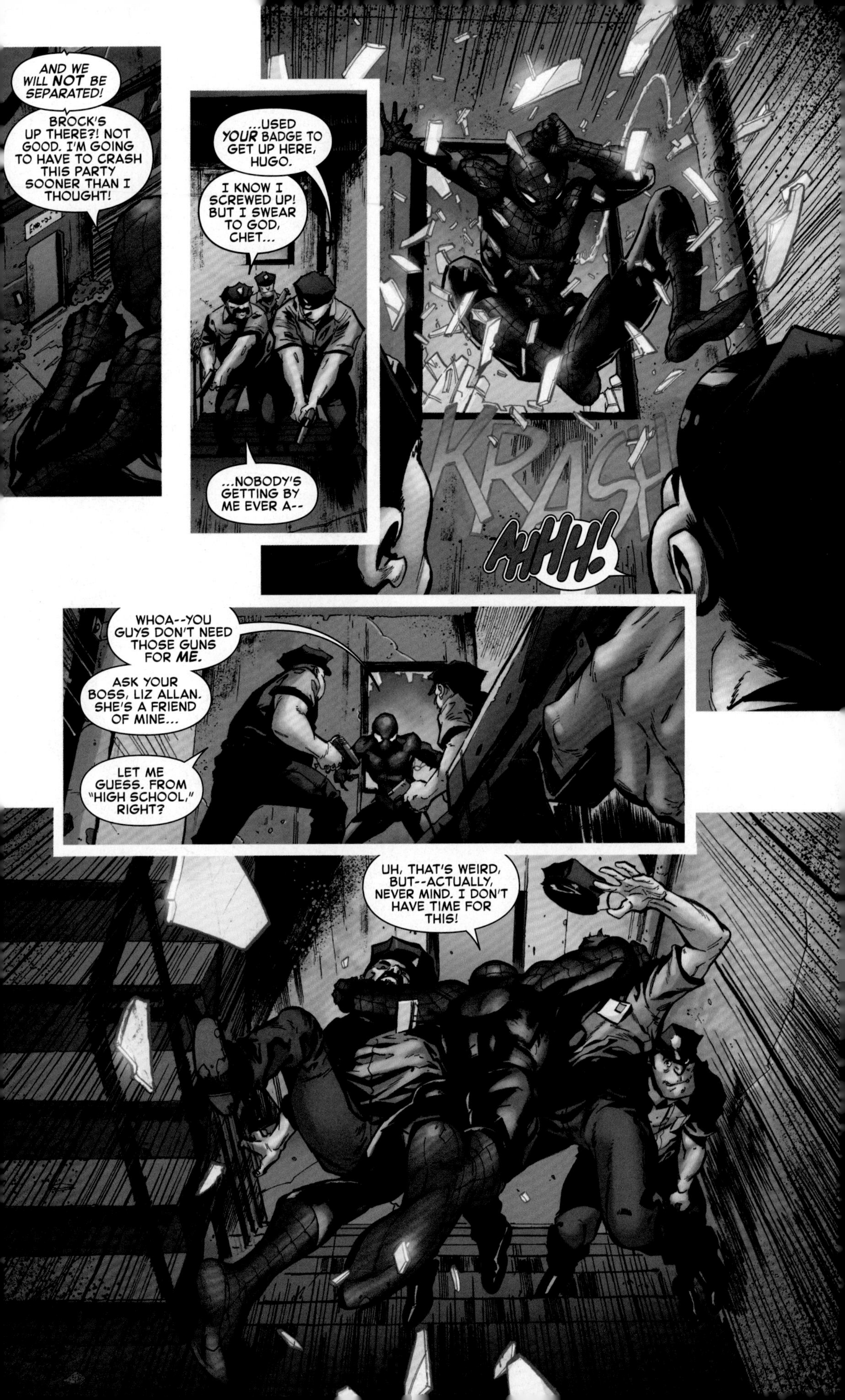
AND WE WILL NOT BE SEPARATED!
BROCK'S UP THERE?! NOT GOOD. I'M GOING TO HAVE TO CRASH THIS PARTY SOONER THAN I THOUGHT!
...USED YOUR BADGE TO GET UP HERE, HUGO.
I KNOW I SCREWED UP! BUT I SWEAR TO GOD, CHET...
...NOBODY'S GETTING BY ME EVER A--
KRASH
AHHH!
WHOA--YOU GUYS DON'T NEED THOSE GUNS FOR ME.
ASK YOUR BOSS, LIZ ALLAN. SHE'S A FRIEND OF MINE...
LET ME GUESS. FROM "HIGH SCHOOL," RIGHT?
UH, THAT'S WEIRD, BUT--ACTUALLY, NEVER MIND. I DON'T HAVE TIME FOR THIS!

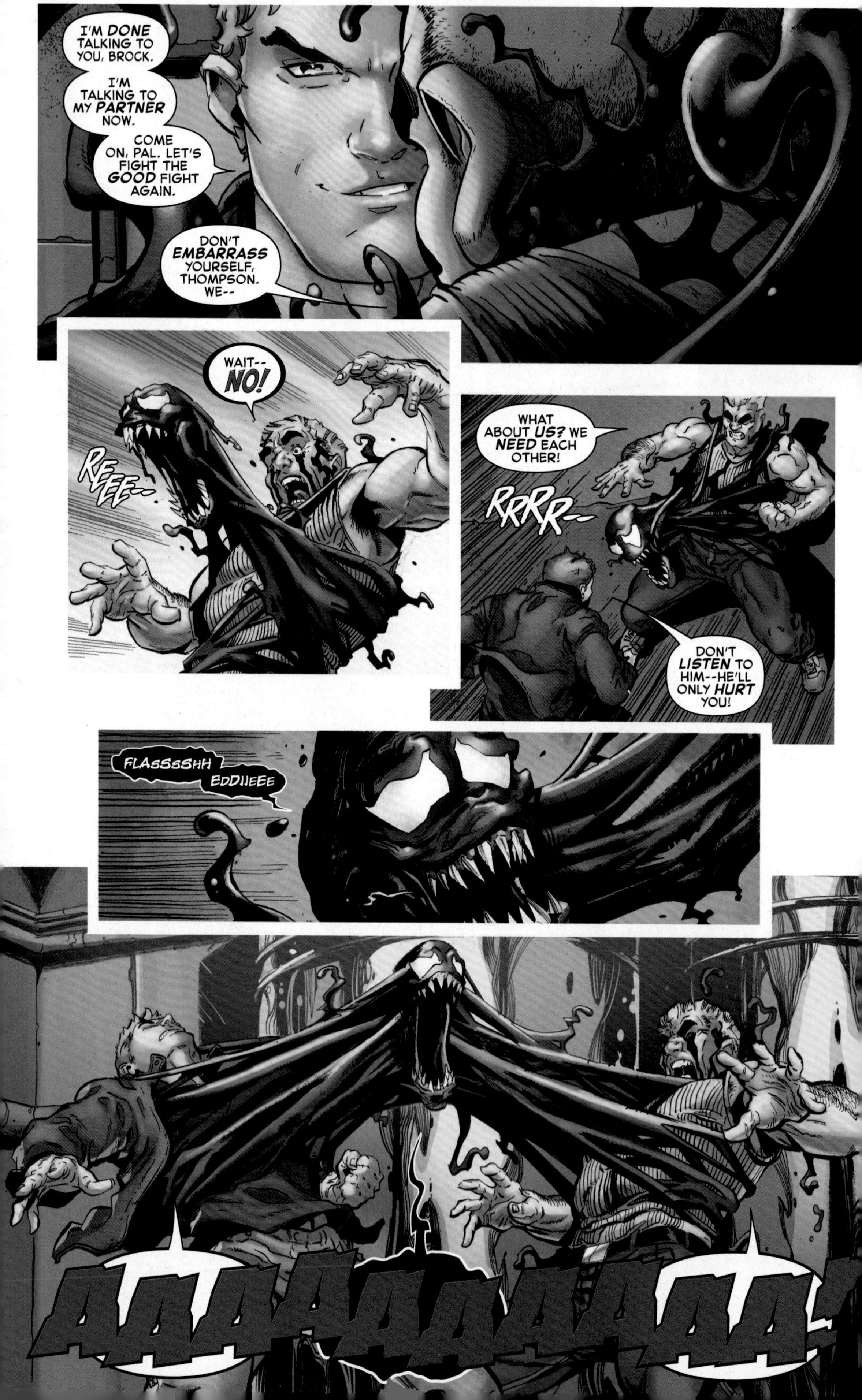

I'M DONE TALKING TO YOU, BROCK.
I'M TALKING TO MY PARTNER NOW.
COME ON, PAL. LET'S FIGHT THE GOOD FIGHT AGAIN.
DON'T EMBARRASS YOURSELF, THOMPSON. WE--
WAIT-- NO!
REEE--
WHAT ABOUT US? WE NEED EACH OTHER!
RRRR--
DON'T LISTEN TO HIM--HE'LL ONLY HURT YOU!
FLASSSSHH
EDDIIEEE

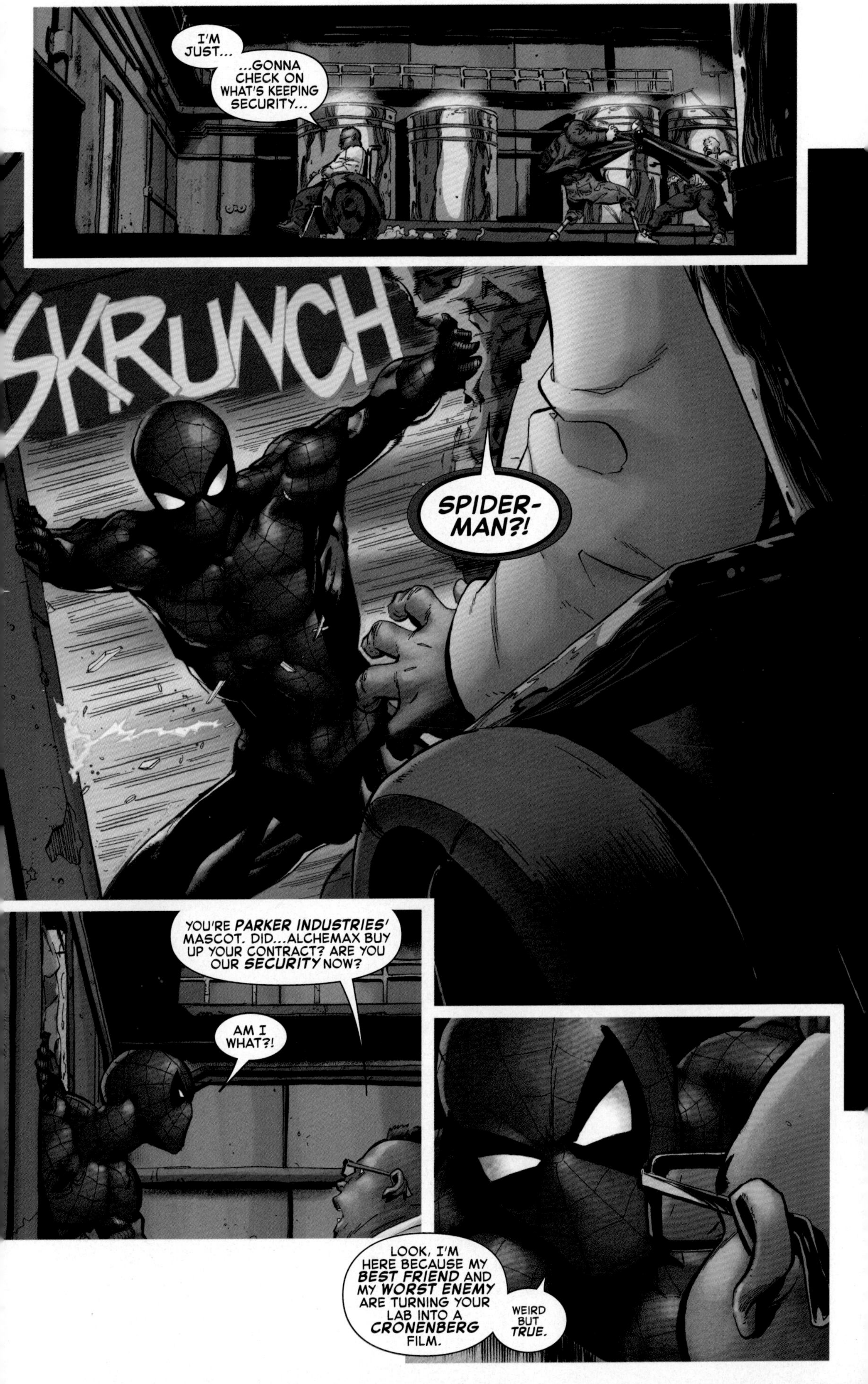
I'M JUST...
...GONNA CHECK ON WHAT'S KEEPING SECURITY...
SKRUNCH
SPIDER-MAN?!
YOU'RE PARKER INDUSTRIES' MASCOT. DID...ALCHEMAX BUY UP YOUR CONTRACT? ARE YOU OUR SECURITY NOW?
AM I WHAT?!
LOOK, I'M HERE BECAUSE MY BEST FRIEND AND MY WORST ENEMY ARE TURNING YOUR LAB INTO A CRONENBERG FILM.
WEIRD BUT TRUE.

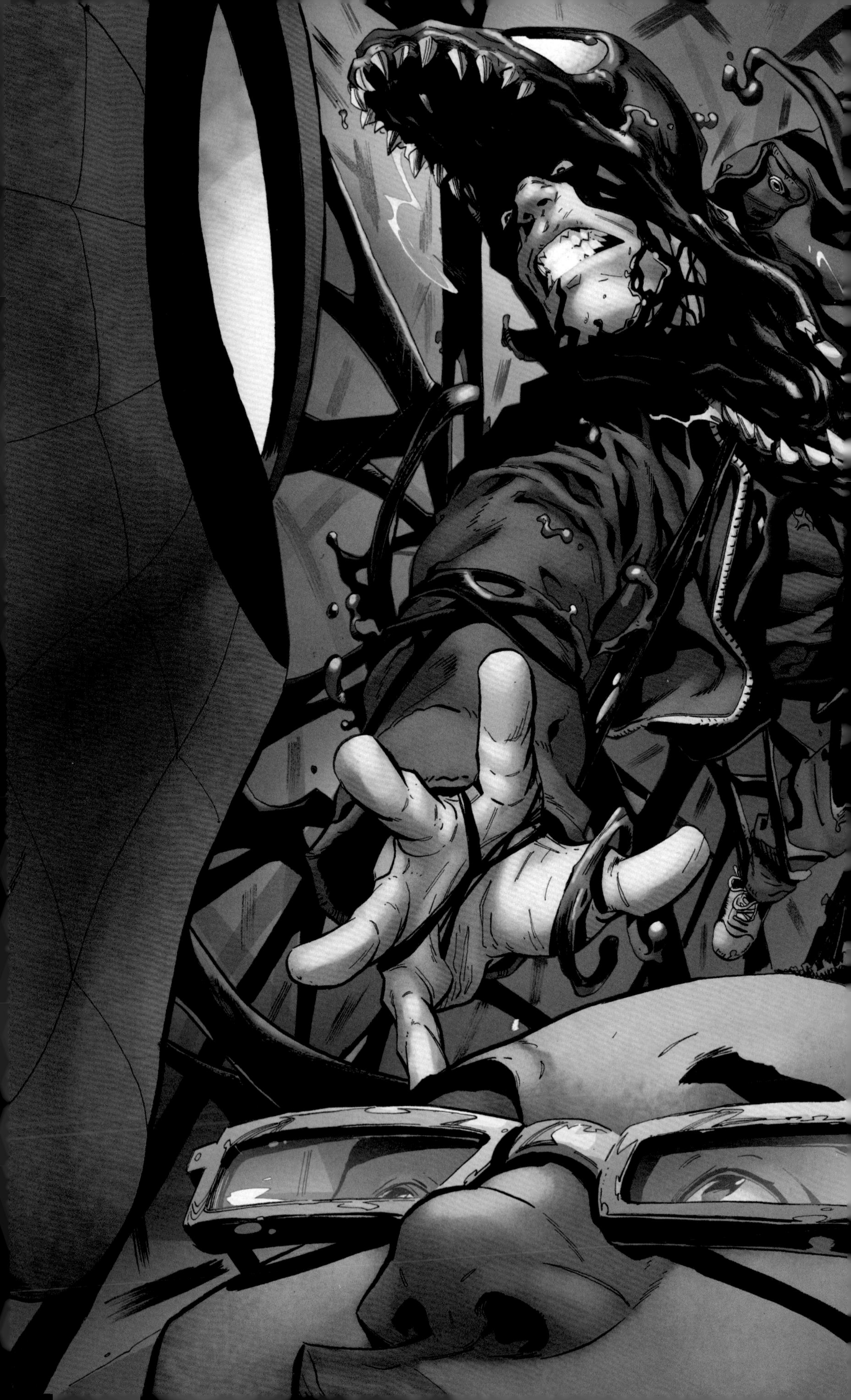

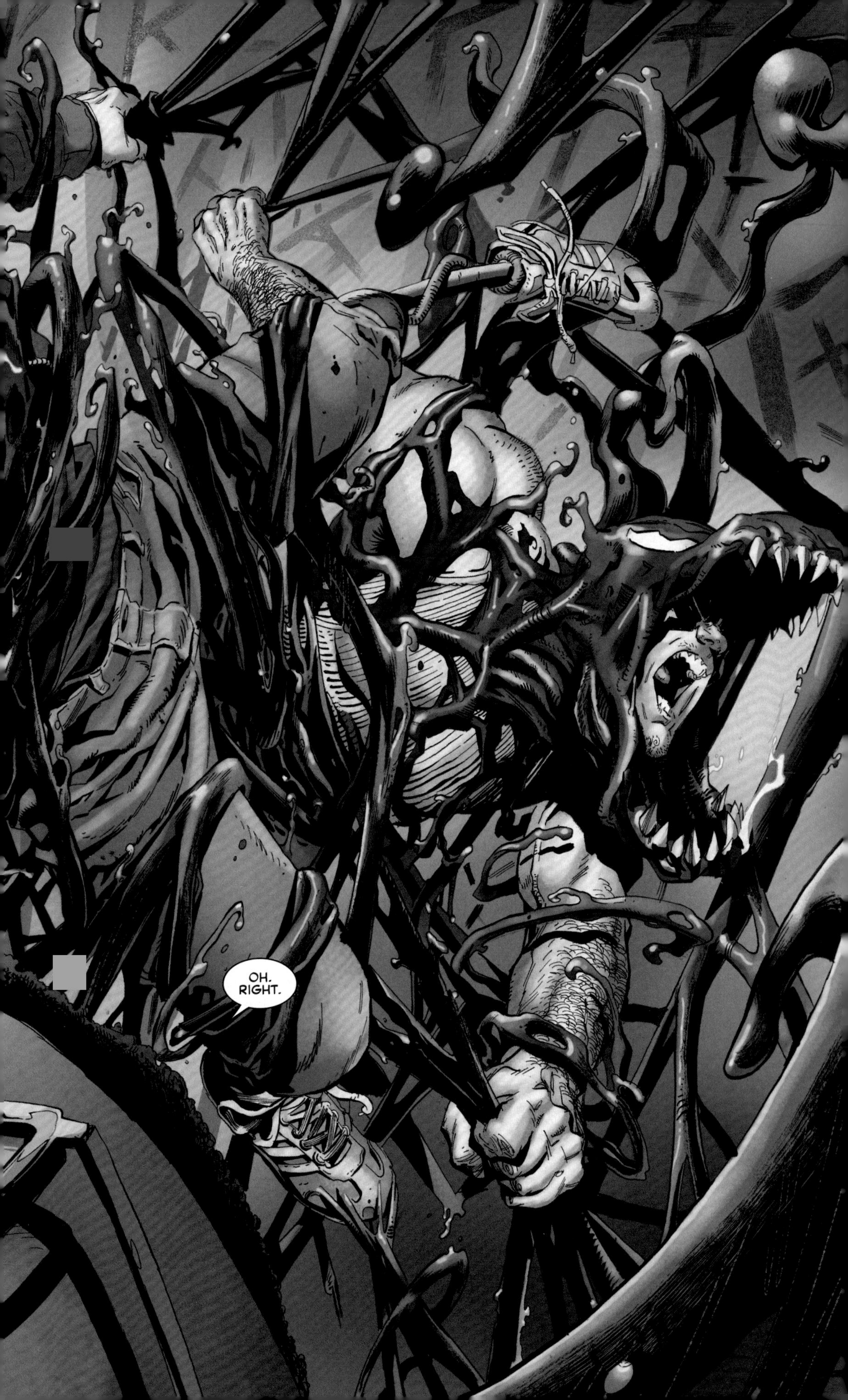
OH. RIGHT.

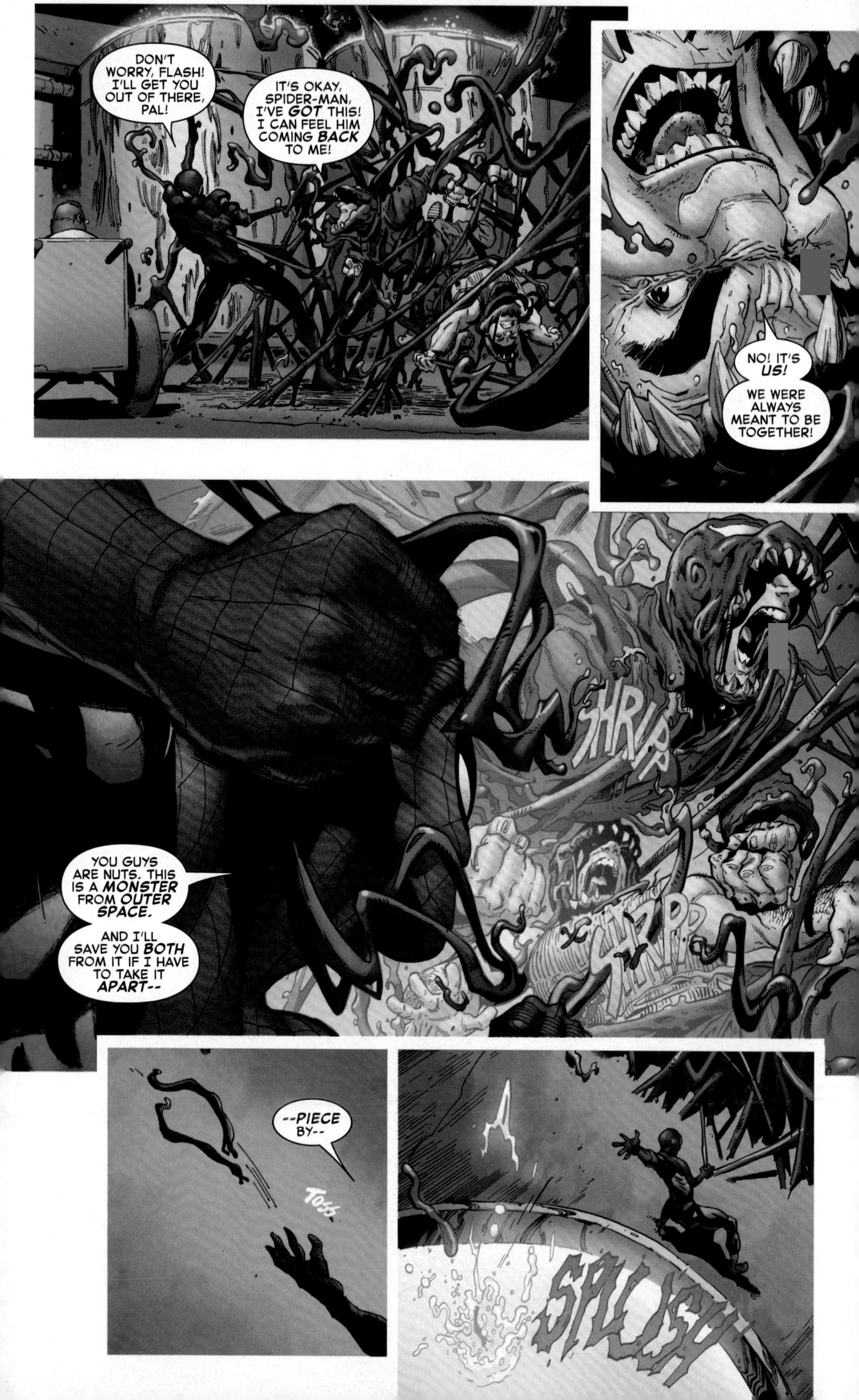

DON'T WORRY, FLASH! I'LL GET YOU OUT OF THERE, PAL!
IT'S OKAY, SPIDER-MAN, I'VE *GOT* THIS! I CAN FEEL HIM COMING *BACK* TO ME!
NO! IT'S *US!*
WE WERE ALWAYS MEANT TO BE TOGETHER!
SHRIPP
YOU GUYS ARE NUTS. THIS IS A *MONSTER* FROM *OUTER SPACE.*
AND I'LL SAVE YOU *BOTH* FROM IT IF I HAVE TO TAKE IT *APART--*
--PIECE BY--
TOSS
SPLISH

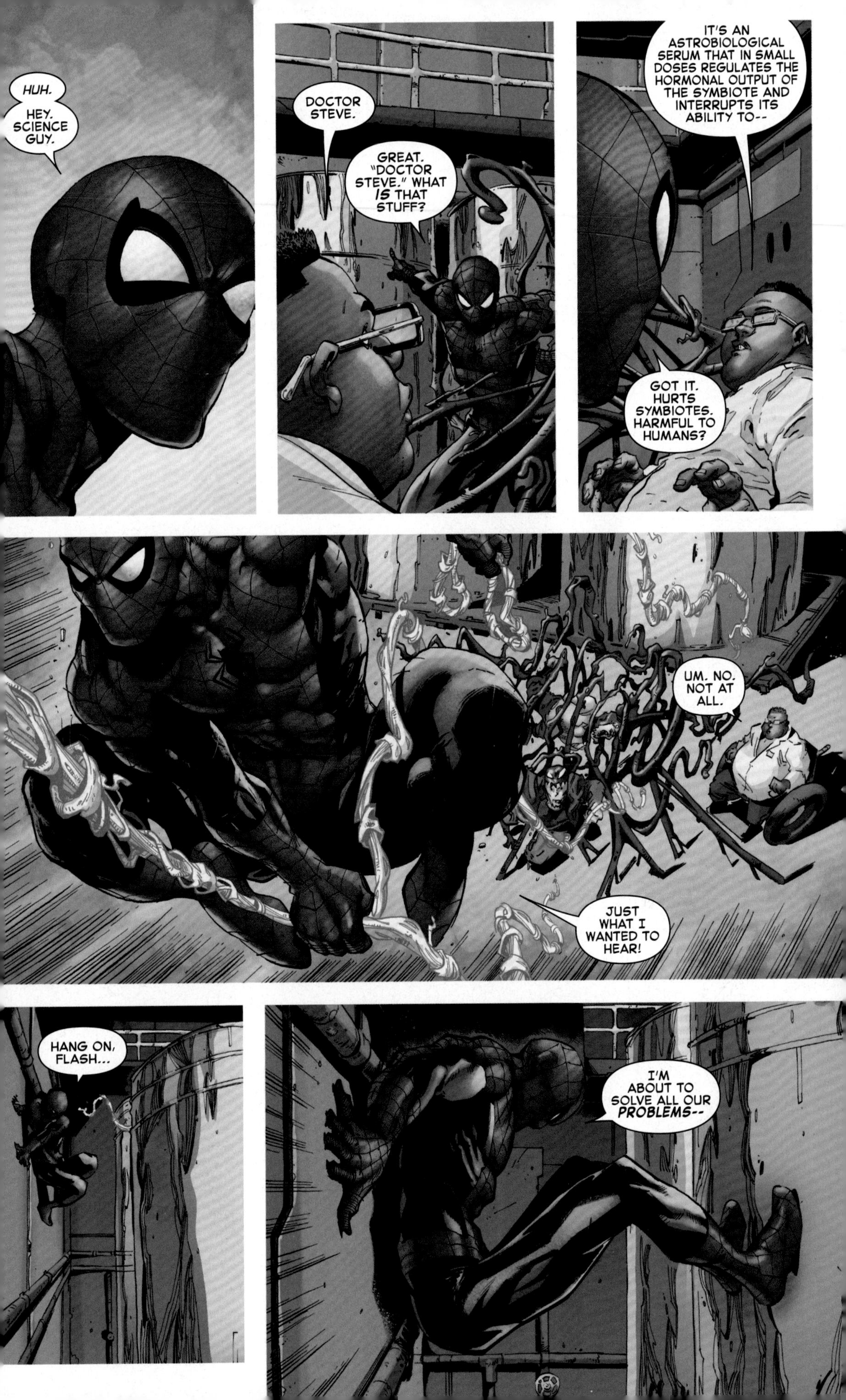
HUH.
HEY. SCIENCE GUY.
DOCTOR STEVE.
GREAT. "DOCTOR STEVE." WHAT IS THAT STUFF?
IT'S AN ASTROBIOLOGICAL SERUM THAT IN SMALL DOSES REGULATES THE HORMONAL OUTPUT OF THE SYMBIOTE AND INTERRUPTS ITS ABILITY TO--
GOT IT. HURTS SYMBIOTES. HARMFUL TO HUMANS?
UM. NO. NOT AT ALL.
JUST WHAT I WANTED TO HEAR!
HANG ON, FLASH...
I'M ABOUT TO SOLVE ALL OUR PROBLEMS--

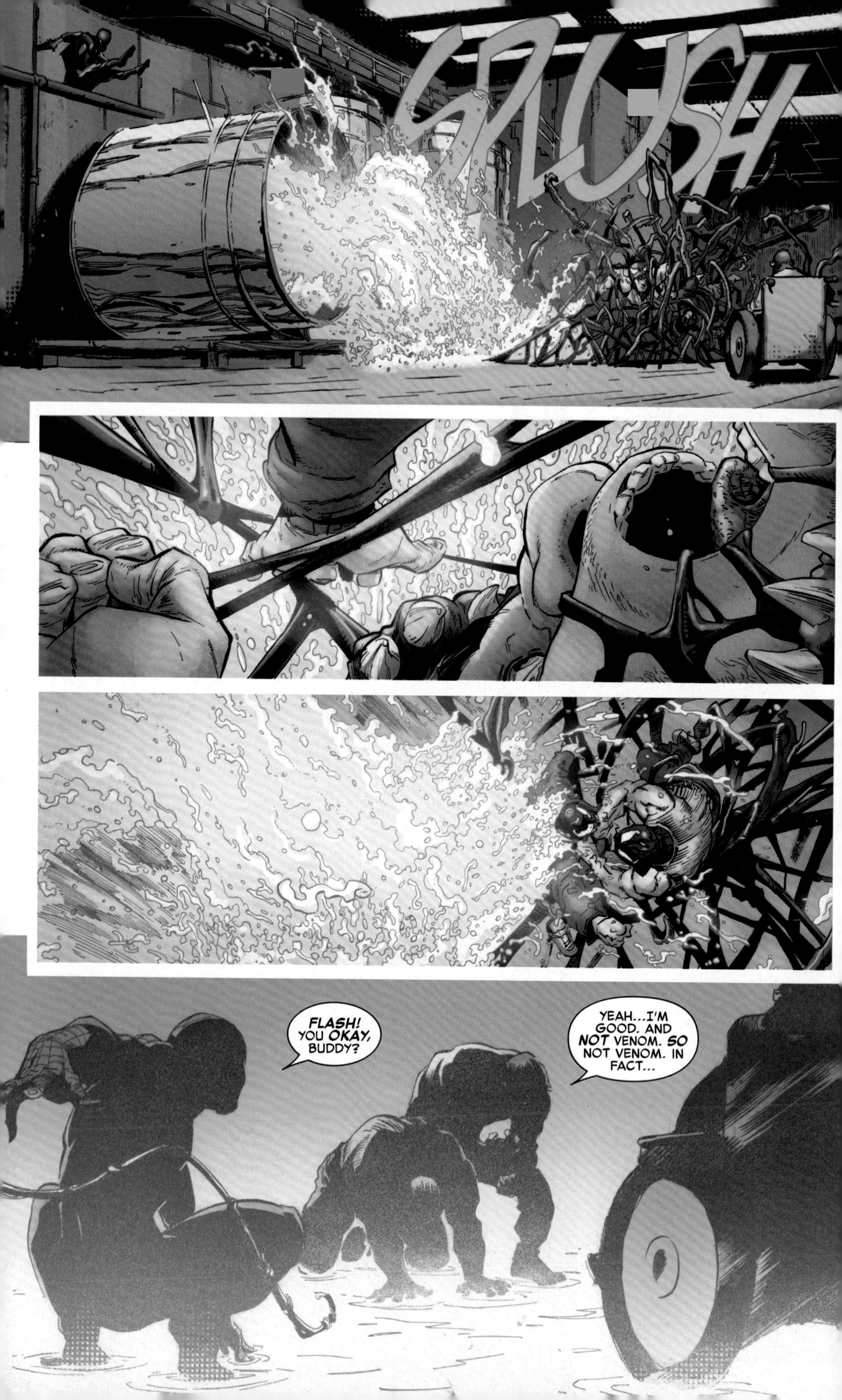

SPLUSH
FLASH! YOU OKAY, BUDDY?
YEAH...I'M GOOD. AND NOT VENOM. SO NOT VENOM. IN FACT...

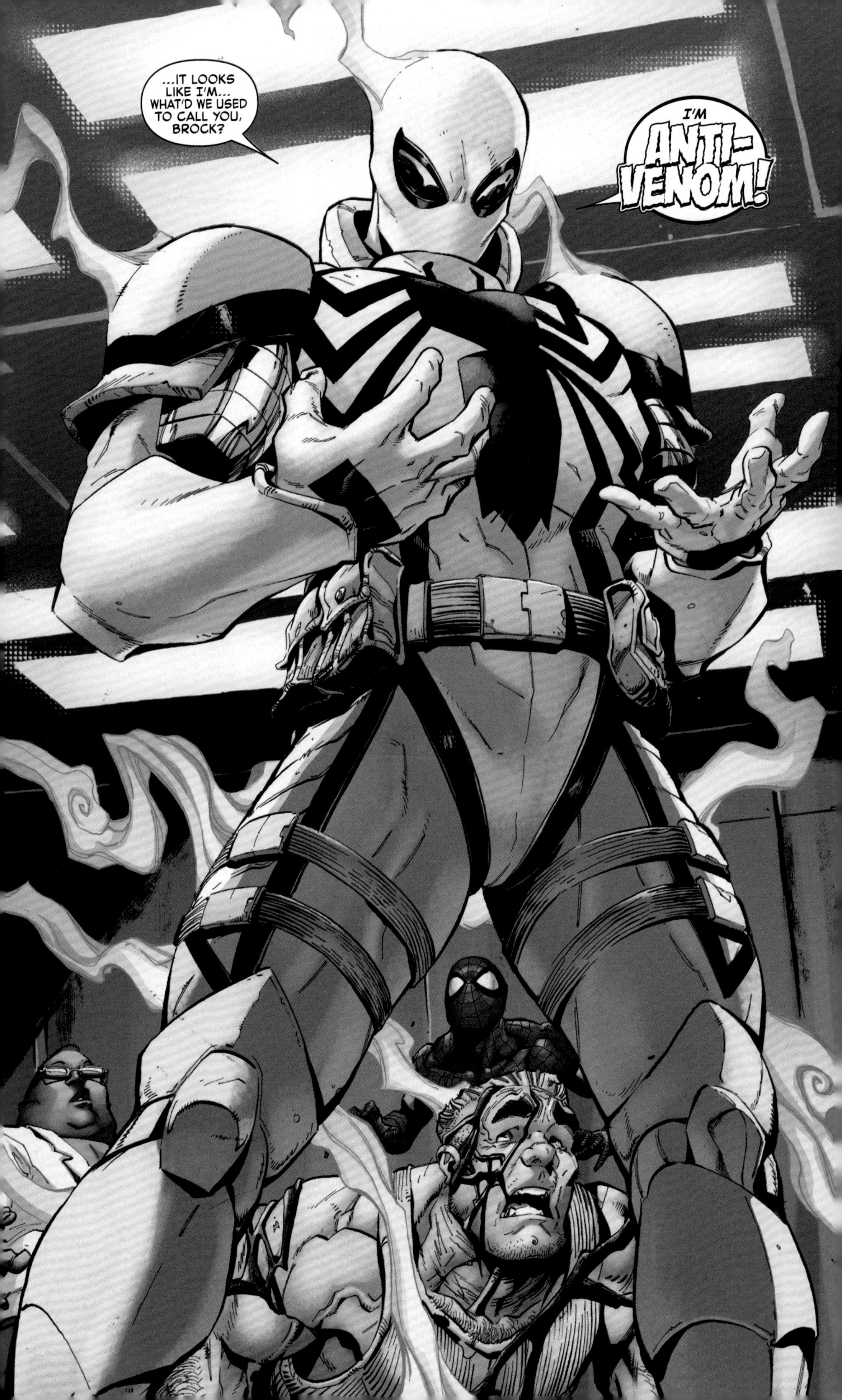
...IT LOOKS LIKE I'M... WHAT'D WE USED TO CALL YOU, BROCK?
I'M ANTI-VENOM!

IT WAS TERRIFYING, MAN. THIS THING WAS GOING TO EAT ME. I THOUGHT I WAS GOING TO DIE!

AND I'M NO PUSHOVER, YOU KNOW? I FOUGHT VALKYRIE ONCE. SHE'S AN ASGARDIAN.

YEAH, YEAH, NORTON. WE ALL KNOW YOU FOUGHT AN ASGARDIAN.

DUDE, YOU SMELL LIKE PEE.

EXCUSE ME, BUT YOU SOUND LIKE THE KIND OF MAN WE COULD USE IN OUR ORGANIZATION.

NOT INTERESTED, PAL.

THE LOOTER LOOTS ALONE.

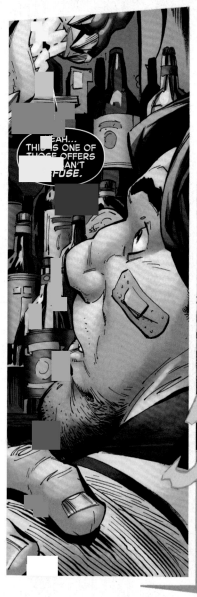

YEAH... THIS IS ONE OF THOSE OFFERS CAN'T REFUSE.

WHAT THE HELL, MAN?! SAY IT, DON'T--

SFTOO

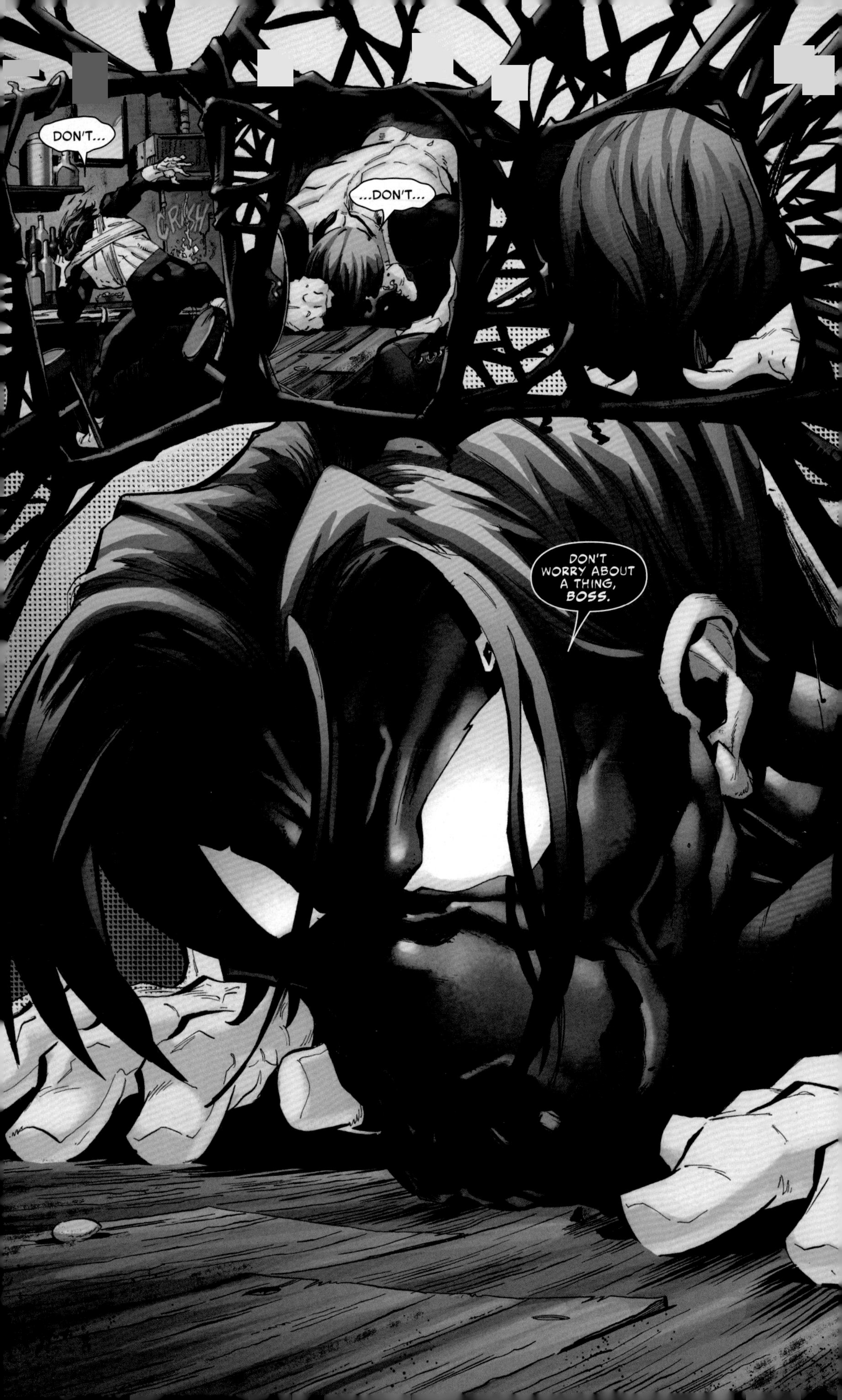
DON'T...
...DON'T...
CRASH
DON'T WORRY ABOUT A THING, BOSS.

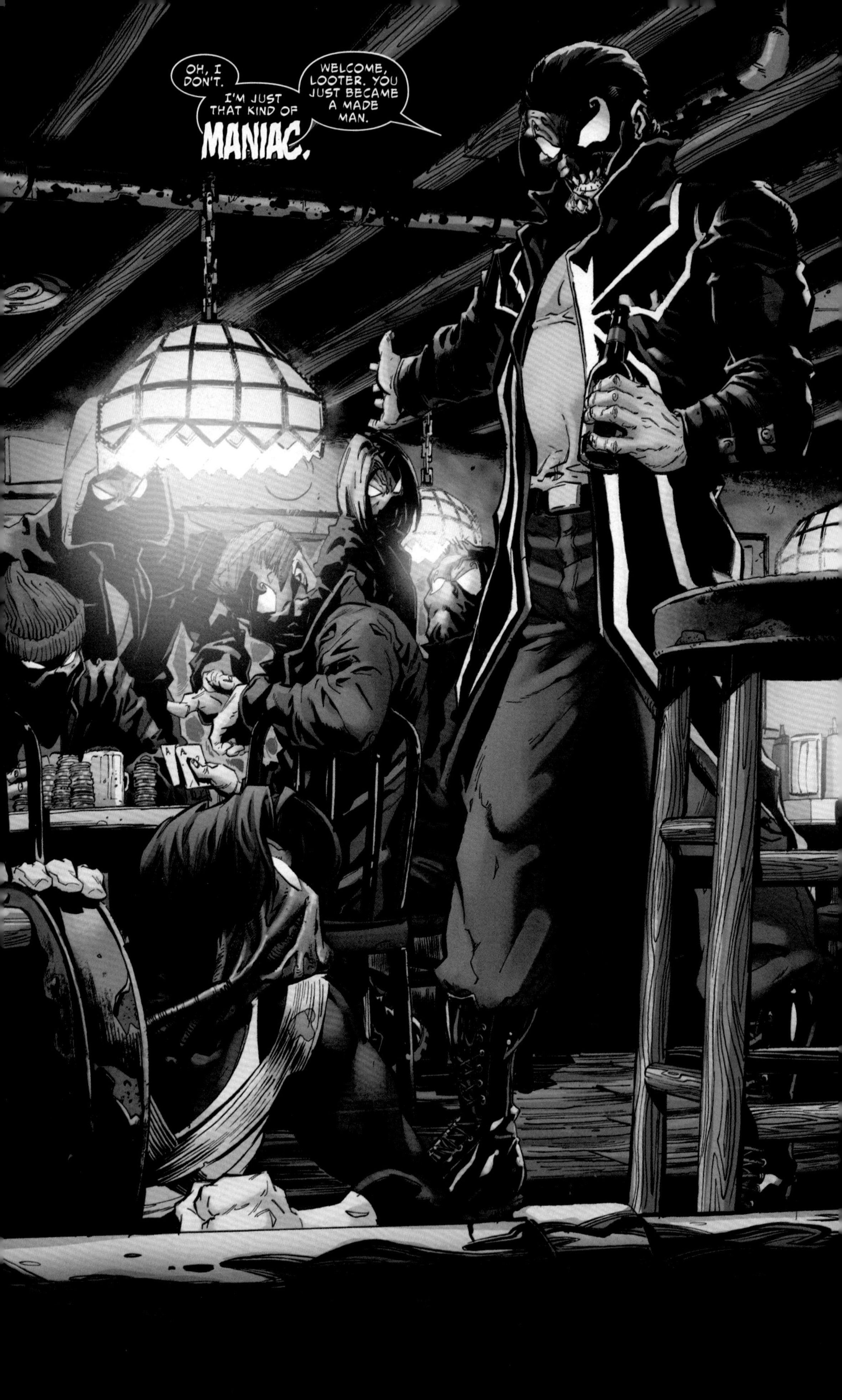

OH, I DON'T.
I'M JUST THAT KIND OF MANIAC.
WELCOME, LOOTER. YOU JUST BECAME A MADE MAN.

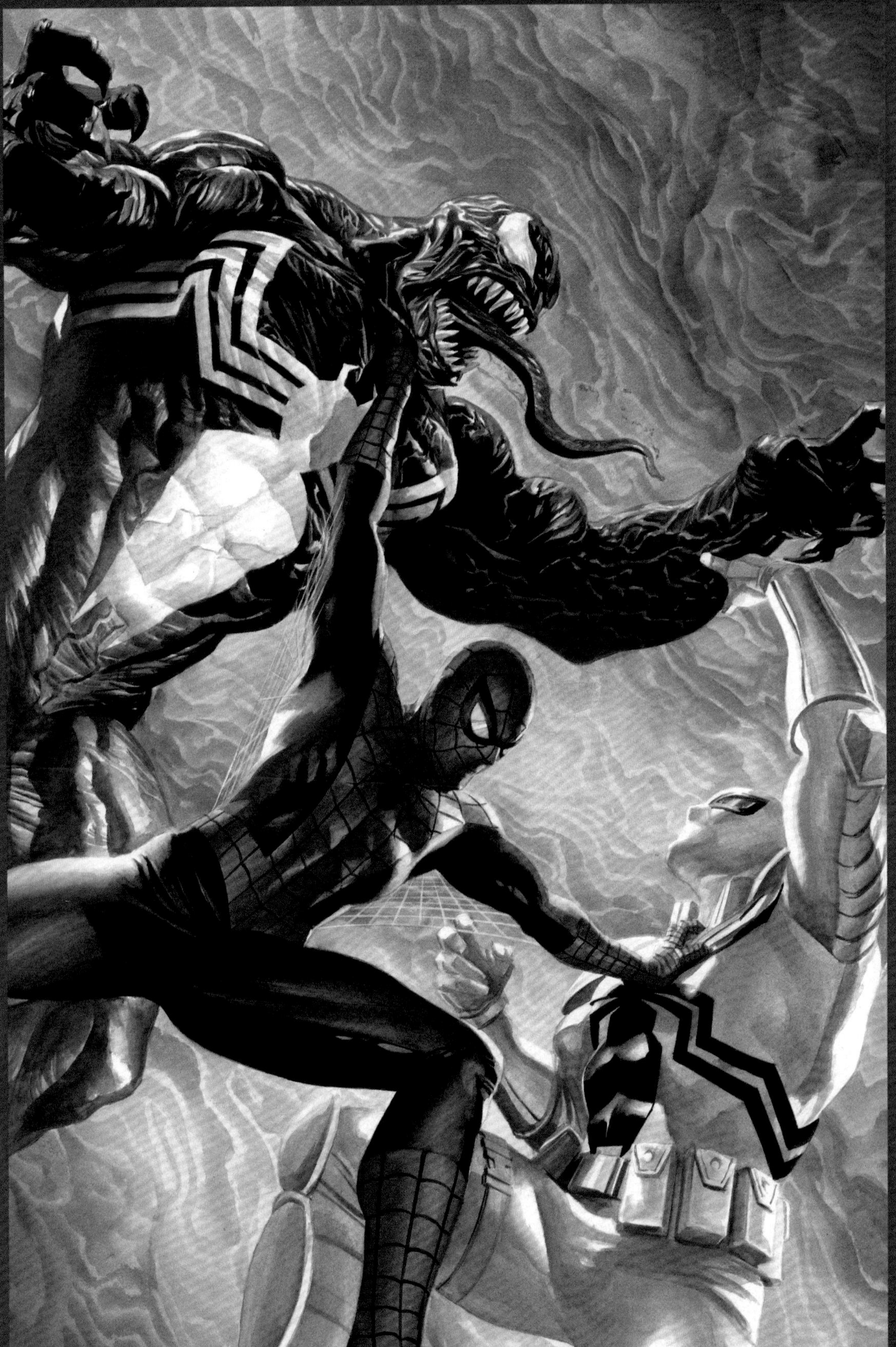

AMAZING SPIDER-MAN 792

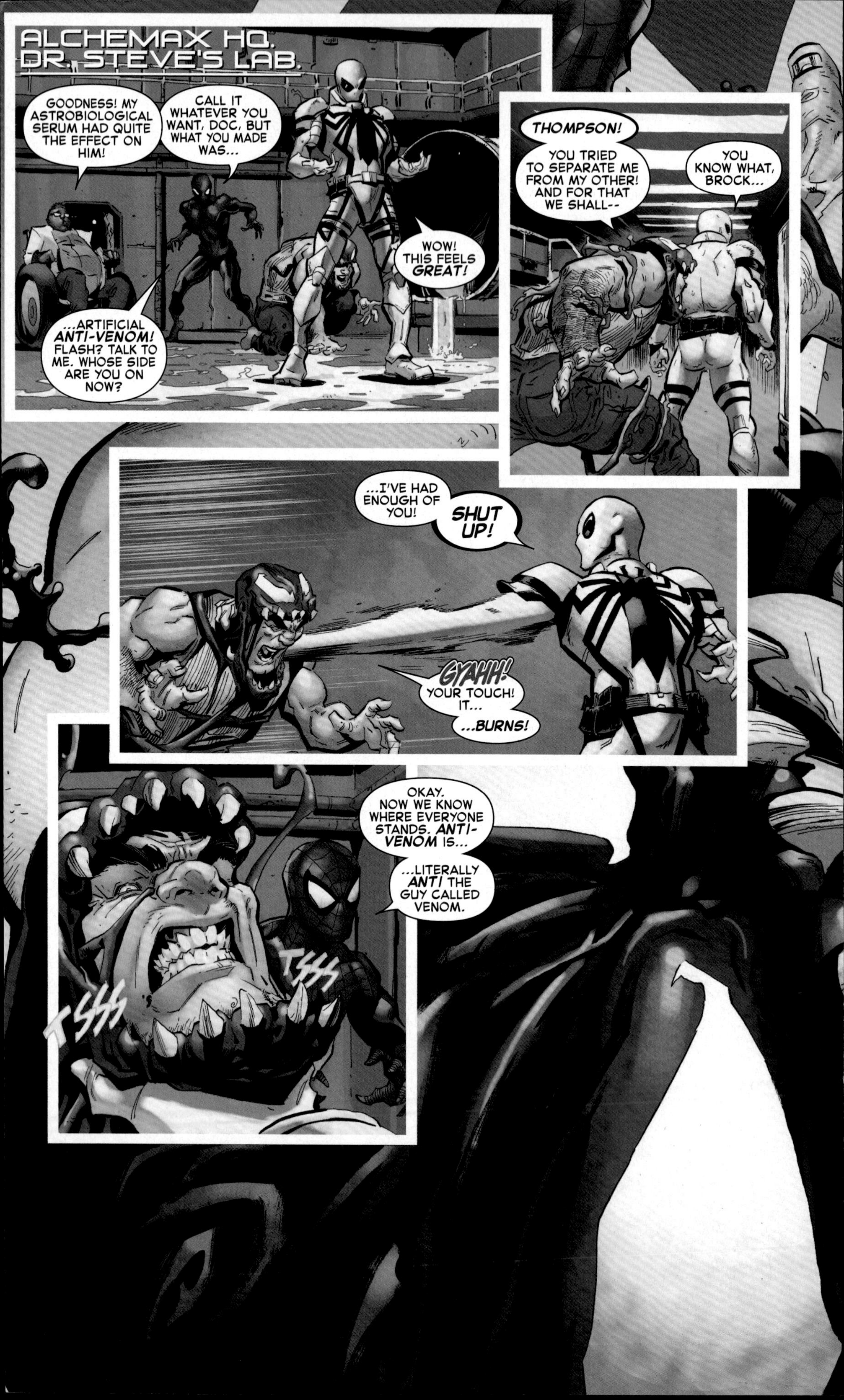
ALCHEMAX HQ.
DR. STEVE'S LAB.
GOODNESS! MY ASTROBIOLOGICAL SERUM HAD QUITE THE EFFECT ON HIM!
CALL IT WHATEVER YOU WANT, DOC, BUT WHAT YOU MADE WAS...
...ARTIFICIAL ANTI-VENOM! FLASH? TALK TO ME. WHOSE SIDE ARE YOU ON NOW?
WOW! THIS FEELS GREAT!
THOMPSON!
YOU TRIED TO SEPARATE ME FROM MY OTHER! AND FOR THAT WE SHALL--
YOU KNOW WHAT, BROCK...
...I'VE HAD ENOUGH OF YOU!
SHUT UP!
GYAHH! YOUR TOUCH! IT...
...BURNS!
OKAY. NOW WE KNOW WHERE EVERYONE STANDS. ANTI-VENOM IS...
...LITERALLY ANTI THE GUY CALLED VENOM.
TSSS
TSSS

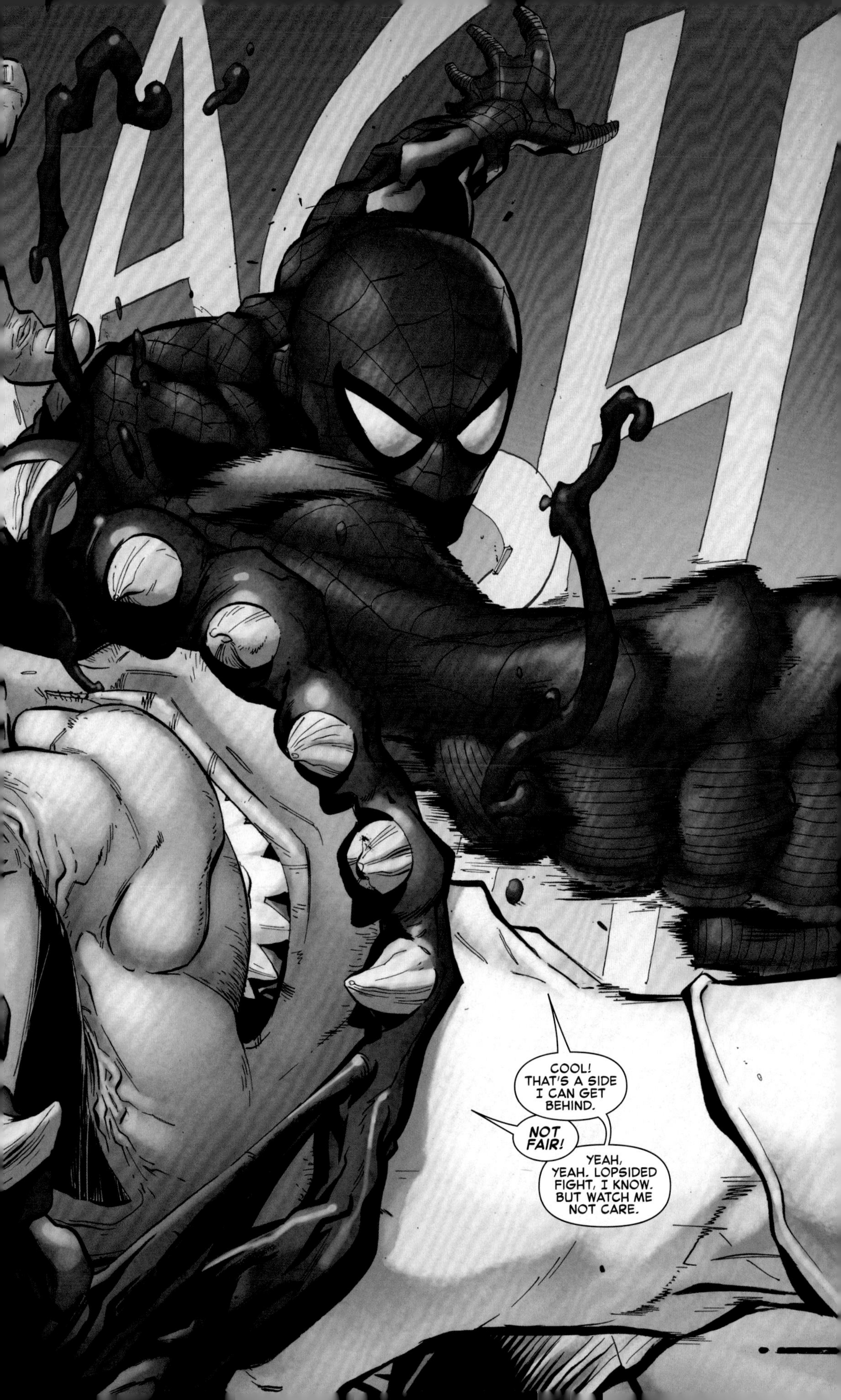
AAAH
COOL! THAT'S A SIDE I CAN GET BEHIND.
NOT FAIR!
YEAH, YEAH. LOPSIDED FIGHT, I KNOW. BUT WATCH ME NOT CARE.

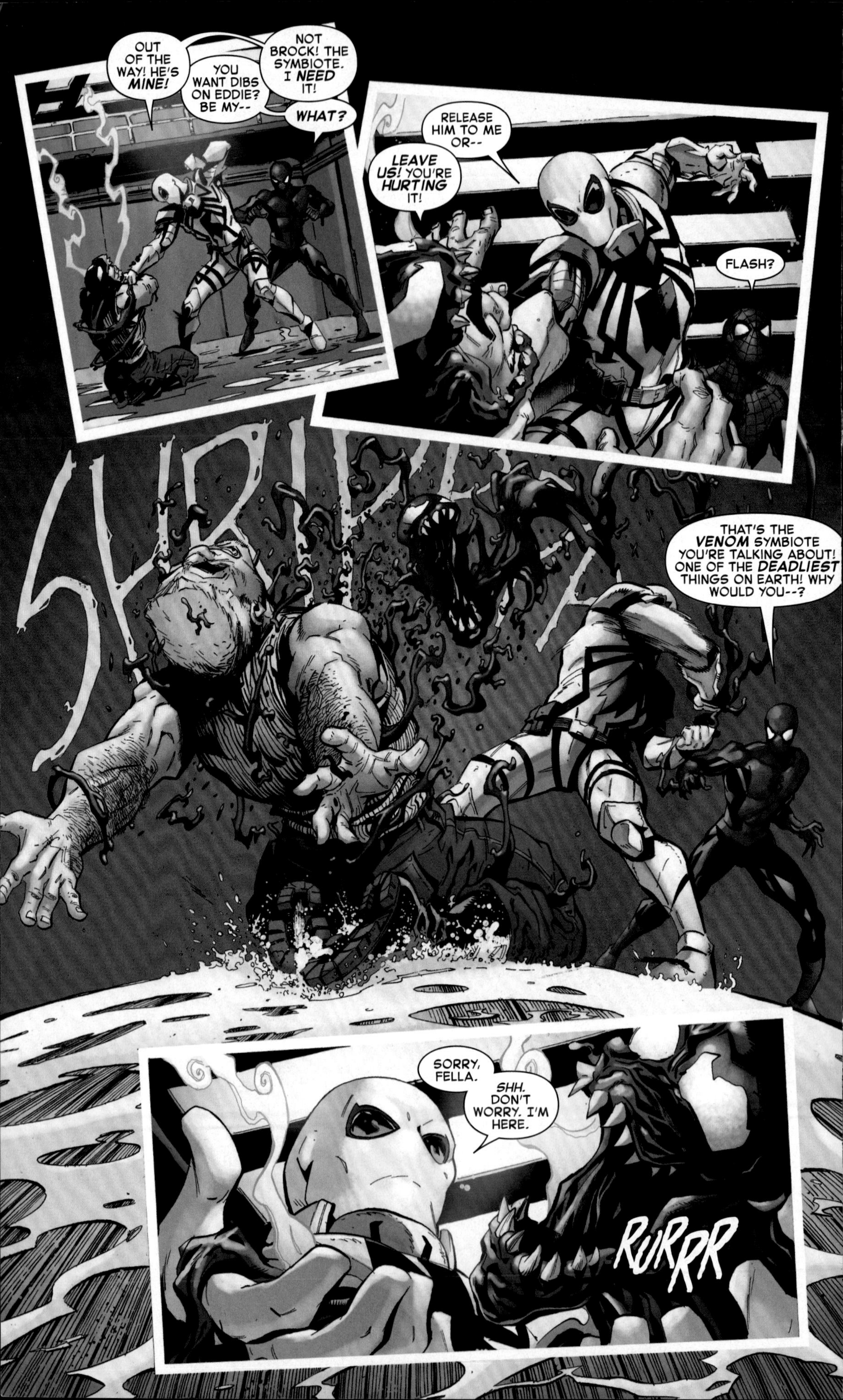
OUT OF THE WAY! HE'S MINE!
YOU WANT DIBS ON EDDIE? BE MY--
NOT BROCK! THE SYMBIOTE. I NEED IT!
WHAT?
RELEASE HIM TO ME OR--
LEAVE US! YOU'RE HURTING IT!
FLASH?
SHRIEEK
THAT'S THE VENOM SYMBIOTE YOU'RE TALKING ABOUT! ONE OF THE DEADLIEST THINGS ON EARTH! WHY WOULD YOU--?
SORRY, FELLA.
SHH. DON'T WORRY. I'M HERE.
RURRR

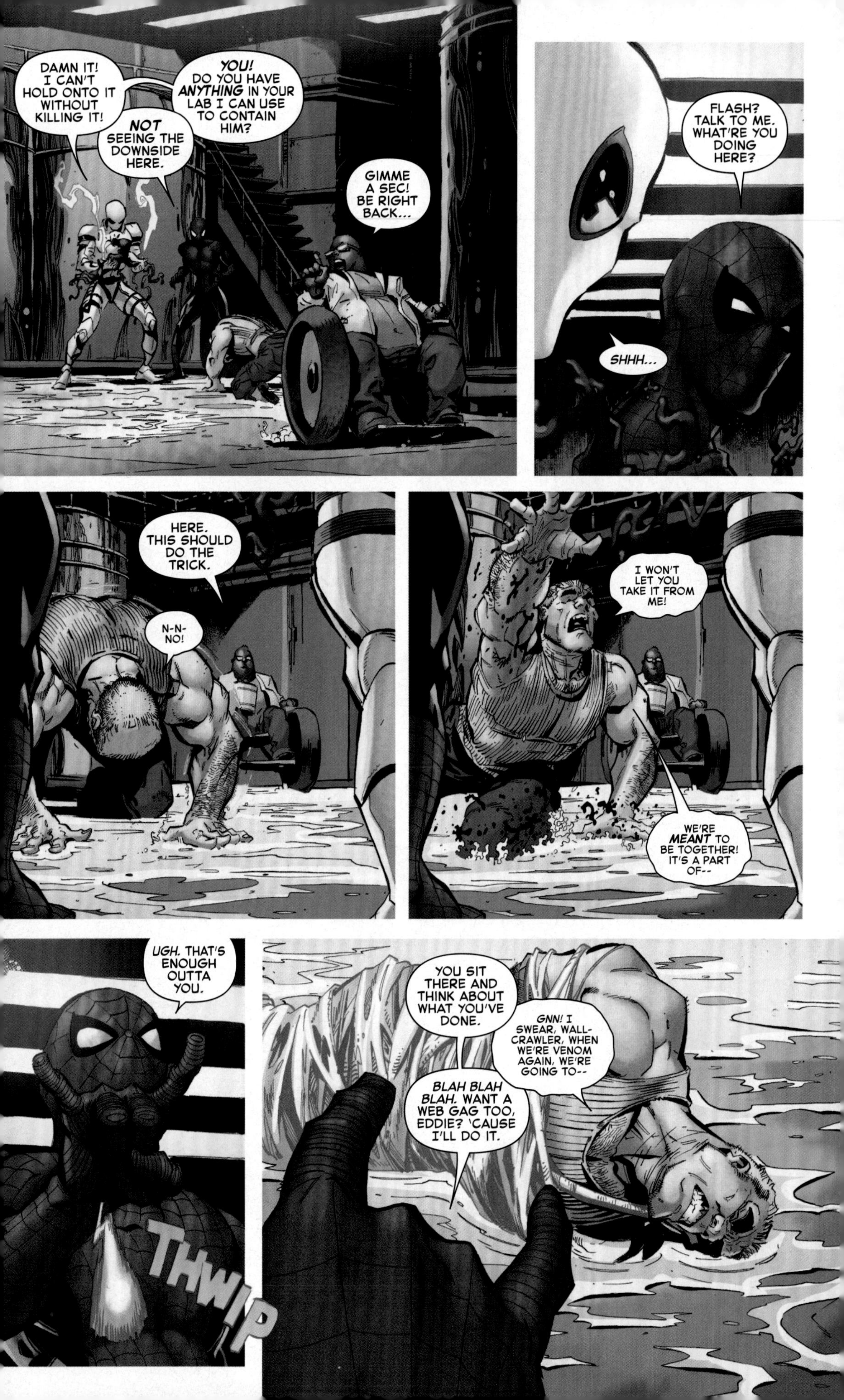
DAMN IT! I CAN'T HOLD ONTO IT WITHOUT KILLING IT!
NOT SEEING THE DOWNSIDE HERE.
YOU! DO YOU HAVE ANYTHING IN YOUR LAB I CAN USE TO CONTAIN HIM?
GIMME A SEC! BE RIGHT BACK...
FLASH? TALK TO ME. WHAT'RE YOU DOING HERE?
SHHH...
HERE. THIS SHOULD DO THE TRICK.
N-N-NO!
I WON'T LET YOU TAKE IT FROM ME!
WE'RE MEANT TO BE TOGETHER! IT'S A PART OF--
UGH. THAT'S ENOUGH OUTTA YOU.
THWIP
YOU SIT THERE AND THINK ABOUT WHAT YOU'VE DONE.
GNN! I SWEAR, WALL-CRAWLER, WHEN WE'RE VENOM AGAIN, WE'RE GOING TO--
BLAH BLAH BLAH. WANT A WEB GAG TOO, EDDIE? 'CAUSE I'LL DO IT.

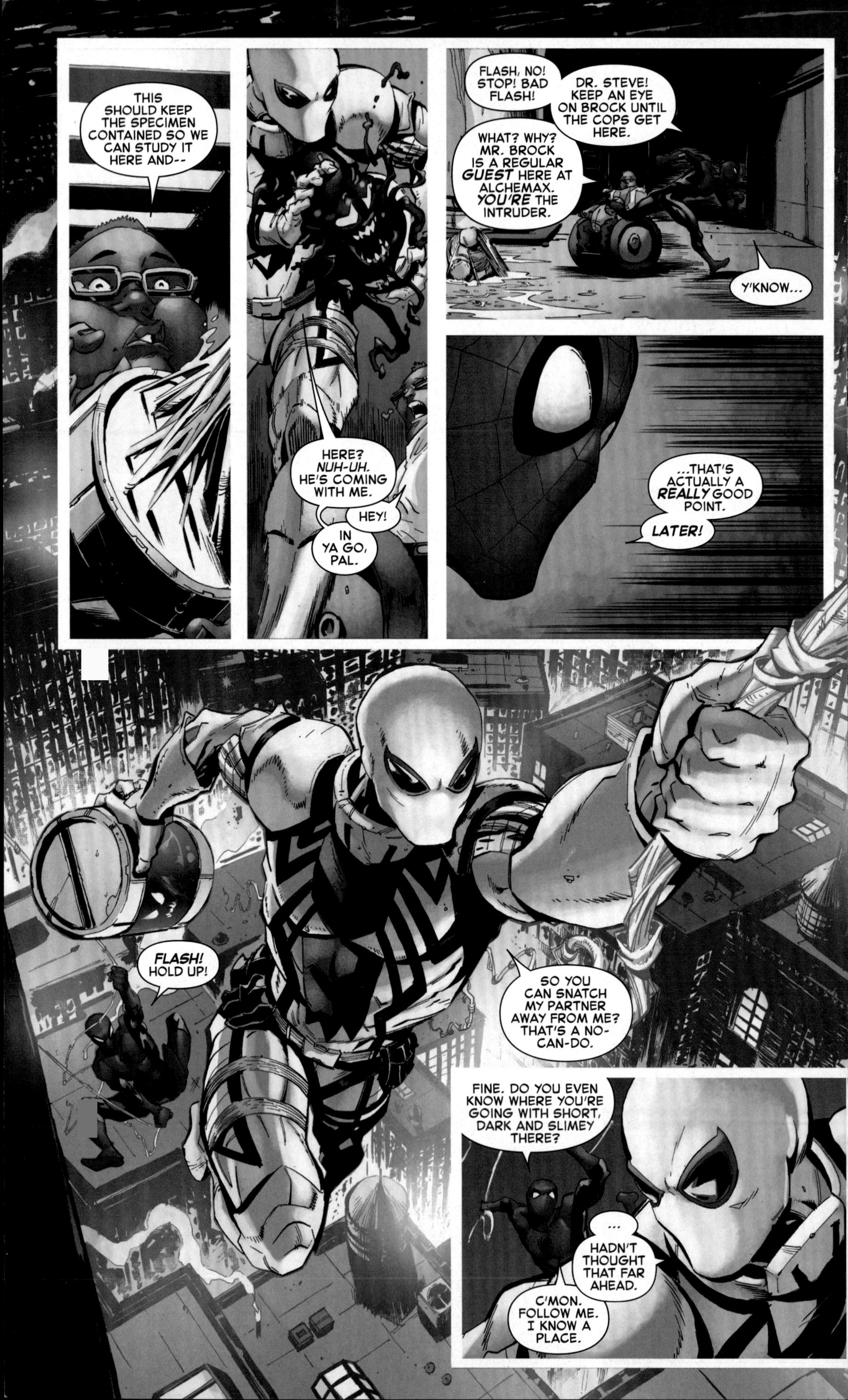
THIS SHOULD KEEP THE SPECIMEN CONTAINED SO WE CAN STUDY IT HERE AND--
HERE? NUH-UH. HE'S COMING WITH ME.
HEY!
IN YA GO, PAL.
FLASH, NO! STOP! BAD FLASH!
DR. STEVE! KEEP AN EYE ON BROCK UNTIL THE COPS GET HERE.
WHAT? WHY? MR. BROCK IS A REGULAR GUEST HERE AT ALCHEMAX. YOU'RE THE INTRUDER.
Y'KNOW...
...THAT'S ACTUALLY A REALLY GOOD POINT.
LATER!
FLASH! HOLD UP!
SO YOU CAN SNATCH MY PARTNER AWAY FROM ME? THAT'S A NO-CAN-DO.
FINE. DO YOU EVEN KNOW WHERE YOU'RE GOING WITH SHORT, DARK AND SLIMEY THERE?
...
HADN'T THOUGHT THAT FAR AHEAD.
C'MON. FOLLOW ME. I KNOW A PLACE.

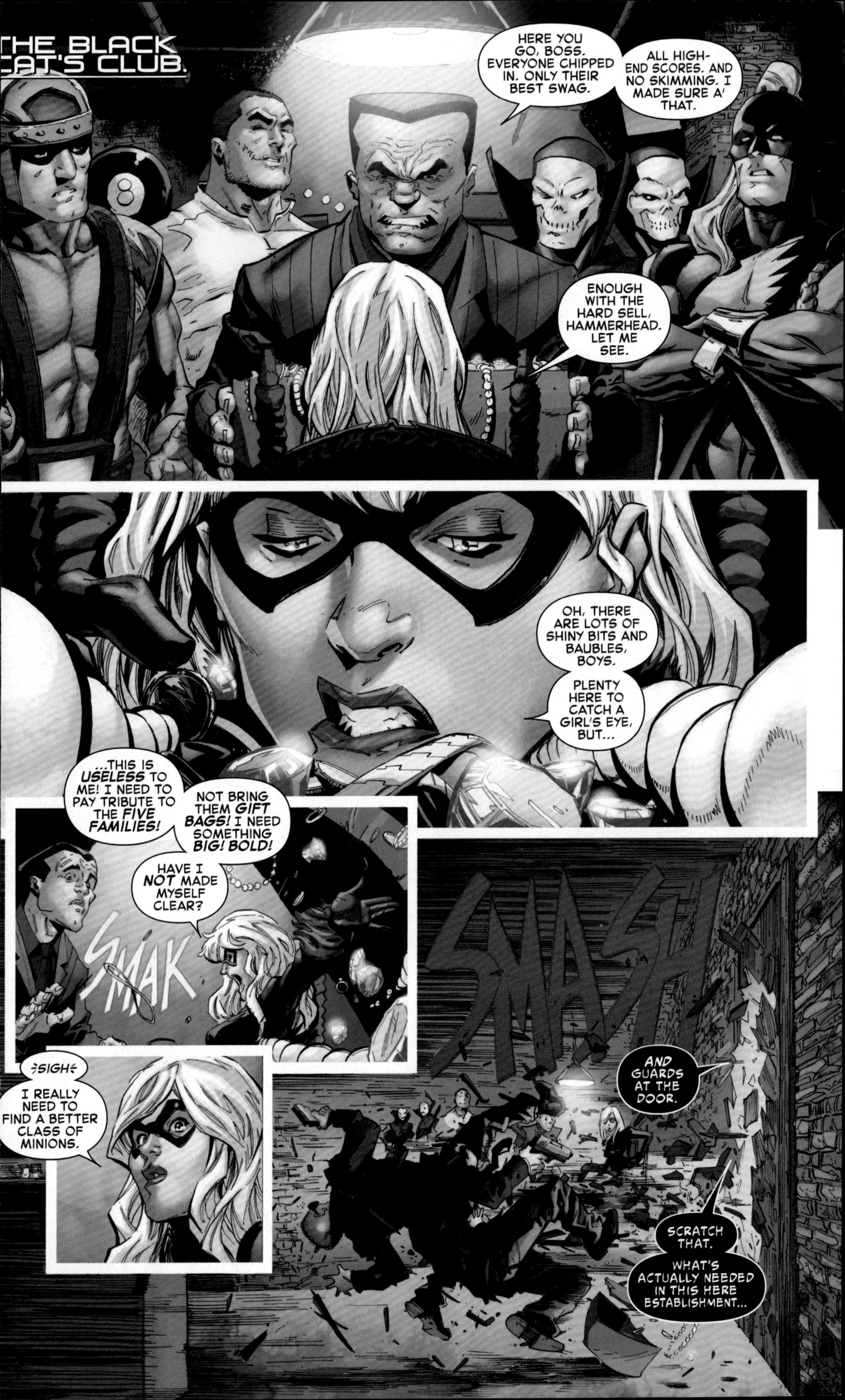
THE BLACK CAT'S CLUB.
HERE YOU GO, BOSS. EVERYONE CHIPPED IN. ONLY THEIR BEST SWAG.
ALL HIGH-END SCORES. AND NO SKIMMING. I MADE SURE A' THAT.
ENOUGH WITH THE HARD SELL, HAMMERHEAD. LET ME SEE.
OH, THERE ARE LOTS OF SHINY BITS AND BAUBLES, BOYS.
PLENTY HERE TO CATCH A GIRL'S EYE, BUT...
...THIS IS USELESS TO ME! I NEED TO PAY TRIBUTE TO THE FIVE FAMILIES!
NOT BRING THEM GIFT BAGS! I NEED SOMETHING BIG! BOLD!
HAVE I NOT MADE MYSELF CLEAR?
SMAK
SIGH
I REALLY NEED TO FIND A BETTER CLASS OF MINIONS.
SMASH
AND GUARDS AT THE DOOR.
SCRATCH THAT.
WHAT'S ACTUALLY NEEDED IN THIS HERE ESTABLISHMENT...

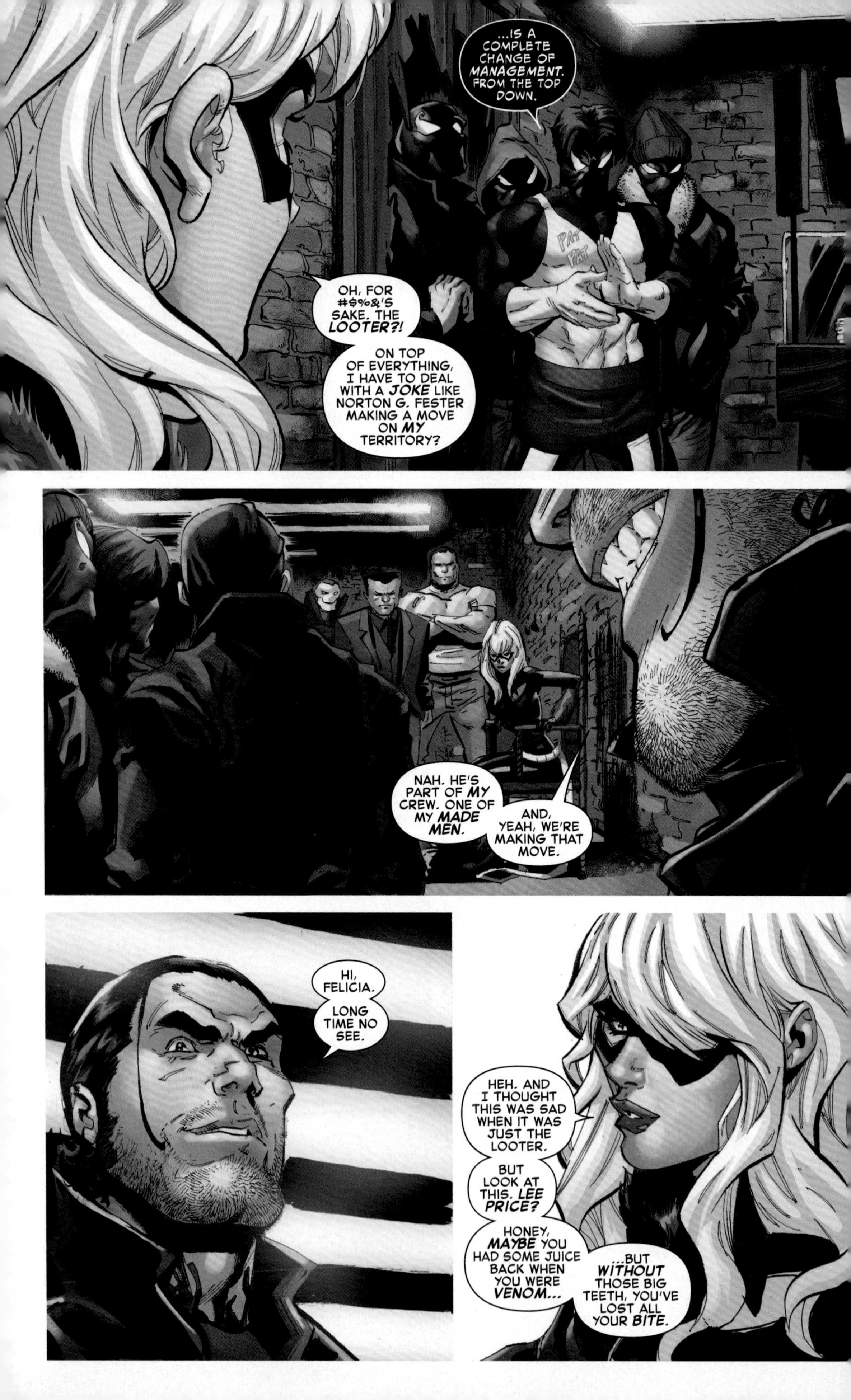
...IS A COMPLETE CHANGE OF MANAGEMENT. FROM THE TOP DOWN.
OH, FOR #$%&'S SAKE. THE LOOTER?!
ON TOP OF EVERYTHING, I HAVE TO DEAL WITH A JOKE LIKE NORTON G. FESTER MAKING A MOVE ON MY TERRITORY?
PAT PAT
NAH. HE'S PART OF MY CREW. ONE OF MY MADE MEN.
AND, YEAH, WE'RE MAKING THAT MOVE.
HI, FELICIA.
LONG TIME NO SEE.
HEH. AND I THOUGHT THIS WAS SAD WHEN IT WAS JUST THE LOOTER.
BUT LOOK AT THIS. LEE PRICE?
HONEY, MAYBE YOU HAD SOME JUICE BACK WHEN YOU WERE VENOM...
...BUT WITHOUT THOSE BIG TEETH, YOU'VE LOST ALL YOUR BITE.

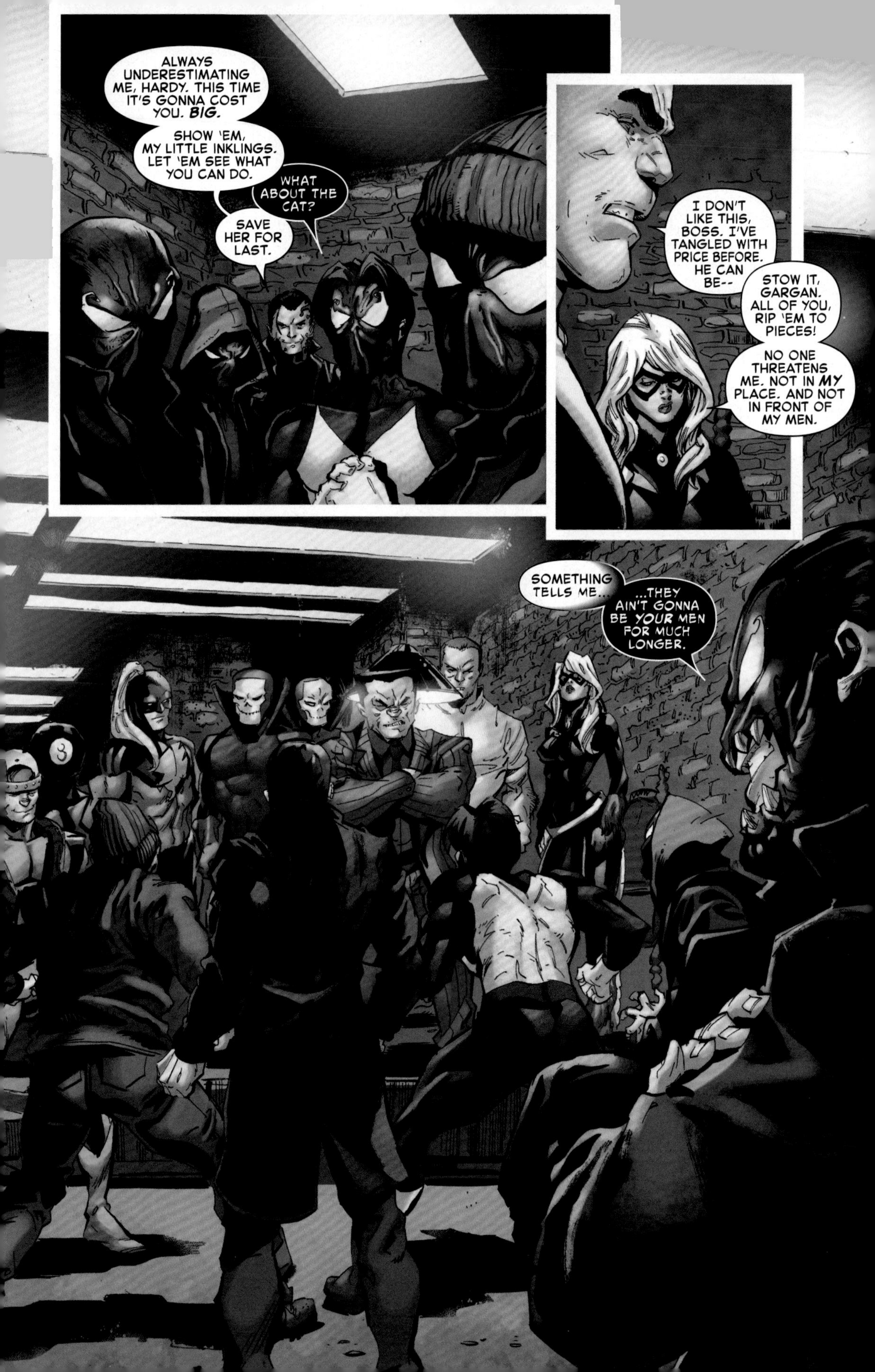

ALWAYS UNDERESTIMATING ME, HARDY. THIS TIME IT'S GONNA COST YOU. BIG.
SHOW 'EM, MY LITTLE INKLINGS. LET 'EM SEE WHAT YOU CAN DO.
WHAT ABOUT THE CAT?
SAVE HER FOR LAST.
I DON'T LIKE THIS, BOSS. I'VE TANGLED WITH PRICE BEFORE. HE CAN BE--
STOW IT, GARGAN. ALL OF YOU, RIP 'EM TO PIECES!
NO ONE THREATENS ME. NOT IN MY PLACE. AND NOT IN FRONT OF MY MEN.
SOMETHING TELLS ME...
...THEY AIN'T GONNA BE YOUR MEN FOR MUCH LONGER.

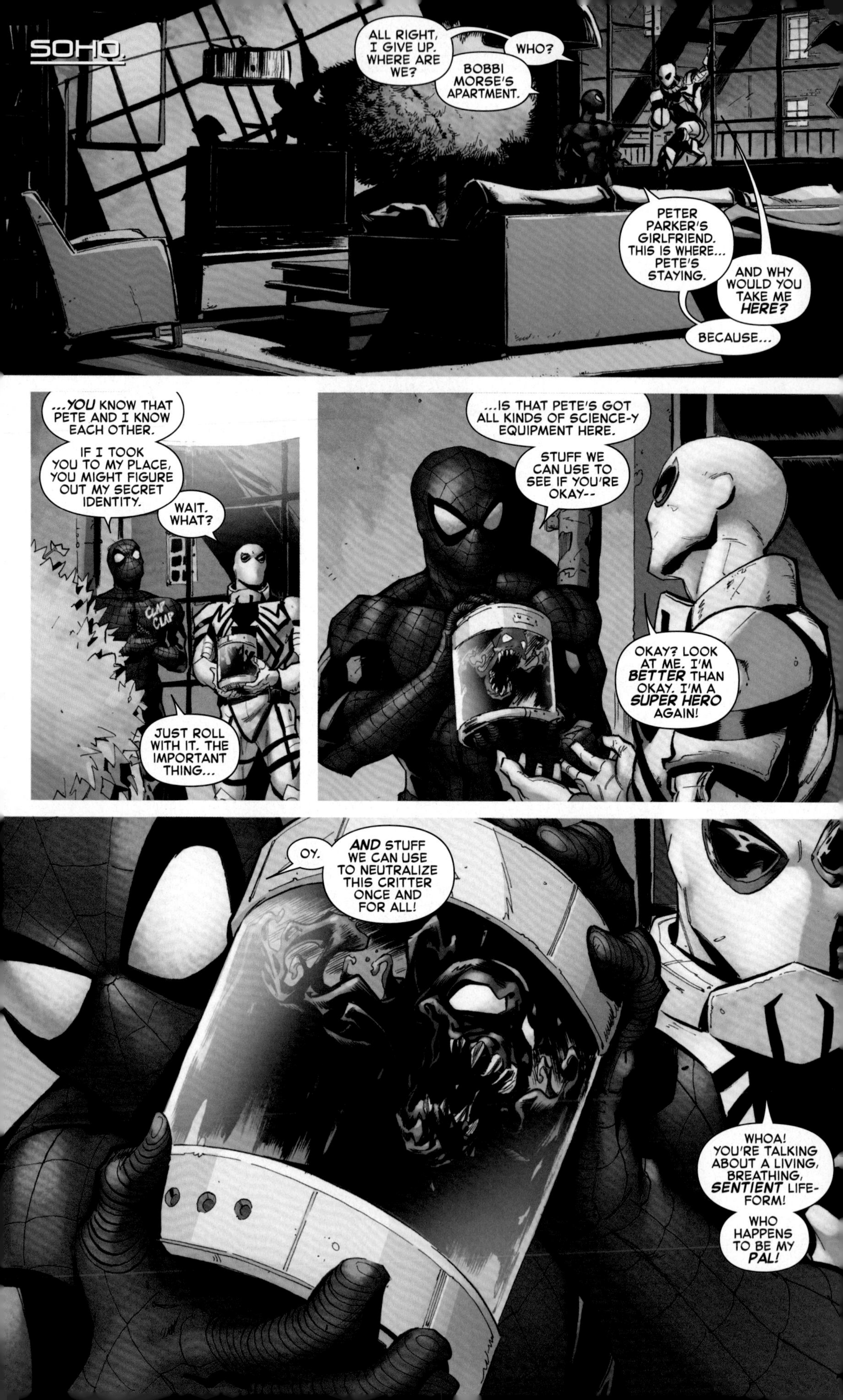
SOHO.
ALL RIGHT, I GIVE UP. WHERE ARE WE?
BOBBI MORSE'S APARTMENT.
WHO?
PETER PARKER'S GIRLFRIEND. THIS IS WHERE... PETE'S STAYING.
AND WHY WOULD YOU TAKE ME HERE?
BECAUSE...
...YOU KNOW THAT PETE AND I KNOW EACH OTHER.
IF I TOOK YOU TO MY PLACE, YOU MIGHT FIGURE OUT MY SECRET IDENTITY.
WAIT. WHAT?
CLAP CLAP
JUST ROLL WITH IT. THE IMPORTANT THING...
...IS THAT PETE'S GOT ALL KINDS OF SCIENCE-Y EQUIPMENT HERE.
STUFF WE CAN USE TO SEE IF YOU'RE OKAY--
OKAY? LOOK AT ME. I'M BETTER THAN OKAY. I'M A SUPER HERO AGAIN!
OY.
AND STUFF WE CAN USE TO NEUTRALIZE THIS CRITTER ONCE AND FOR ALL!
WHOA! YOU'RE TALKING ABOUT A LIVING, BREATHING, SENTIENT LIFE-FORM!
WHO HAPPENS TO BE MY PAL!

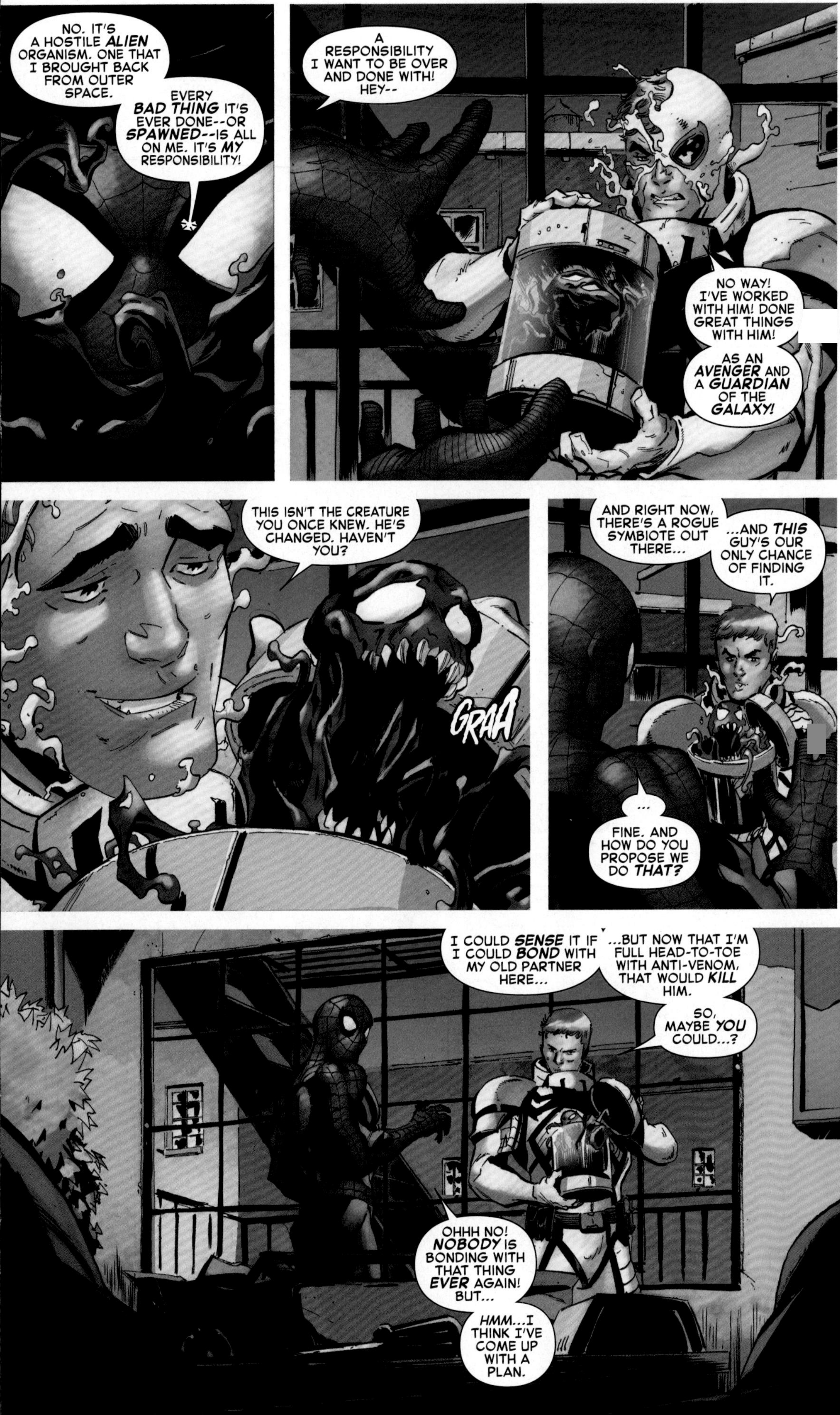
NO. IT'S A HOSTILE ALIEN ORGANISM. ONE THAT I BROUGHT BACK FROM OUTER SPACE.
EVERY BAD THING IT'S EVER DONE--OR SPAWNED--IS ALL ON ME. IT'S MY RESPONSIBILITY!
A RESPONSIBILITY I WANT TO BE OVER AND DONE WITH! HEY--
NO WAY! I'VE WORKED WITH HIM! DONE GREAT THINGS WITH HIM!
AS AN AVENGER AND A GUARDIAN OF THE GALAXY!
THIS ISN'T THE CREATURE YOU ONCE KNEW. HE'S CHANGED. HAVEN'T YOU?
GRAA
AND RIGHT NOW, THERE'S A ROGUE SYMBIOTE OUT THERE...
...AND THIS GUY'S OUR ONLY CHANCE OF FINDING IT.
...
FINE. AND HOW DO YOU PROPOSE WE DO THAT?
I COULD SENSE IT IF I COULD BOND WITH MY OLD PARTNER HERE...
...BUT NOW THAT I'M FULL HEAD-TO-TOE WITH ANTI-VENOM, THAT WOULD KILL HIM.
SO, MAYBE YOU COULD...?
OHHH NO! NOBODY IS BONDING WITH THAT THING EVER AGAIN! BUT...
HMM...I THINK I'VE COME UP WITH A PLAN.

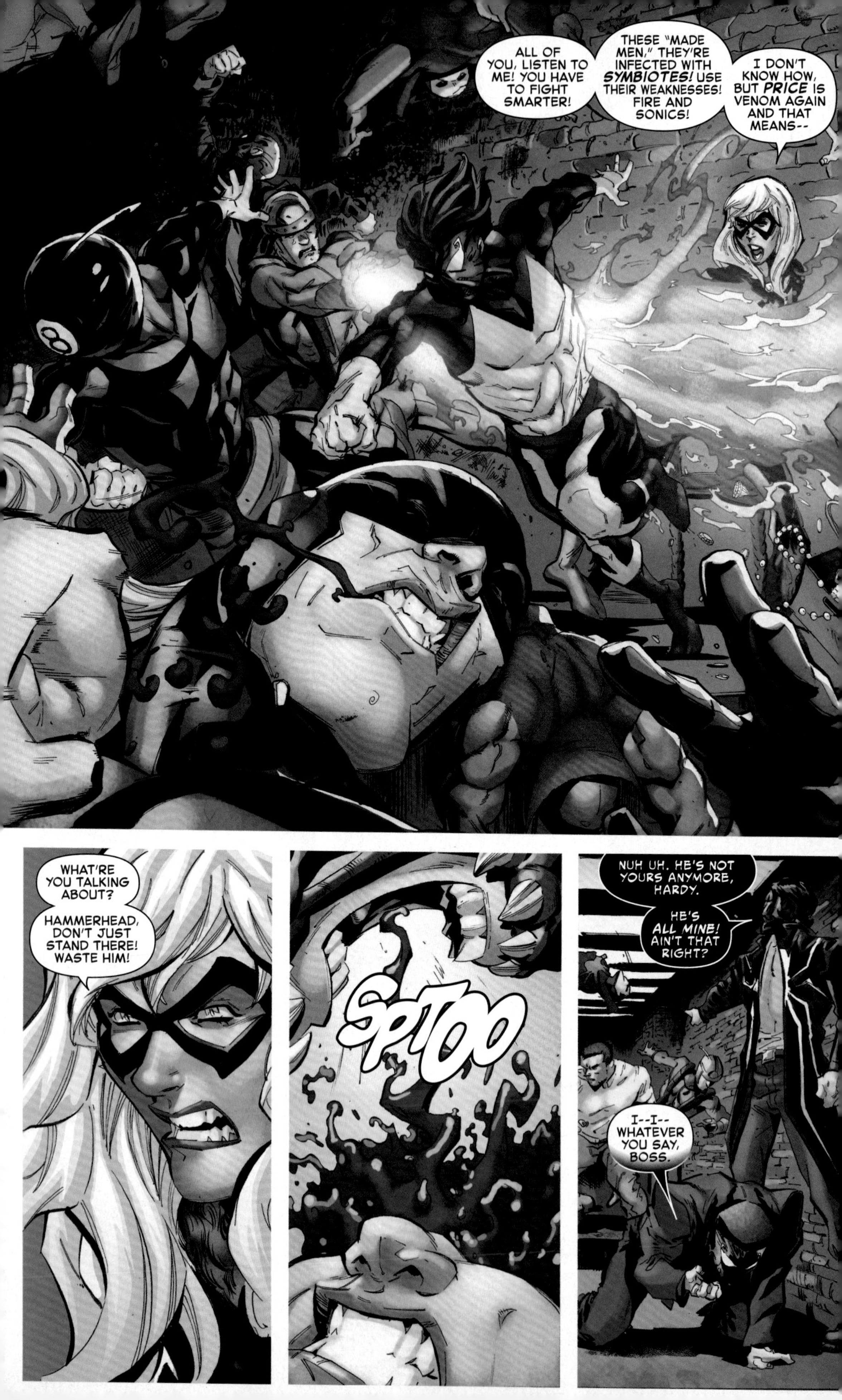
ALL OF YOU, LISTEN TO ME! YOU HAVE TO FIGHT SMARTER!
THESE "MADE MEN," THEY'RE INFECTED WITH *SYMBIOTES!* USE THEIR WEAKNESSES! FIRE AND SONICS!
I DON'T KNOW HOW, BUT *PRICE* IS VENOM AGAIN AND THAT MEANS--
WHAT'RE YOU TALKING ABOUT?
HAMMERHEAD, DON'T JUST STAND THERE! WASTE HIM!
SPTOO
NUH UH. HE'S NOT YOURS ANYMORE, HARDY.
HE'S *ALL MINE!* AIN'T THAT RIGHT?
I--I-- WHATEVER YOU SAY, BOSS.

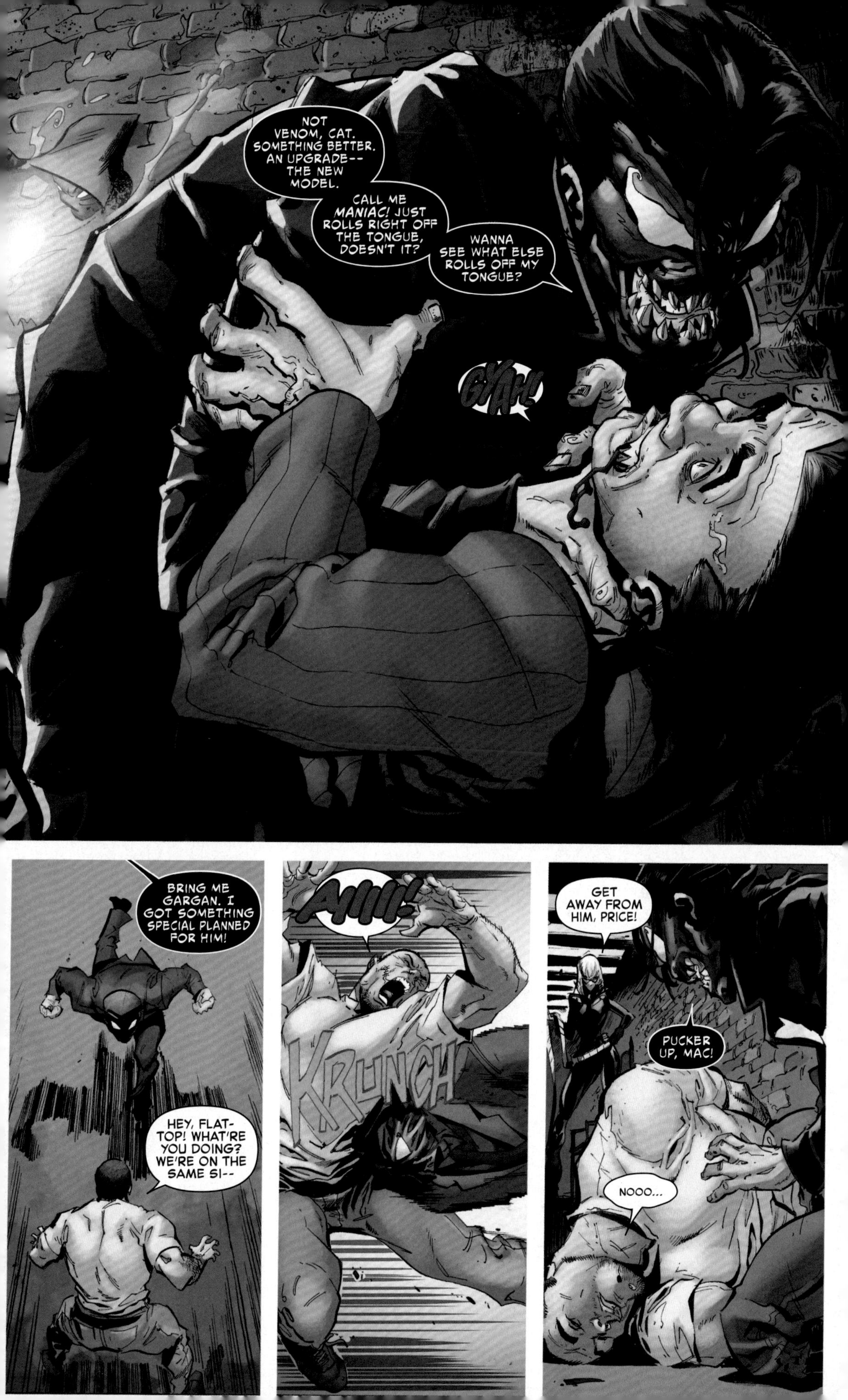
NOT VENOM, CAT. SOMETHING BETTER. AN UPGRADE-- THE NEW MODEL.
CALL ME MANIAC! JUST ROLLS RIGHT OFF THE TONGUE, DOESN'T IT?
WANNA SEE WHAT ELSE ROLLS OFF MY TONGUE?
GYAH!
BRING ME GARGAN. I GOT SOMETHING SPECIAL PLANNED FOR HIM!
HEY, FLAT-TOP! WHAT'RE YOU DOING? WE'RE ON THE SAME SI--
AIIII!
KRUNCH
GET AWAY FROM HIM, PRICE!
PUCKER UP, MAC!
NOOO...

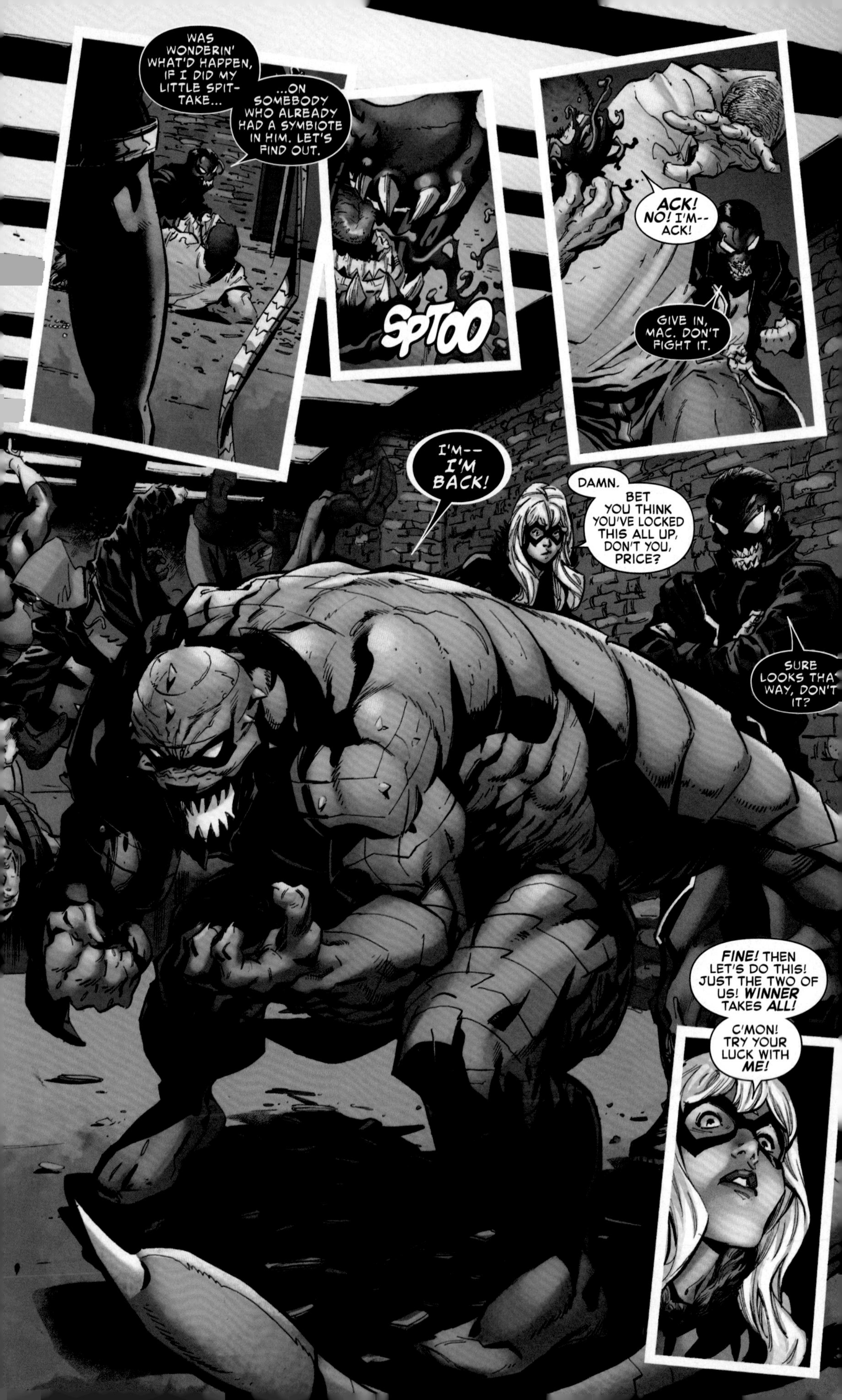

WAS WONDERIN' WHAT'D HAPPEN, IF I DID MY LITTLE SPIT-TAKE...
...ON SOMEBODY WHO ALREADY HAD A SYMBIOTE IN HIM. LET'S FIND OUT.
SPTOO
ACK! NO! I'M--ACK!
GIVE IN, MAC. DON'T FIGHT IT.
I'M-- I'M BACK!
DAMN.
BET YOU THINK YOU'VE LOCKED THIS ALL UP, DON'T YOU, PRICE?
SURE LOOKS THA WAY, DON'T IT?
FINE! THEN LET'S DO THIS! JUST THE TWO OF US! WINNER TAKES ALL!
C'MON! TRY YOUR LUCK WITH ME!

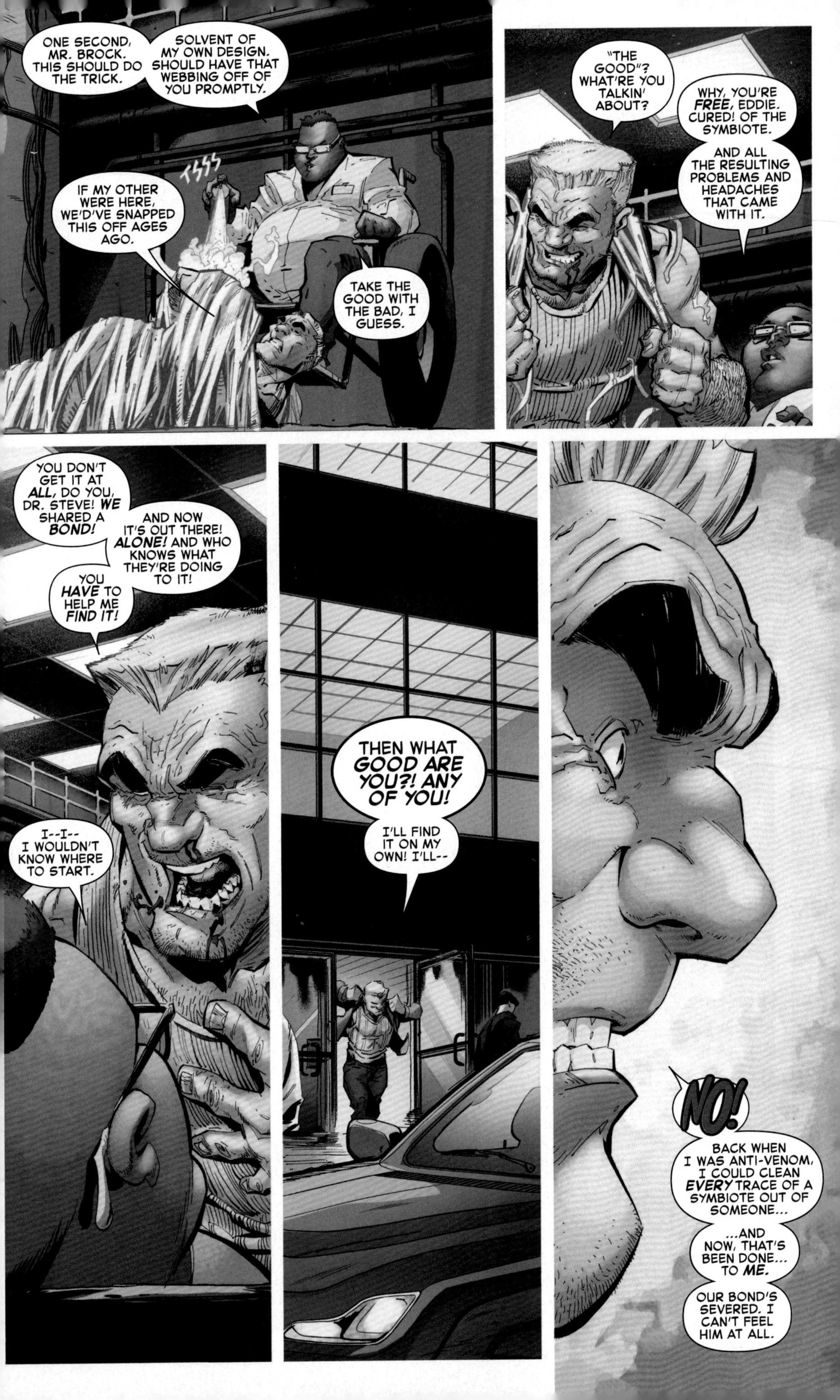

ONE SECOND, MR. BROCK. THIS SHOULD DO THE TRICK.
SOLVENT OF MY OWN DESIGN. SHOULD HAVE THAT WEBBING OFF OF YOU PROMPTLY.
TSSS
IF MY OTHER WERE HERE, WE'D'VE SNAPPED THIS OFF AGES AGO.
TAKE THE GOOD WITH THE BAD, I GUESS.
"THE GOOD"? WHAT'RE YOU TALKIN' ABOUT?
WHY, YOU'RE FREE, EDDIE. CURED! OF THE SYMBIOTE.
AND ALL THE RESULTING PROBLEMS AND HEADACHES THAT CAME WITH IT.
YOU DON'T GET IT AT ALL, DO YOU, DR. STEVE! WE SHARED A BOND!
AND NOW IT'S OUT THERE! ALONE! AND WHO KNOWS WHAT THEY'RE DOING TO IT!
YOU HAVE TO HELP ME FIND IT!
I--I-- I WOULDN'T KNOW WHERE TO START.
THEN WHAT GOOD ARE YOU?! ANY OF YOU!
I'LL FIND IT ON MY OWN! I'LL--
NO!
BACK WHEN I WAS ANTI-VENOM, I COULD CLEAN EVERY TRACE OF A SYMBIOTE OUT OF SOMEONE...
...AND NOW, THAT'S BEEN DONE... TO ME.
OUR BOND'S SEVERED. I CAN'T FEEL HIM AT ALL.

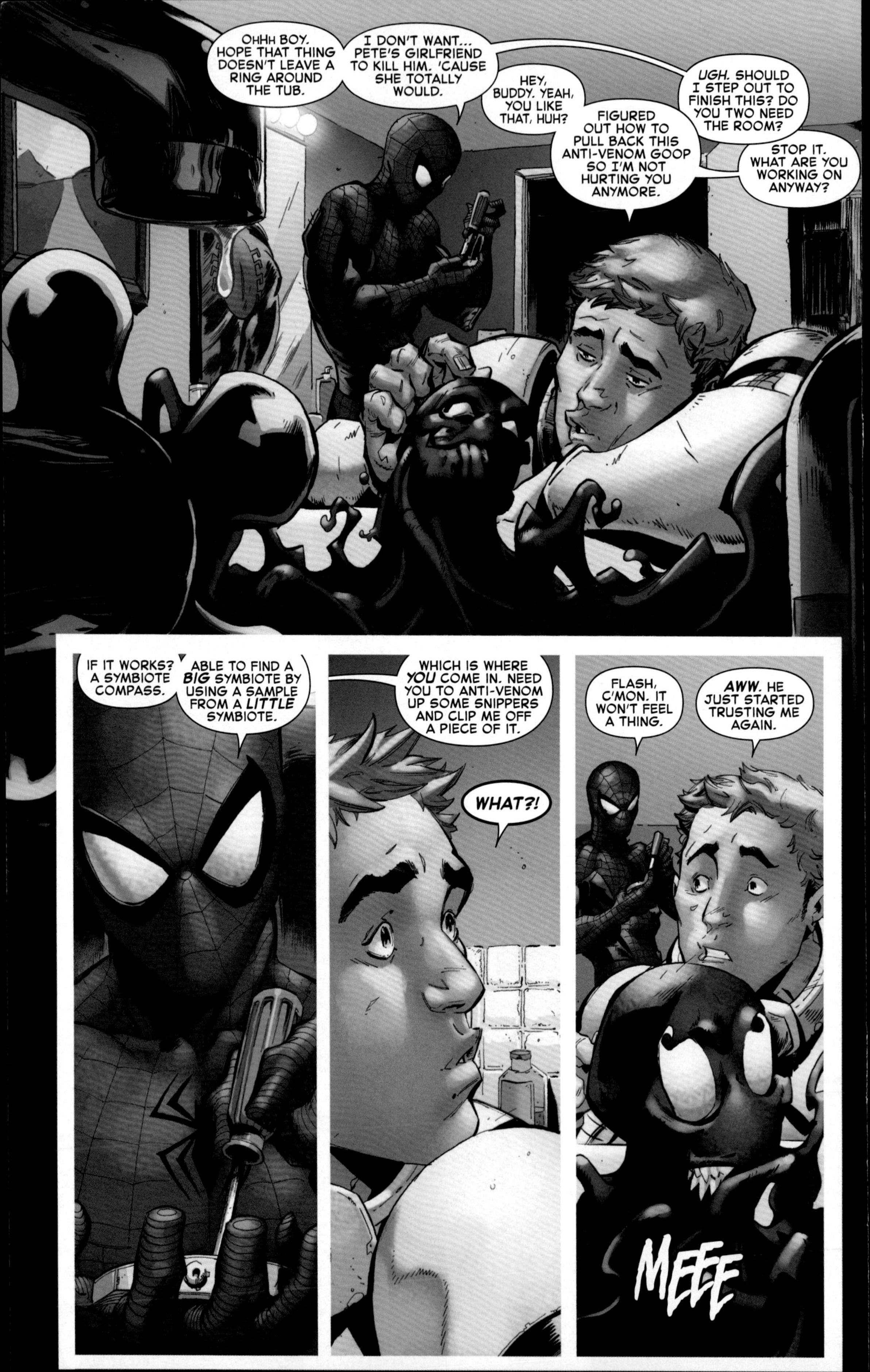
OHHH BOY. HOPE THAT THING DOESN'T LEAVE A RING AROUND THE TUB.
I DON'T WANT... PETE'S GIRLFRIEND TO KILL HIM. 'CAUSE SHE TOTALLY WOULD.
HEY, BUDDY. YEAH, YOU LIKE THAT, HUH?
FIGURED OUT HOW TO PULL BACK THIS ANTI-VENOM GOOP SO I'M NOT HURTING YOU ANYMORE.
UGH. SHOULD I STEP OUT TO FINISH THIS? DO YOU TWO NEED THE ROOM?
STOP IT. WHAT ARE YOU WORKING ON ANYWAY?
IF IT WORKS? A SYMBIOTE COMPASS.
ABLE TO FIND A BIG SYMBIOTE BY USING A SAMPLE FROM A LITTLE SYMBIOTE.
WHICH IS WHERE YOU COME IN. NEED YOU TO ANTI-VENOM UP SOME SNIPPERS AND CLIP ME OFF A PIECE OF IT.
WHAT?!
FLASH, C'MON. IT WON'T FEEL A THING.
AWW. HE JUST STARTED TRUSTING ME AGAIN.
MEEE

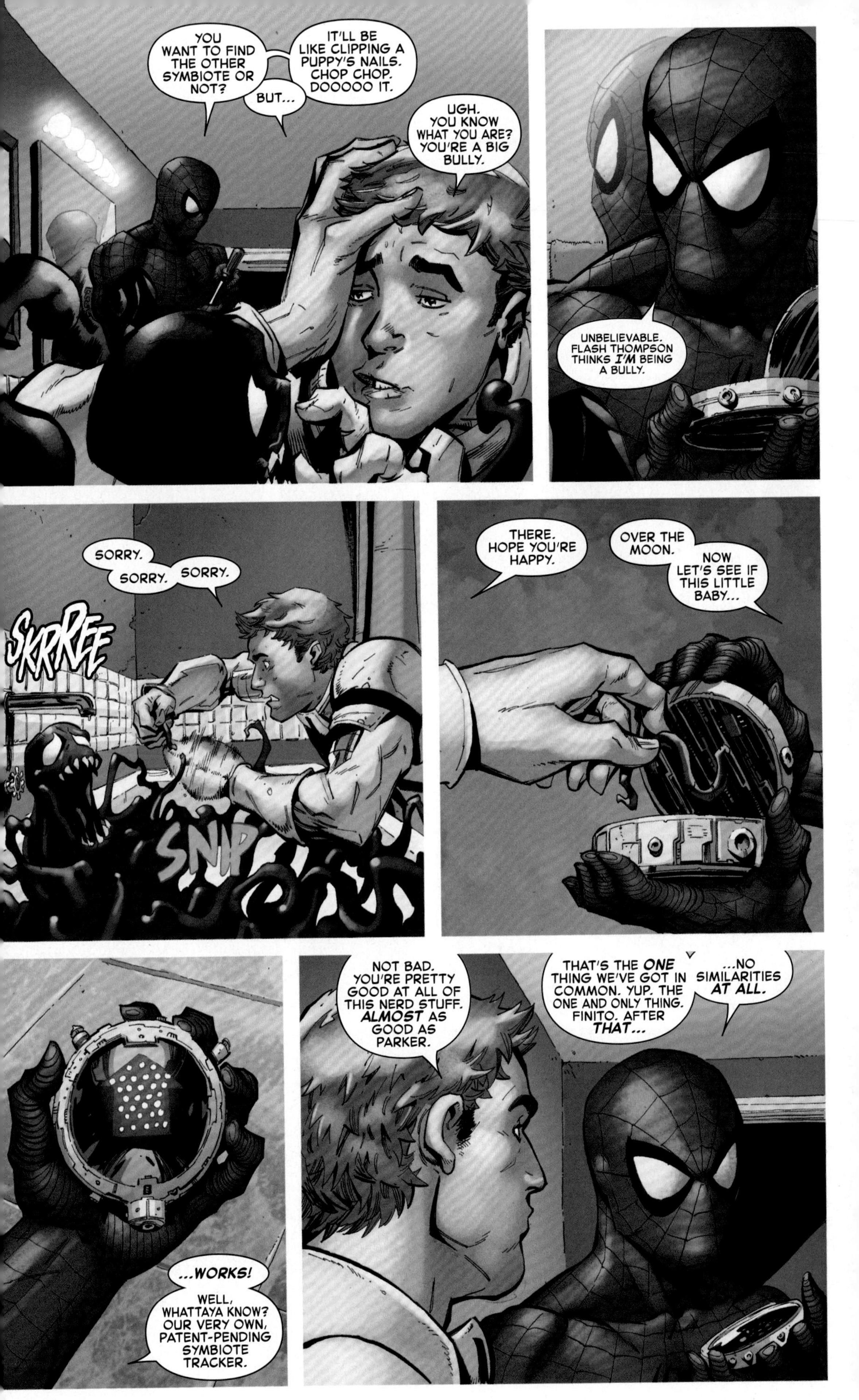
YOU WANT TO FIND THE OTHER SYMBIOTE OR NOT?
BUT...
IT'LL BE LIKE CLIPPING A PUPPY'S NAILS. CHOP CHOP. DOOOOO IT.
UGH. YOU KNOW WHAT YOU ARE? YOU'RE A BIG BULLY.
UNBELIEVABLE. FLASH THOMPSON THINKS *I'M* BEING A BULLY.
SORRY.
SORRY.
SORRY.
SKRREE
SNIP
THERE. HOPE YOU'RE HAPPY.
OVER THE MOON.
NOW LET'S SEE IF THIS LITTLE BABY...
...*WORKS!*
WELL, WHATTAYA KNOW? OUR VERY OWN, PATENT-PENDING SYMBIOTE TRACKER.
NOT BAD. YOU'RE PRETTY GOOD AT ALL OF THIS NERD STUFF. *ALMOST* AS GOOD AS PARKER.
THAT'S THE *ONE* THING WE'VE GOT IN COMMON. YUP. THE ONE AND ONLY THING. FINITO. AFTER *THAT...*
...NO SIMILARITIES *AT ALL.*

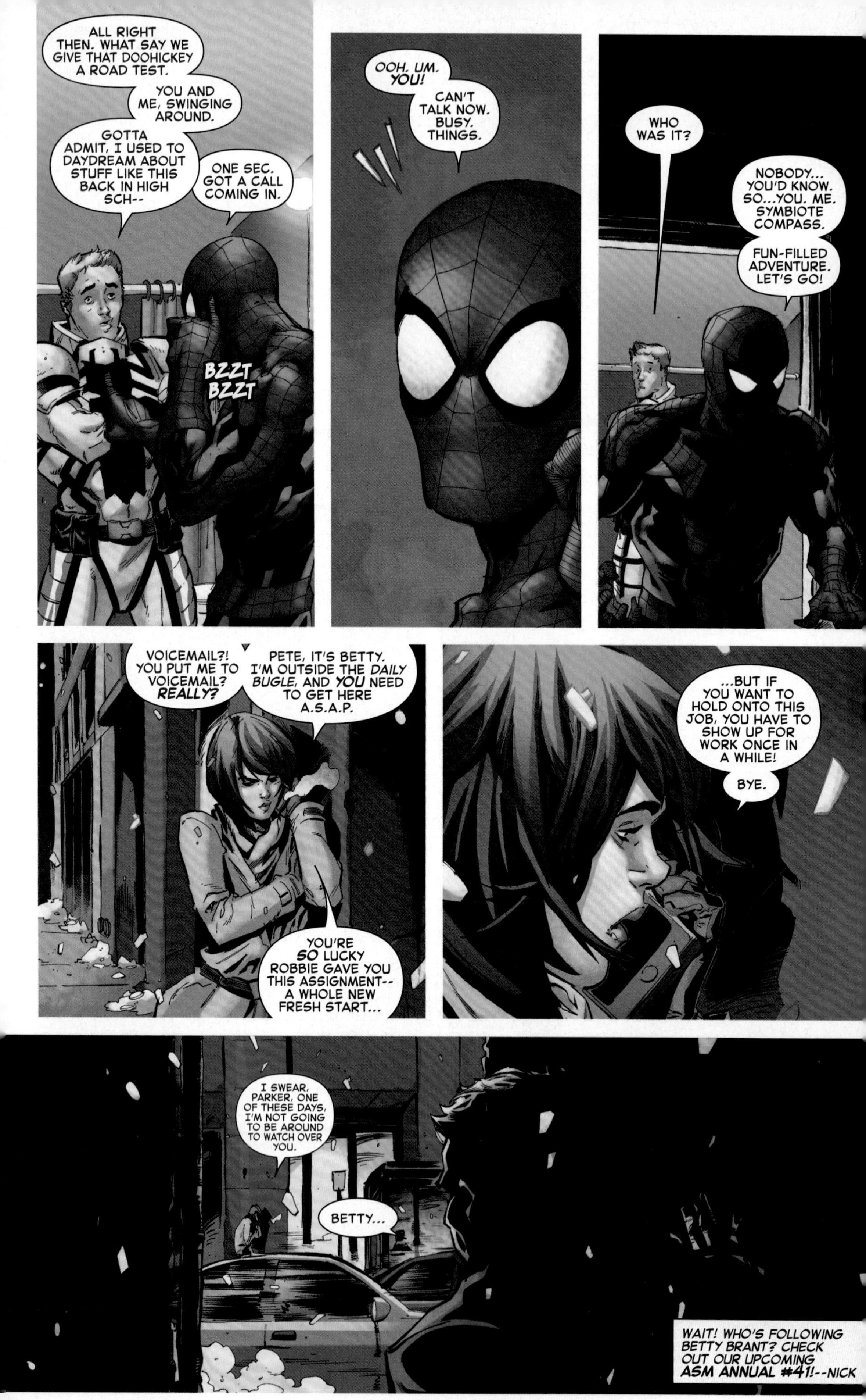
ALL RIGHT THEN. WHAT SAY WE GIVE THAT DOOHICKEY A ROAD TEST.
YOU AND ME, SWINGING AROUND.
GOTTA ADMIT, I USED TO DAYDREAM ABOUT STUFF LIKE THIS BACK IN HIGH SCH--
ONE SEC. GOT A CALL COMING IN.
BZZT BZZT
OOH. UM. YOU!
CAN'T TALK NOW. BUSY. THINGS.
WHO WAS IT?
NOBODY... YOU'D KNOW. SO...YOU. ME. SYMBIOTE COMPASS.
FUN-FILLED ADVENTURE. LET'S GO!
PETE, IT'S BETTY. I'M OUTSIDE THE DAILY BUGLE, AND YOU NEED TO GET HERE A.S.A.P.
VOICEMAIL?! YOU PUT ME TO VOICEMAIL? REALLY?
YOU'RE SO LUCKY ROBBIE GAVE YOU THIS ASSIGNMENT-- A WHOLE NEW FRESH START...
...BUT IF YOU WANT TO HOLD ONTO THIS JOB, YOU HAVE TO SHOW UP FOR WORK ONCE IN A WHILE!
BYE.
I SWEAR, PARKER, ONE OF THESE DAYS, I'M NOT GOING TO BE AROUND TO WATCH OVER YOU.
BETTY...
WAIT! WHO'S FOLLOWING BETTY BRANT? CHECK OUT OUR UPCOMING ASM ANNUAL #41!--NICK

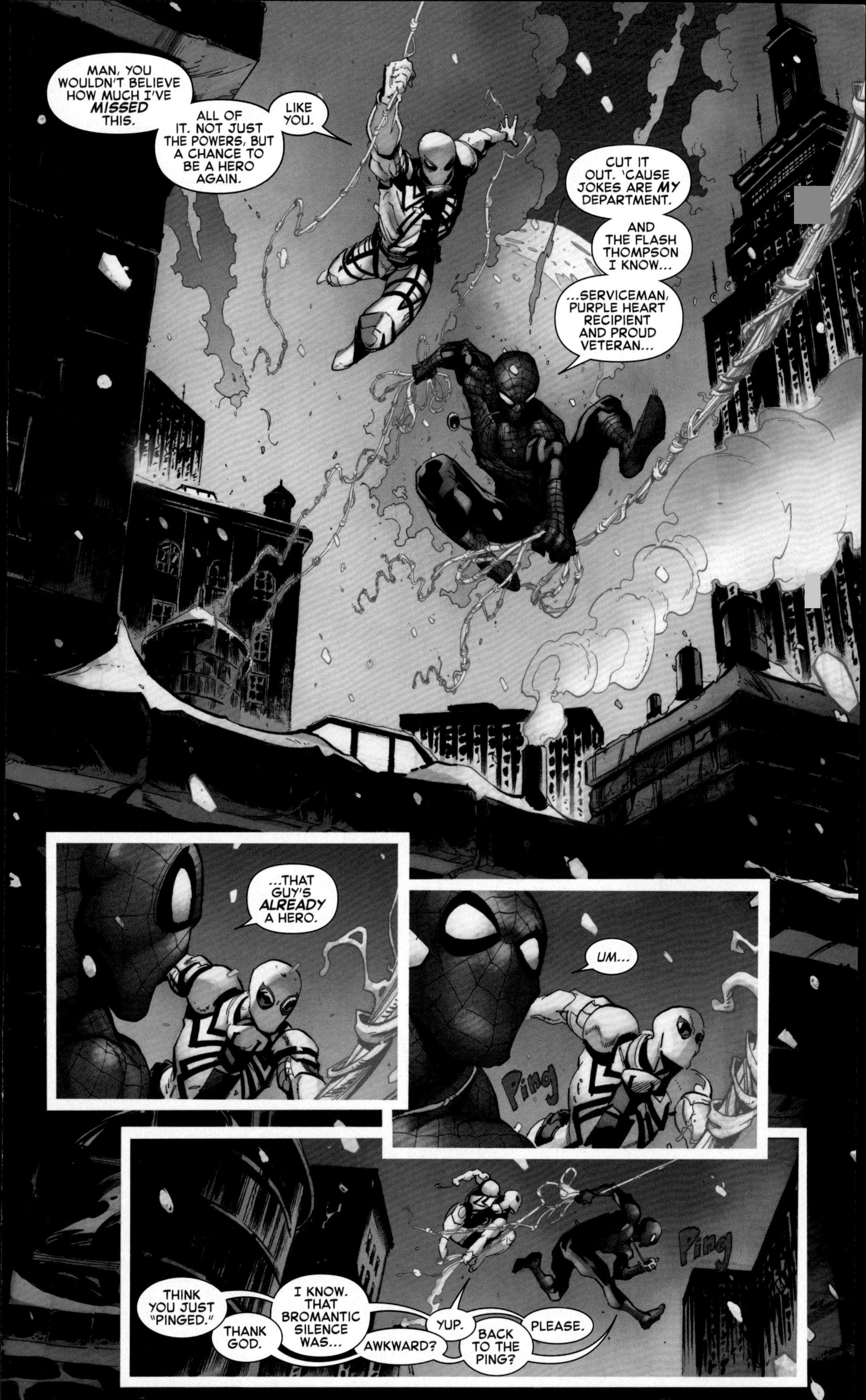
MAN, YOU WOULDN'T BELIEVE HOW MUCH I'VE *MISSED* THIS.
ALL OF IT. NOT JUST THE POWERS, BUT A CHANCE TO BE A HERO AGAIN.
LIKE YOU.
CUT IT OUT. 'CAUSE JOKES ARE *MY* DEPARTMENT.
AND THE FLASH THOMPSON I KNOW...
...SERVICEMAN, PURPLE HEART RECIPIENT AND PROUD VETERAN...
...THAT GUY'S *ALREADY* A HERO.
UM...
Ping
Ping
THINK YOU JUST "PINGED."
THANK GOD.
I KNOW. THAT BROMANTIC SILENCE WAS...
AWKWARD?
YUP.
BACK TO THE PING?
PLEASE.

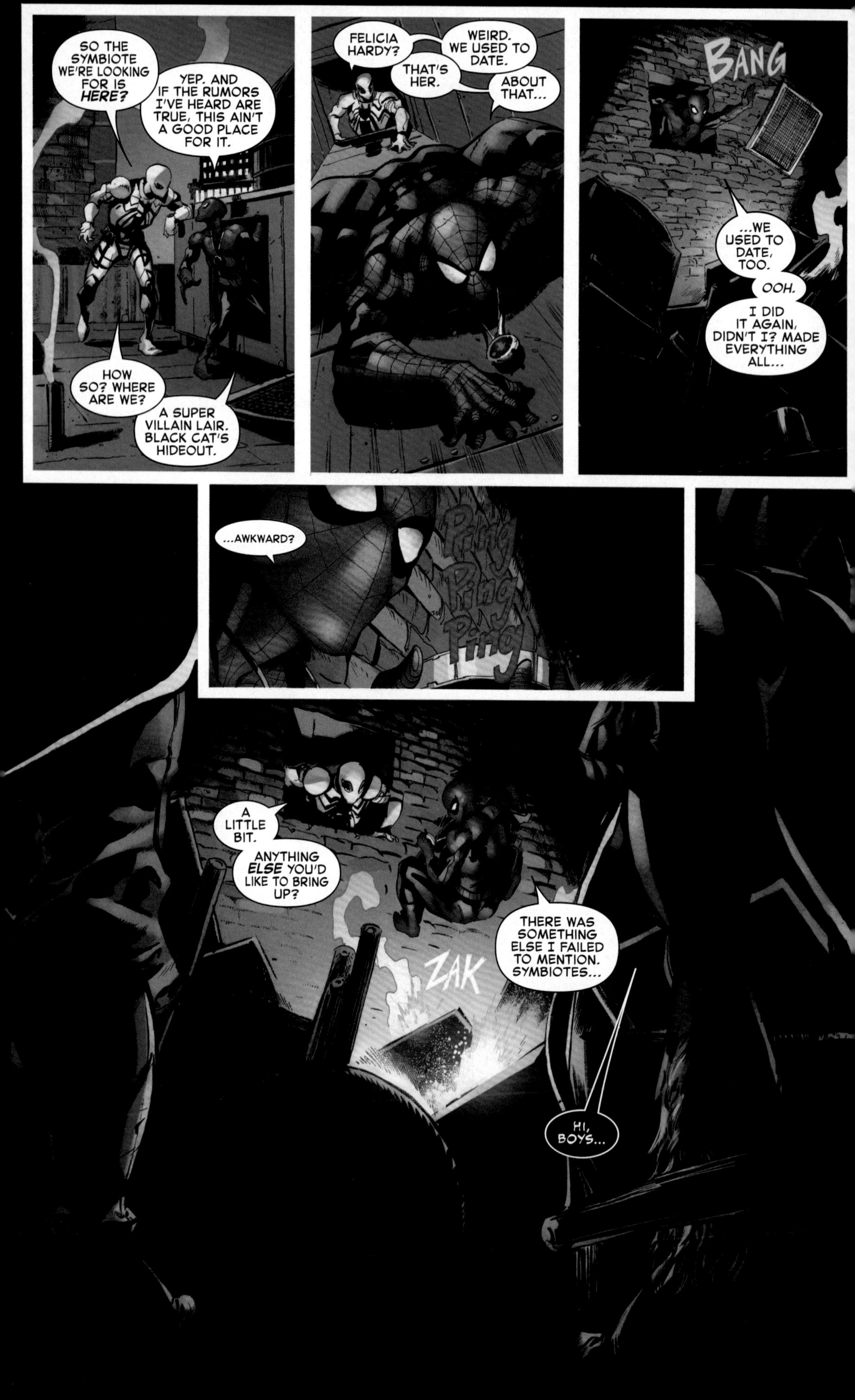
SO THE SYMBIOTE WE'RE LOOKING FOR IS HERE?
YEP. AND IF THE RUMORS I'VE HEARD ARE TRUE, THIS AIN'T A GOOD PLACE FOR IT.
HOW SO? WHERE ARE WE?
A SUPER VILLAIN LAIR. BLACK CAT'S HIDEOUT.
FELICIA HARDY?
WEIRD. WE USED TO DATE.
THAT'S HER.
ABOUT THAT...
BANG
...WE USED TO DATE, TOO.
OOH.
I DID IT AGAIN, DIDN'T I? MADE EVERYTHING ALL...
...AWKWARD?
Ping Ping Ping
A LITTLE BIT.
ANYTHING ELSE YOU'D LIKE TO BRING UP?
THERE WAS SOMETHING ELSE I FAILED TO MENTION. SYMBIOTES...
ZAK
HI, BOYS...

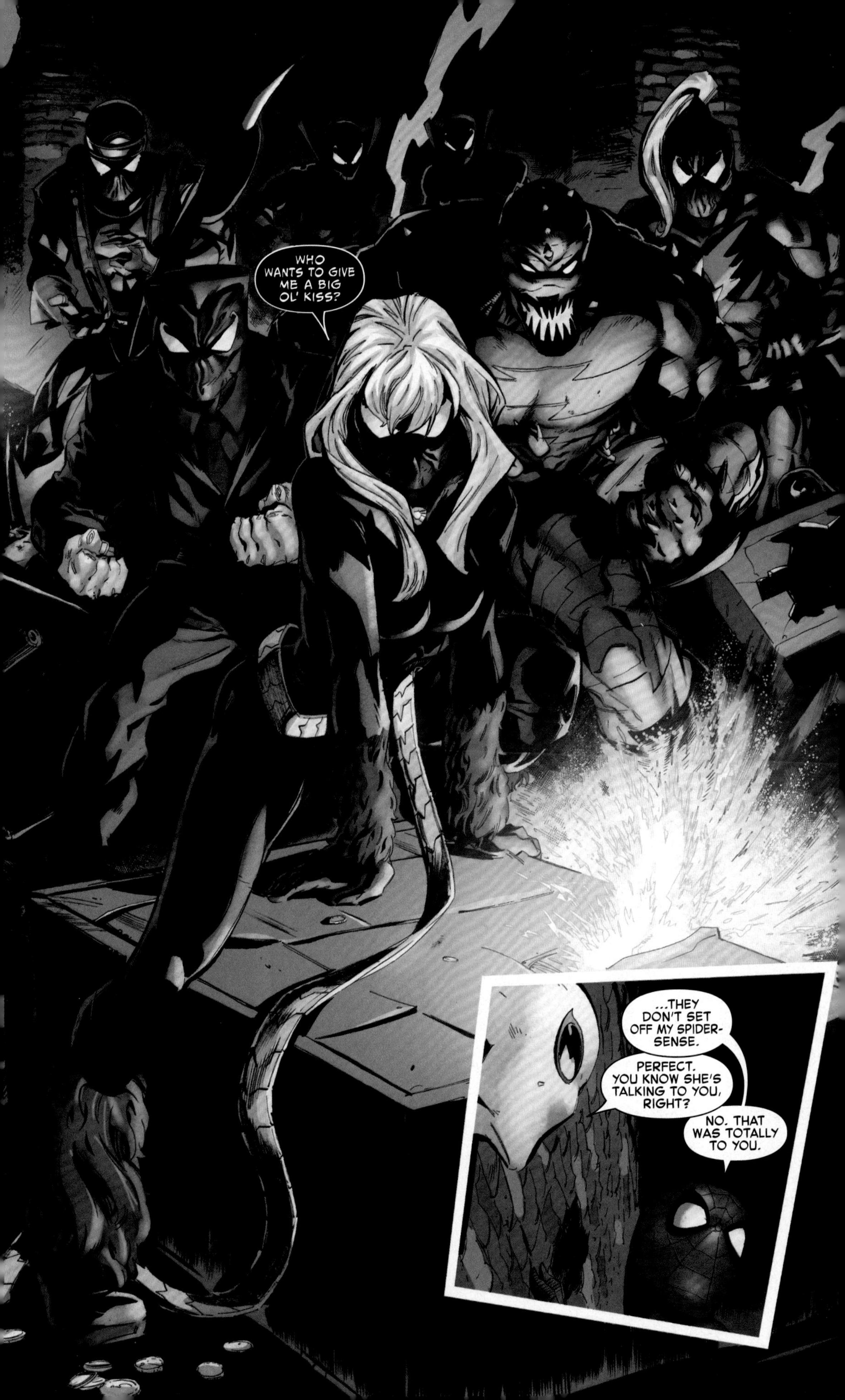
WHO WANTS TO GIVE ME A BIG OL' KISS?
...THEY DON'T SET OFF MY SPIDER-SENSE.
PERFECT. YOU KNOW SHE'S TALKING TO YOU, RIGHT?
NO. THAT WAS TOTALLY TO YOU.

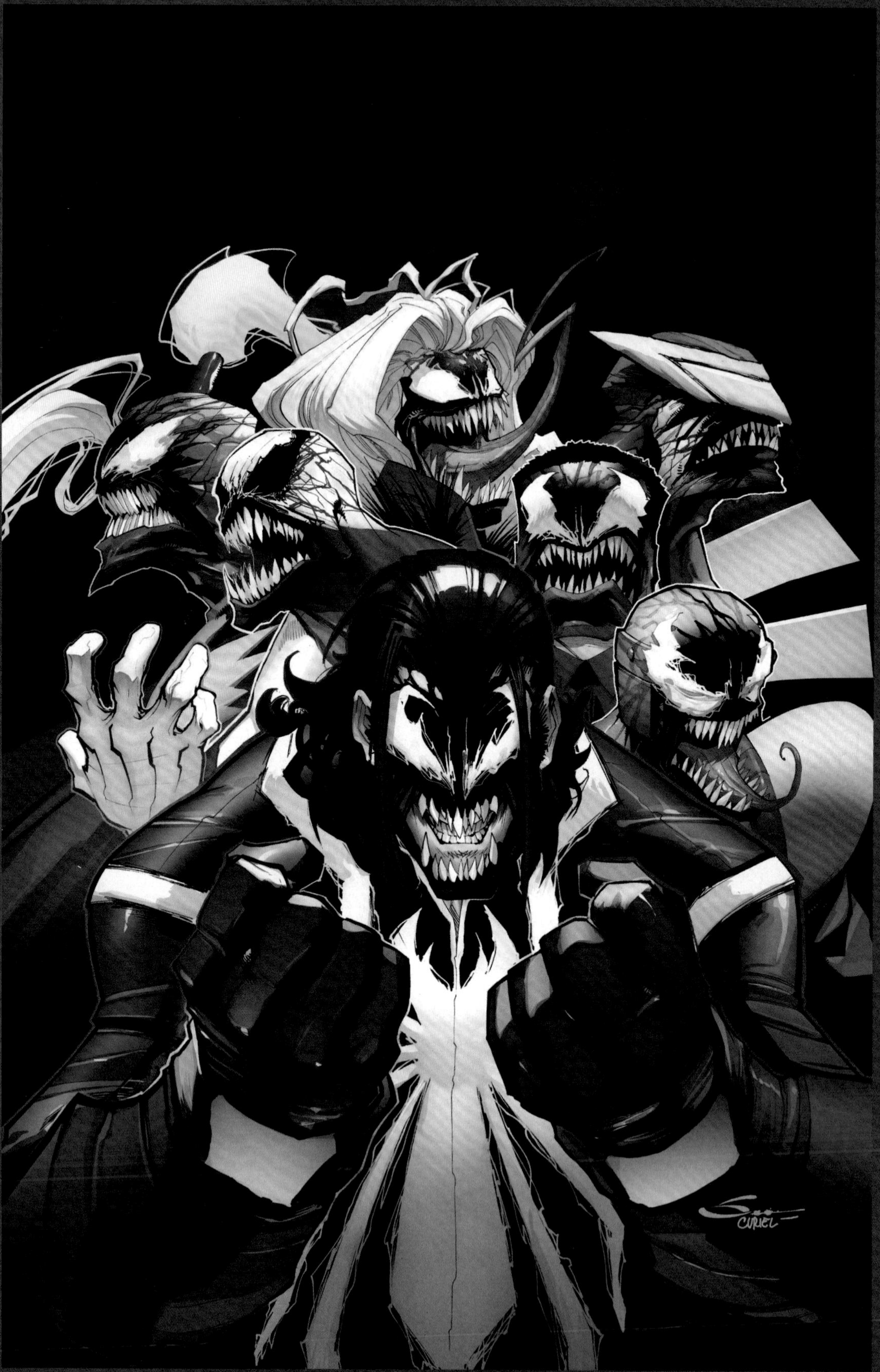
CURIEL

VENOM 159

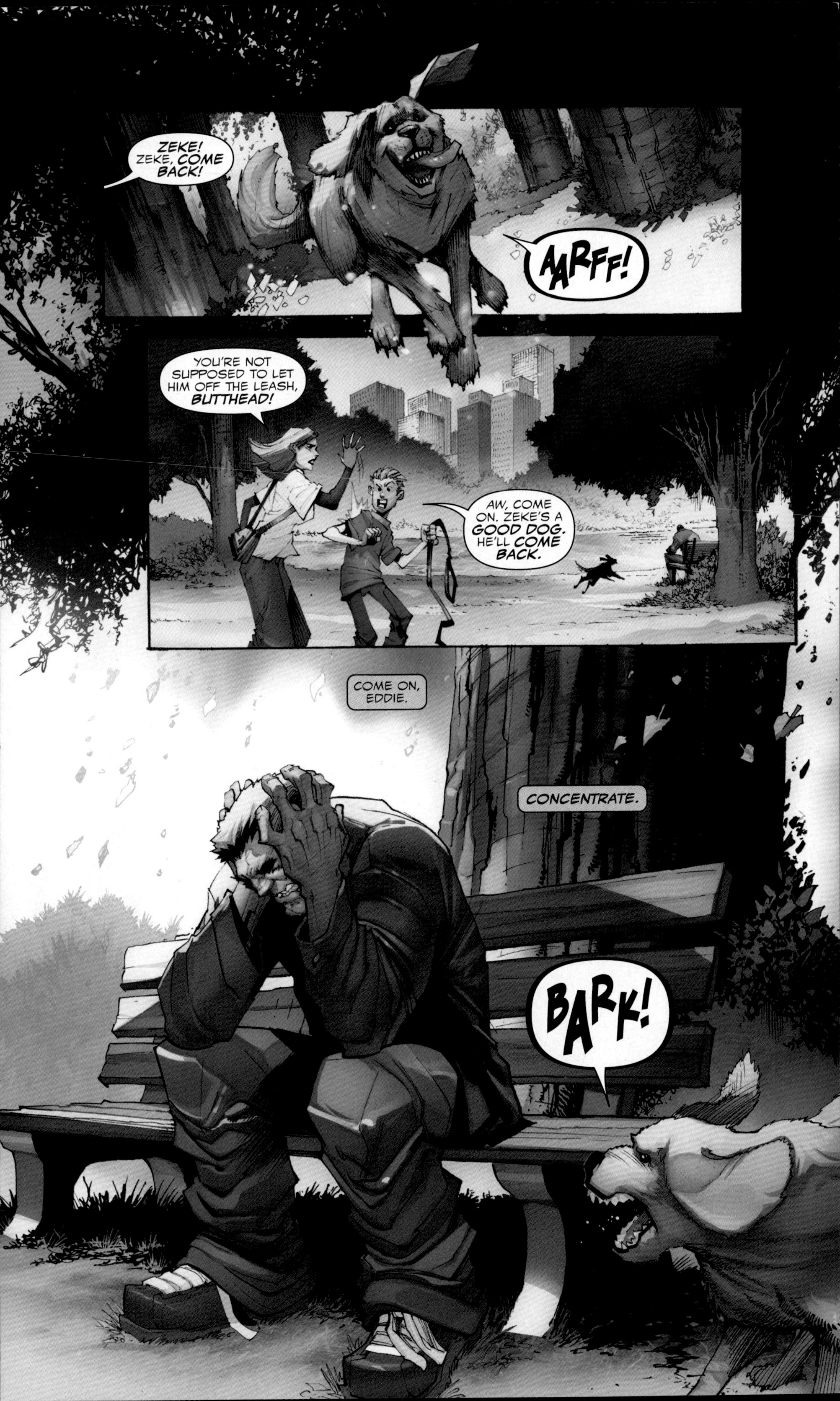
ZEKE! ZEKE, COME BACK!
AARFF!
YOU'RE NOT SUPPOSED TO LET HIM OFF THE LEASH, BUTTHEAD!
AW, COME ON. ZEKE'S A GOOD DOG. HE'LL COME BACK.
COME ON, EDDIE.
CONCENTRATE.
BARK!

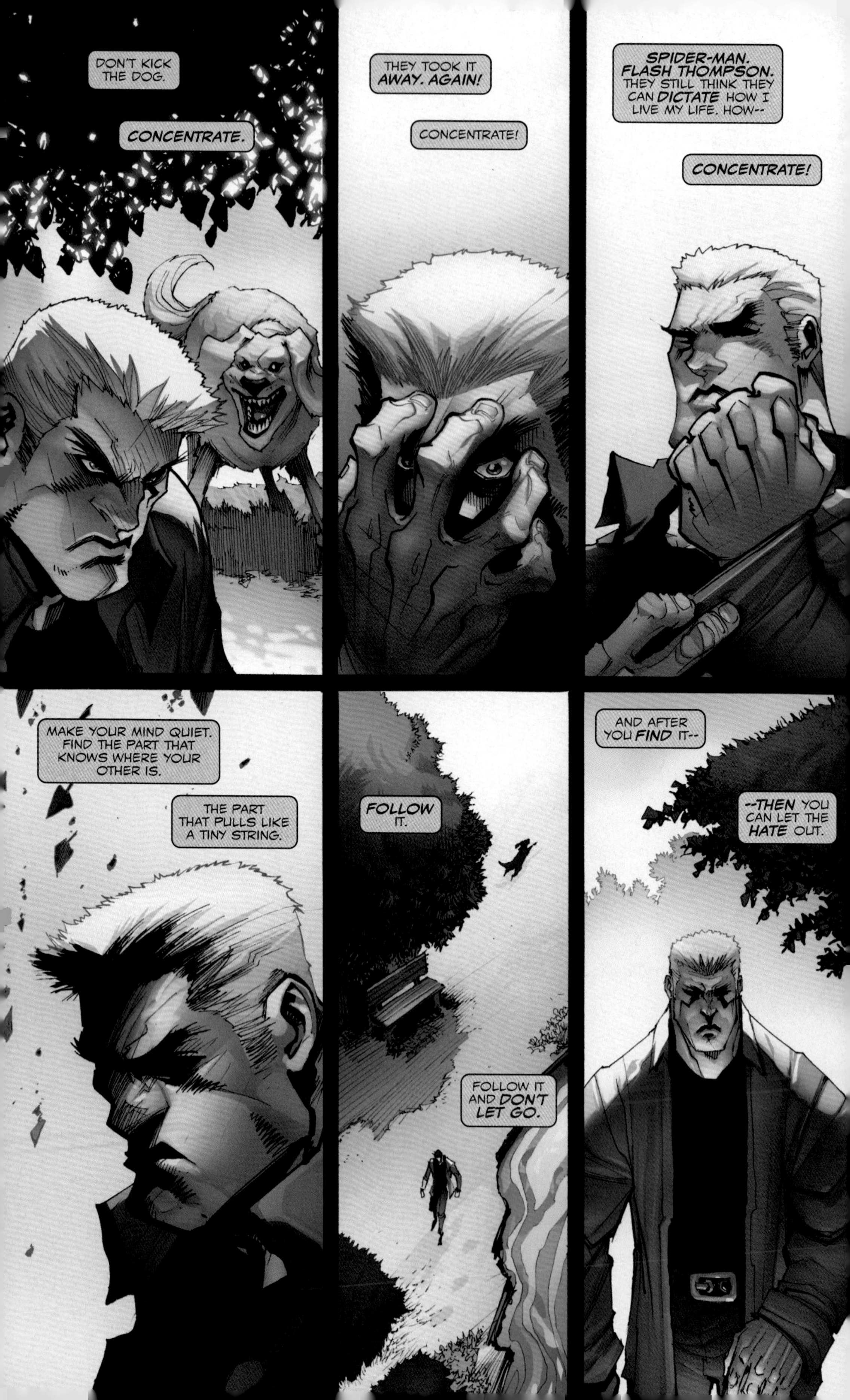
DON'T KICK THE DOG.
CONCENTRATE.
THEY TOOK IT AWAY. AGAIN!
CONCENTRATE!
SPIDER-MAN. FLASH THOMPSON. THEY STILL THINK THEY CAN DICTATE HOW I LIVE MY LIFE. HOW--
CONCENTRATE!
MAKE YOUR MIND QUIET. FIND THE PART THAT KNOWS WHERE YOUR OTHER IS.
THE PART THAT PULLS LIKE A TINY STRING.
FOLLOW IT.
FOLLOW IT AND DON'T LET GO.
AND AFTER YOU FIND IT--
--THEN YOU CAN LET THE HATE OUT.

GRRAAAAGGHHH!
HM...
CLEARLY WE AREN'T WEARING THE RIGHT COSTUMES TO THIS PARTY.
SO LET'S SAY MY PAL AND I JUST KINDA BACK OUT SLOWLY, AND ALL OF US CAN FORGET THIS EMBARRASSING FAUX PAS EVER HAPPENED.

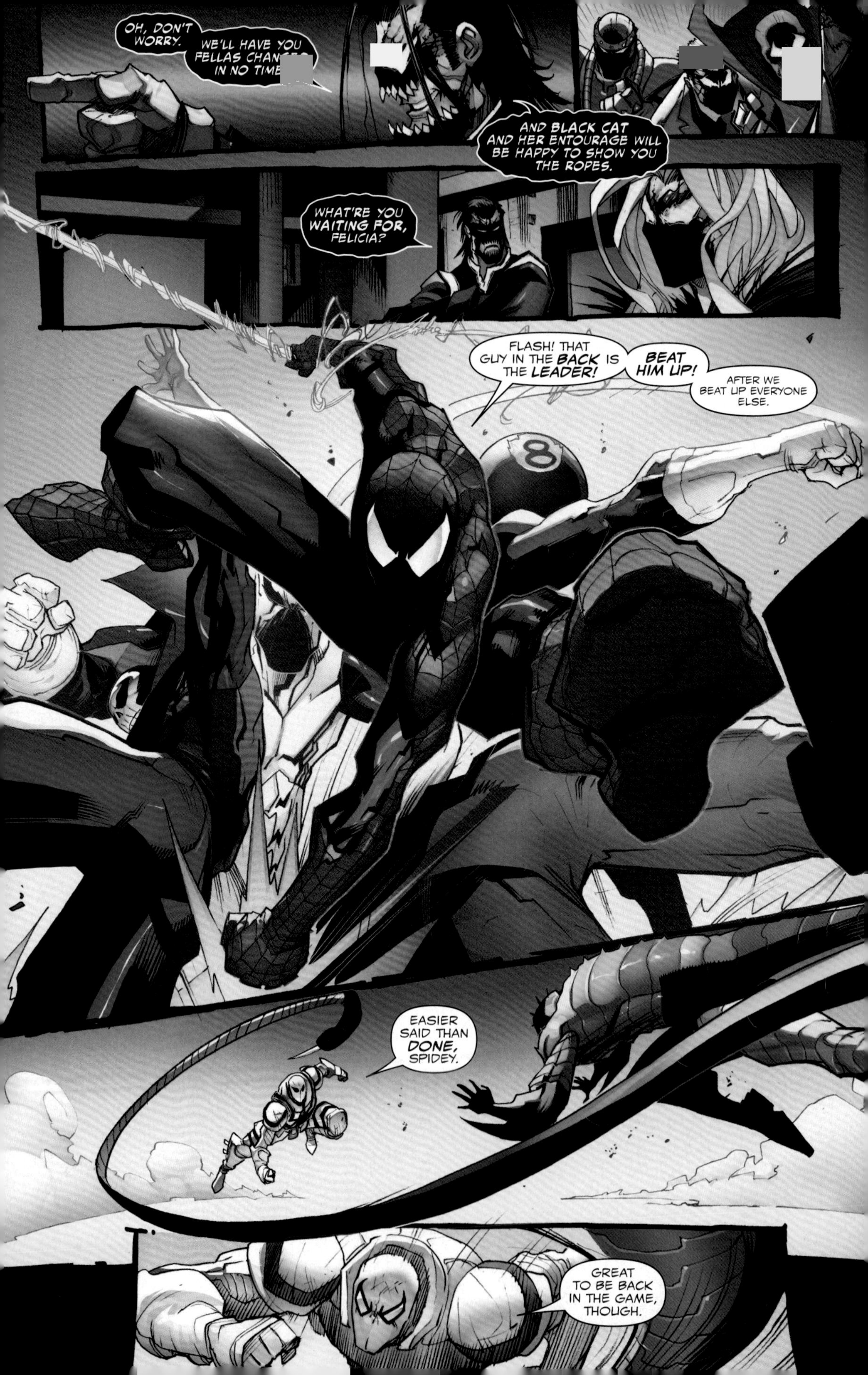
OH, DON'T WORRY.
WE'LL HAVE YOU FELLAS CHAN
IN NO TIME
AND BLACK CAT AND HER ENTOURAGE WILL BE HAPPY TO SHOW YOU THE ROPES.
WHAT'RE YOU WAITING FOR, FELICIA?
FLASH! THAT GUY IN THE BACK IS THE LEADER!
BEAT HIM UP!
AFTER WE BEAT UP EVERYONE ELSE.
EASIER SAID THAN DONE, SPIDEY.
GREAT TO BE BACK IN THE GAME, THOUGH.

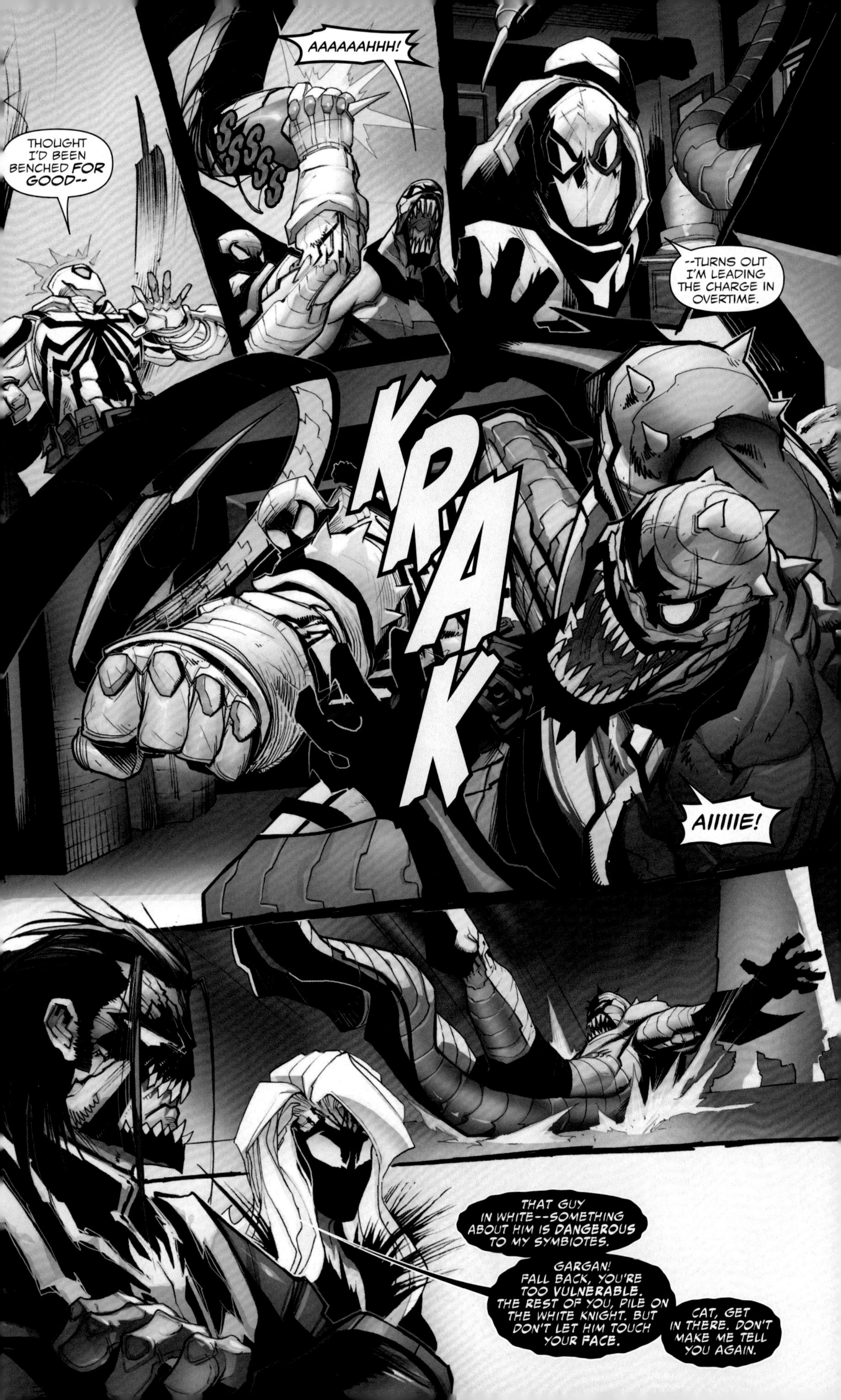
THOUGHT I'D BEEN BENCHED FOR GOOD--
AAAAAAHHH!
SSSSS
--TURNS OUT I'M LEADING THE CHARGE IN OVERTIME.
KRAK
AIIIIIE!
THAT GUY IN WHITE--SOMETHING ABOUT HIM IS DANGEROUS TO MY SYMBIOTES.
GARGAN! FALL BACK, YOU'RE TOO VULNERABLE. THE REST OF YOU, PILE ON THE WHITE KNIGHT. BUT DON'T LET HIM TOUCH YOUR FACE.
CAT, GET IN THERE. DON'T MAKE ME TELL YOU AGAIN.

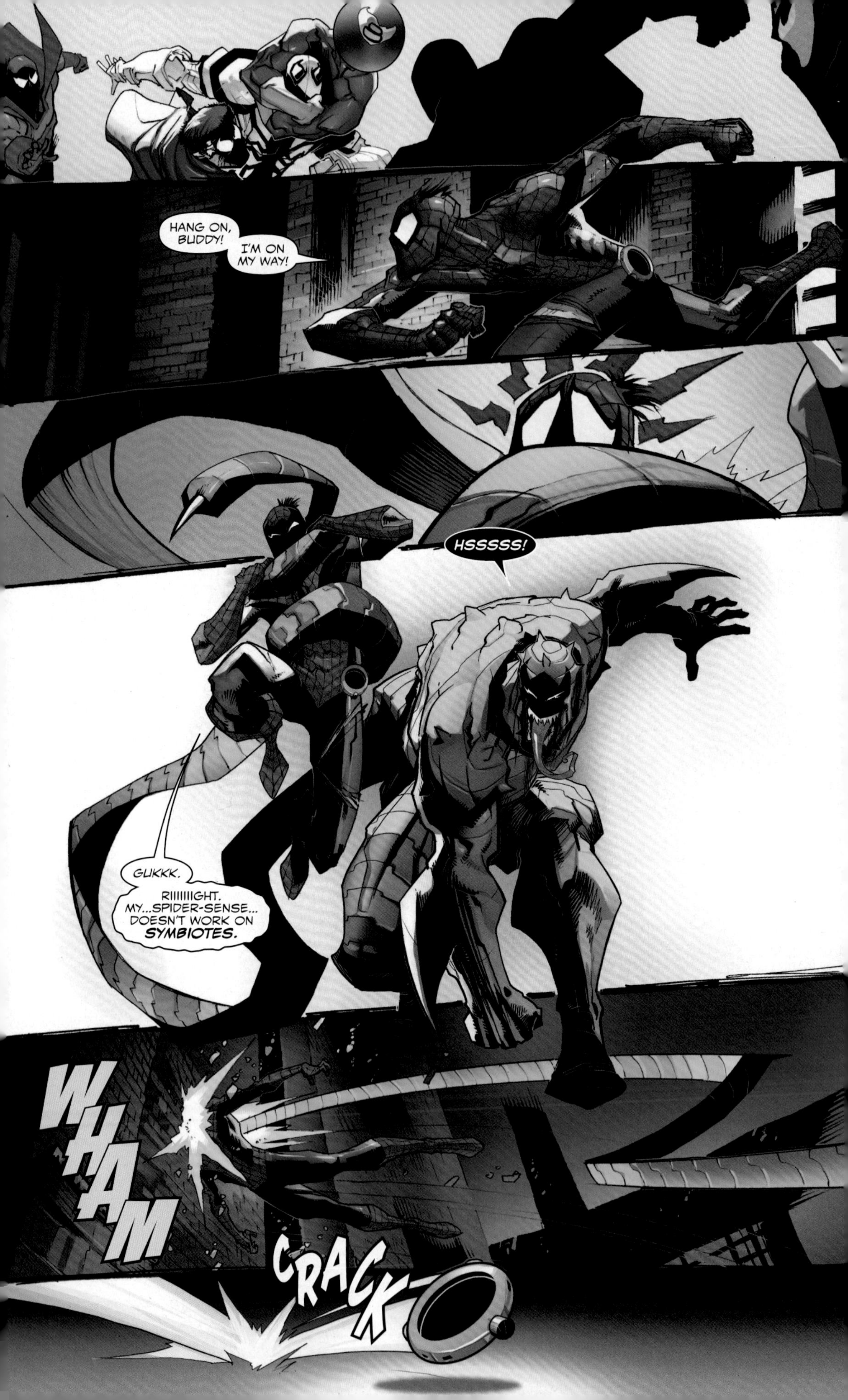
HANG ON, BUDDY!
I'M ON MY WAY!
HSSSSS!
GUKKK.
RIIIIIIGHT. MY...SPIDER-SENSE... DOESN'T WORK ON SYMBIOTES.
WHAM
CRACK

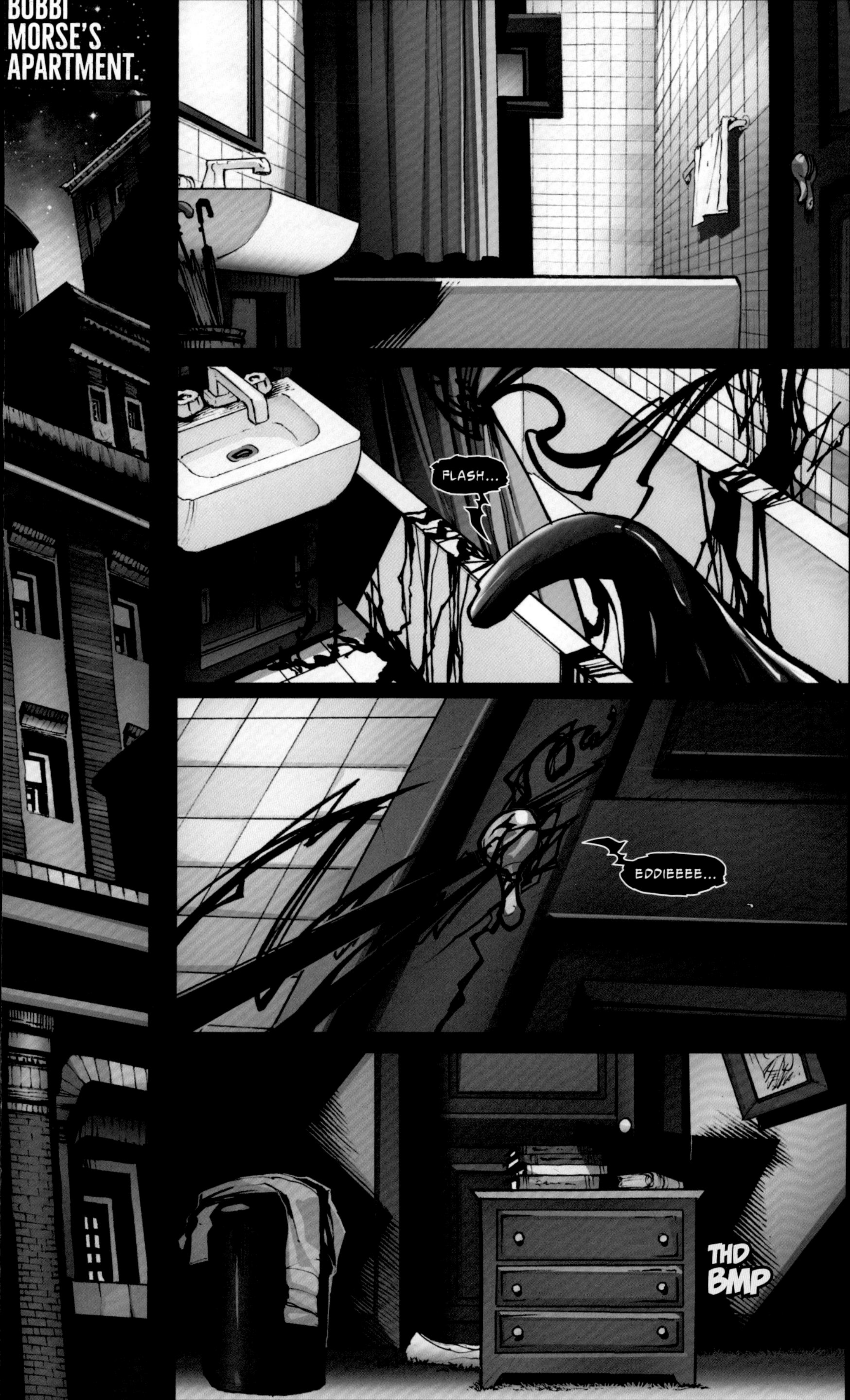

BOBBI MORSE'S APARTMENT.
FLASH...
EDDIEEEE...
THD BMP

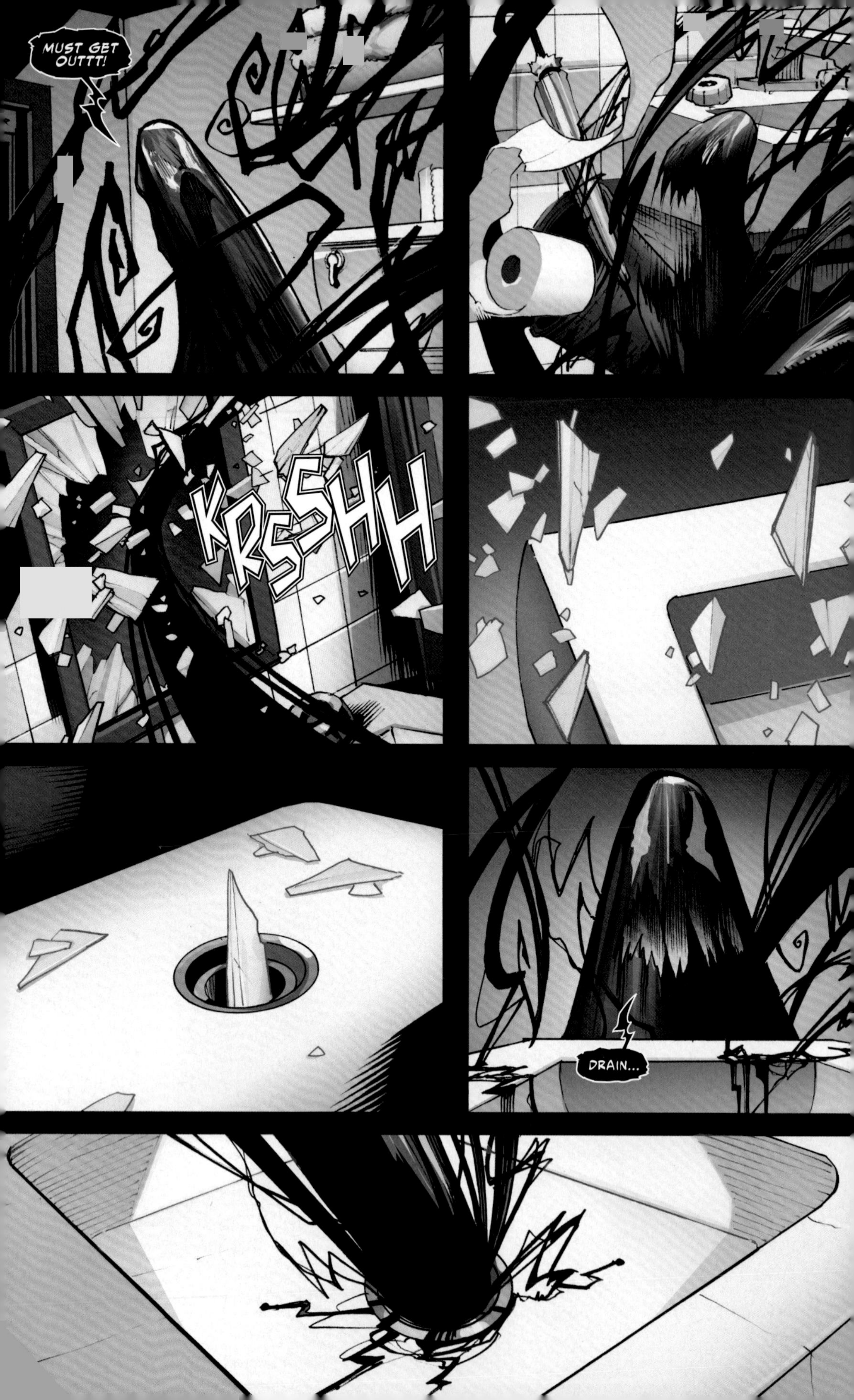
MUST GET OUTTT!
KRSSHH
DRAIN...

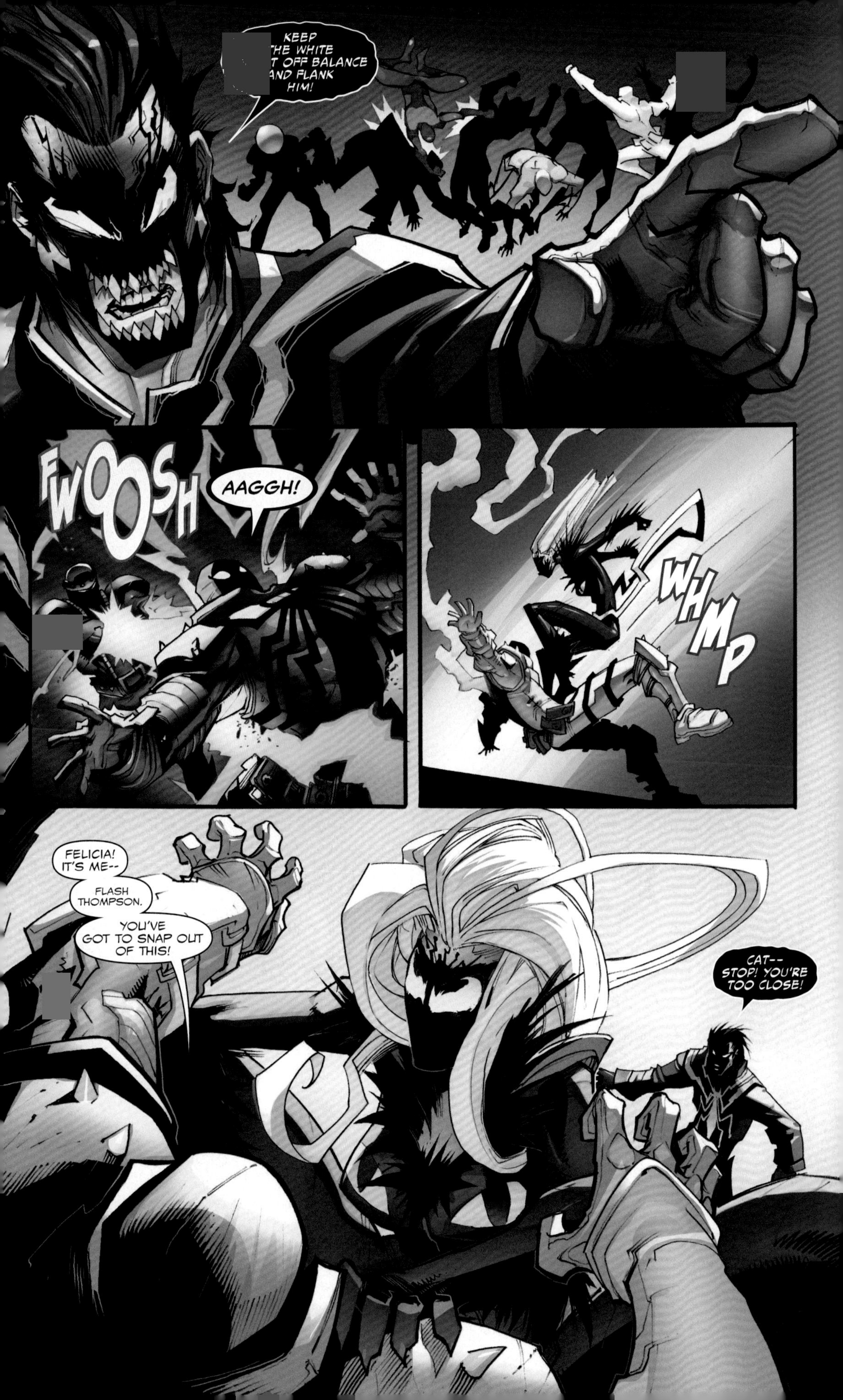
KEEP THE WHITE OFF BALANCE AND FLANK HIM!
FWOOSH
AAGGH!
WHMP
FELICIA! IT'S ME--
FLASH THOMPSON.
YOU'VE GOT TO SNAP OUT OF THIS!
CAT-- STOP! YOU'RE TOO CLOSE!

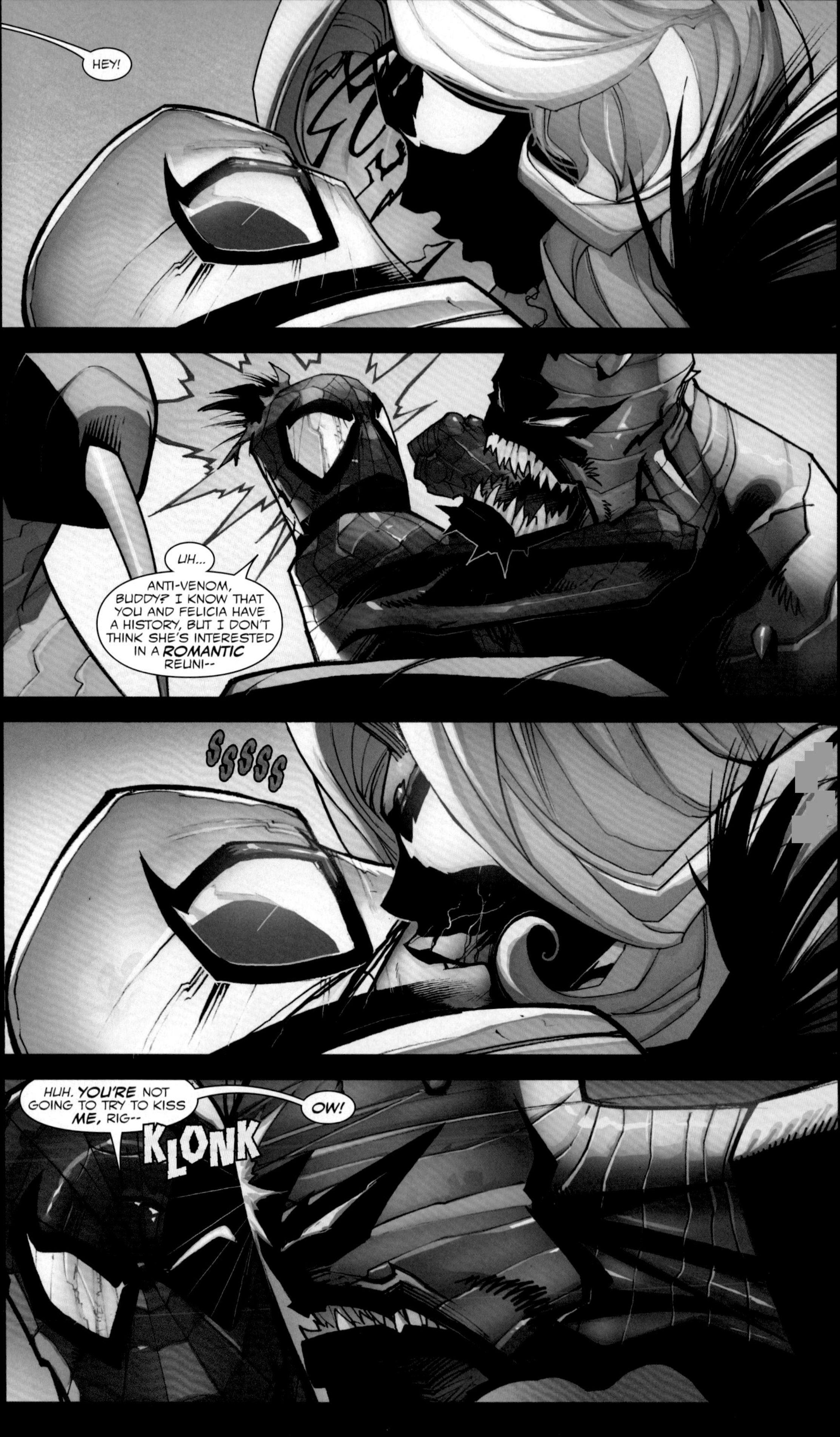

HEY!
UH...
ANTI-VENOM, BUDDY? I KNOW THAT YOU AND FELICIA HAVE A HISTORY, BUT I DON'T THINK SHE'S INTERESTED IN A ROMANTIC REUNI--
SSSSS
HUH. YOU'RE NOT GOING TO TRY TO KISS ME, RIG--
KLONK
OW!

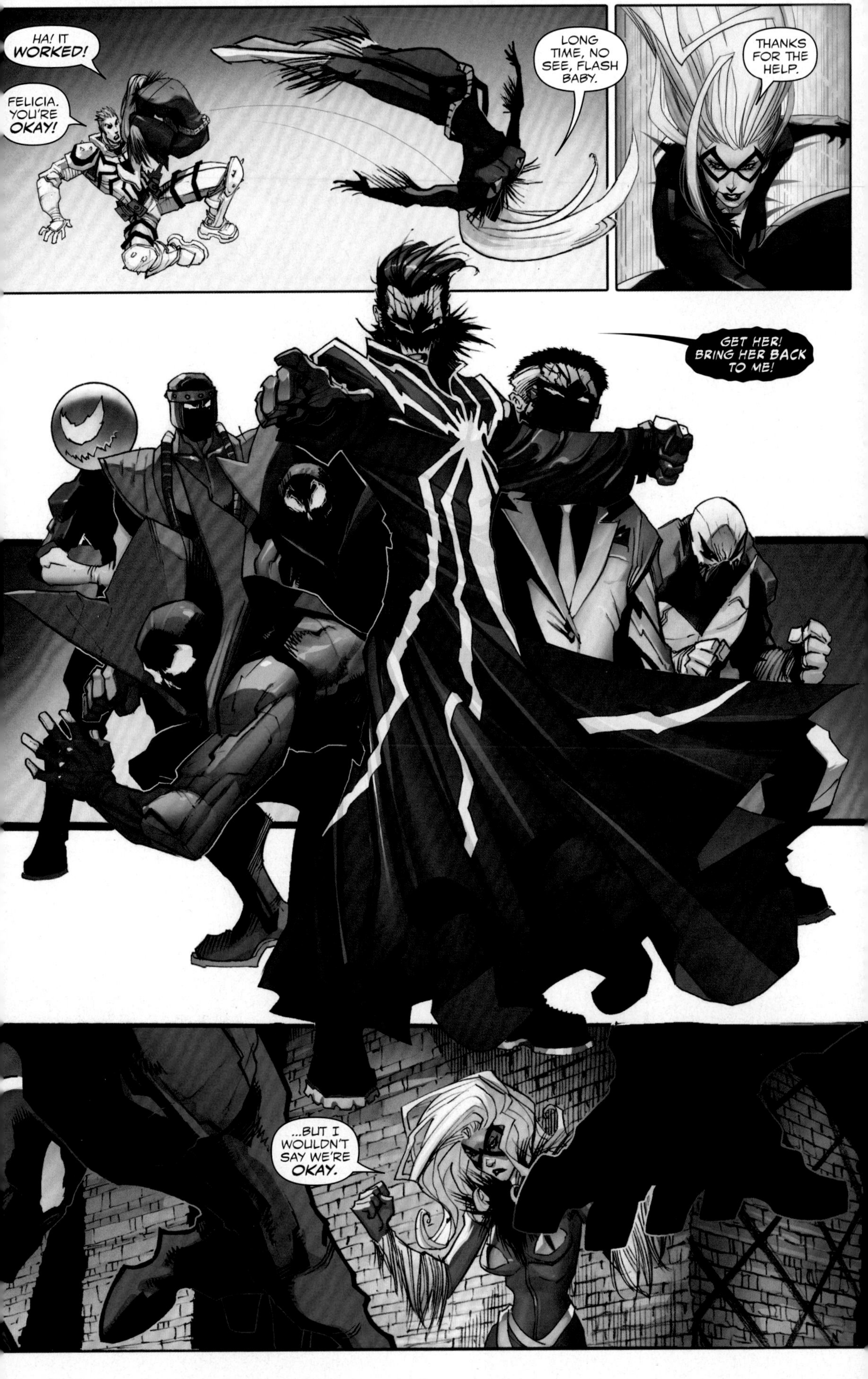
HA! IT WORKED!
FELICIA. YOU'RE OKAY!
LONG TIME, NO SEE, FLASH BABY.
THANKS FOR THE HELP.
GET HER! BRING HER BACK TO ME!
...BUT I WOULDN'T SAY WE'RE OKAY.

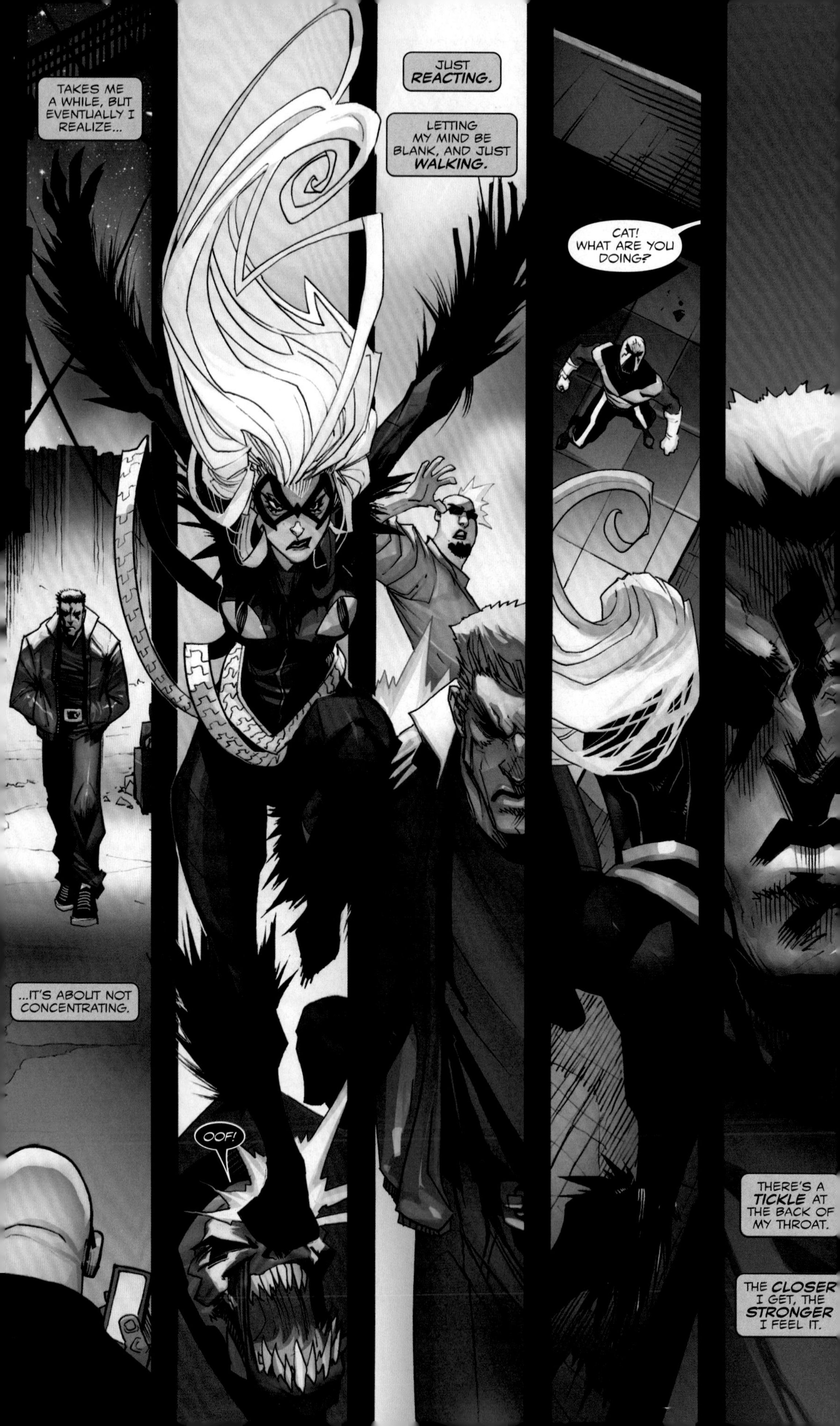

TAKES ME A WHILE, BUT EVENTUALLY I REALIZE...
...IT'S ABOUT NOT CONCENTRATING.
OOF!
JUST REACTING.
LETTING MY MIND BE BLANK, AND JUST WALKING.
CAT! WHAT ARE YOU DOING?
THERE'S A TICKLE AT THE BACK OF MY THROAT.
THE CLOSER I GET, THE STRONGER I FEEL IT.

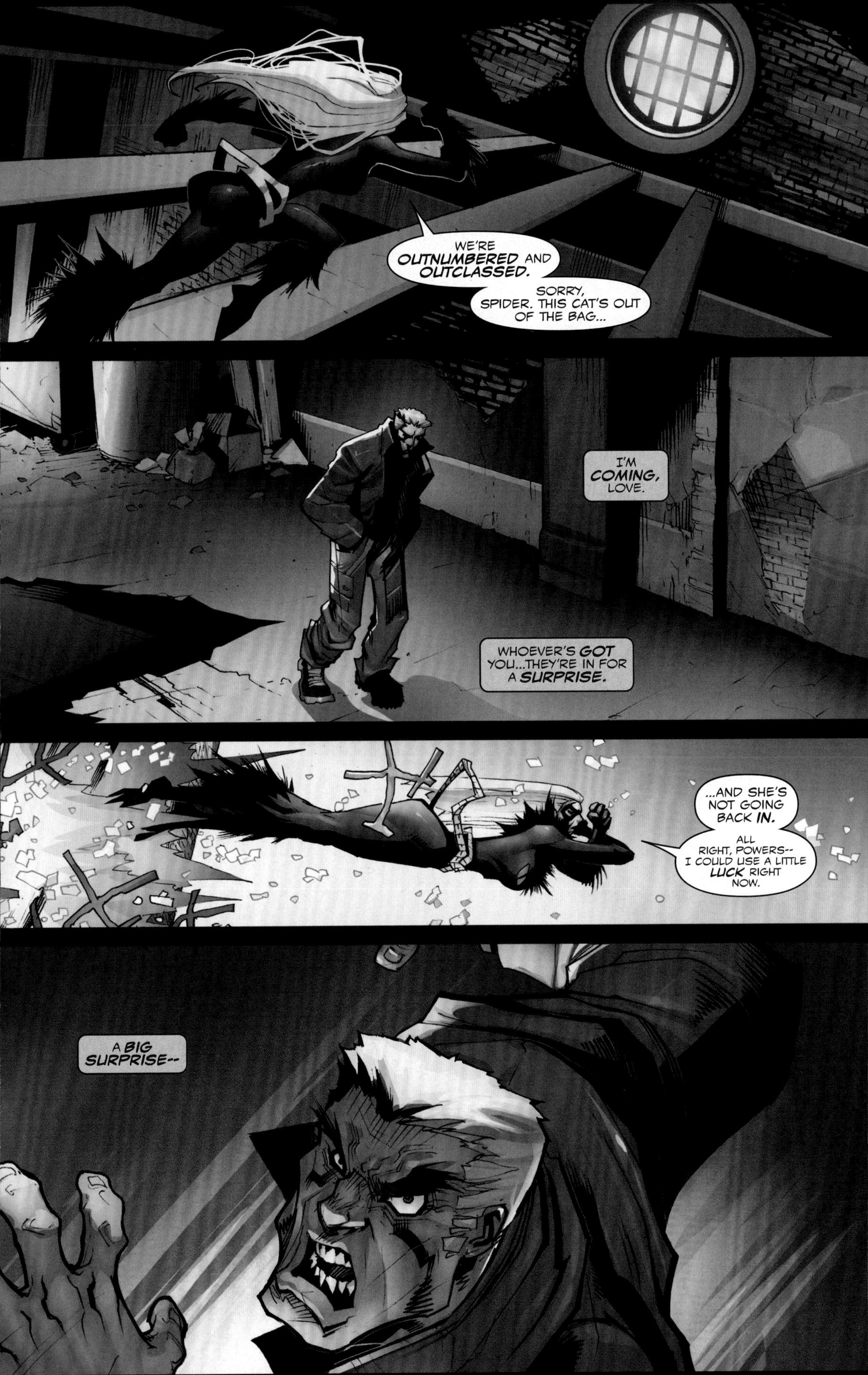
WE'RE OUTNUMBERED AND OUTCLASSED.
SORRY, SPIDER. THIS CAT'S OUT OF THE BAG...
I'M COMING, LOVE.
WHOEVER'S GOT YOU...THEY'RE IN FOR A SURPRISE.
...AND SHE'S NOT GOING BACK IN.
ALL RIGHT, POWERS-- I COULD USE A LITTLE LUCK RIGHT NOW.
A BIG SURPRISE--

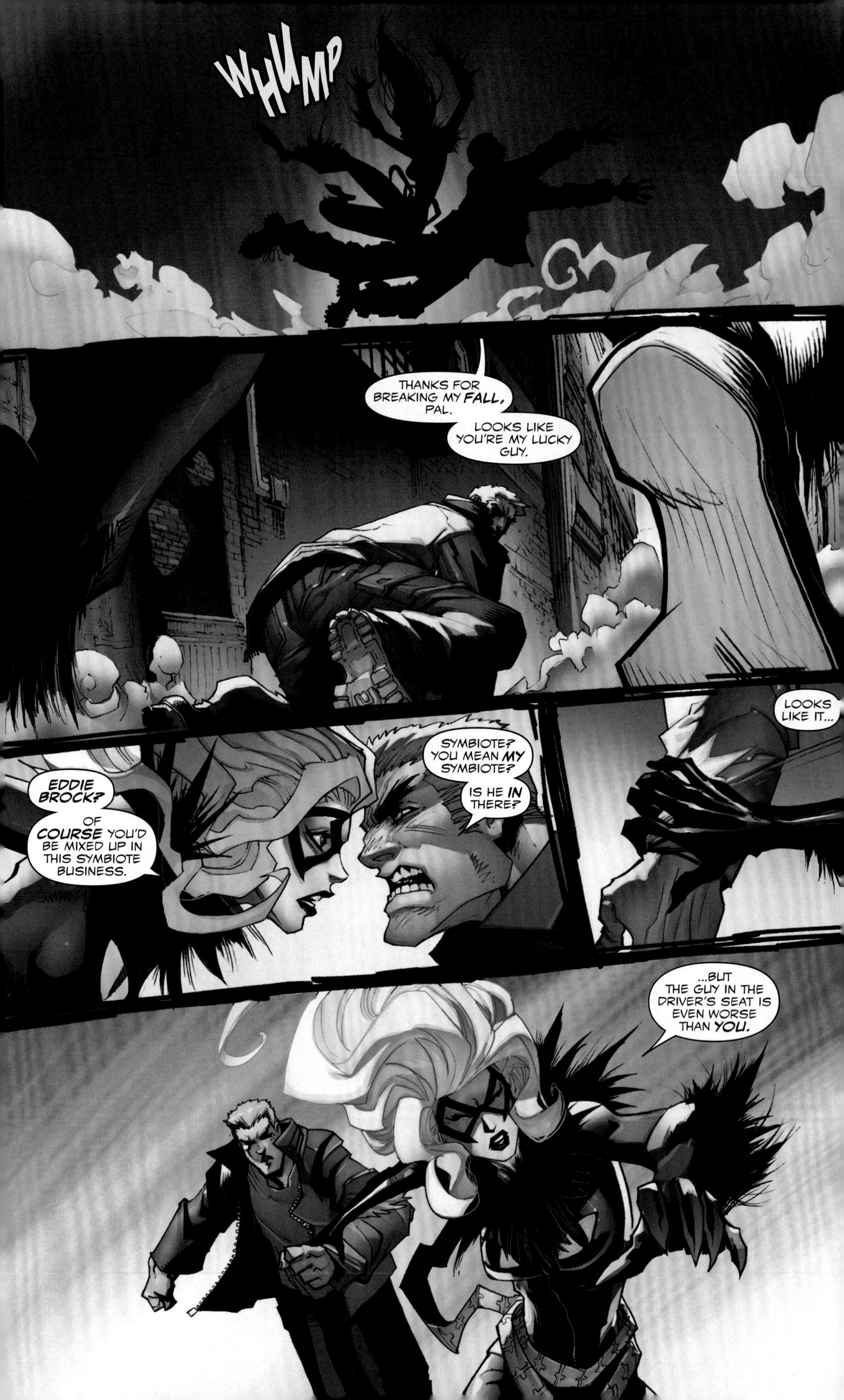
WHUMP
THANKS FOR BREAKING MY FALL, PAL.
LOOKS LIKE YOU'RE MY LUCKY GUY.
EDDIE BROCK?
OF COURSE YOU'D BE MIXED UP IN THIS SYMBIOTE BUSINESS.
SYMBIOTE? YOU MEAN MY SYMBIOTE?
IS HE IN THERE?
LOOKS LIKE IT...
...BUT THE GUY IN THE DRIVER'S SEAT IS EVEN WORSE THAN YOU.

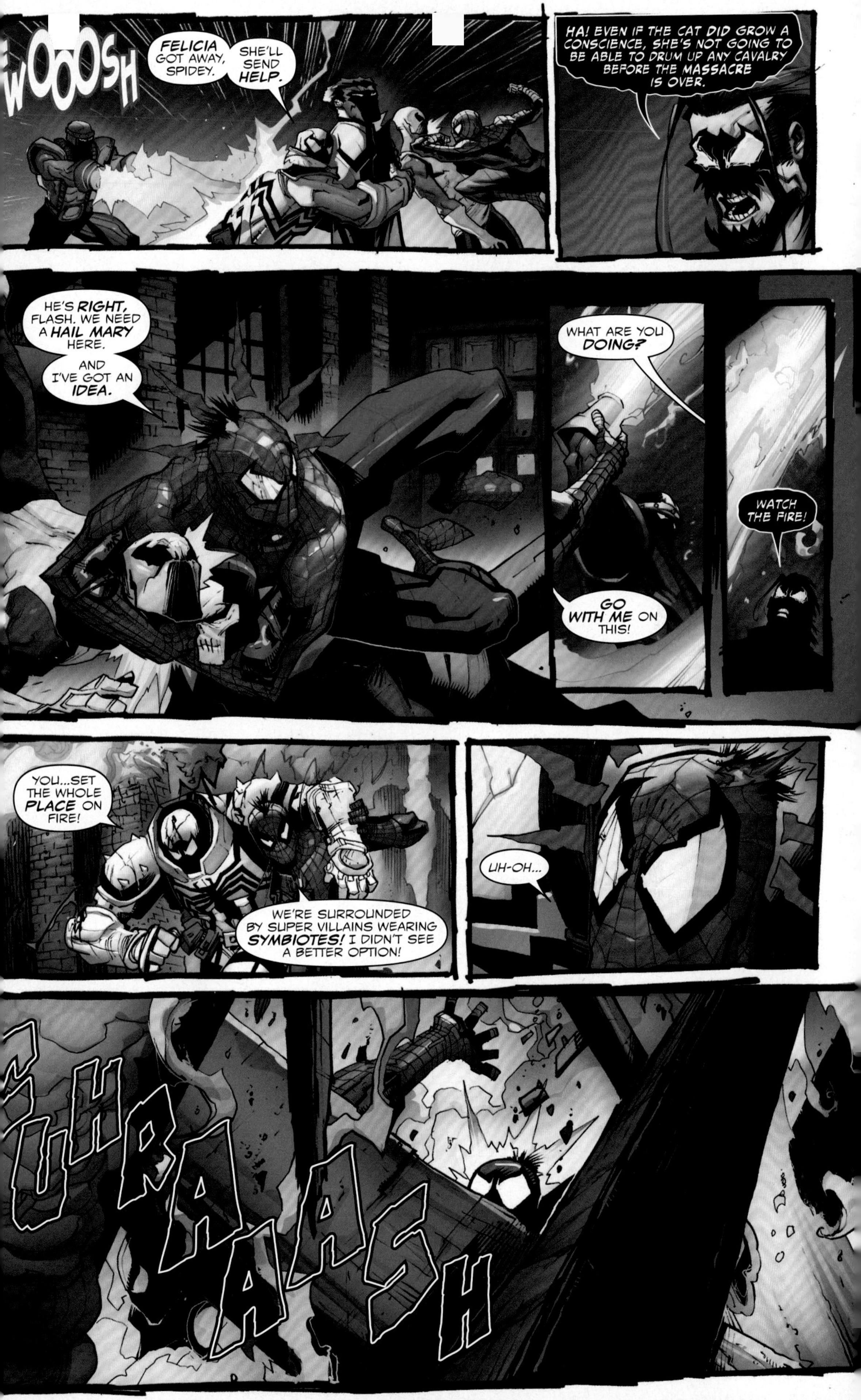
WOOOSH
FELICIA GOT AWAY, SPIDEY.
SHE'LL SEND HELP.
HA! EVEN IF THE CAT DID GROW A CONSCIENCE, SHE'S NOT GOING TO BE ABLE TO DRUM UP ANY CAVALRY BEFORE THE MASSACRE IS OVER.
HE'S RIGHT, FLASH. WE NEED A HAIL MARY HERE.
AND I'VE GOT AN IDEA.
WHAT ARE YOU DOING?
GO WITH ME ON THIS!
WATCH THE FIRE!
YOU...SET THE WHOLE PLACE ON FIRE!
WE'RE SURROUNDED BY SUPER VILLAINS WEARING SYMBIOTES! I DIDN'T SEE A BETTER OPTION!
UH-OH...
CHRAAASH

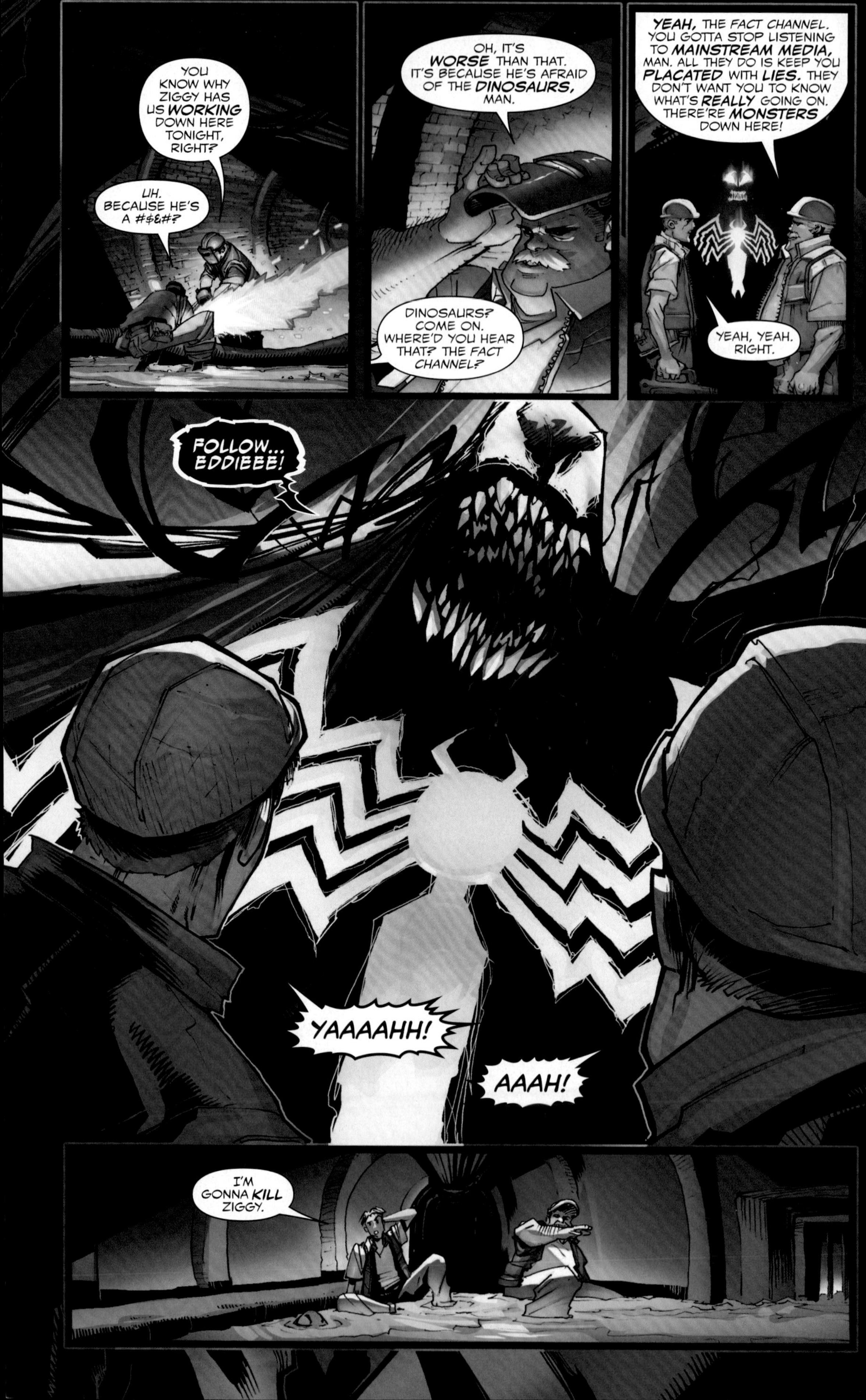
YOU KNOW WHY ZIGGY HAS US WORKING DOWN HERE TONIGHT, RIGHT?
UH. BECAUSE HE'S A #$&#?
OH, IT'S WORSE THAN THAT. IT'S BECAUSE HE'S AFRAID OF THE DINOSAURS, MAN.
DINOSAURS? COME ON. WHERE'D YOU HEAR THAT? THE FACT CHANNEL?
YEAH, THE FACT CHANNEL. YOU GOTTA STOP LISTENING TO MAINSTREAM MEDIA, MAN. ALL THEY DO IS KEEP YOU PLACATED WITH LIES. THEY DON'T WANT YOU TO KNOW WHAT'S REALLY GOING ON. THERE'RE MONSTERS DOWN HERE!
YEAH, YEAH. RIGHT.
FOLLOW... EDDIEEE!
YAAAAHH!
AAAH!
I'M GONNA KILL ZIGGY.

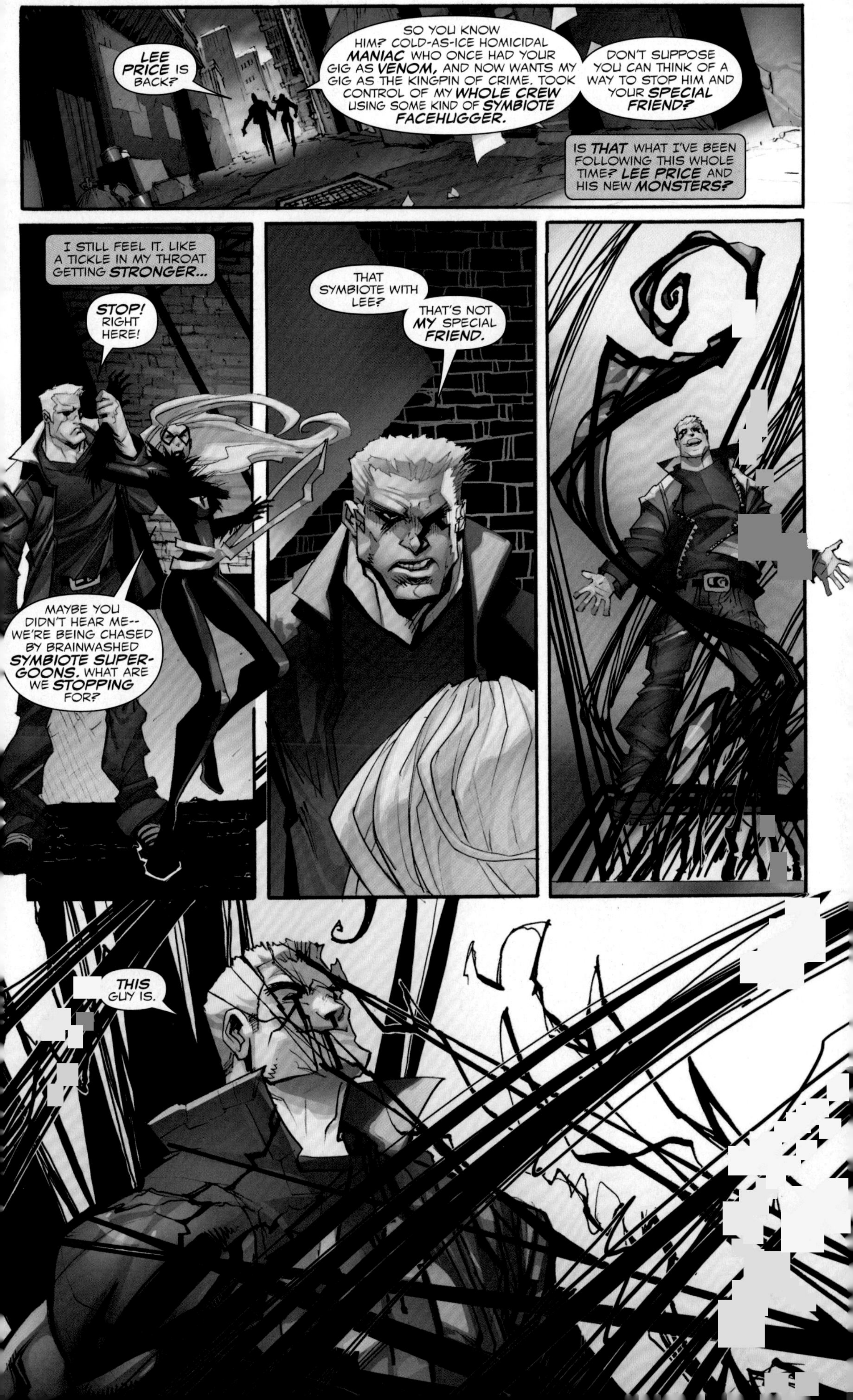

LEE PRICE IS BACK?
SO YOU KNOW HIM? COLD-AS-ICE HOMICIDAL MANIAC WHO ONCE HAD YOUR GIG AS VENOM, AND NOW WANTS MY GIG AS THE KINGPIN OF CRIME. TOOK CONTROL OF MY WHOLE CREW USING SOME KIND OF SYMBIOTE FACEHUGGER.
DON'T SUPPOSE YOU CAN THINK OF A WAY TO STOP HIM AND YOUR SPECIAL FRIEND?
IS THAT WHAT I'VE BEEN FOLLOWING THIS WHOLE TIME? LEE PRICE AND HIS NEW MONSTERS?
I STILL FEEL IT. LIKE A TICKLE IN MY THROAT GETTING STRONGER...
STOP! RIGHT HERE!
MAYBE YOU DIDN'T HEAR ME--WE'RE BEING CHASED BY BRAINWASHED SYMBIOTE SUPER-GOONS. WHAT ARE WE STOPPING FOR?
THAT SYMBIOTE WITH LEE?
THAT'S NOT MY SPECIAL FRIEND.
THIS GUY IS.

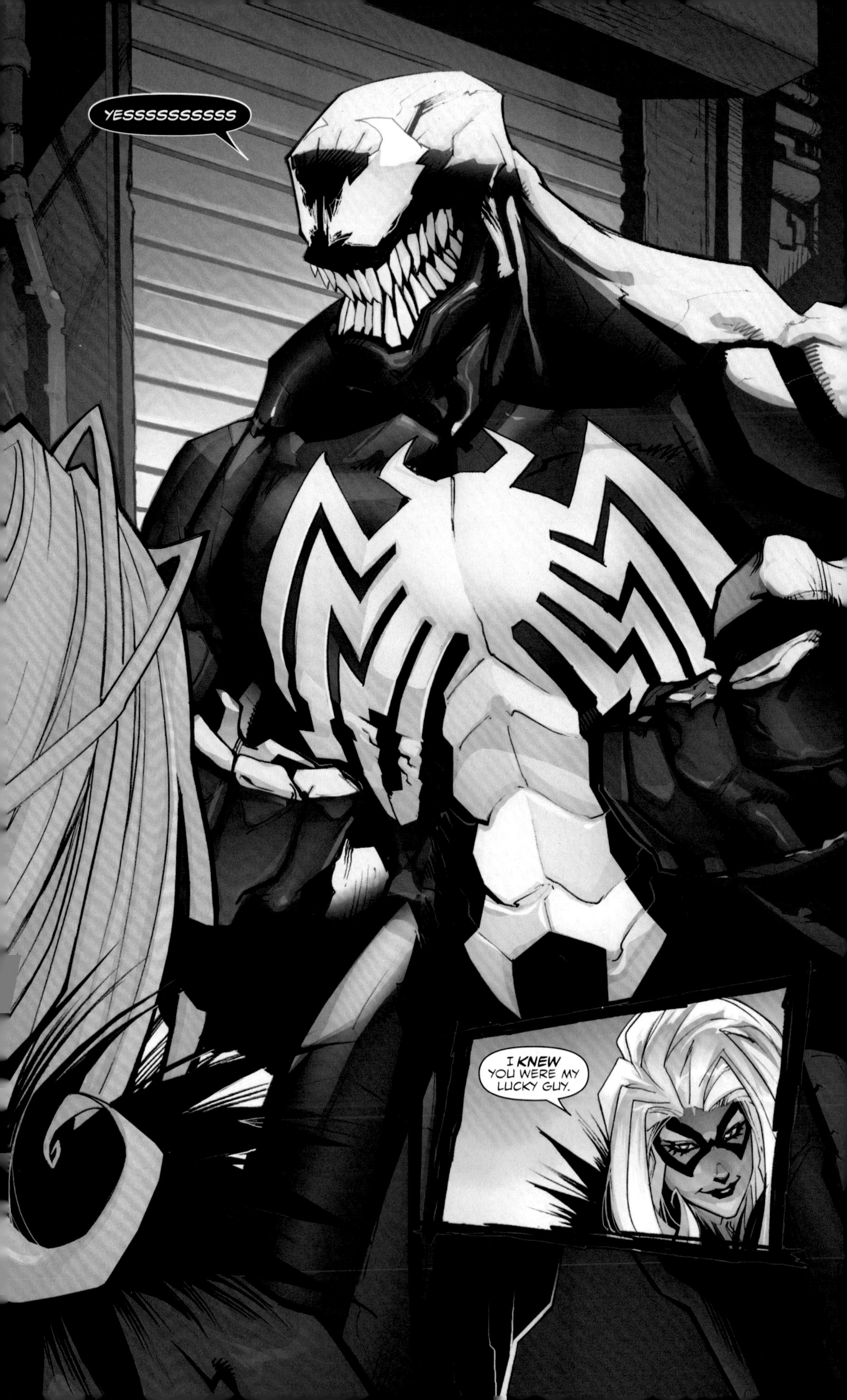
YESSSSSSSSSSS
I KNEW YOU WERE MY LUCKY GUY.

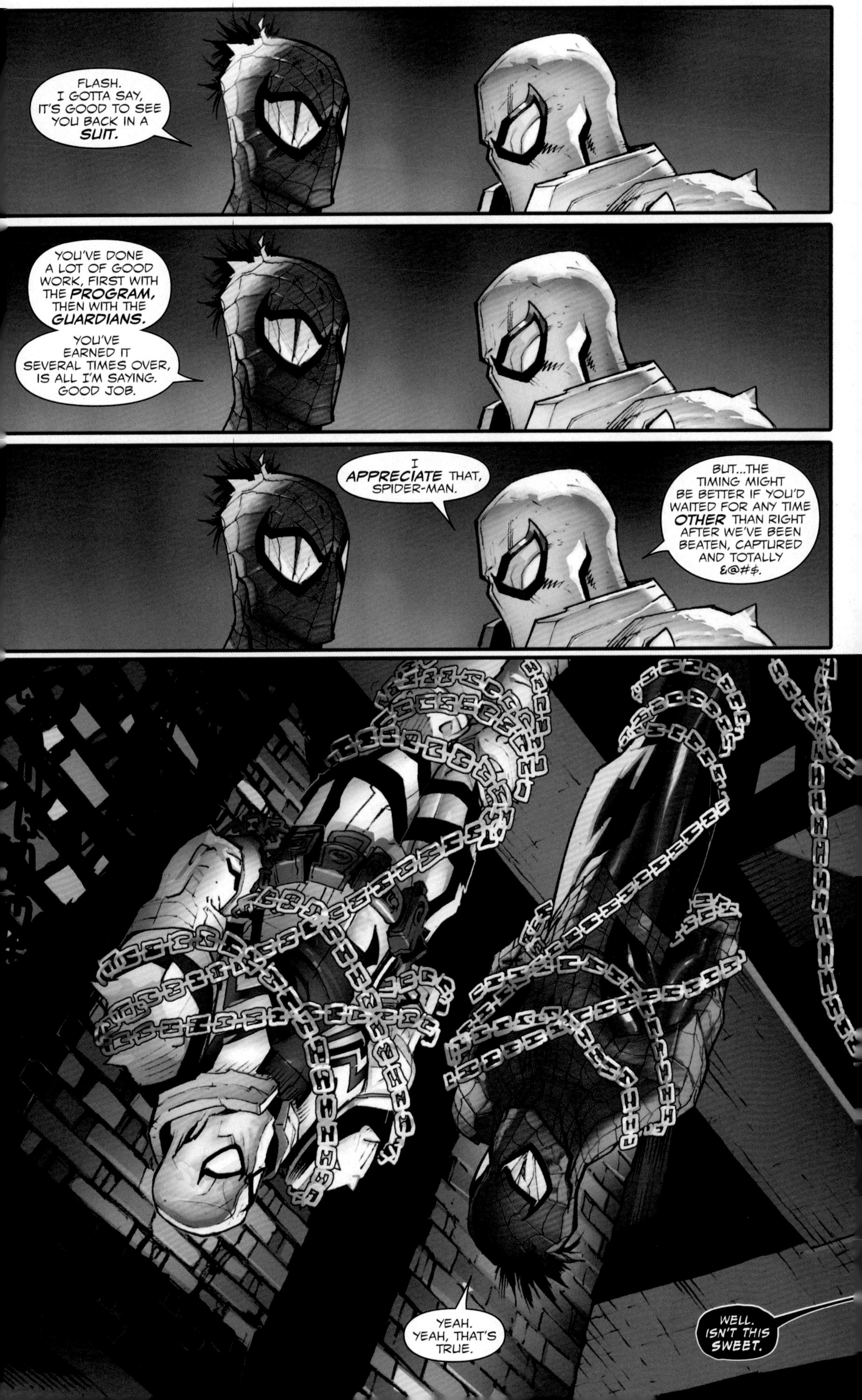
FLASH. I GOTTA SAY, IT'S GOOD TO SEE YOU BACK IN A SUIT.
YOU'VE DONE A LOT OF GOOD WORK, FIRST WITH THE PROGRAM, THEN WITH THE GUARDIANS.
YOU'VE EARNED IT SEVERAL TIMES OVER, IS ALL I'M SAYING. GOOD JOB.
I APPRECIATE THAT, SPIDER-MAN.
BUT...THE TIMING MIGHT BE BETTER IF YOU'D WAITED FOR ANY TIME OTHER THAN RIGHT AFTER WE'VE BEEN BEATEN, CAPTURED AND TOTALLY &@#$.
YEAH. YEAH, THAT'S TRUE.
WELL. ISN'T THIS SWEET.

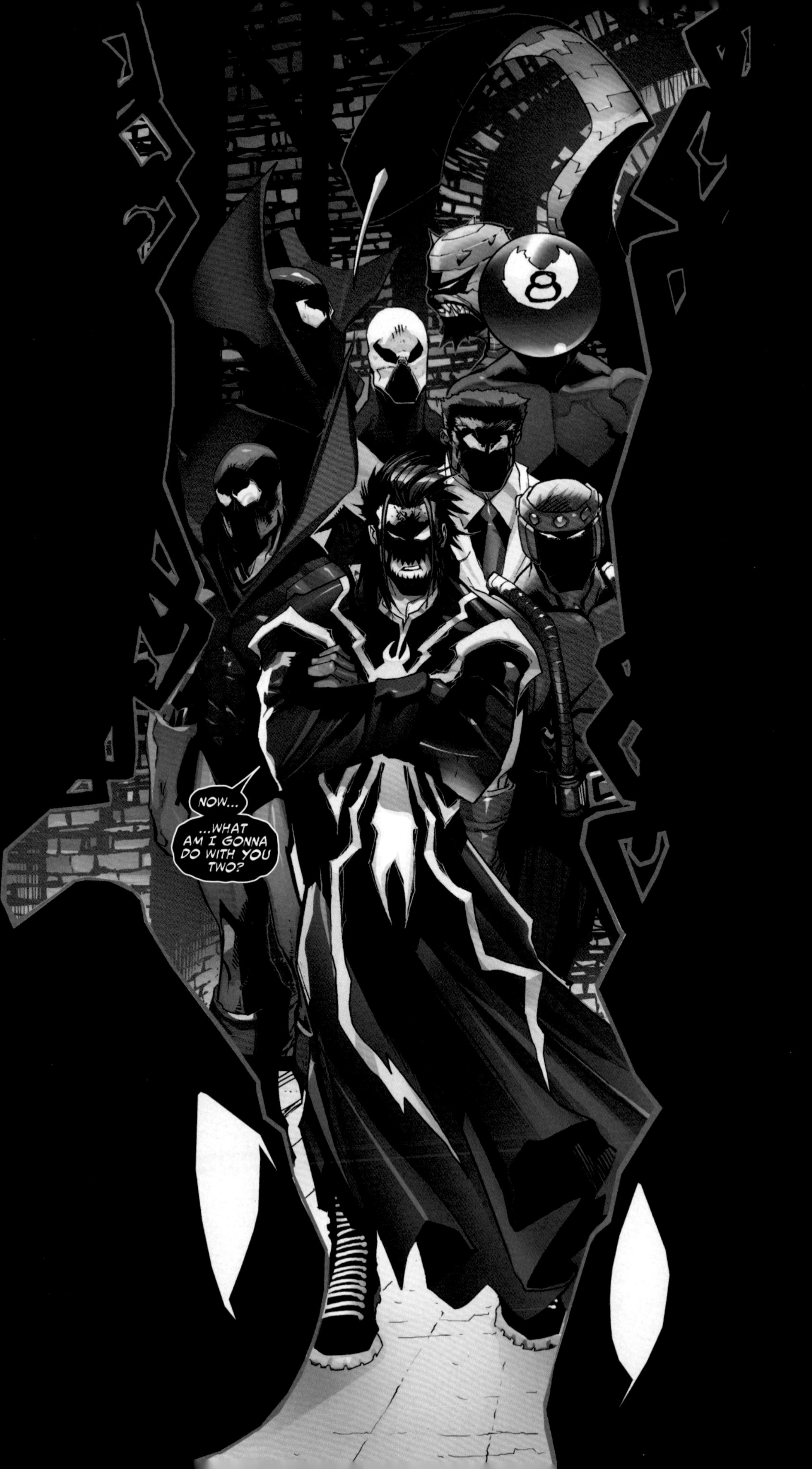
NOW...
...WHAT AM I GONNA DO WITH YOU TWO?

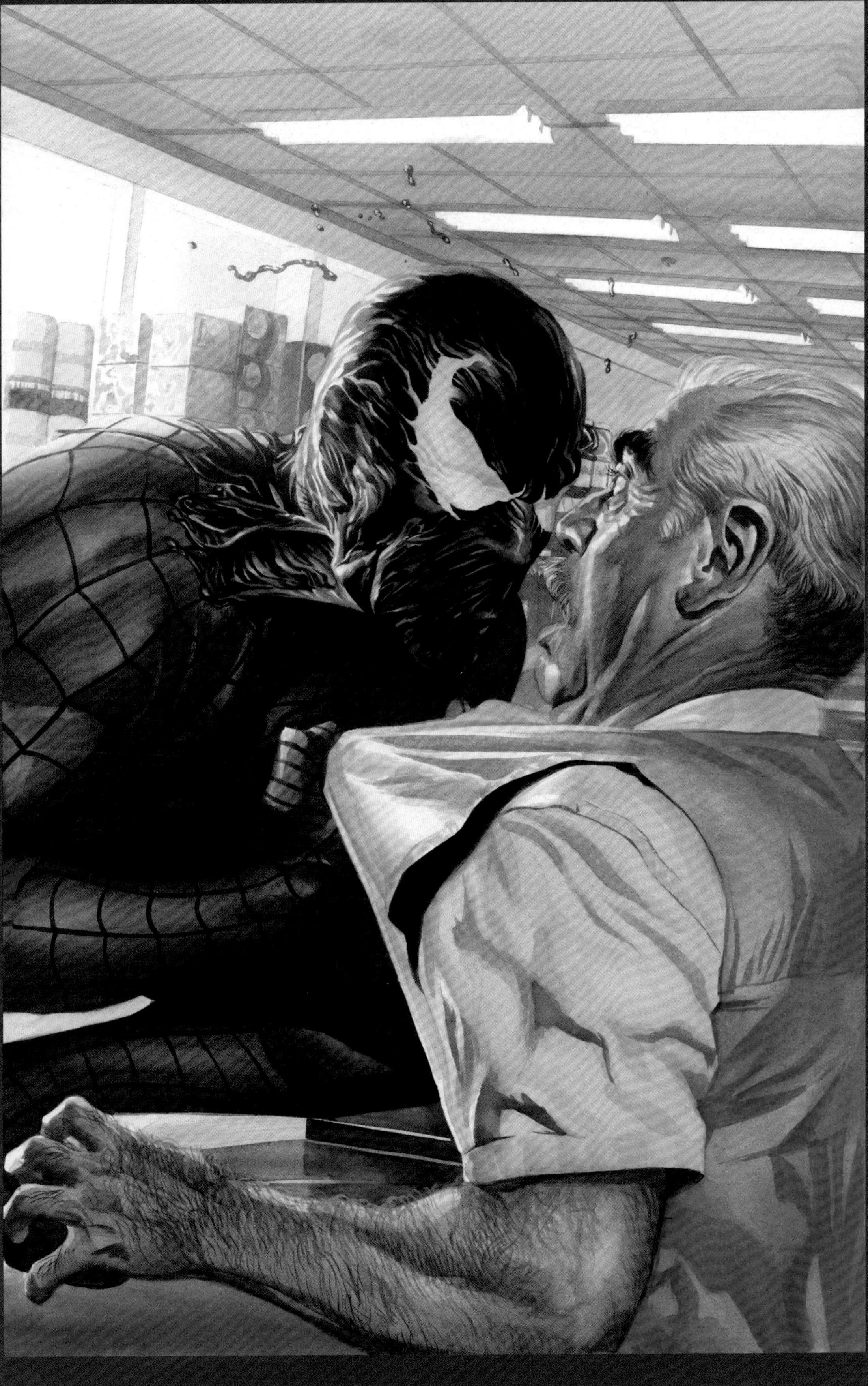

AMAZING SPIDER-MAN 793

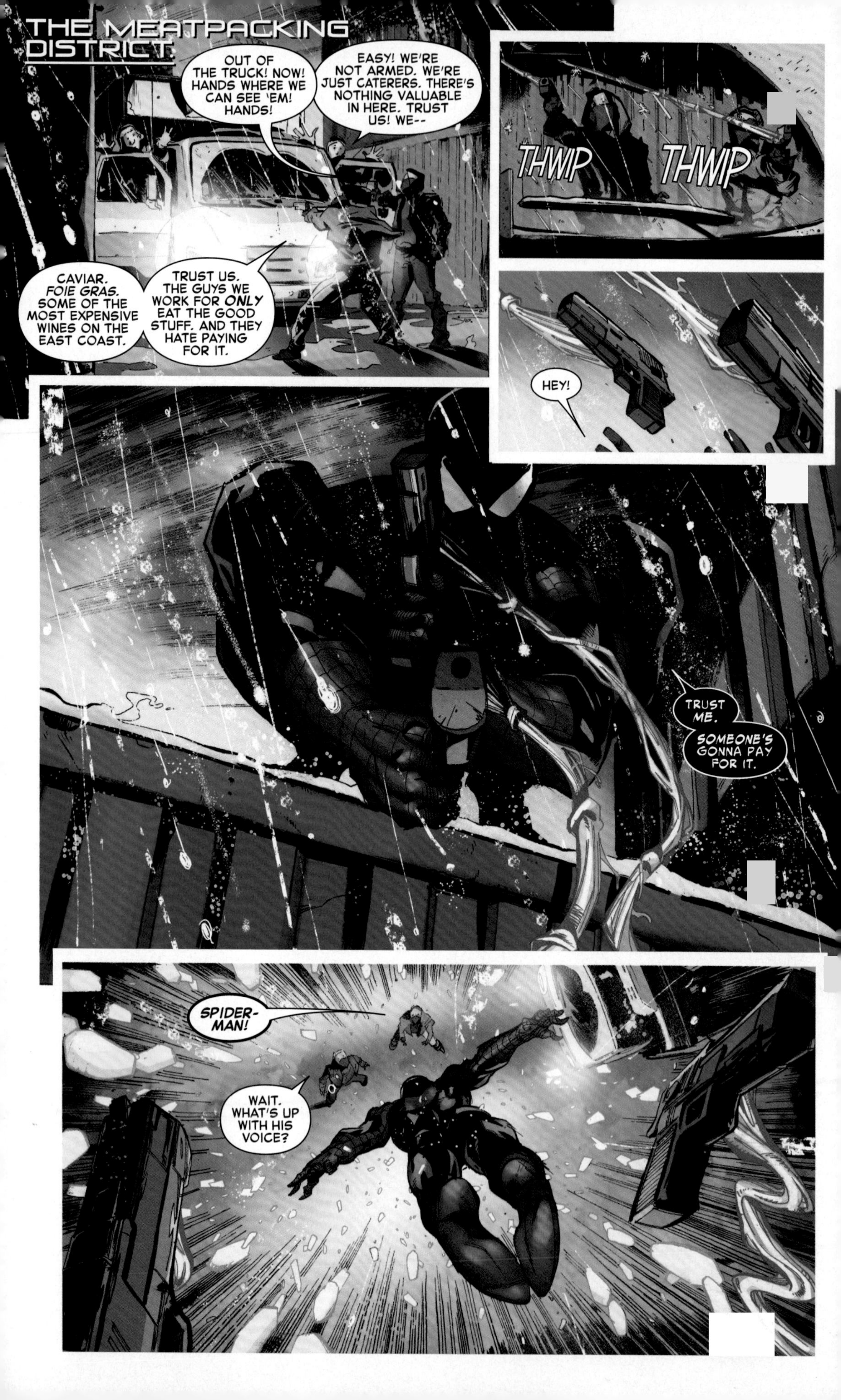
THE MEATPACKING DISTRICT.
OUT OF THE TRUCK! NOW! HANDS WHERE WE CAN SEE 'EM! HANDS!
EASY! WE'RE NOT ARMED. WE'RE JUST CATERERS. THERE'S NOTHING VALUABLE IN HERE. TRUST US! WE--
CAVIAR. FOIE GRAS. SOME OF THE MOST EXPENSIVE WINES ON THE EAST COAST.
TRUST US. THE GUYS WE WORK FOR ONLY EAT THE GOOD STUFF. AND THEY HATE PAYING FOR IT.
THWIP
THWIP
HEY!
TRUST ME.
SOMEONE'S GONNA PAY FOR IT.
SPIDER-MAN!
WAIT. WHAT'S UP WITH HIS VOICE?

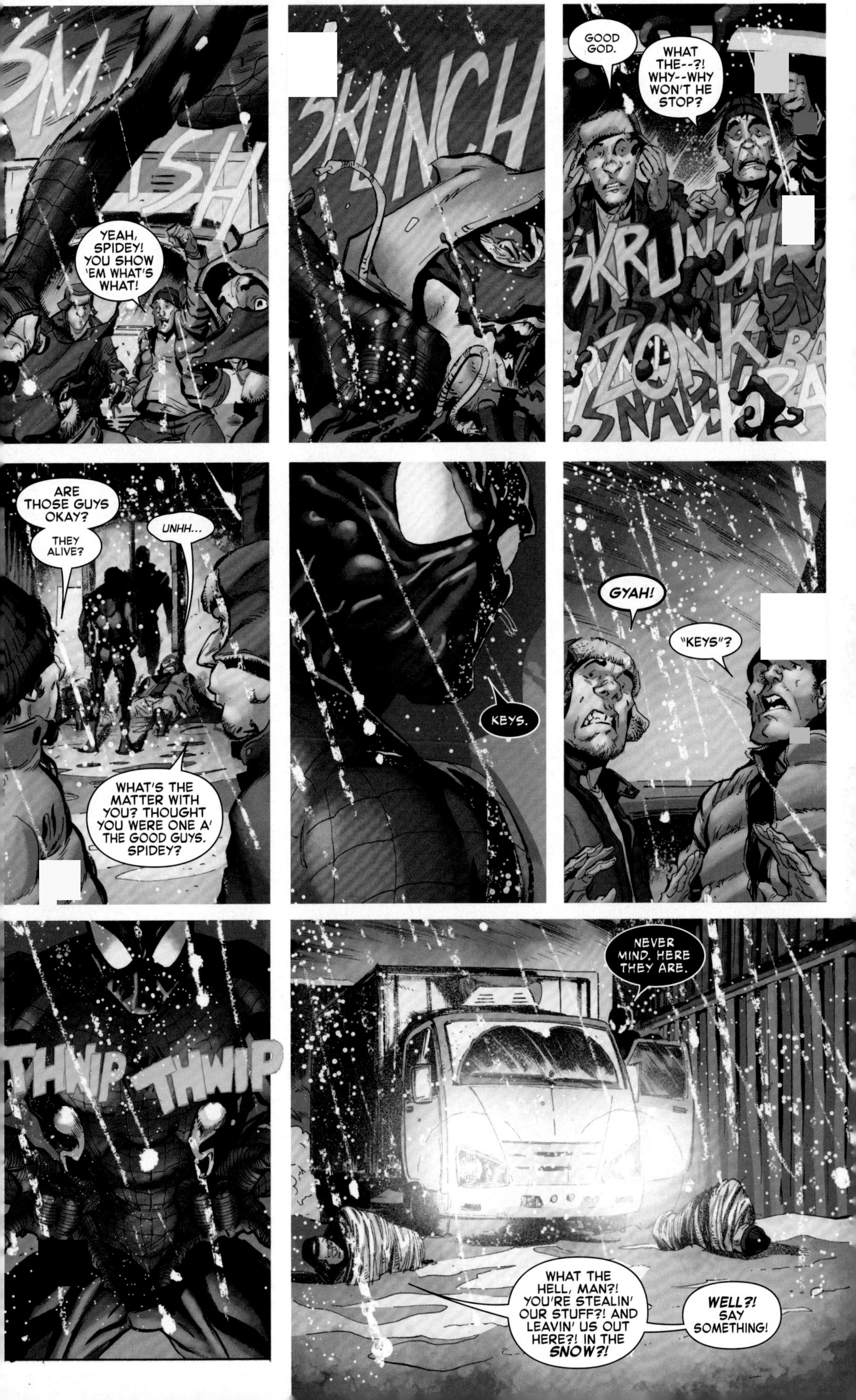
SMASH
YEAH, SPIDEY! YOU SHOW 'EM WHAT'S WHAT!
SKLINCH
GOOD GOD.
WHAT THE--?! WHY--WHY WON'T HE STOP?
SKRUNCH
ZONK
ARE THOSE GUYS OKAY?
THEY ALIVE?
UNHH...
WHAT'S THE MATTER WITH YOU? THOUGHT YOU WERE ONE A' THE GOOD GUYS. SPIDEY?
KEYS.
GYAH!
"KEYS"?
THWIP THWIP
NEVER MIND. HERE THEY ARE.
WHAT THE HELL, MAN?! YOU'RE STEALIN' OUR STUFF?! AND LEAVIN' US OUT HERE?! IN THE SNOW?!
WELL?! SAY SOMETHING!

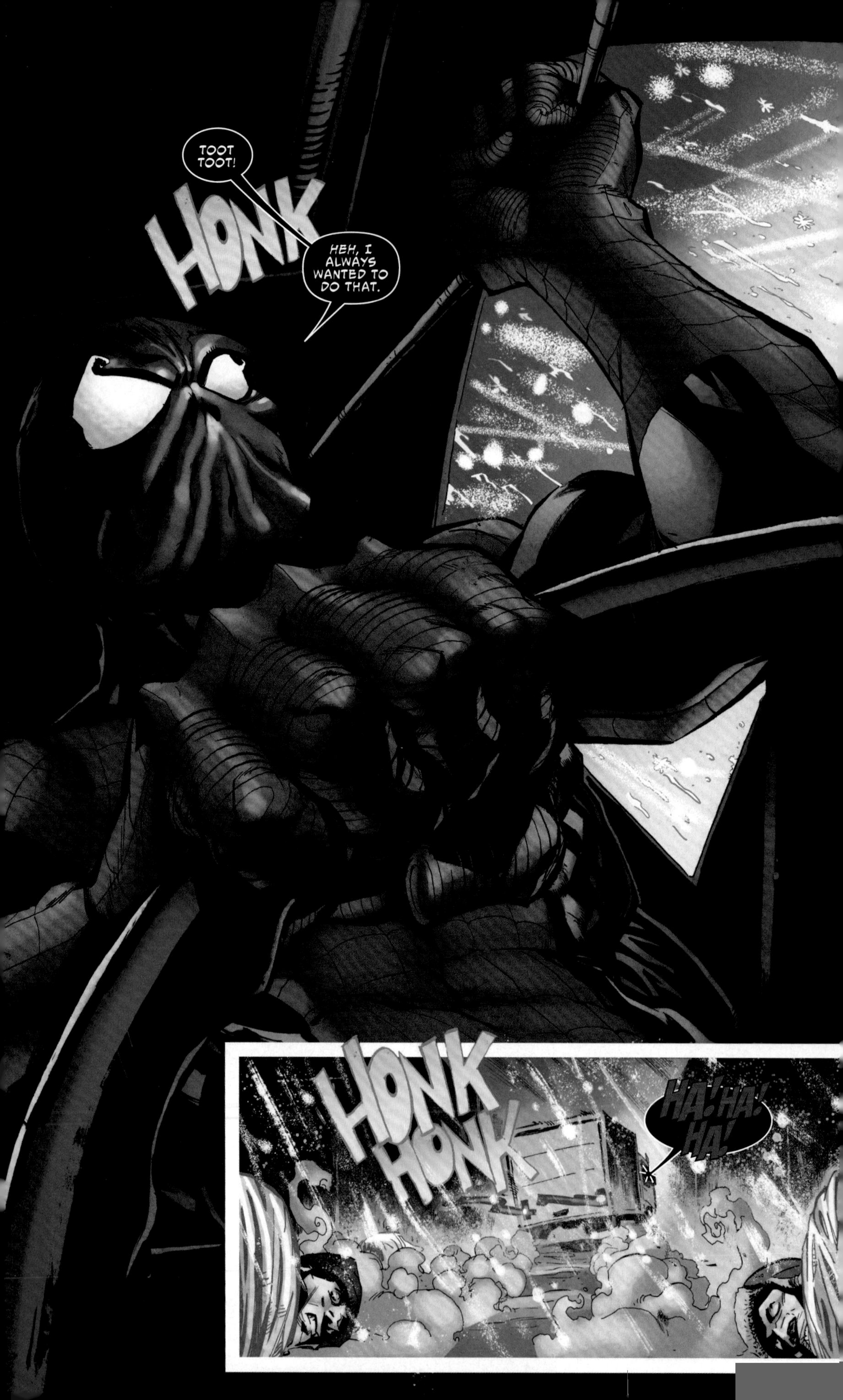
TOOT TOOT!
HONK
HEH, I ALWAYS WANTED TO DO THAT.
HONK
HONK
HA! HA! HA!

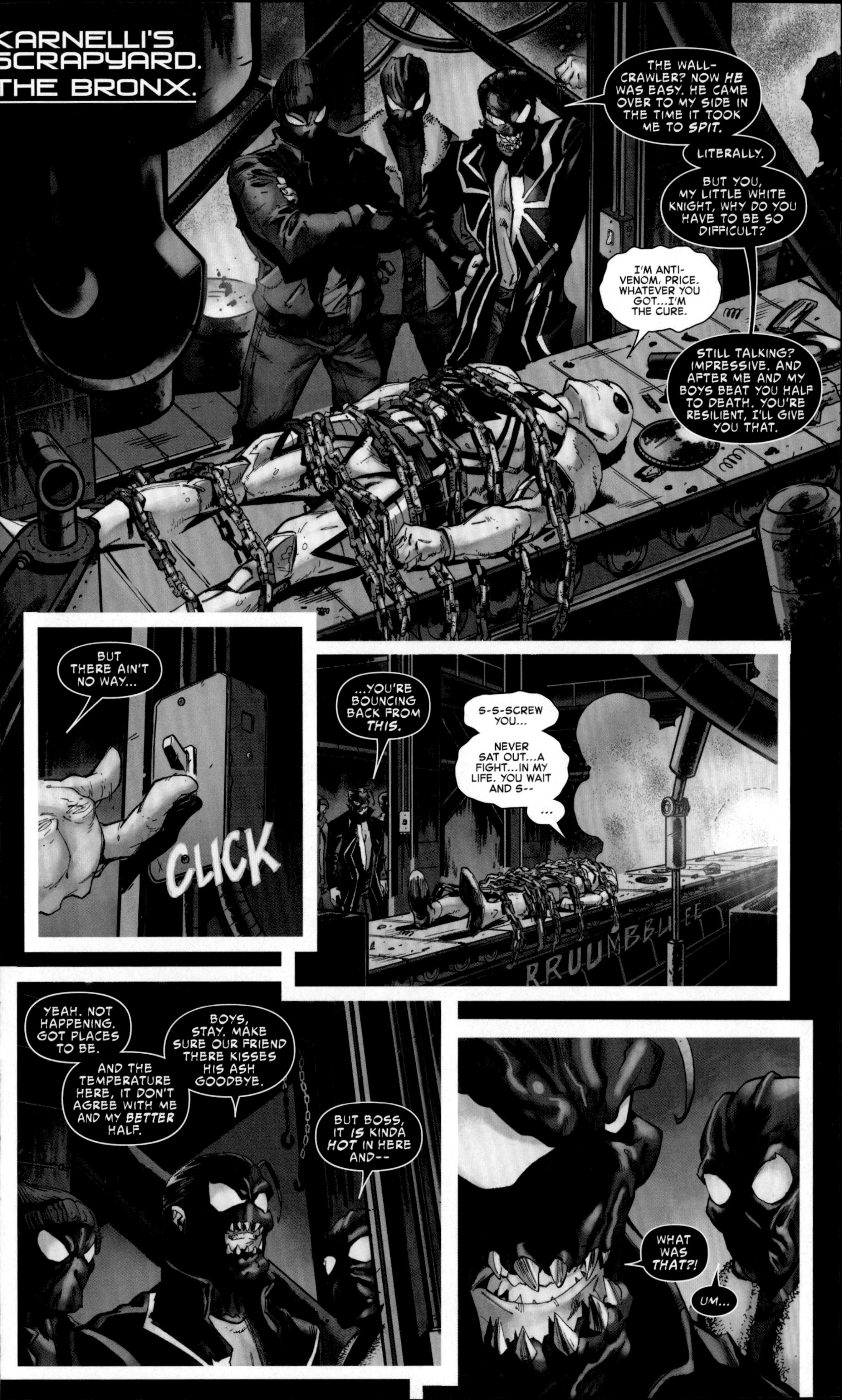

KARNELLI'S SCRAPYARD. THE BRONX.
THE WALL-CRAWLER? NOW HE WAS EASY. HE CAME OVER TO MY SIDE IN THE TIME IT TOOK ME TO SPIT.
LITERALLY.
BUT YOU, MY LITTLE WHITE KNIGHT, WHY DO YOU HAVE TO BE SO DIFFICULT?
I'M ANTI-VENOM, PRICE. WHATEVER YOU GOT...I'M THE CURE.
STILL TALKING? IMPRESSIVE. AND AFTER ME AND MY BOYS BEAT YOU HALF TO DEATH. YOU'RE RESILIENT, I'LL GIVE YOU THAT.
BUT THERE AIN'T NO WAY...
CLICK
...YOU'RE BOUNCING BACK FROM THIS.
S-S-SCREW YOU...
NEVER SAT OUT...A FIGHT...IN MY LIFE. YOU WAIT AND S--
...
RRUUMBBLEE
YEAH. NOT HAPPENING. GOT PLACES TO BE.
AND THE TEMPERATURE HERE, IT DON'T AGREE WITH ME AND MY BETTER HALF.
BOYS, STAY. MAKE SURE OUR FRIEND THERE KISSES HIS ASH GOODBYE.
BUT BOSS, IT IS KINDA HOT IN HERE AND--
WHAT WAS THAT?!
UM...

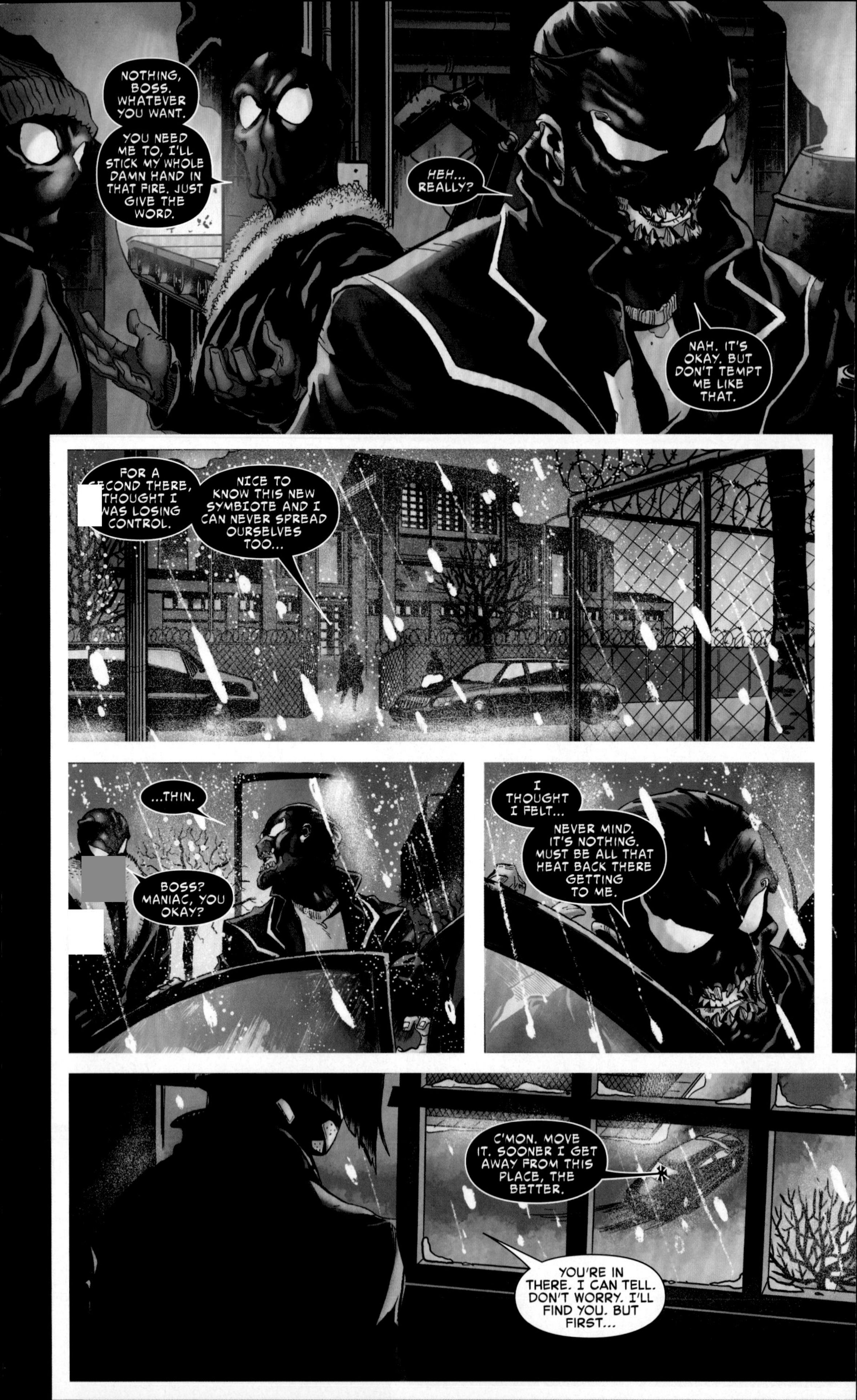
NOTHING, BOSS. WHATEVER YOU WANT.
YOU NEED ME TO, I'LL STICK MY WHOLE DAMN HAND IN THAT FIRE. JUST GIVE THE WORD.
HEH... REALLY?
NAH. IT'S OKAY. BUT DON'T TEMPT ME LIKE THAT.
FOR A ECOND THERE, THOUGHT I WAS LOSING CONTROL.
NICE TO KNOW THIS NEW SYMBIOTE AND I CAN NEVER SPREAD OURSELVES TOO...
...THIN.
BOSS? MANIAC, YOU OKAY?
I THOUGHT I FELT...
NEVER MIND. IT'S NOTHING. MUST BE ALL THAT HEAT BACK THERE GETTING TO ME.
C'MON. MOVE IT. SOONER I GET AWAY FROM THIS PLACE, THE BETTER.
YOU'RE IN THERE. I CAN TELL. DON'T WORRY. I'LL FIND YOU. BUT FIRST...

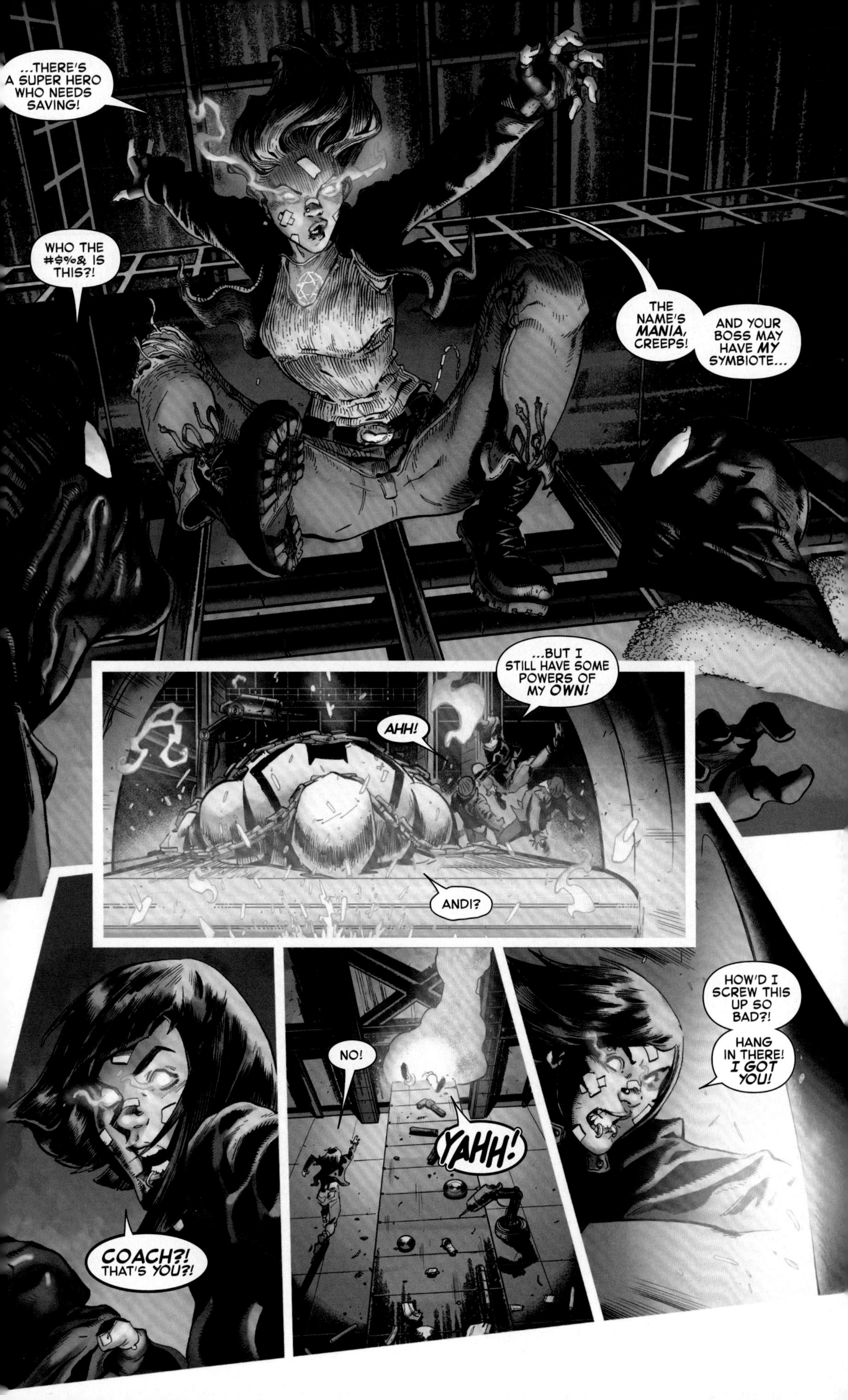
...THERE'S A SUPER HERO WHO NEEDS SAVING!
WHO THE #$%& IS THIS?!
THE NAME'S MANIA, CREEPS!
AND YOUR BOSS MAY HAVE MY SYMBIOTE...
...BUT I STILL HAVE SOME POWERS OF MY OWN!
AHH!
ANDI?
COACH?! THAT'S YOU?!
NO!
YAHH!
HOW'D I SCREW THIS UP SO BAD?!
HANG IN THERE! I GOT YOU!

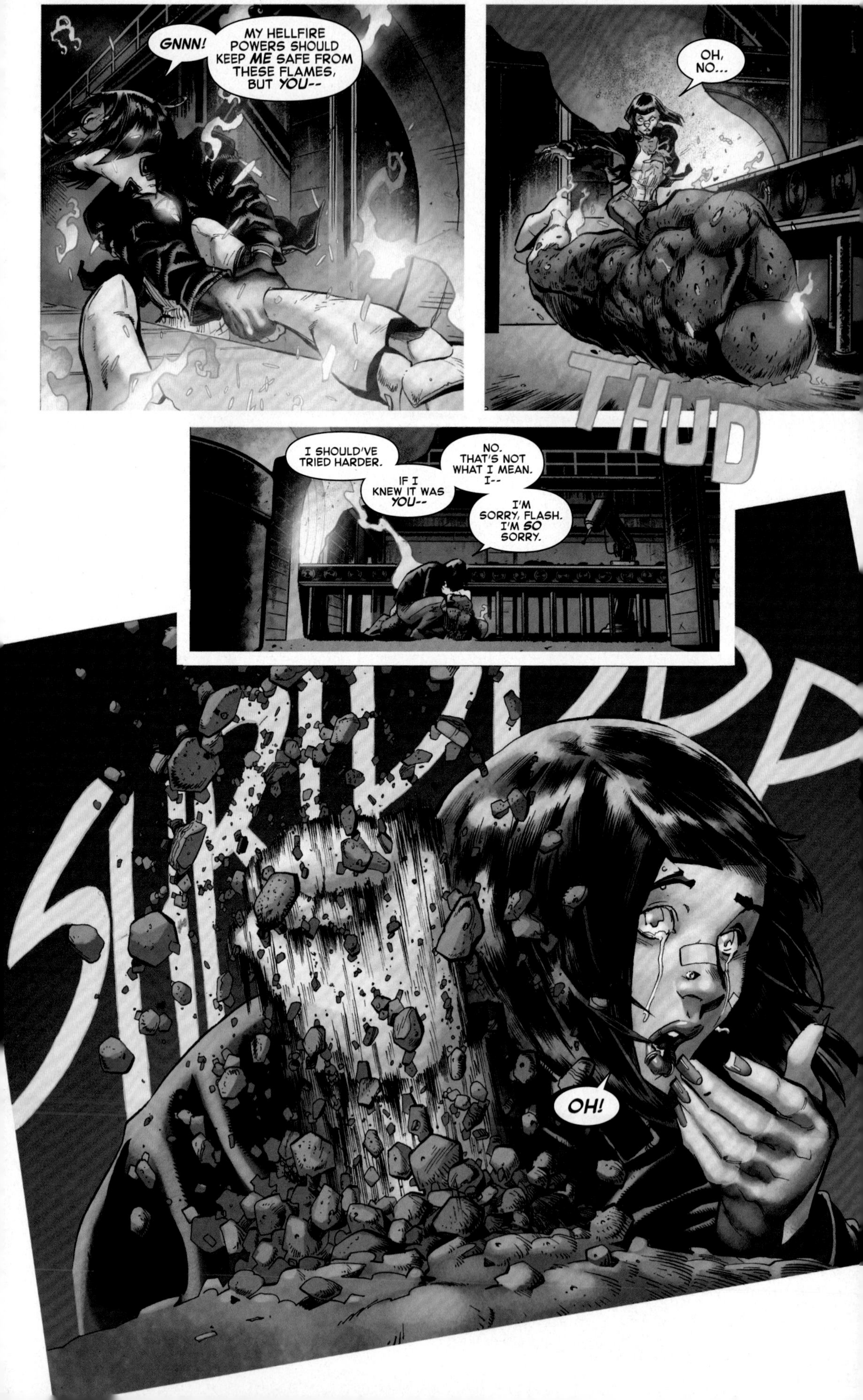

GNNN!
MY HELLFIRE POWERS SHOULD KEEP ME SAFE FROM THESE FLAMES, BUT YOU--
OH, NO...
THUD
I SHOULD'VE TRIED HARDER.
IF I KNEW IT WAS YOU--
NO. THAT'S NOT WHAT I MEAN. I--
I'M SORRY, FLASH. I'M SO SORRY.
OH!

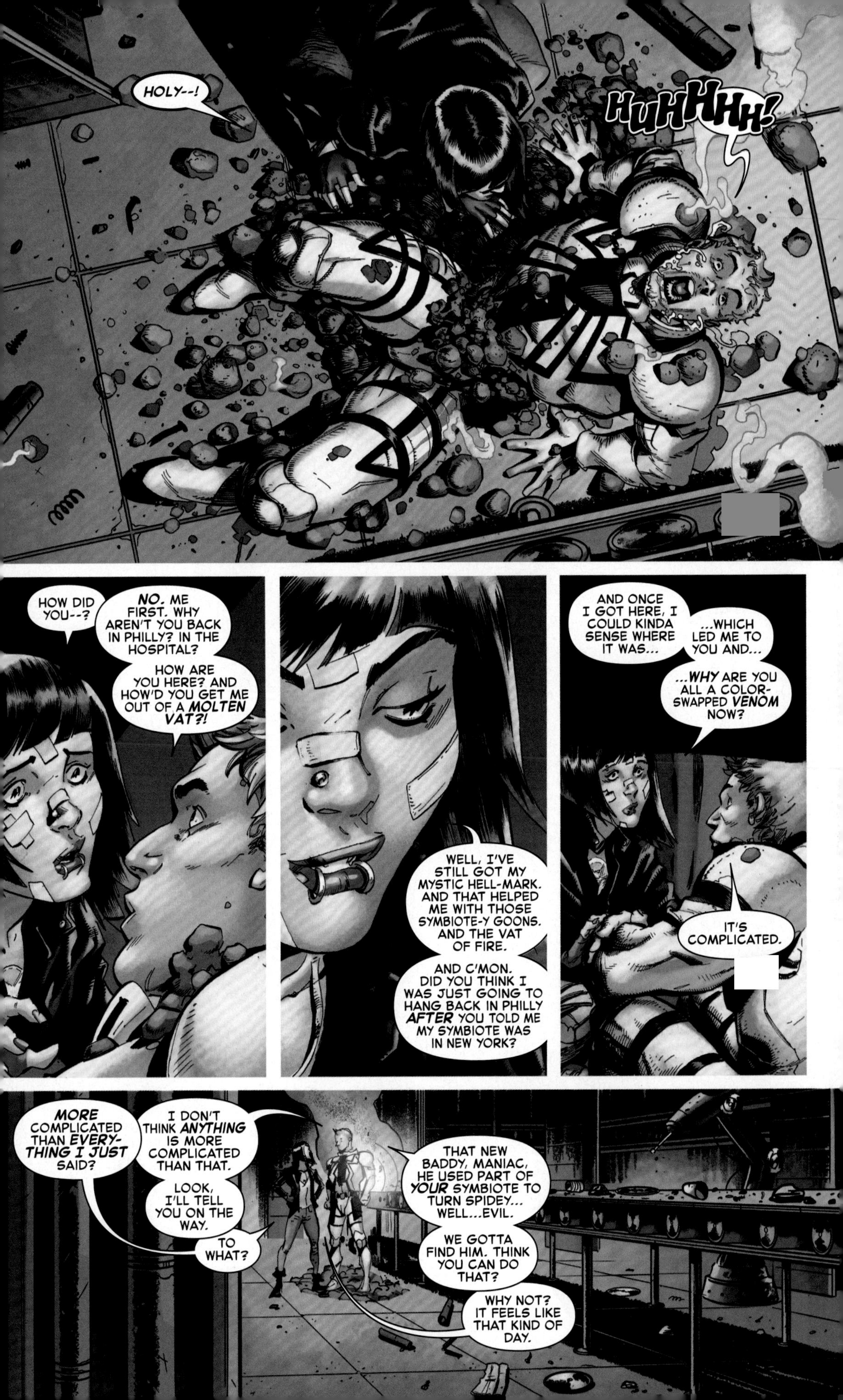
HOLY--!
HUHHHHH!
HOW DID YOU--?
NO. ME FIRST. WHY AREN'T YOU BACK IN PHILLY? IN THE HOSPITAL?
HOW ARE YOU HERE? AND HOW'D YOU GET ME OUT OF A MOLTEN VAT?!
WELL, I'VE STILL GOT MY MYSTIC HELL-MARK. AND THAT HELPED ME WITH THOSE SYMBIOTE-Y GOONS. AND THE VAT OF FIRE.
AND C'MON. DID YOU THINK I WAS JUST GOING TO HANG BACK IN PHILLY AFTER YOU TOLD ME MY SYMBIOTE WAS IN NEW YORK?
AND ONCE I GOT HERE, I COULD KINDA SENSE WHERE IT WAS...
...WHICH LED ME TO YOU AND...
...WHY ARE YOU ALL A COLOR-SWAPPED VENOM NOW?
IT'S COMPLICATED.
MORE COMPLICATED THAN EVERY-THING I JUST SAID?
I DON'T THINK ANYTHING IS MORE COMPLICATED THAN THAT.
LOOK, I'LL TELL YOU ON THE WAY.
TO WHAT?
THAT NEW BADDY, MANIAC, HE USED PART OF YOUR SYMBIOTE TO TURN SPIDEY... WELL...EVIL.
WE GOTTA FIND HIM. THINK YOU CAN DO THAT?
WHY NOT? IT FEELS LIKE THAT KIND OF DAY.

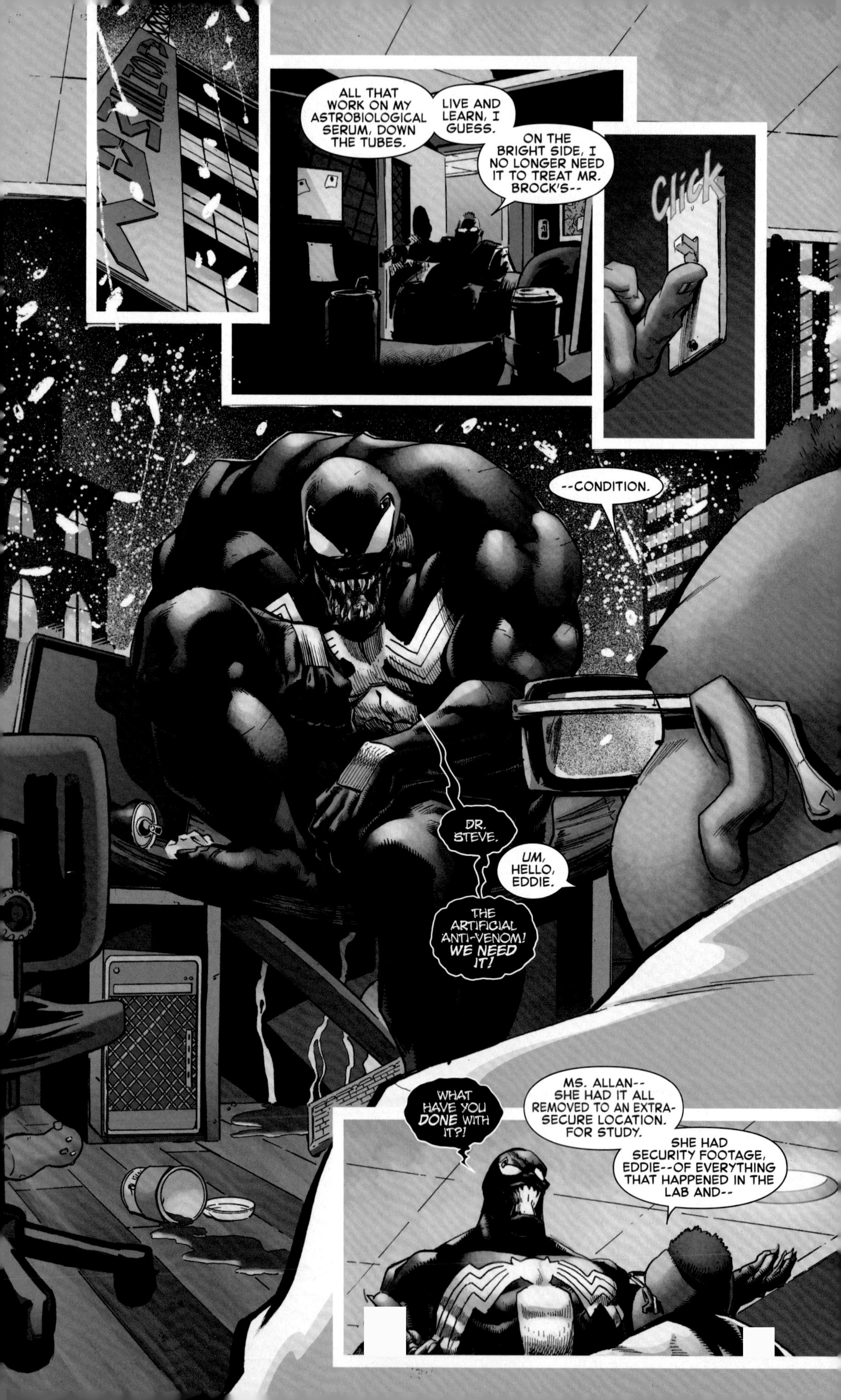

ALL THAT WORK ON MY ASTROBIOLOGICAL SERUM, DOWN THE TUBES.
LIVE AND LEARN, I GUESS.
ON THE BRIGHT SIDE, I NO LONGER NEED IT TO TREAT MR. BROCK'S--
CLICK
--CONDITION.
DR. STEVE.
UM, HELLO, EDDIE.
THE ARTIFICIAL ANTI-VENOM! WE NEED IT!
WHAT HAVE YOU DONE WITH IT?!
MS. ALLAN-- SHE HAD IT ALL REMOVED TO AN EXTRA-SECURE LOCATION. FOR STUDY.
SHE HAD SECURITY FOOTAGE, EDDIE--OF EVERYTHING THAT HAPPENED IN THE LAB AND--

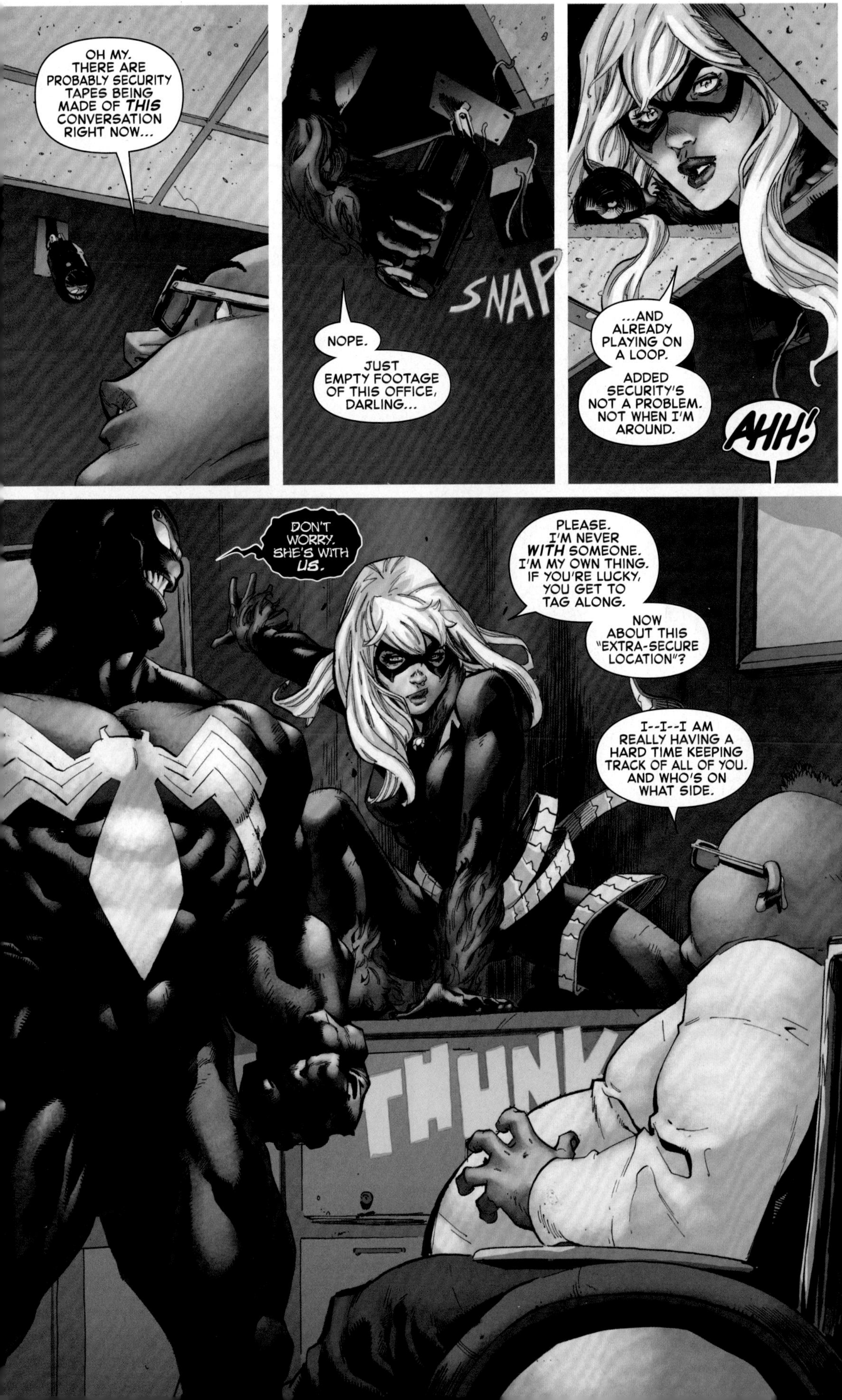
OH MY. THERE ARE PROBABLY SECURITY TAPES BEING MADE OF THIS CONVERSATION RIGHT NOW...
SNAP
NOPE.
JUST EMPTY FOOTAGE OF THIS OFFICE, DARLING...
...AND ALREADY PLAYING ON A LOOP.
ADDED SECURITY'S NOT A PROBLEM. NOT WHEN I'M AROUND.
AHH!
DON'T WORRY. SHE'S WITH US.
PLEASE. I'M NEVER WITH SOMEONE. I'M MY OWN THING. IF YOU'RE LUCKY, YOU GET TO TAG ALONG.
NOW ABOUT THIS "EXTRA-SECURE LOCATION"?
I--I--I AM REALLY HAVING A HARD TIME KEEPING TRACK OF ALL OF YOU. AND WHO'S ON WHAT SIDE.
THUNK

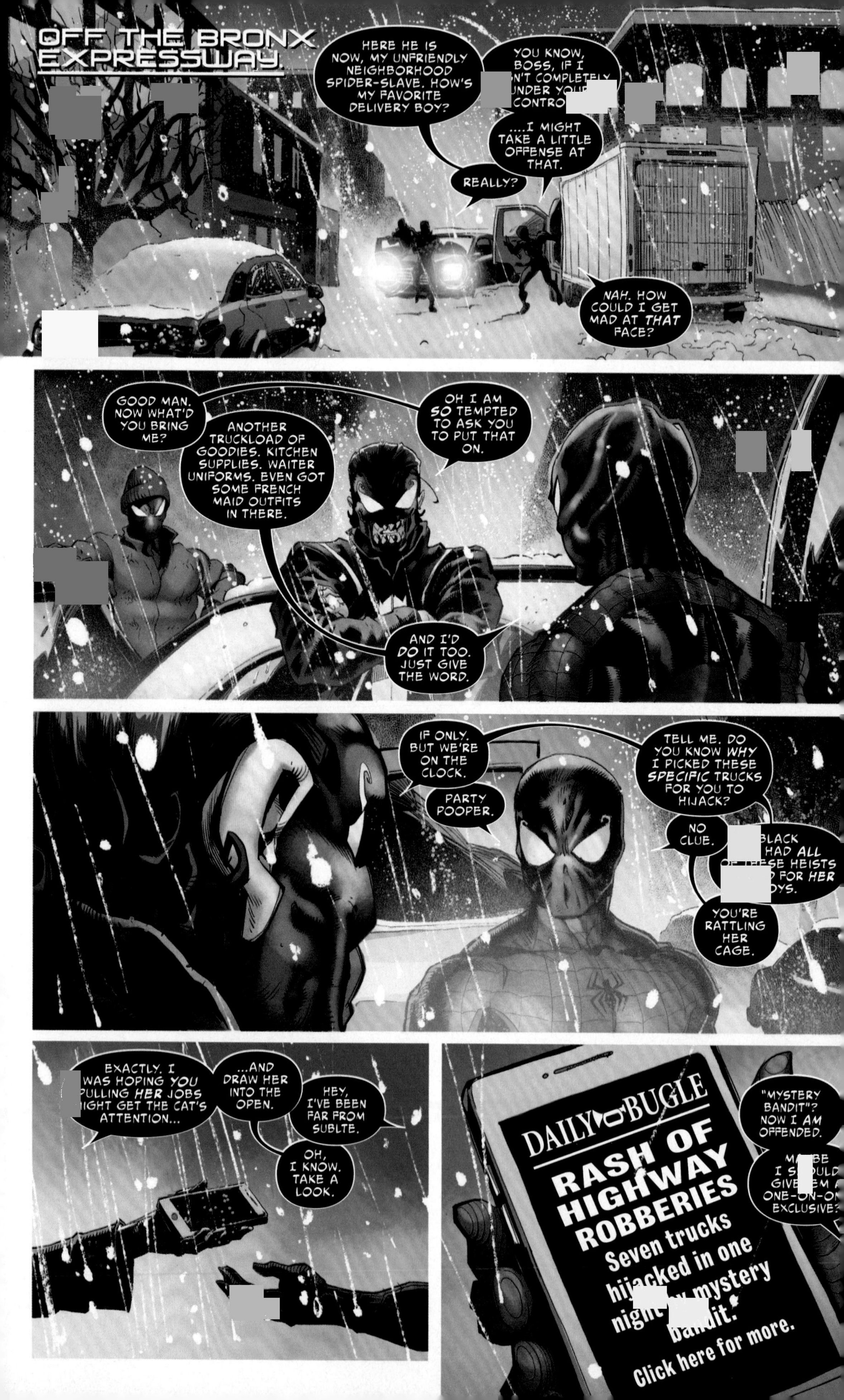

OFF THE BRONX EXPRESSWAY.
HERE HE IS NOW, MY UNFRIENDLY NEIGHBORHOOD SPIDER-SLAVE. HOW'S MY FAVORITE DELIVERY BOY?
YOU KNOW, BOSS, IF I N'T COMPLETELY NDER YOUR CONTRO
...I MIGHT TAKE A LITTLE OFFENSE AT THAT.
REALLY?
NAH. HOW COULD I GET MAD AT THAT FACE?
GOOD MAN. NOW WHAT'D YOU BRING ME?
ANOTHER TRUCKLOAD OF GOODIES. KITCHEN SUPPLIES. WAITER UNIFORMS. EVEN GOT SOME FRENCH MAID OUTFITS IN THERE.
OH I AM SO TEMPTED TO ASK YOU TO PUT THAT ON.
AND I'D DO IT TOO. JUST GIVE THE WORD.
IF ONLY. BUT WE'RE ON THE CLOCK.
PARTY POOPER.
TELL ME. DO YOU KNOW WHY I PICKED THESE SPECIFIC TRUCKS FOR YOU TO HIJACK?
NO CLUE.
BLACK HAD ALL SE HEISTS D FOR HER OYS.
YOU'RE RATTLING HER CAGE.
EXACTLY. I WAS HOPING YOU ULLING HER JOBS IGHT GET THE CAT'S ATTENTION...
...AND DRAW HER INTO THE OPEN.
HEY, I'VE BEEN FAR FROM SUBLTE.
OH, I KNOW. TAKE A LOOK.
DAILY BUGLE
RASH OF HIGHWAY ROBBERIES
Seven trucks
hijacked in one
hi mystery
nigh bandit.
Click here for more.
"MYSTERY BANDIT"? NOW I AM OFFENDED.
EXCLUSIVE?

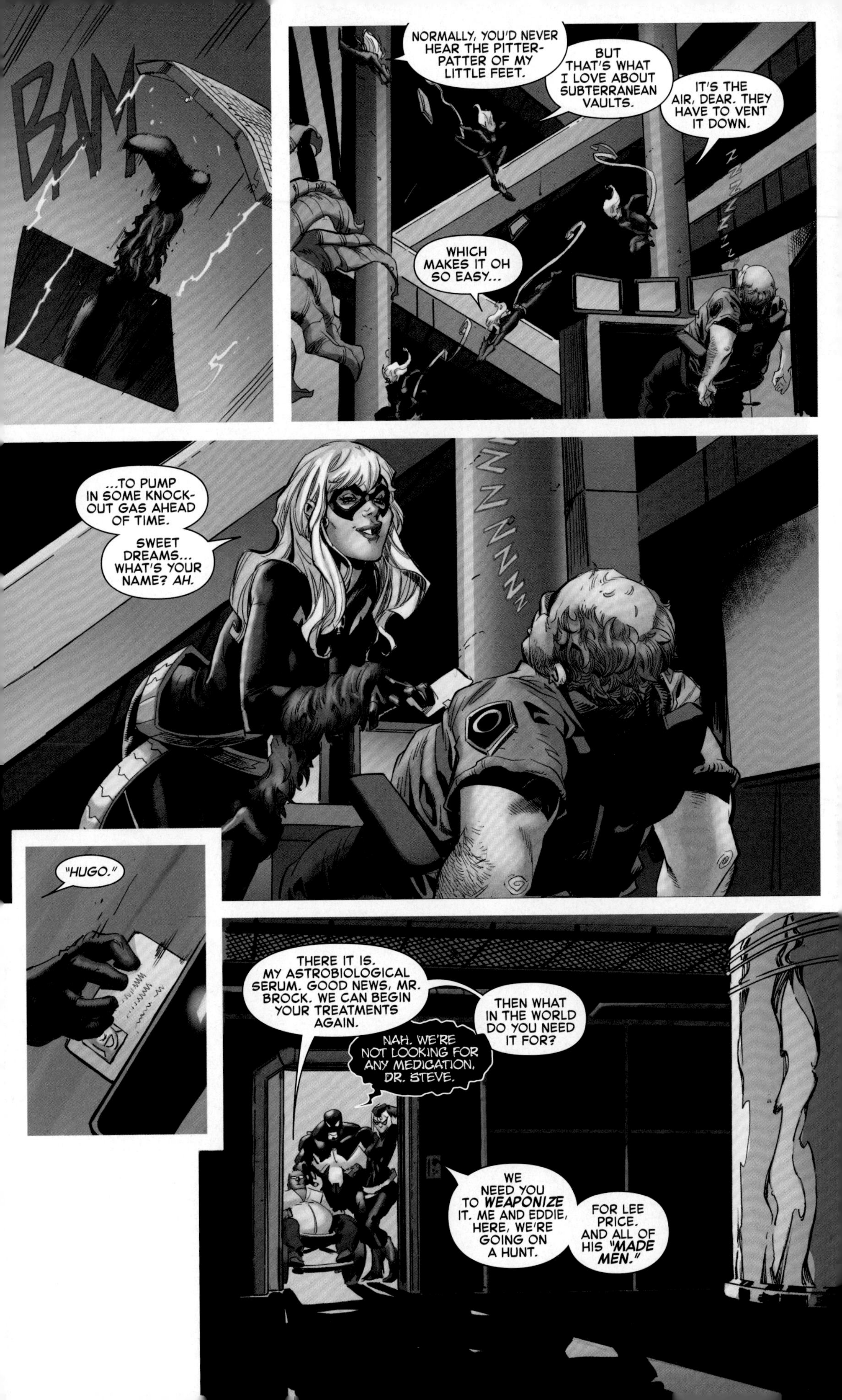
BAM
NORMALLY, YOU'D NEVER HEAR THE PITTER-PATTER OF MY LITTLE FEET.
BUT THAT'S WHAT I LOVE ABOUT SUBTERRANEAN VAULTS.
IT'S THE AIR, DEAR. THEY HAVE TO VENT IT DOWN.
WHICH MAKES IT OH SO EASY...
...TO PUMP IN SOME KNOCK-OUT GAS AHEAD OF TIME.
SWEET DREAMS... WHAT'S YOUR NAME? AH.
"HUGO."
THERE IT IS. MY ASTROBIOLOGICAL SERUM. GOOD NEWS, MR. BROCK. WE CAN BEGIN YOUR TREATMENTS AGAIN.
NAH. WE'RE NOT LOOKING FOR ANY MEDICATION, DR. STEVE.
THEN WHAT IN THE WORLD DO YOU NEED IT FOR?
WE NEED YOU TO WEAPONIZE IT. ME AND EDDIE, HERE, WE'RE GOING ON A HUNT.
FOR LEE PRICE. AND ALL OF HIS "MADE MEN."

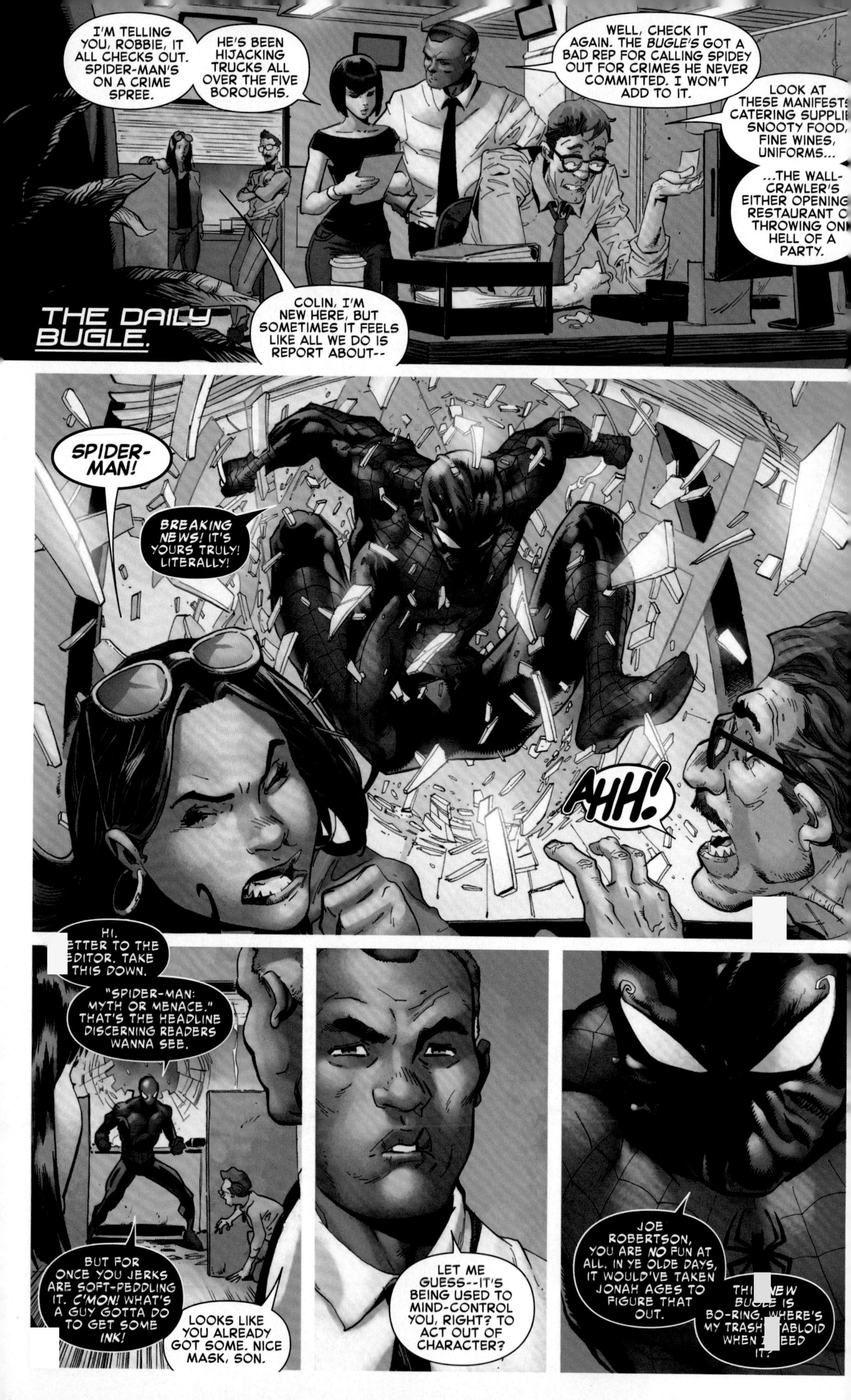
I'M TELLING YOU, ROBBIE, IT ALL CHECKS OUT. SPIDER-MAN'S ON A CRIME SPREE.
HE'S BEEN HIJACKING TRUCKS ALL OVER THE FIVE BOROUGHS.
WELL, CHECK IT AGAIN. THE BUGLE'S GOT A BAD REP FOR CALLING SPIDEY OUT FOR CRIMES HE NEVER COMMITTED. I WON'T ADD TO IT.
LOOK AT THESE MANIFEST CATERING SUPPLI SNOOTY FOOD, FINE WINES, UNIFORMS...
...THE WALL-CRAWLER'S EITHER OPENING RESTAURANT O THROWING ON HELL OF A PARTY.
THE DAILY BUGLE.
COLIN, I'M NEW HERE, BUT SOMETIMES IT FEELS LIKE ALL WE DO IS REPORT ABOUT--
SPIDER-MAN!
BREAKING NEWS! IT'S YOURS TRULY! LITERALLY!
AHH!
HI. ETTER TO THE DITOR. TAKE THIS DOWN.
"SPIDER-MAN: MYTH OR MENACE." THAT'S THE HEADLINE DISCERNING READERS WANNA SEE.
BUT FOR ONCE YOU JERKS ARE SOFT-PEDDLING IT. C'MON! WHAT'S A GUY GOTTA DO TO GET SOME INK!
LOOKS LIKE YOU ALREADY GOT SOME. NICE MASK, SON.
LET ME GUESS--IT'S BEING USED TO MIND-CONTROL YOU, RIGHT? TO ACT OUT OF CHARACTER?
JOE ROBERTSON, YOU ARE NO FUN AT ALL. IN YE OLDE DAYS, IT WOULD'VE TAKEN JONAH AGES TO FIGURE THAT OUT.
THI NEW BUGLE IS BO-RING. WHERE'S MY TRASH TABLOID WHEN I EED IT?

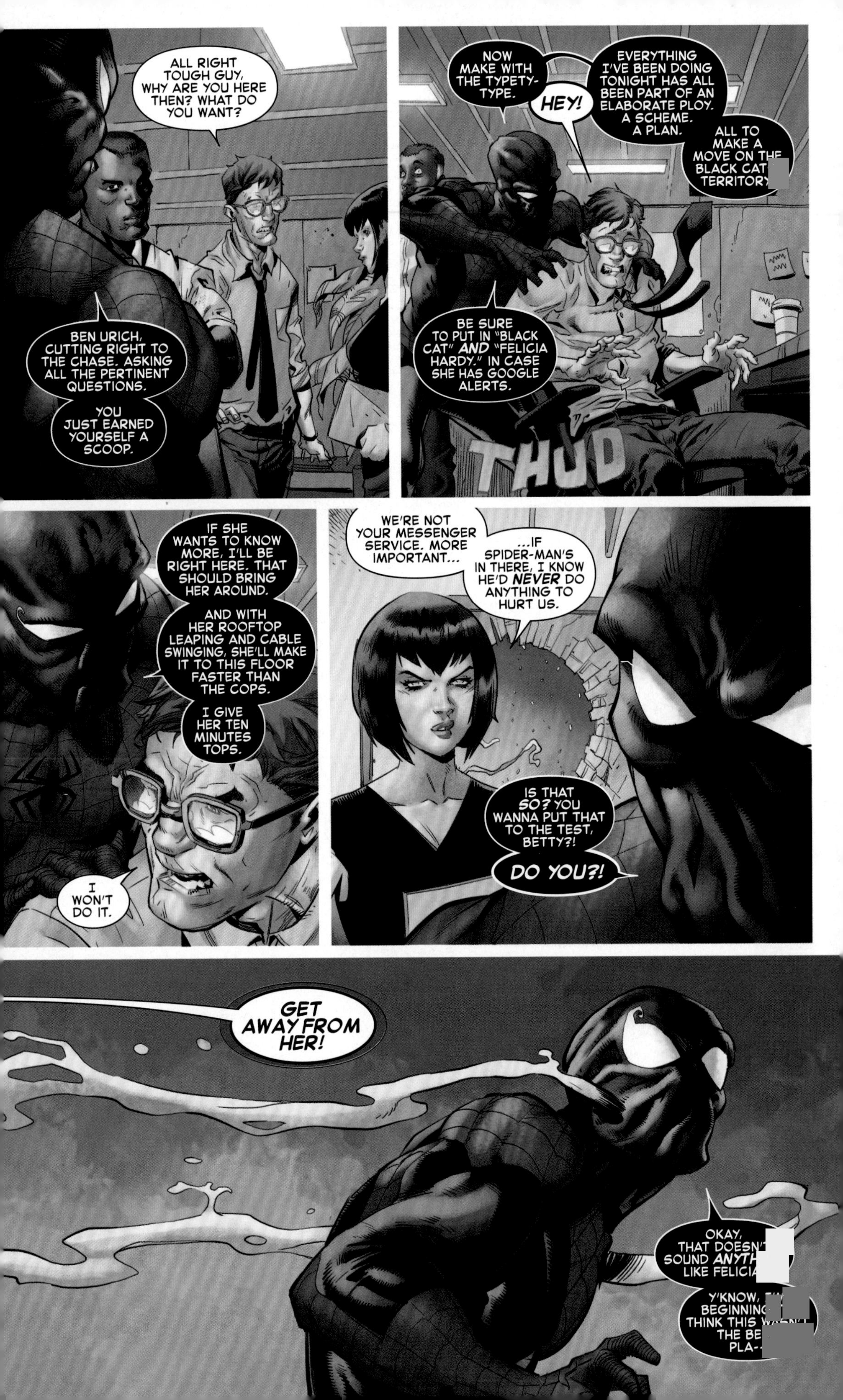

ALL RIGHT TOUGH GUY, WHY ARE YOU HERE THEN? WHAT DO YOU WANT?
BEN URICH, CUTTING RIGHT TO THE CHASE. ASKING ALL THE PERTINENT QUESTIONS.
YOU JUST EARNED YOURSELF A SCOOP.
NOW MAKE WITH THE TYPETY-TYPE.
HEY!
EVERYTHING I'VE BEEN DOING TONIGHT HAS ALL BEEN PART OF AN ELABORATE PLOY. A SCHEME. A PLAN.
ALL TO MAKE A MOVE ON THE BLACK CAT TERRITORY
BE SURE TO PUT IN "BLACK CAT" AND "FELICIA HARDY." IN CASE SHE HAS GOOGLE ALERTS.
THUD
IF SHE WANTS TO KNOW MORE, I'LL BE RIGHT HERE. THAT SHOULD BRING HER AROUND.
AND WITH HER ROOFTOP LEAPING AND CABLE SWINGING, SHE'LL MAKE IT TO THIS FLOOR FASTER THAN THE COPS.
I GIVE HER TEN MINUTES TOPS.
I WON'T DO IT.
WE'RE NOT YOUR MESSENGER SERVICE. MORE IMPORTANT...
...IF SPIDER-MAN'S IN THERE, I KNOW HE'D NEVER DO ANYTHING TO HURT US.
IS THAT SO? YOU WANNA PUT THAT TO THE TEST, BETTY?!
DO YOU?!
GET AWAY FROM HER!
OKAY, THAT SOUND LIKE
Y'KNOW, THINK THIS THE PLA--

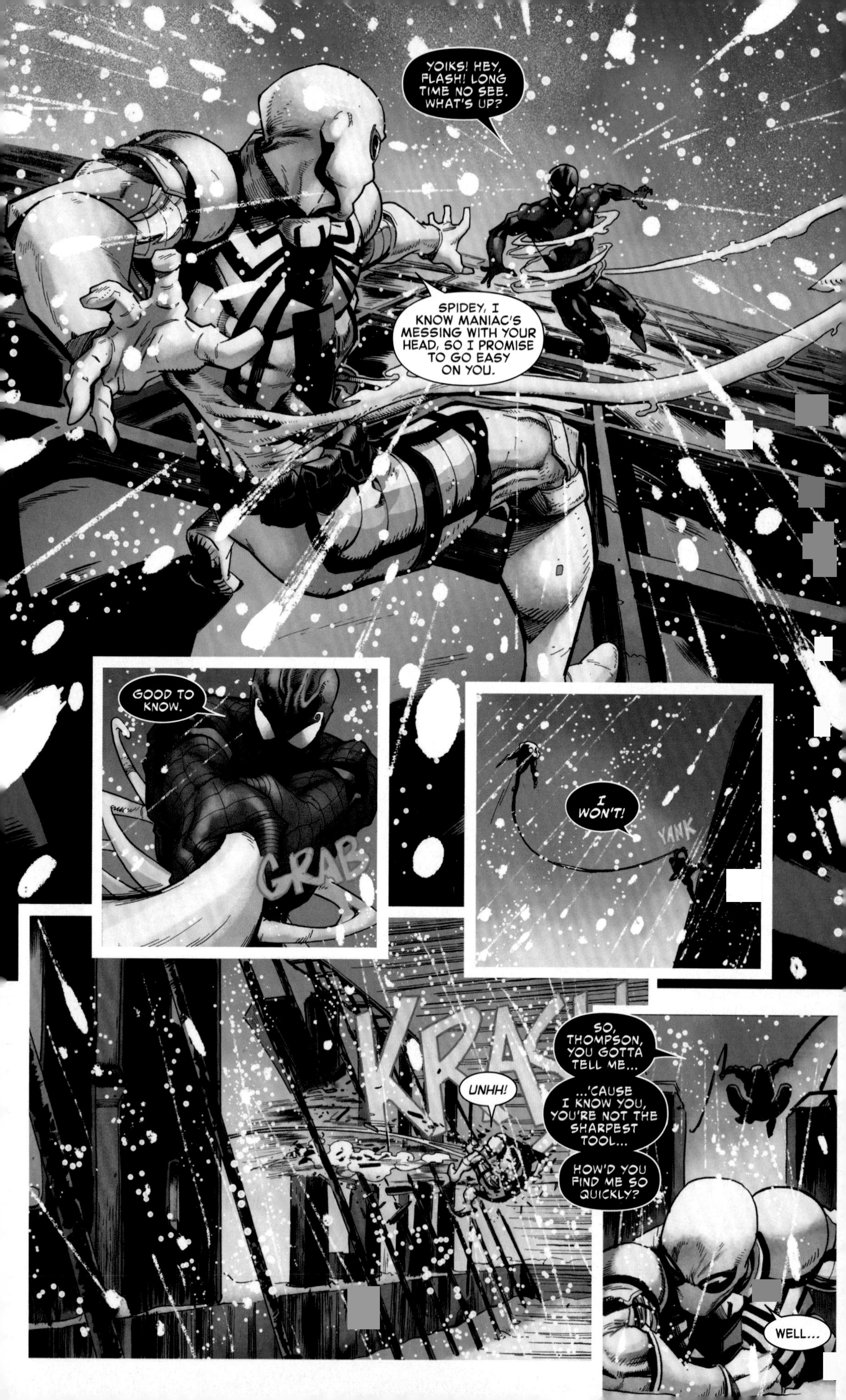
YOIKS! HEY, FLASH! LONG TIME NO SEE. WHAT'S UP?
SPIDEY, I KNOW MANIAC'S MESSING WITH YOUR HEAD, SO I PROMISE TO GO EASY ON YOU.
GOOD TO KNOW.
GRAB
I WON'T!
YANK
KRA
UNHH!
SO, THOMPSON, YOU GOTTA TELL ME...
...'CAUSE I KNOW YOU, YOU'RE NOT THE SHARPEST TOOL...
HOW'D YOU FIND ME SO QUICKLY?
WELL...

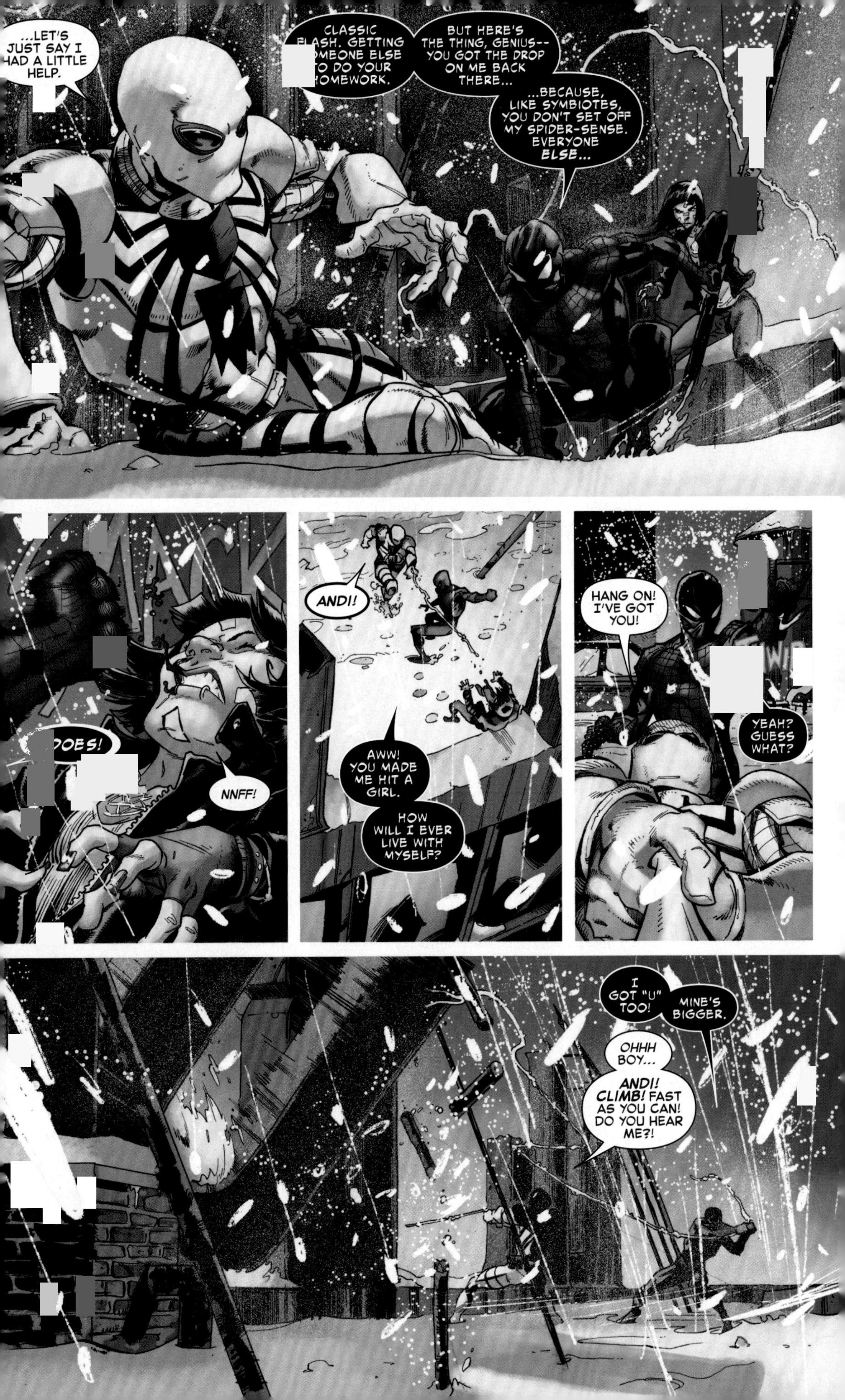
...LET'S JUST SAY I HAD A LITTLE HELP.
CLASSIC LASH. GETTING OMEONE ELSE TO DO YOUR OMEWORK.
BUT HERE'S THE THING, GENIUS-- YOU GOT THE DROP ON ME BACK THERE...
...BECAUSE, LIKE SYMBIOTES, YOU DON'T SET OFF MY SPIDER-SENSE. EVERYONE ELSE...
DOES!
NNFF!
ANDI!
AWW! YOU MADE ME HIT A GIRL.
HOW WILL I EVER LIVE WITH MYSELF?
HANG ON! I'VE GOT YOU!
YEAH? GUESS WHAT?
I GOT "U" TOO!
MINE'S BIGGER.
OHHH BOY...
ANDI! CLIMB! FAST AS YOU CAN! DO YOU HEAR ME?!

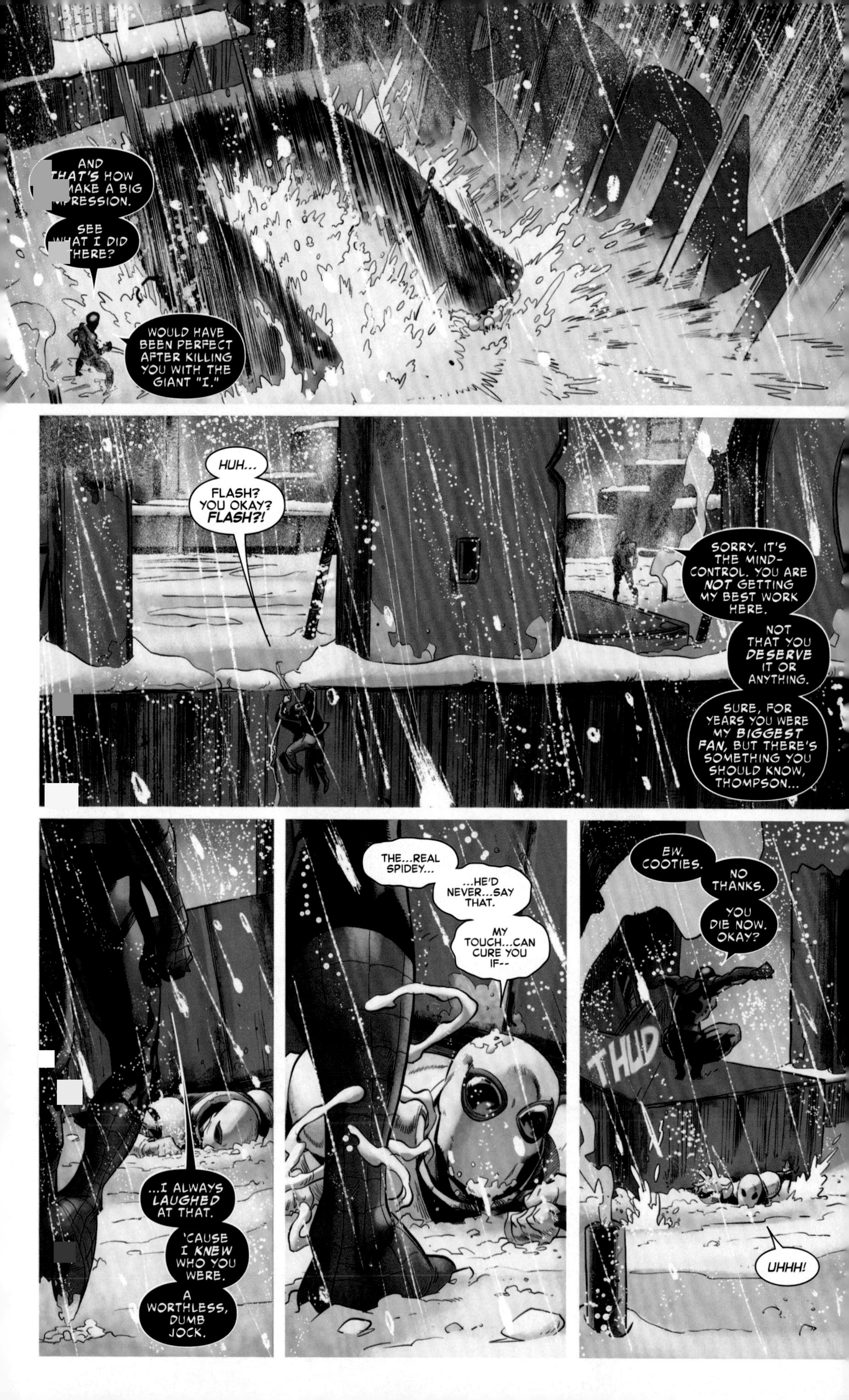
AND THAT'S HOW I MAKE A BIG IMPRESSION.
SEE WHAT I DID THERE?
WOULD HAVE BEEN PERFECT AFTER KILLING YOU WITH THE GIANT "I."
HUH...
FLASH? YOU OKAY? FLASH?!
SORRY. IT'S THE MIND-CONTROL. YOU ARE NOT GETTING MY BEST WORK HERE.
NOT THAT YOU DESERVE IT OR ANYTHING.
SURE, FOR YEARS YOU WERE MY BIGGEST FAN, BUT THERE'S SOMETHING YOU SHOULD KNOW, THOMPSON...
...I ALWAYS LAUGHED AT THAT.
'CAUSE I KNEW WHO YOU WERE.
A WORTHLESS, DUMB JOCK.
THE...REAL SPIDEY...
...HE'D NEVER...SAY THAT.
MY TOUCH...CAN CURE YOU IF--
EW. COOTIES.
NO THANKS.
YOU DIE NOW. OKAY?
THUD
UHHH!

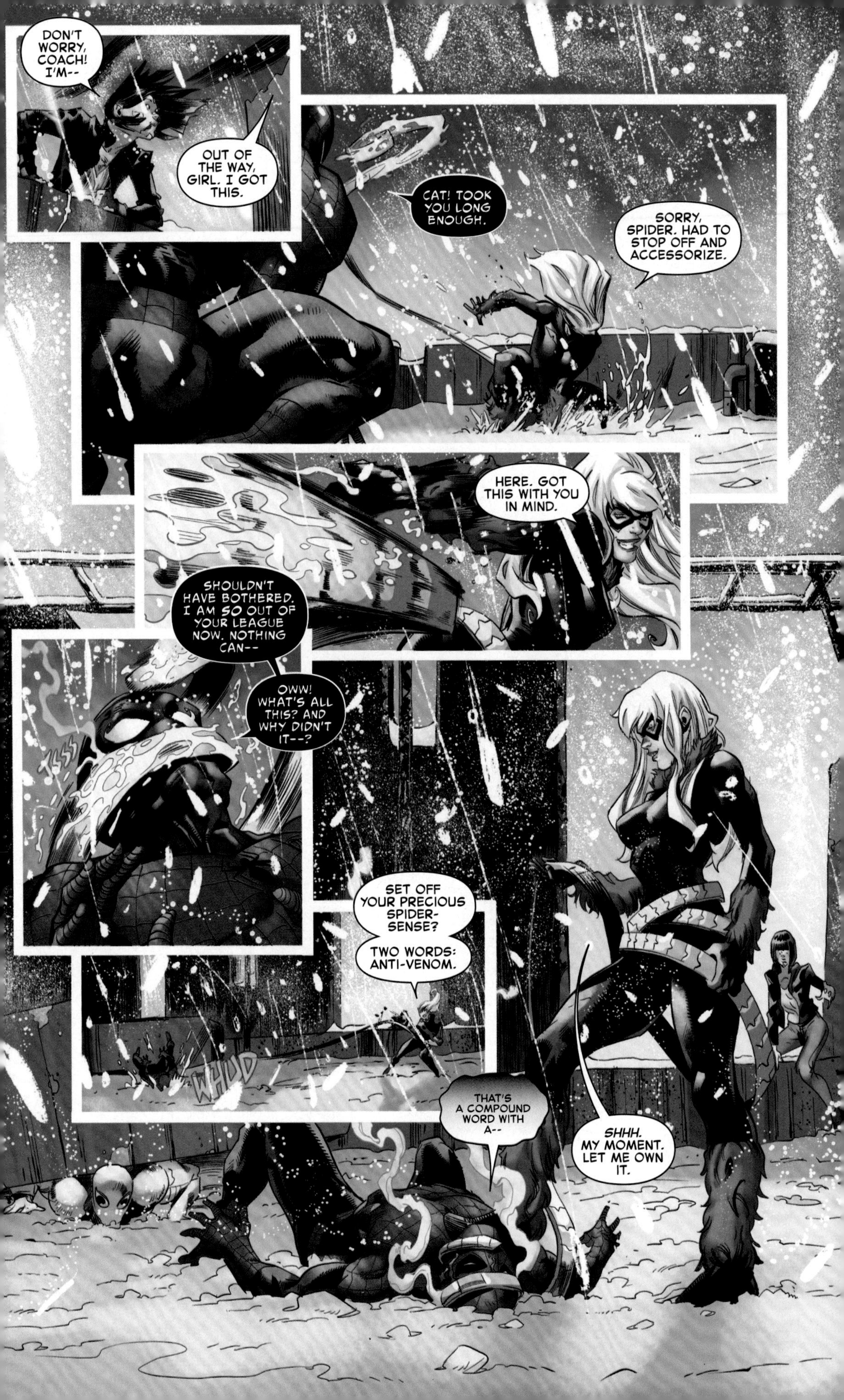
DON'T WORRY, COACH! I'M--
OUT OF THE WAY, GIRL. I GOT THIS.
CAT! TOOK YOU LONG ENOUGH.
SORRY, SPIDER. HAD TO STOP OFF AND ACCESSORIZE.
HERE. GOT THIS WITH YOU IN MIND.
SHOULDN'T HAVE BOTHERED. I AM *SO* OUT OF YOUR LEAGUE NOW. NOTHING CAN--
OWW! WHAT'S ALL THIS? AND WHY DIDN'T IT--?
TSSS
SET OFF YOUR PRECIOUS SPIDER-SENSE?
TWO WORDS: ANTI-VENOM.
WHUD
THAT'S A COMPOUND WORD WITH A--
SHHH. MY MOMENT. LET ME OWN IT.

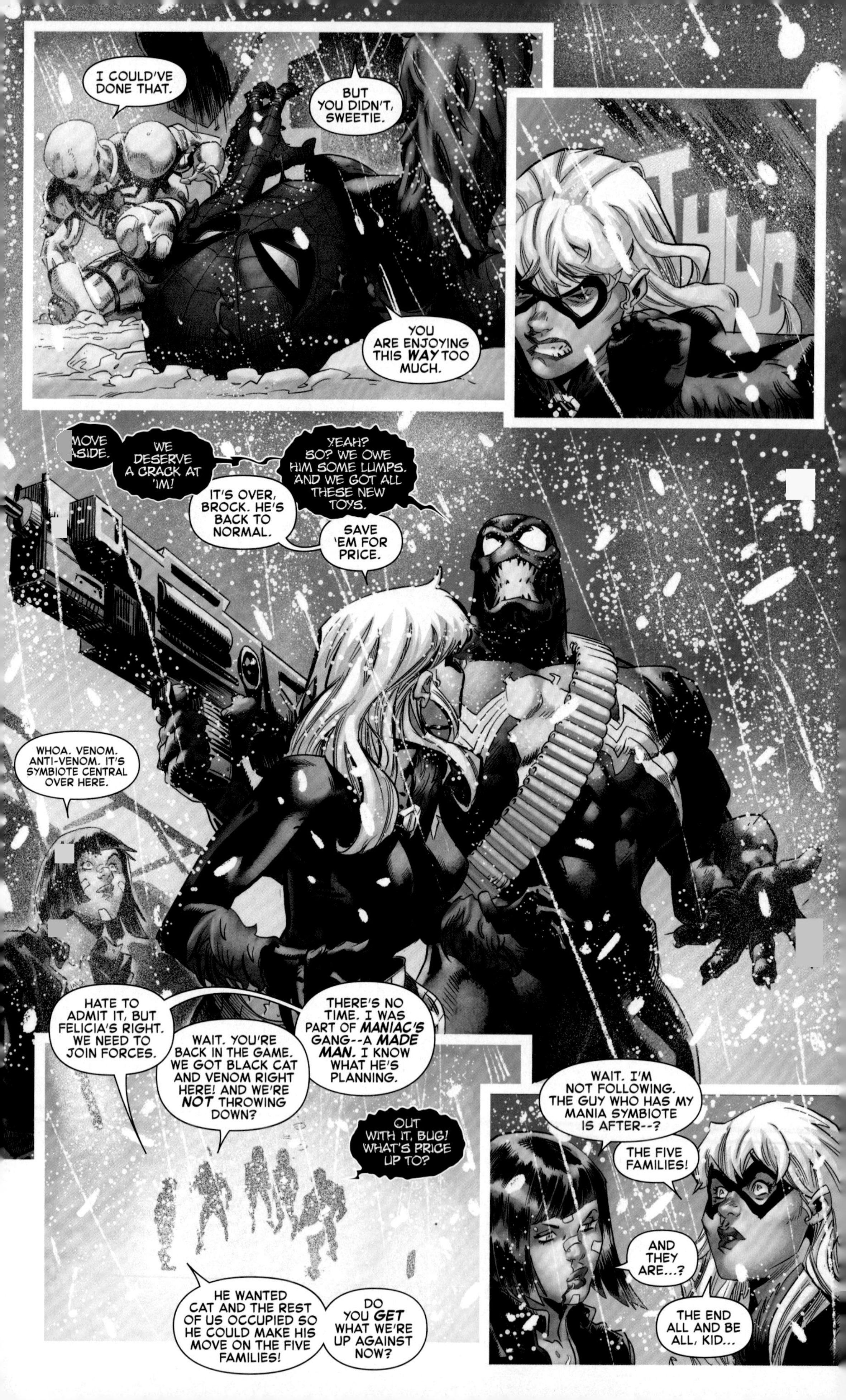
I COULD'VE DONE THAT.
BUT YOU DIDN'T, SWEETIE.
YOU ARE ENJOYING THIS WAY TOO MUCH.
THUD
MOVE ASIDE.
WE DESERVE A CRACK AT 'IM!
YEAH? SO? WE OWE HIM SOME LUMPS. AND WE GOT ALL THESE NEW TOYS.
IT'S OVER, BROCK. HE'S BACK TO NORMAL.
SAVE 'EM FOR PRICE.
WHOA. VENOM. ANTI-VENOM. IT'S SYMBIOTE CENTRAL OVER HERE.
HATE TO ADMIT IT, BUT FELICIA'S RIGHT. WE NEED TO JOIN FORCES.
WAIT. YOU'RE BACK IN THE GAME. WE GOT BLACK CAT AND VENOM RIGHT HERE! AND WE'RE NOT THROWING DOWN?
THERE'S NO TIME. I WAS PART OF MANIAC'S GANG--A MADE MAN. I KNOW WHAT HE'S PLANNING.
OUT WITH IT, BUG! WHAT'S PRICE UP TO?
HE WANTED CAT AND THE REST OF US OCCUPIED SO HE COULD MAKE HIS MOVE ON THE FIVE FAMILIES!
DO YOU GET WHAT WE'RE UP AGAINST NOW?
WAIT. I'M NOT FOLLOWING. THE GUY WHO HAS MY MANIA SYMBIOTE IS AFTER--?
THE FIVE FAMILIES!
AND THEY ARE...?
THE END ALL AND BE ALL, KID...

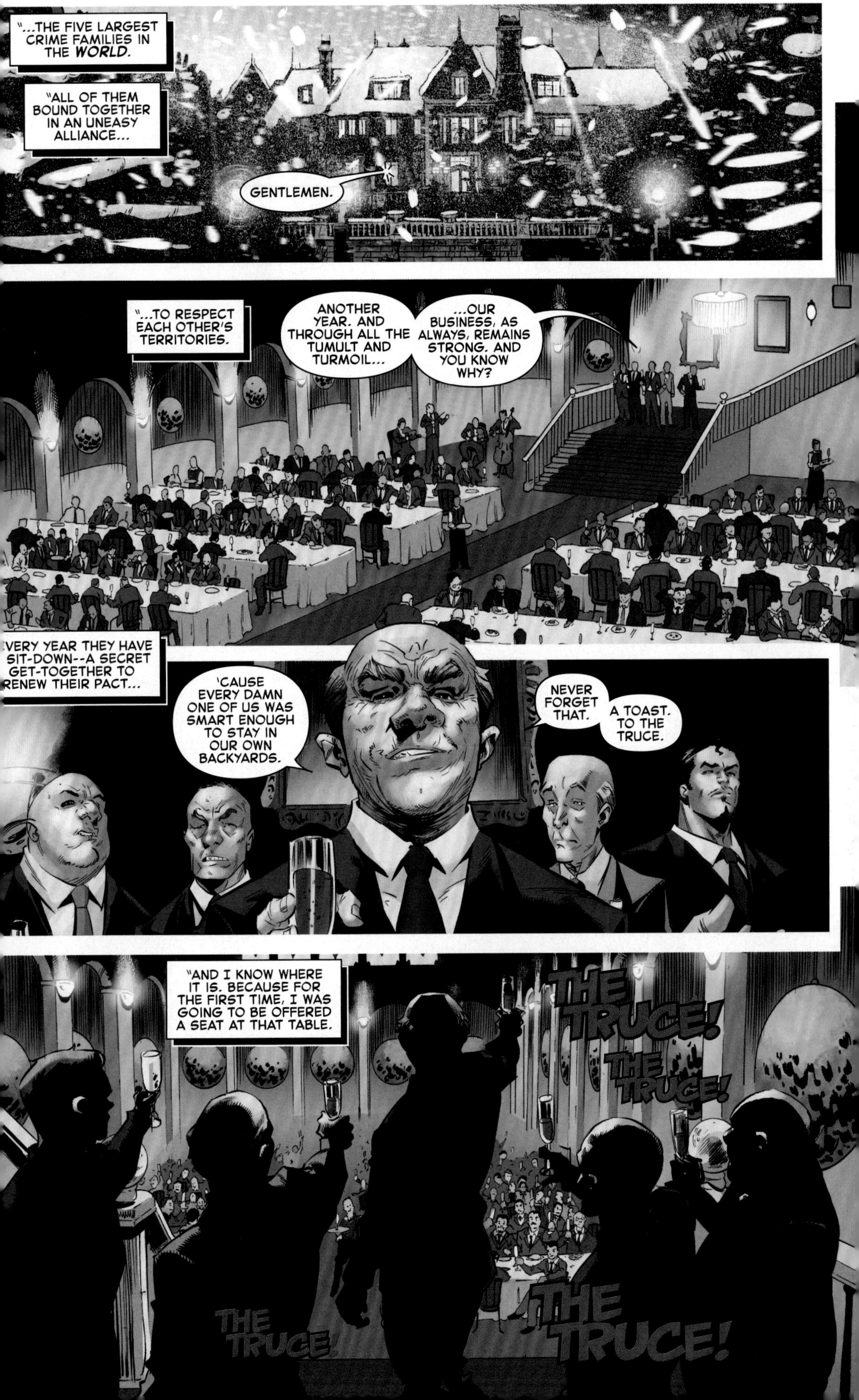
"...THE FIVE LARGEST CRIME FAMILIES IN THE *WORLD*.
"ALL OF THEM BOUND TOGETHER IN AN UNEASY ALLIANCE...
GENTLEMEN.
"...TO RESPECT EACH OTHER'S TERRITORIES.
ANOTHER YEAR. AND THROUGH ALL THE TUMULT AND TURMOIL...
...OUR BUSINESS, AS ALWAYS, REMAINS STRONG. AND YOU KNOW WHY?
VERY YEAR THEY HAVE SIT-DOWN--A SECRET GET-TOGETHER TO RENEW THEIR PACT...
'CAUSE EVERY DAMN ONE OF US WAS SMART ENOUGH TO STAY IN OUR OWN BACKYARDS.
NEVER FORGET THAT.
A TOAST. TO THE TRUCE.
"AND I KNOW WHERE IT IS. BECAUSE FOR THE FIRST TIME, I WAS GOING TO BE OFFERED A SEAT AT THAT TABLE.
THE TRUCE!
THE TRUCE!
THE TRUCE
THE TRUCE!

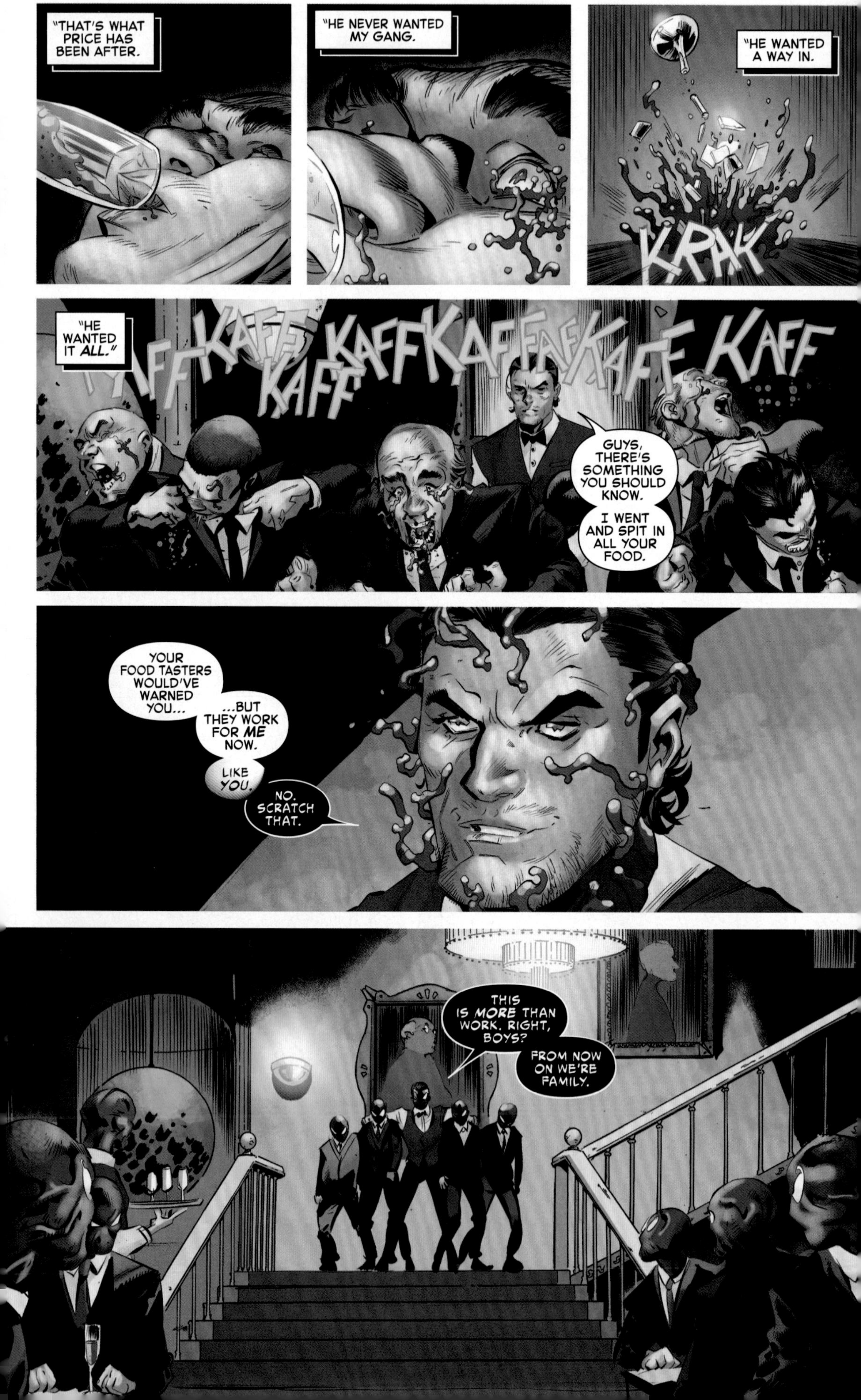
"THAT'S WHAT PRICE HAS BEEN AFTER.
"HE NEVER WANTED MY GANG.
"HE WANTED A WAY IN.
KRAK
"HE WANTED IT ALL."
KAFF KAFF KAFF KAFF KAFF
GUYS, THERE'S SOMETHING YOU SHOULD KNOW.
I WENT AND SPIT IN ALL YOUR FOOD.
YOUR FOOD TASTERS WOULD'VE WARNED YOU...
...BUT THEY WORK FOR *ME* NOW.
LIKE *YOU.*
NO. SCRATCH THAT.
THIS IS *MORE* THAN WORK. RIGHT, BOYS?
FROM NOW ON WE'RE FAMILY.

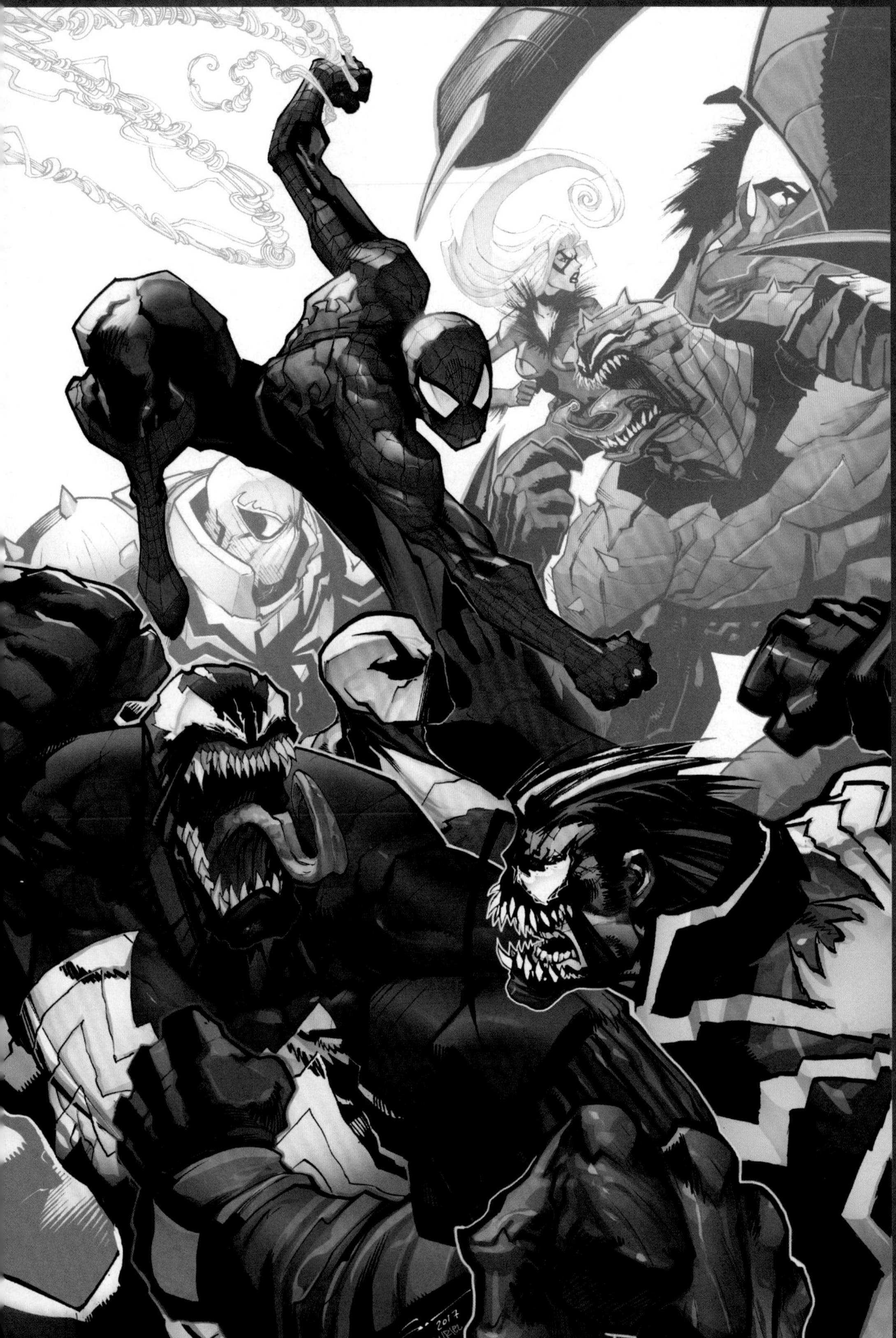

VENOM 160

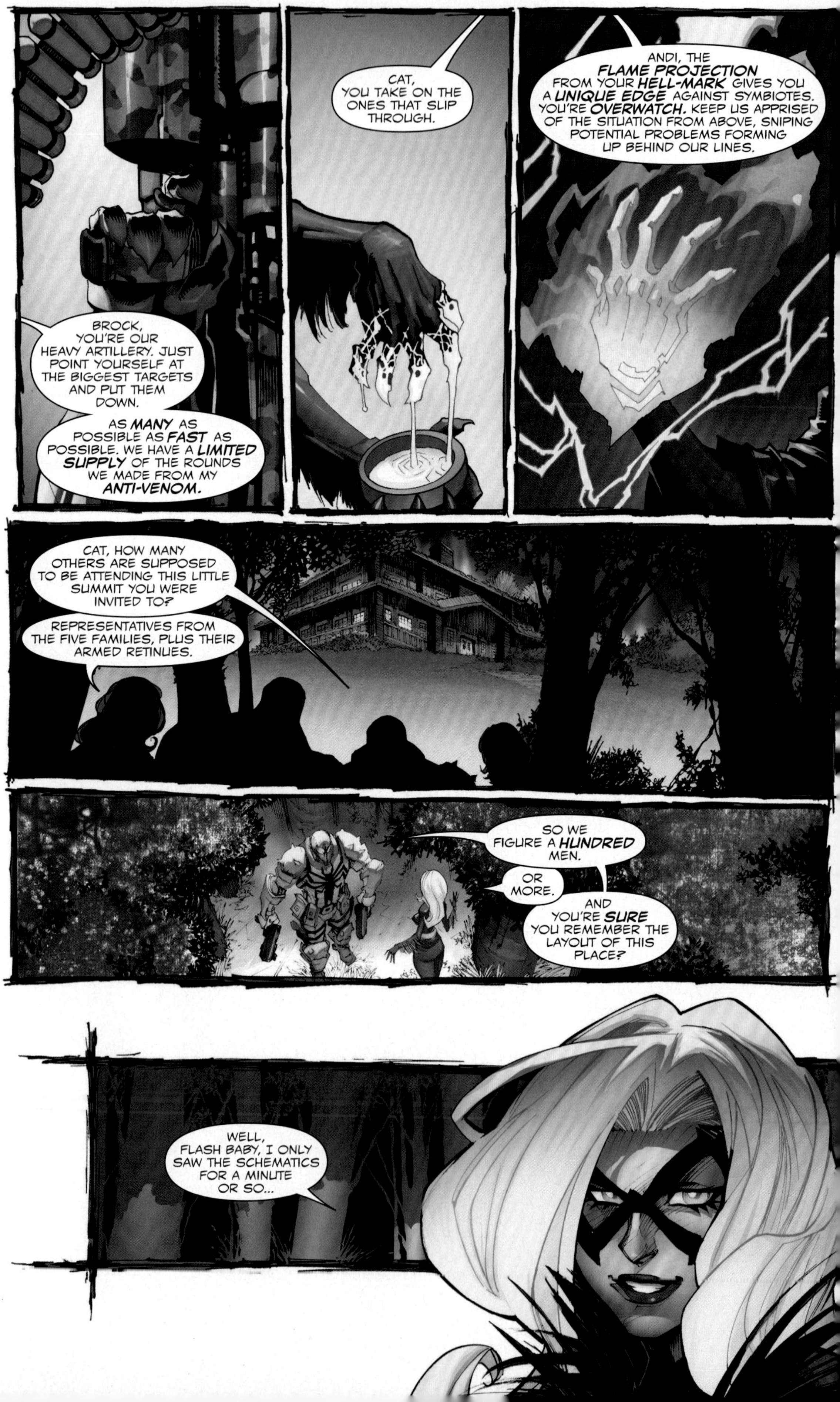
BROCK, YOU'RE OUR HEAVY ARTILLERY. JUST POINT YOURSELF AT THE BIGGEST TARGETS AND PUT THEM DOWN.
AS MANY AS POSSIBLE AS FAST AS POSSIBLE. WE HAVE A LIMITED SUPPLY OF THE ROUNDS WE MADE FROM MY ANTI-VENOM.
CAT, YOU TAKE ON THE ONES THAT SLIP THROUGH.
ANDI, THE FLAME PROJECTION FROM YOUR HELL-MARK GIVES YOU A UNIQUE EDGE AGAINST SYMBIOTES. YOU'RE OVERWATCH. KEEP US APPRISED OF THE SITUATION FROM ABOVE, SNIPING POTENTIAL PROBLEMS FORMING UP BEHIND OUR LINES.
CAT, HOW MANY OTHERS ARE SUPPOSED TO BE ATTENDING THIS LITTLE SUMMIT YOU WERE INVITED TO?
REPRESENTATIVES FROM THE FIVE FAMILIES, PLUS THEIR ARMED RETINUES.
SO WE FIGURE A HUNDRED MEN.
OR MORE.
AND YOU'RE SURE YOU REMEMBER THE LAYOUT OF THIS PLACE?
WELL, FLASH BABY, I ONLY SAW THE SCHEMATICS FOR A MINUTE OR SO...

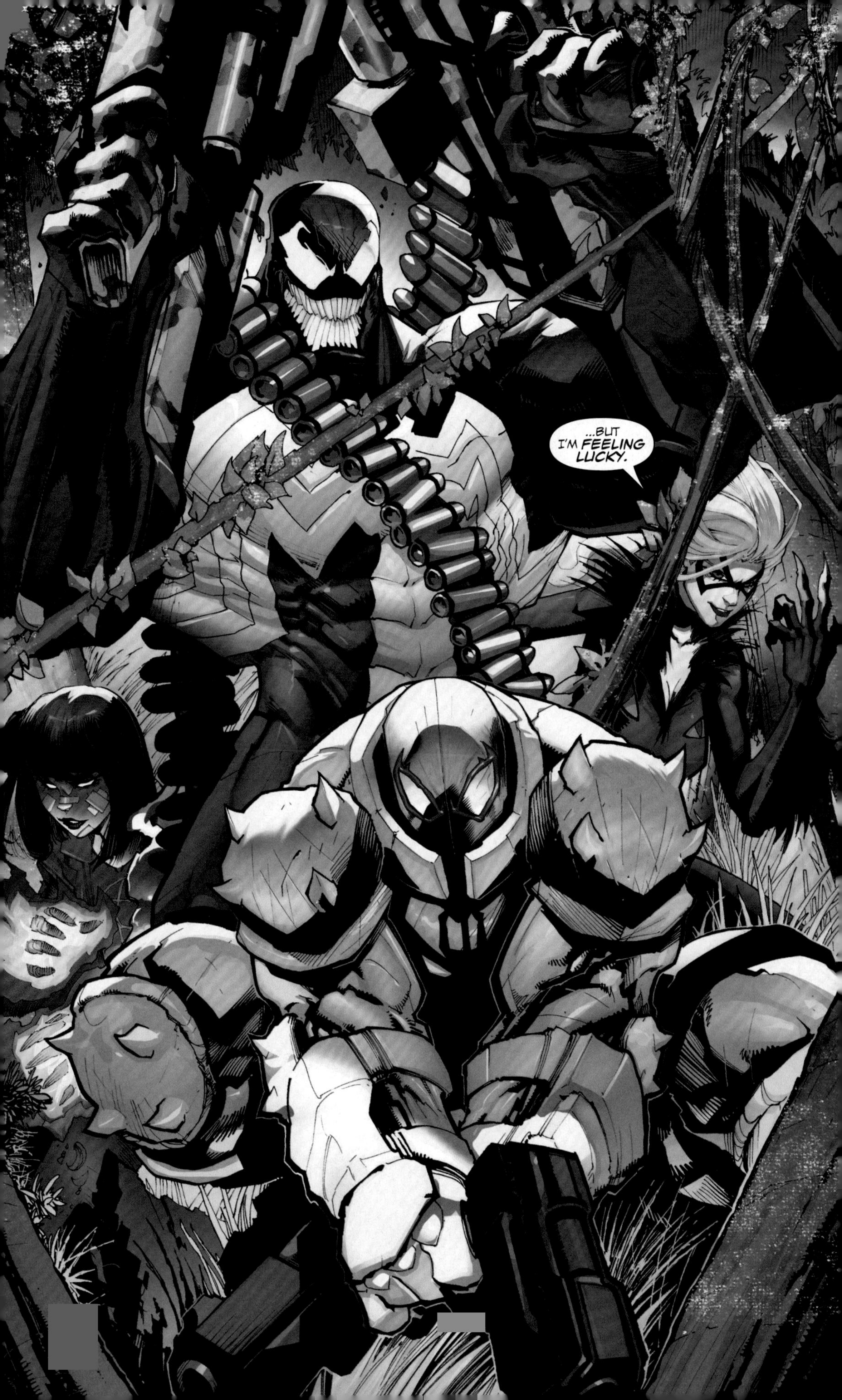
...BUT I'M FEELING LUCKY.

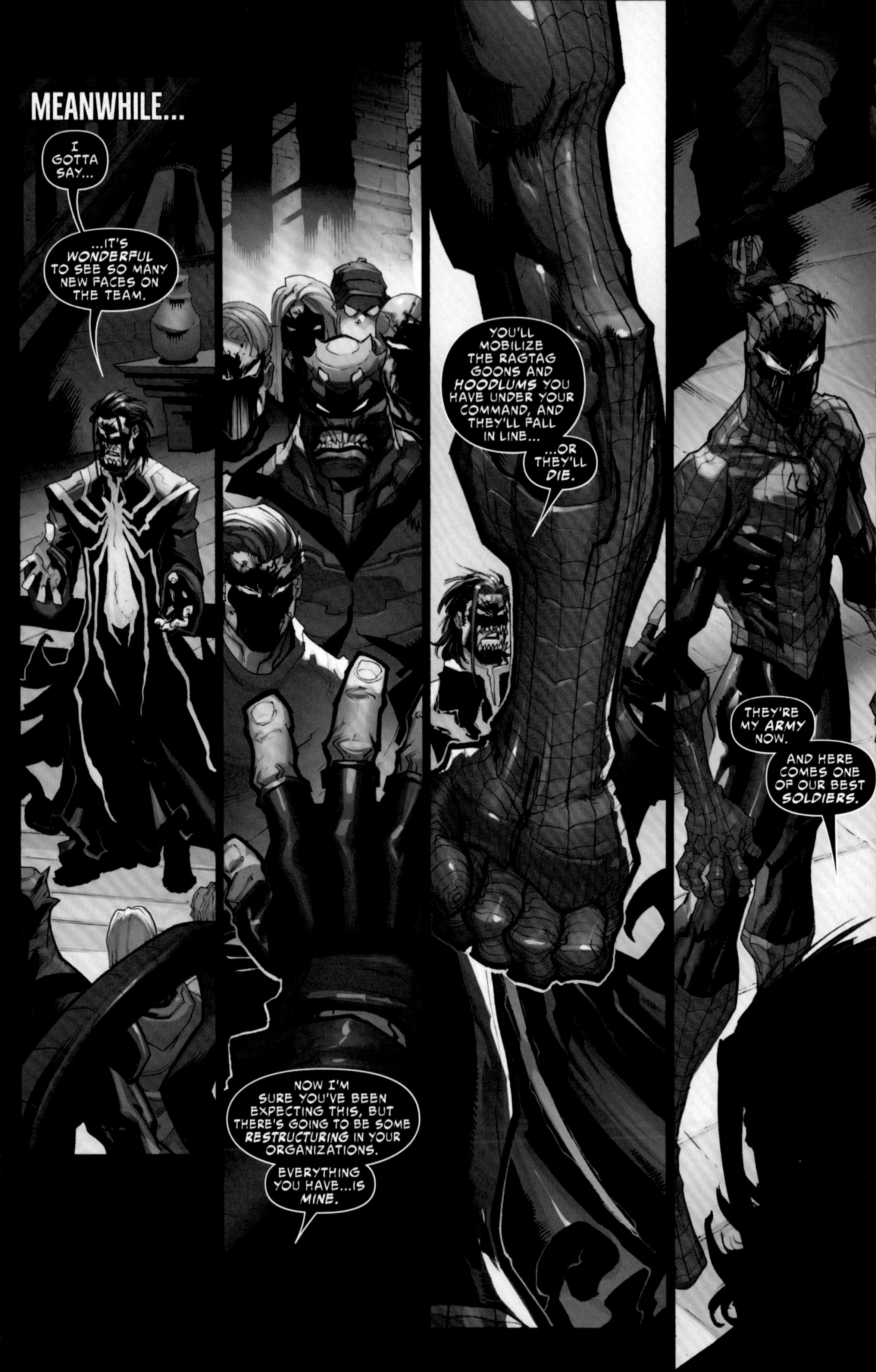
MEANWHILE...
I GOTTA SAY...
...IT'S WONDERFUL TO SEE SO MANY NEW FACES ON THE TEAM.
NOW I'M SURE YOU'VE BEEN EXPECTING THIS, BUT THERE'S GOING TO BE SOME RESTRUCTURING IN YOUR ORGANIZATIONS.
EVERYTHING YOU HAVE...IS MINE.
YOU'LL MOBILIZE THE RAGTAG GOONS AND HOODLUMS YOU HAVE UNDER YOUR COMMAND, AND THEY'LL FALL IN LINE...
...OR THEY'LL DIE.
THEY'RE MY ARMY NOW.
AND HERE COMES ONE OF OUR BEST SOLDIERS.

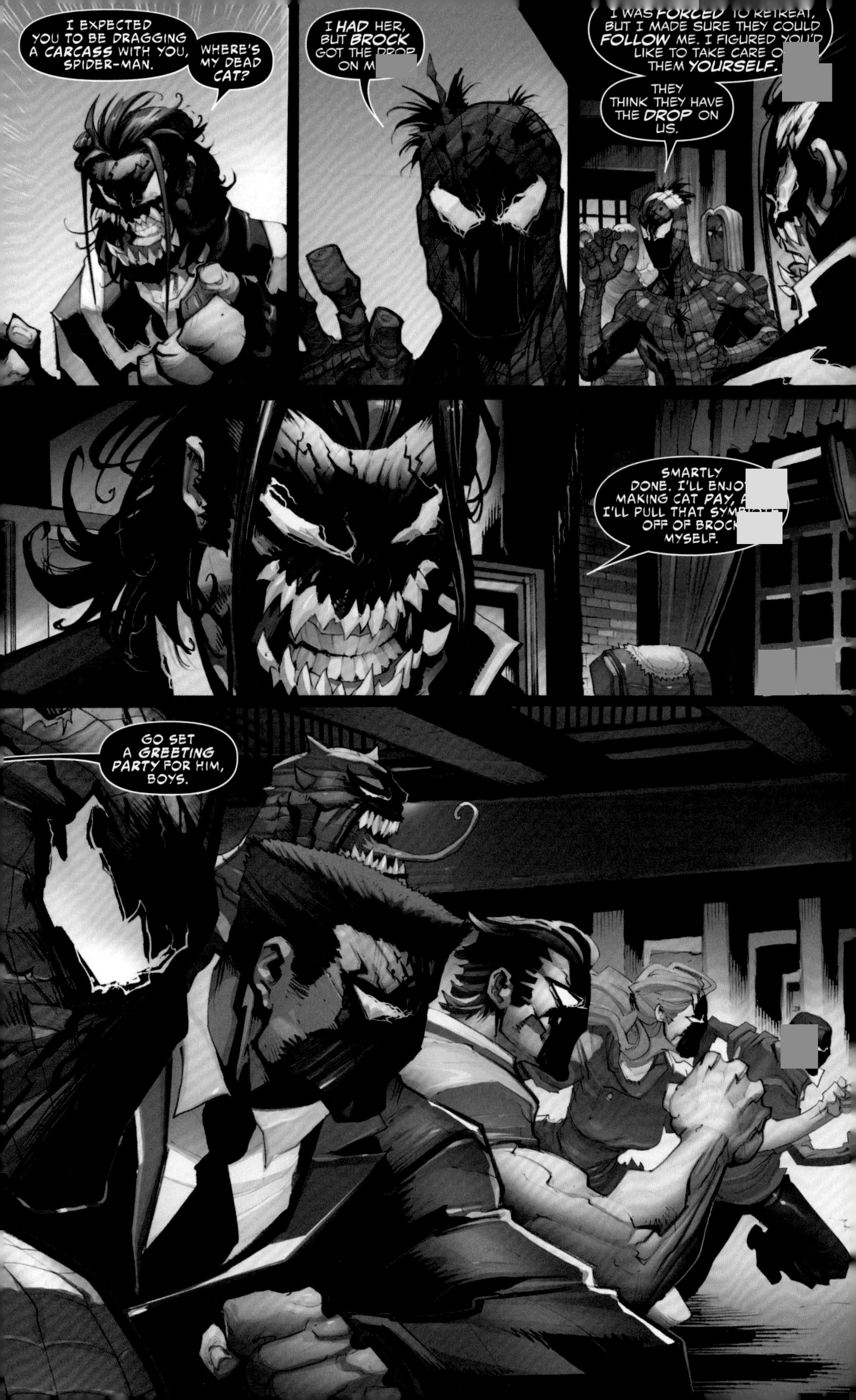

I EXPECTED YOU TO BE DRAGGING A CARCASS WITH YOU, SPIDER-MAN.
WHERE'S MY DEAD CAT?
I HAD HER, BUT BROCK GOT THE DROP ON
I WAS FORCED TO RETREAT, BUT I MADE SURE THEY COULD FOLLOW ME. I FIGURED YOU'D LIKE TO TAKE CARE O THEM YOURSELF.
THEY THINK THEY HAVE THE DROP ON US.
SMARTLY DONE. I'LL ENJO MAKING CAT PAY, A I'LL PULL THAT SYM OFF OF BROC MYSELF.
GO SET A GREETING PARTY FOR HIM, BOYS.

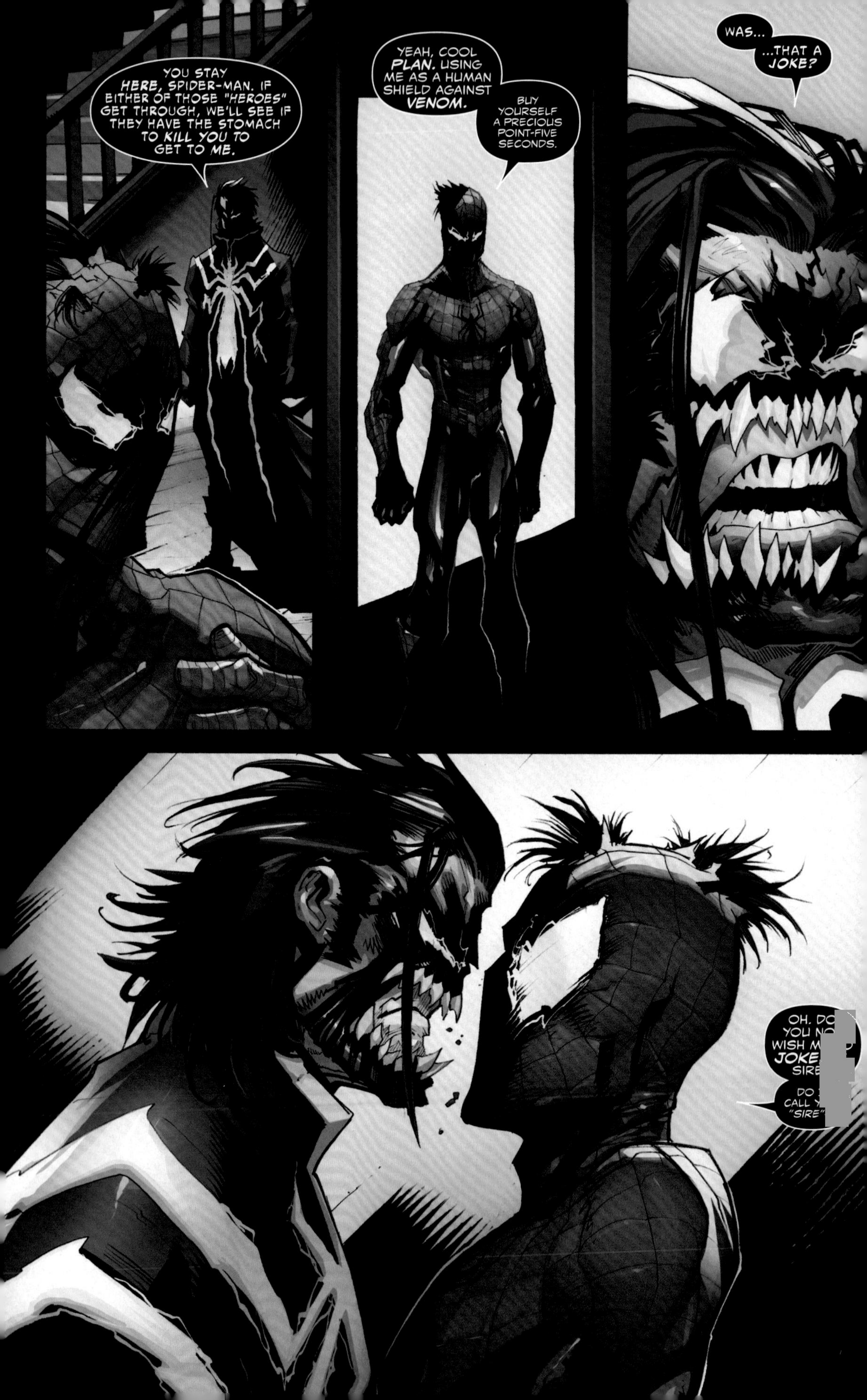
YOU STAY HERE, SPIDER-MAN. IF EITHER OF THOSE "HEROES" GET THROUGH, WE'LL SEE IF THEY HAVE THE STOMACH TO KILL YOU TO GET TO ME.
YEAH, COOL PLAN. USING ME AS A HUMAN SHIELD AGAINST VENOM.
BUY YOURSELF A PRECIOUS POINT-FIVE SECONDS.
WAS...
...THAT A JOKE?
OH. DO YOU NO WISH M JOKE SIRE
DO CALL Y "SIRE"

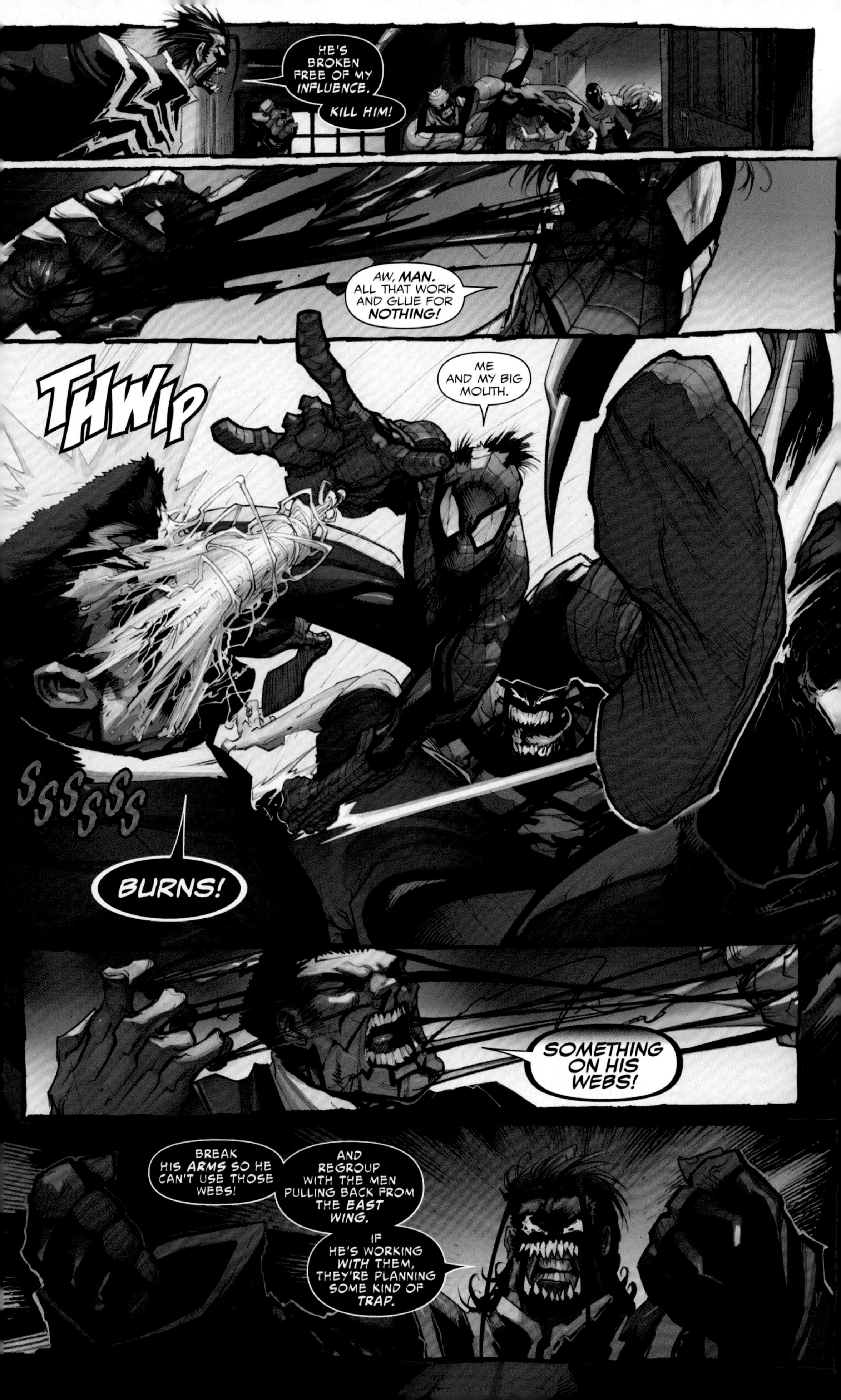
HE'S BROKEN FREE OF MY INFLUENCE.
KILL HIM!
AW, MAN. ALL THAT WORK AND GLUE FOR NOTHING!
THWIP
ME AND MY BIG MOUTH.
SSSSSS
BURNS!
SOMETHING ON HIS WEBS!
BREAK HIS ARMS SO HE CAN'T USE THOSE WEBS!
AND REGROUP WITH THE MEN PULLING BACK FROM THE EAST WING.
IF HE'S WORKING WITH THEM, THEY'RE PLANNING SOME KIND OF TRAP.

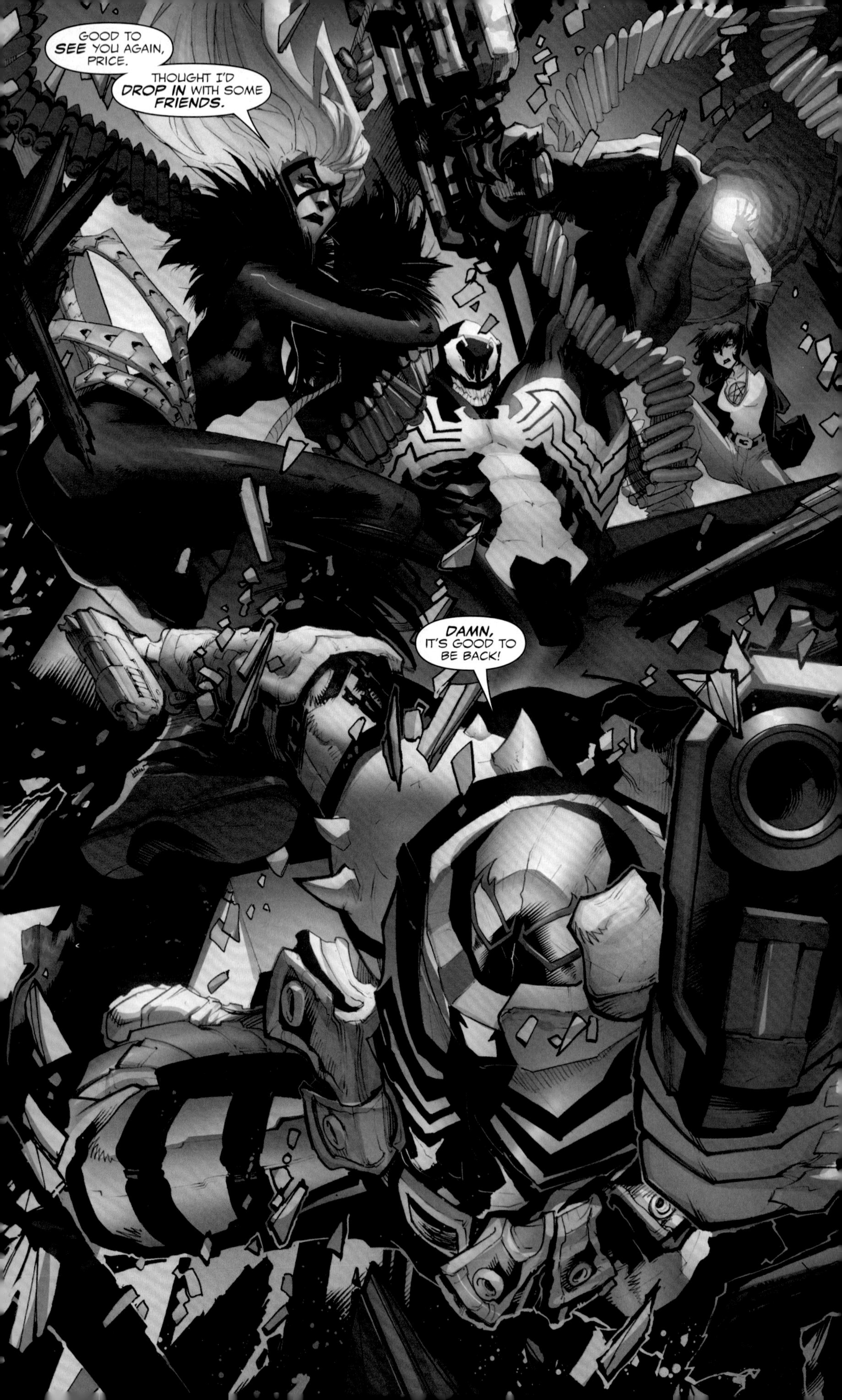
GOOD TO SEE YOU AGAIN, PRICE.
THOUGHT I'D DROP IN WITH SOME FRIENDS.
DAMN, IT'S GOOD TO BE BACK!

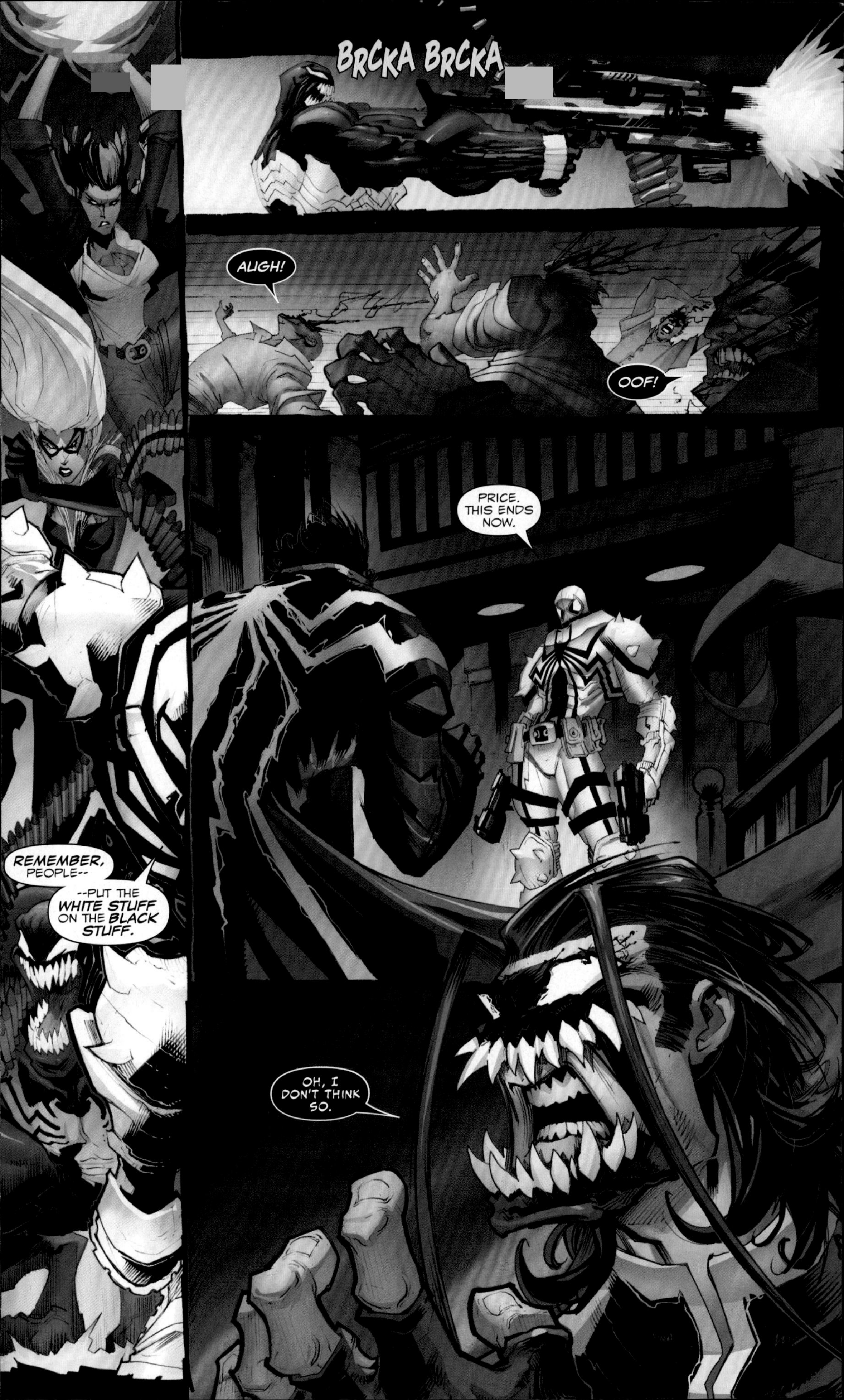
BRCKA BRCKA
AUGH!
OOF!
REMEMBER, PEOPLE--
--PUT THE WHITE STUFF ON THE BLACK STUFF.
PRICE. THIS ENDS NOW.
OH, I DON'T THINK SO.

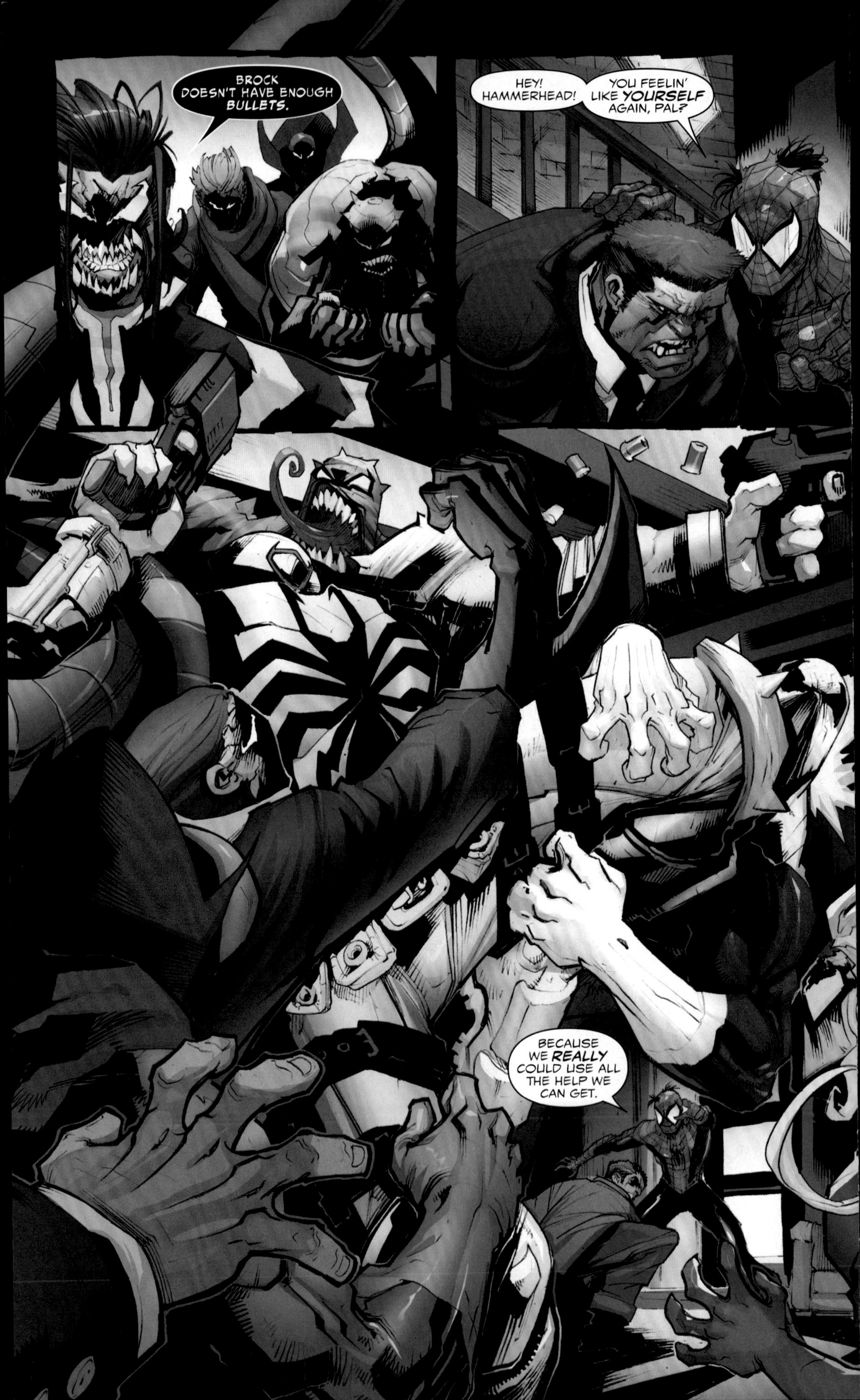

BROCK DOESN'T HAVE ENOUGH BULLETS.
HEY! HAMMERHEAD!
YOU FEELIN' LIKE YOURSELF AGAIN, PAL?
BECAUSE WE REALLY COULD USE ALL THE HELP WE CAN GET.

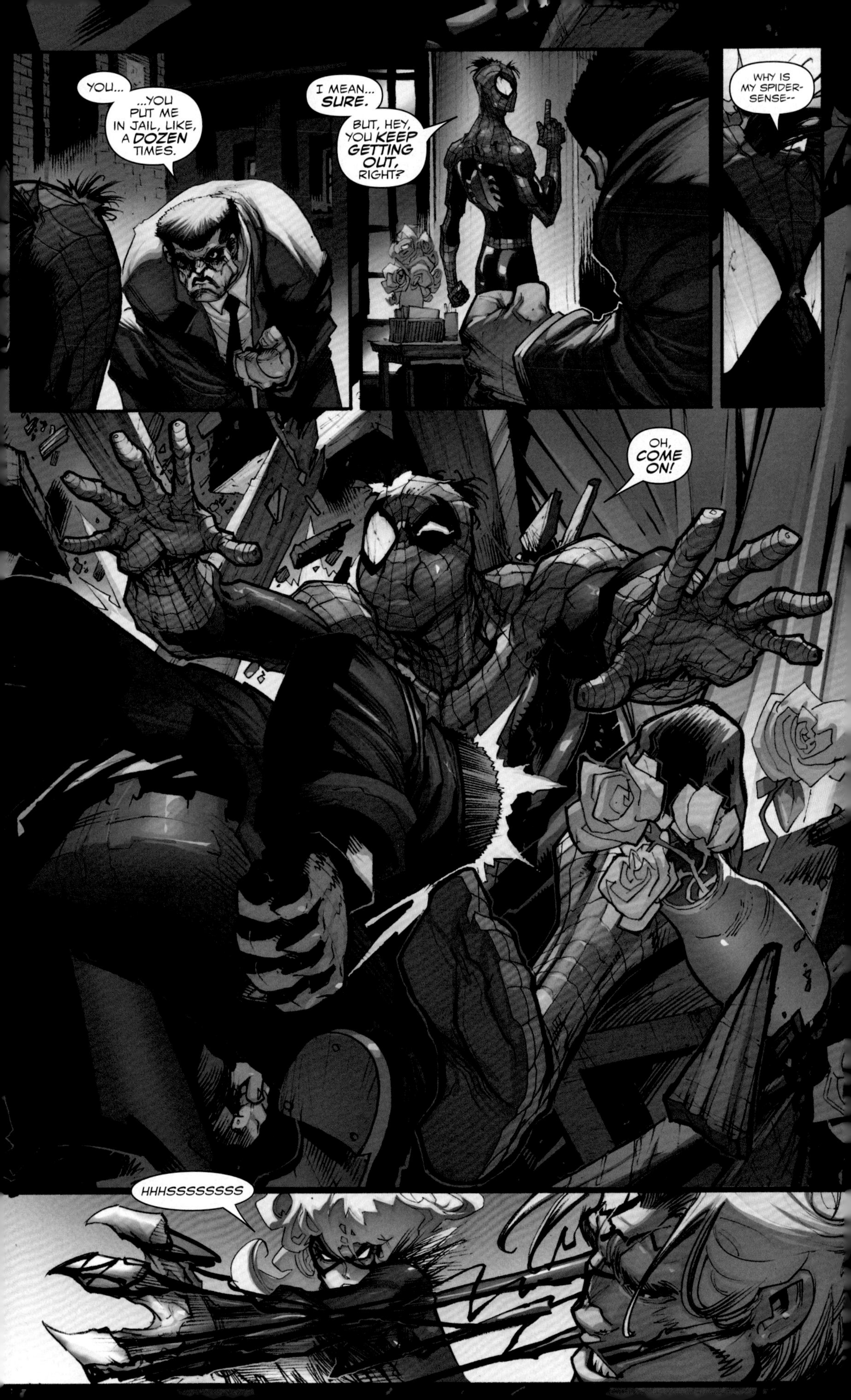
YOU...
...YOU PUT ME IN JAIL, LIKE, A DOZEN TIMES.
I MEAN... SURE.
BUT, HEY, YOU KEEP GETTING OUT, RIGHT?
WHY IS MY SPIDER-SENSE--
OH, COME ON!
HHHSSSSSSSS

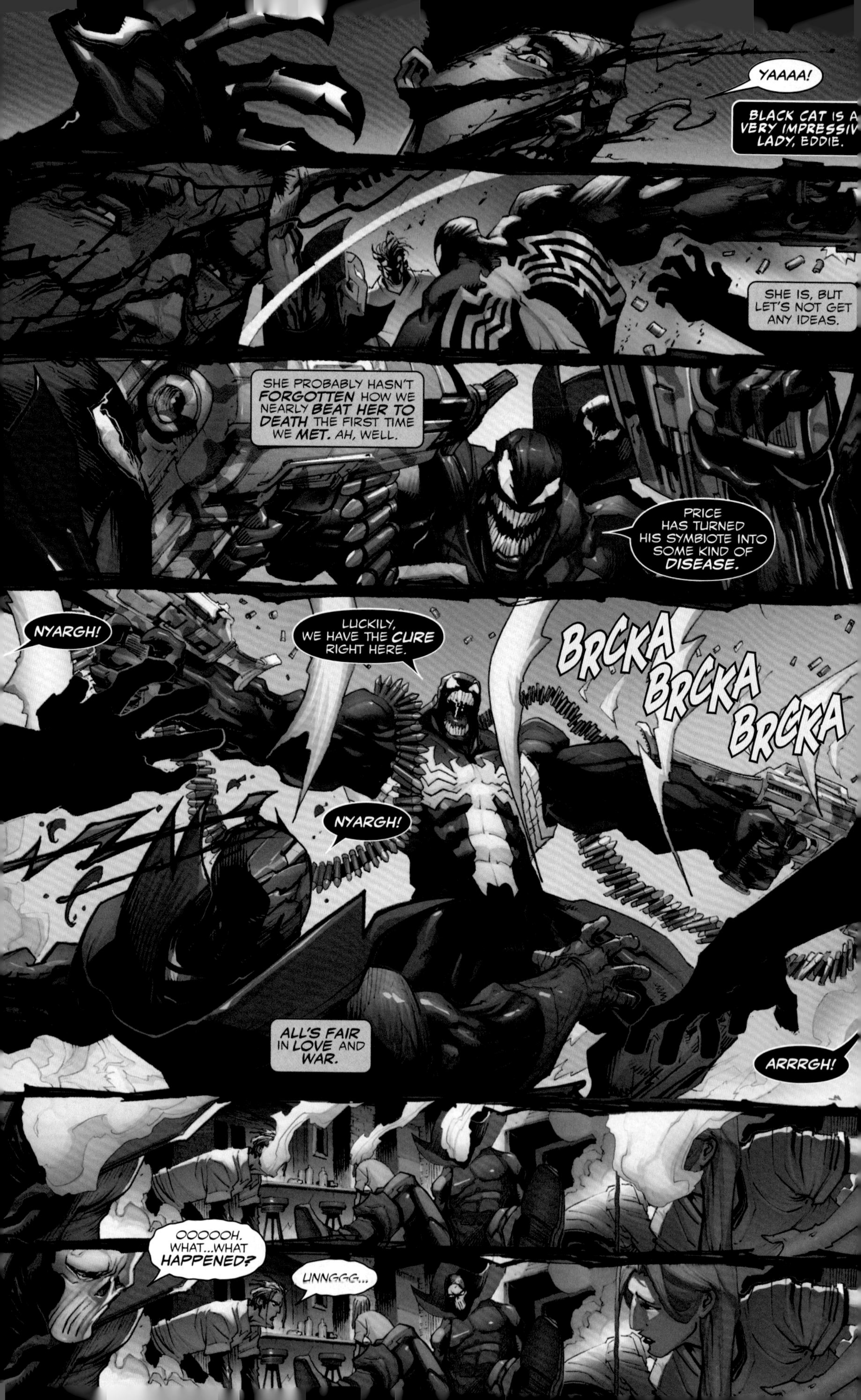
YAAAA!
BLACK CAT IS A VERY IMPRESSIV LADY, EDDIE.
SHE IS, BUT LET'S NOT GET ANY IDEAS.
SHE PROBABLY HASN'T FORGOTTEN HOW WE NEARLY BEAT HER TO DEATH THE FIRST TIME WE MET. AH, WELL.
PRICE HAS TURNED HIS SYMBIOTE INTO SOME KIND OF DISEASE.
NYARGH!
LUCKILY, WE HAVE THE CURE RIGHT HERE.
BRCKA BRCKA BRCKA
NYARGH!
ALL'S FAIR IN LOVE AND WAR.
ARRRGH!
OOOOOH. WHAT...WHAT HAPPENED?
UNNGGG...

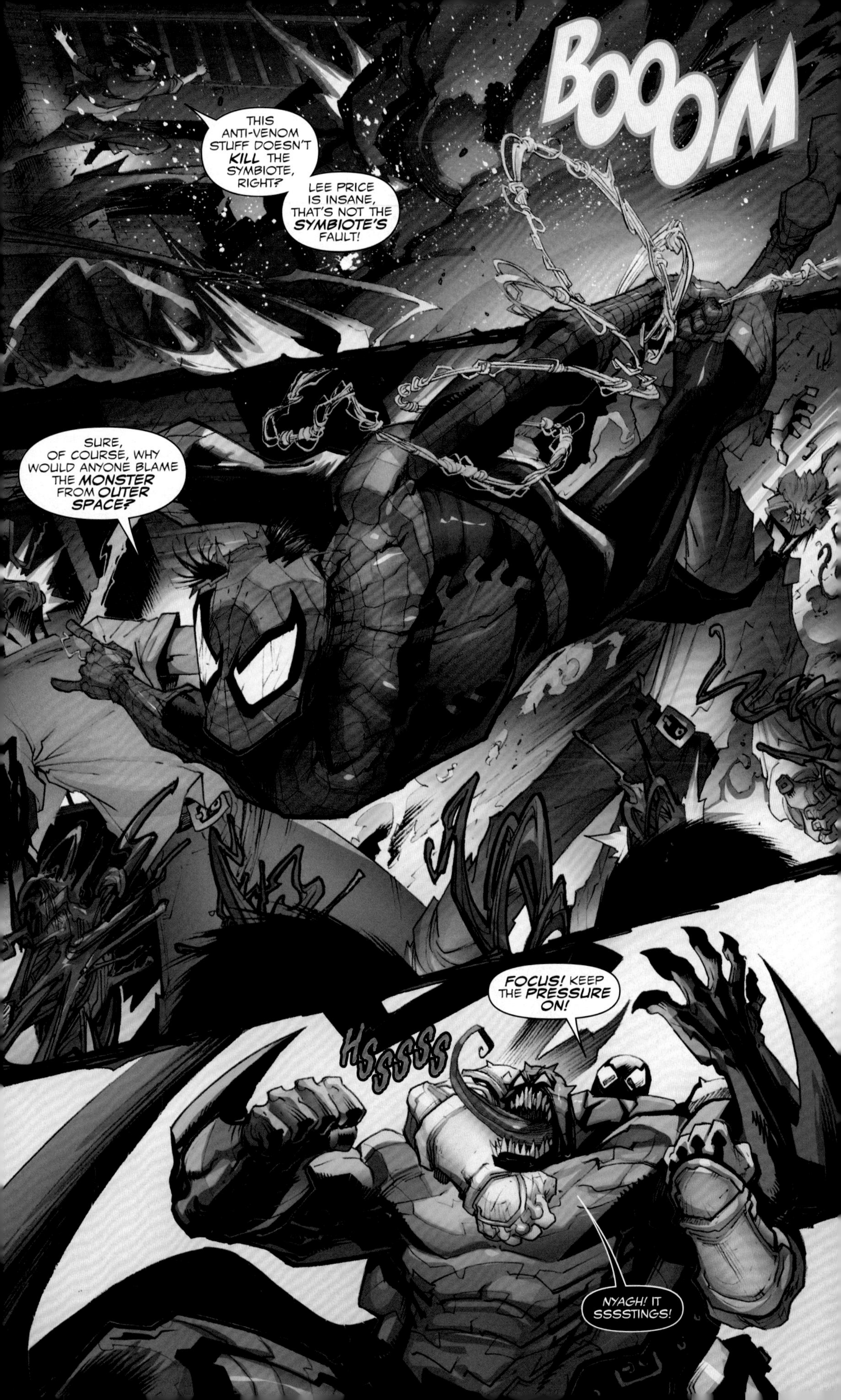
BOOOOM
THIS ANTI-VENOM STUFF DOESN'T KILL THE SYMBIOTE, RIGHT?
LEE PRICE IS INSANE, THAT'S NOT THE SYMBIOTE'S FAULT!
SURE, OF COURSE, WHY WOULD ANYONE BLAME THE MONSTER FROM OUTER SPACE?
FOCUS! KEEP THE PRESSURE ON!
HSSSSS
NYAGH! IT SSSSTINGS!

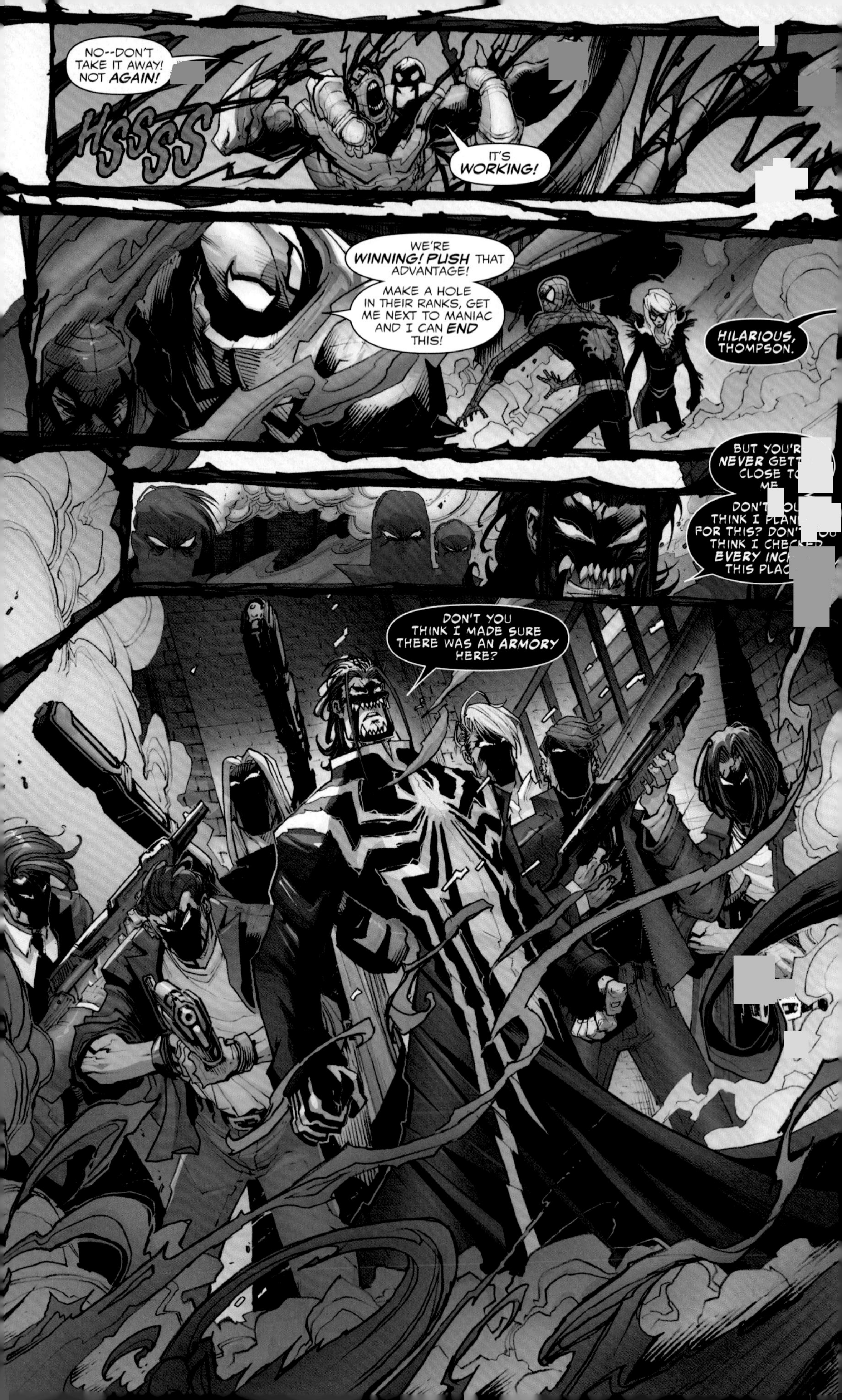

NO--DON'T TAKE IT AWAY! NOT AGAIN!
HSSSS
IT'S WORKING!
WE'RE WINNING! PUSH THAT ADVANTAGE!
MAKE A HOLE IN THEIR RANKS, GET ME NEXT TO MANIAC AND I CAN END THIS!
HILARIOUS, THOMPSON.
BUT YOU'R NEVER GETT CLOSE TO ME.
DON'T OU THINK I PLAN FOR THIS? DON'T OU THINK I CHECKED EVERY INC THIS PLAC
DON'T YOU THINK I MADE SURE THERE WAS AN ARMORY HERE?

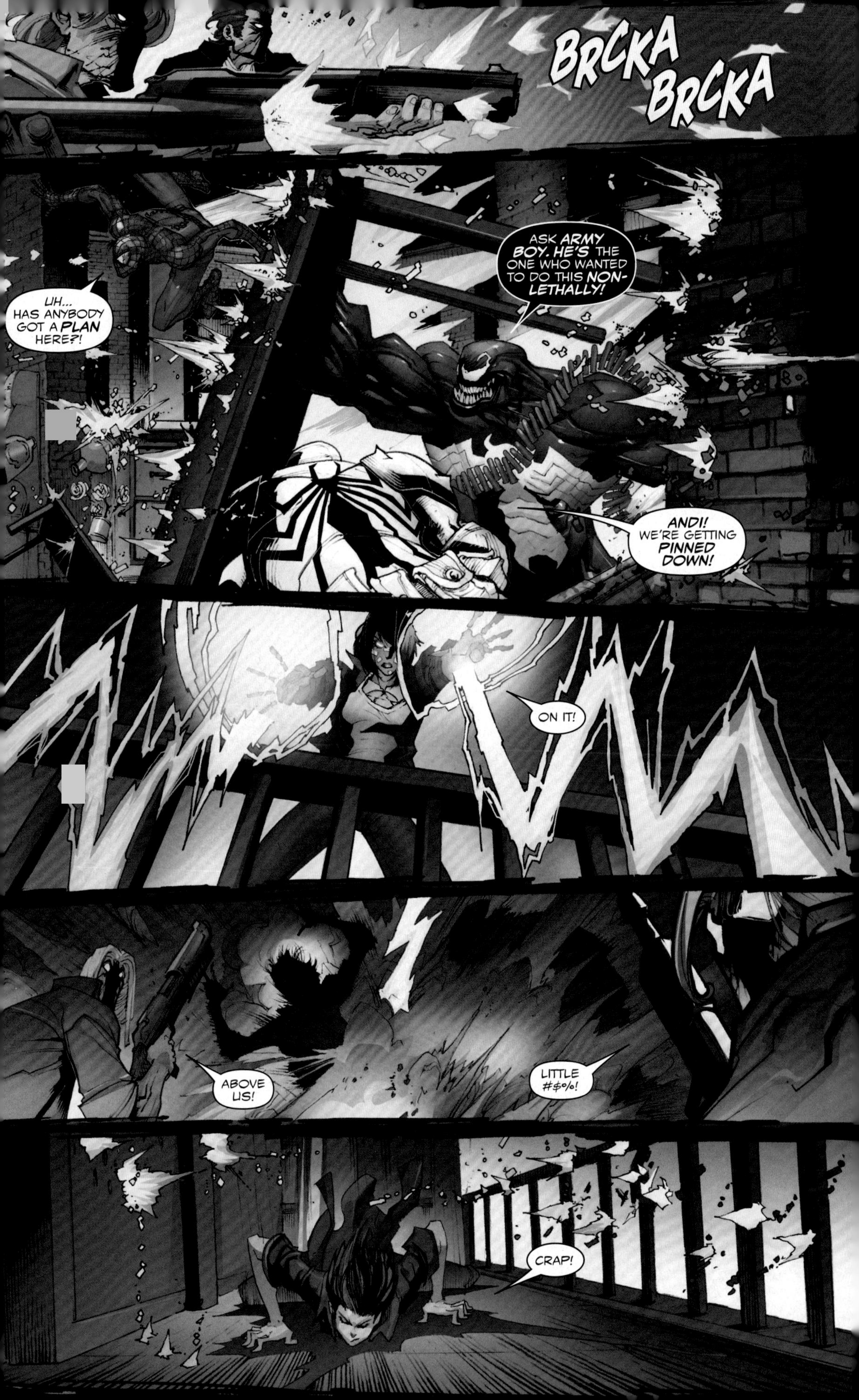
BRCKA BRCKA
UH... HAS ANYBODY GOT A PLAN HERE?!
ASK ARMY BOY. HE'S THE ONE WHO WANTED TO DO THIS NON-LETHALLY!
ANDI! WE'RE GETTING PINNED DOWN!
ON IT!
ABOVE US!
LITTLE #$%!
CRAP!

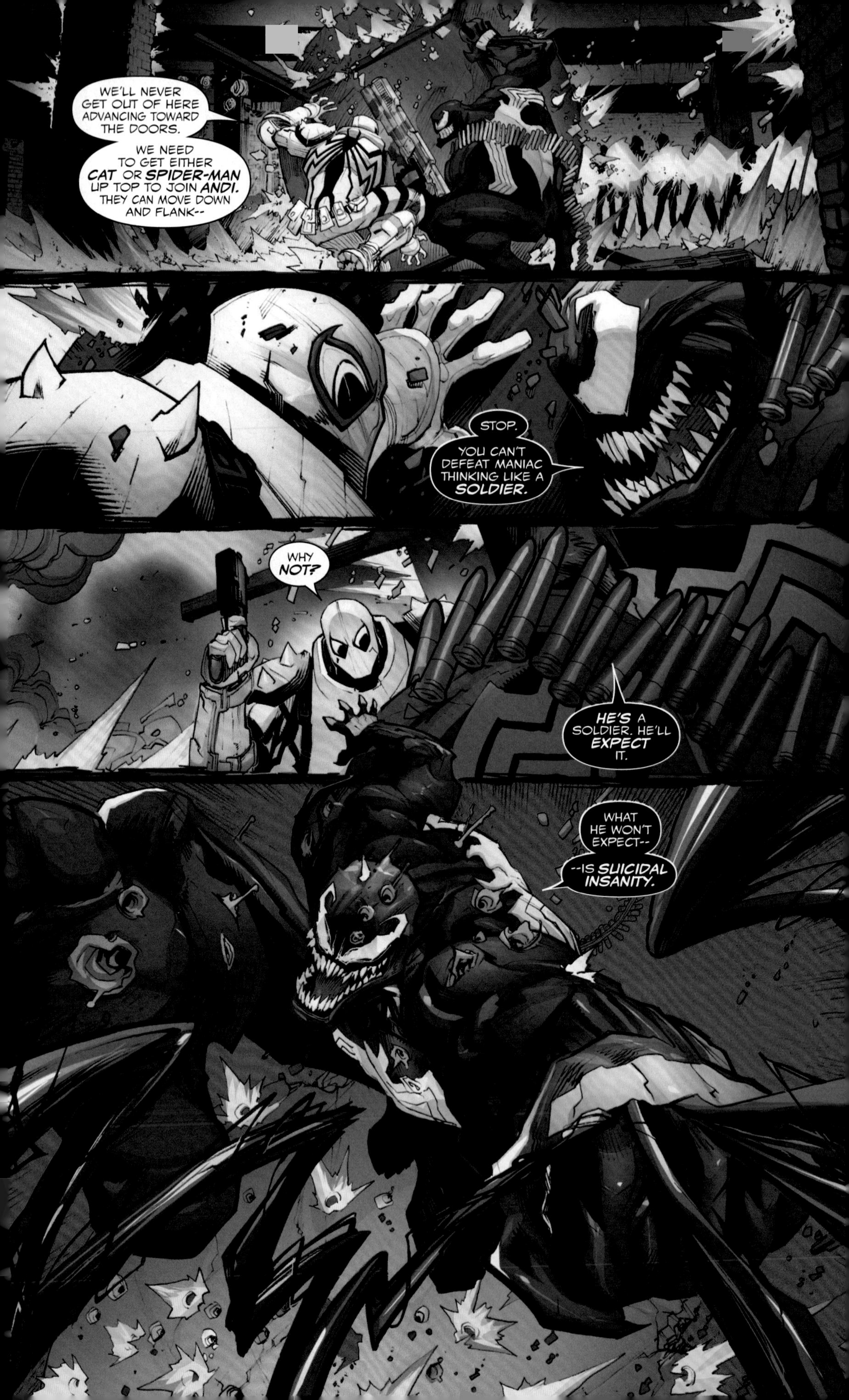
WE'LL NEVER GET OUT OF HERE ADVANCING TOWARD THE DOORS.
WE NEED TO GET EITHER **CAT** OR **SPIDER-MAN** UP TOP TO JOIN **ANDI.** THEY CAN MOVE DOWN AND FLANK--
STOP.
YOU CAN'T DEFEAT MANIAC THINKING LIKE A **SOLDIER.**
WHY **NOT?**
HE'S A SOLDIER. HE'LL **EXPECT** IT.
WHAT HE WON'T EXPECT--
--IS **SUICIDAL INSANITY.**

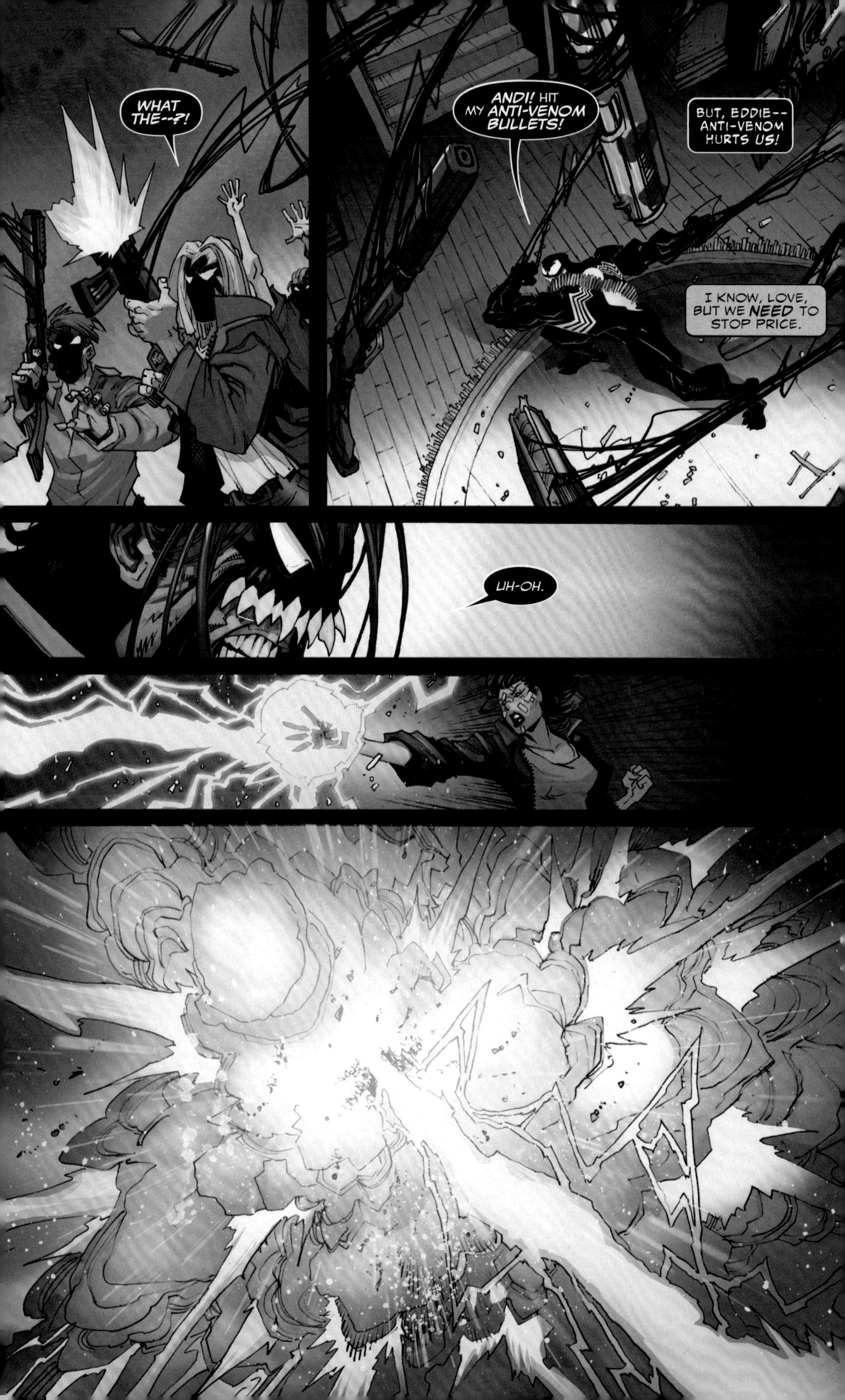
WHAT THE--?!
ANDI! HIT MY ANTI-VENOM BULLETS!
BUT, EDDIE-- ANTI-VENOM HURTS US!
I KNOW, LOVE, BUT WE NEED TO STOP PRICE.
UH-OH.

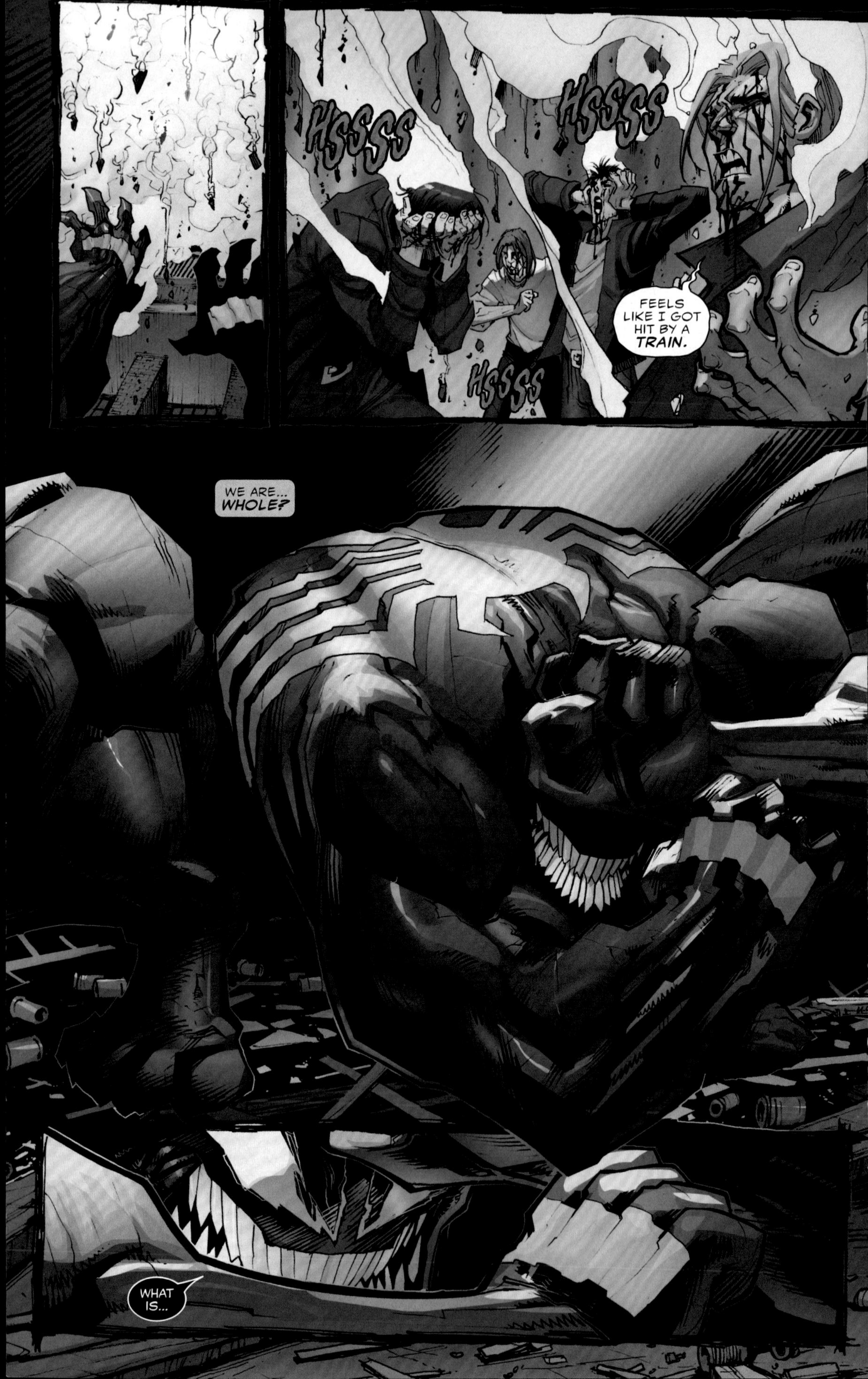
HSSSS
HSSSS
FEELS LIKE I GOT HIT BY A TRAIN.
HSSSS
WE ARE... WHOLE?
WHAT IS...

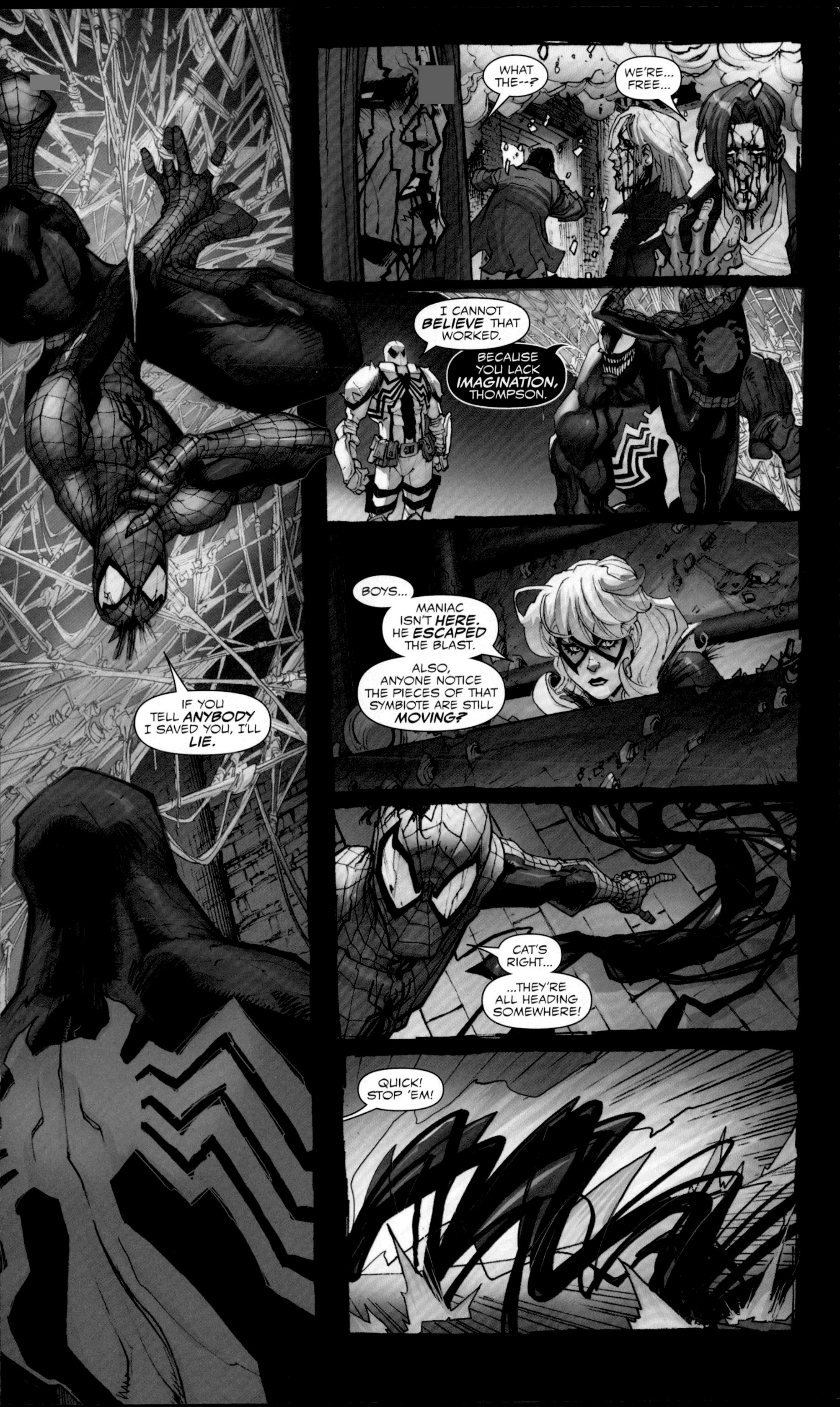
WHAT THE--?
WE'RE... FREE...
I CANNOT BELIEVE THAT WORKED.
BECAUSE YOU LACK IMAGINATION, THOMPSON.
IF YOU TELL ANYBODY I SAVED YOU, I'LL LIE.
BOYS...
MANIAC ISN'T HERE. HE ESCAPED THE BLAST.
ALSO, ANYONE NOTICE THE PIECES OF THAT SYMBIOTE ARE STILL MOVING?
CAT'S RIGHT...
...THEY'RE ALL HEADING SOMEWHERE!
QUICK! STOP 'EM!

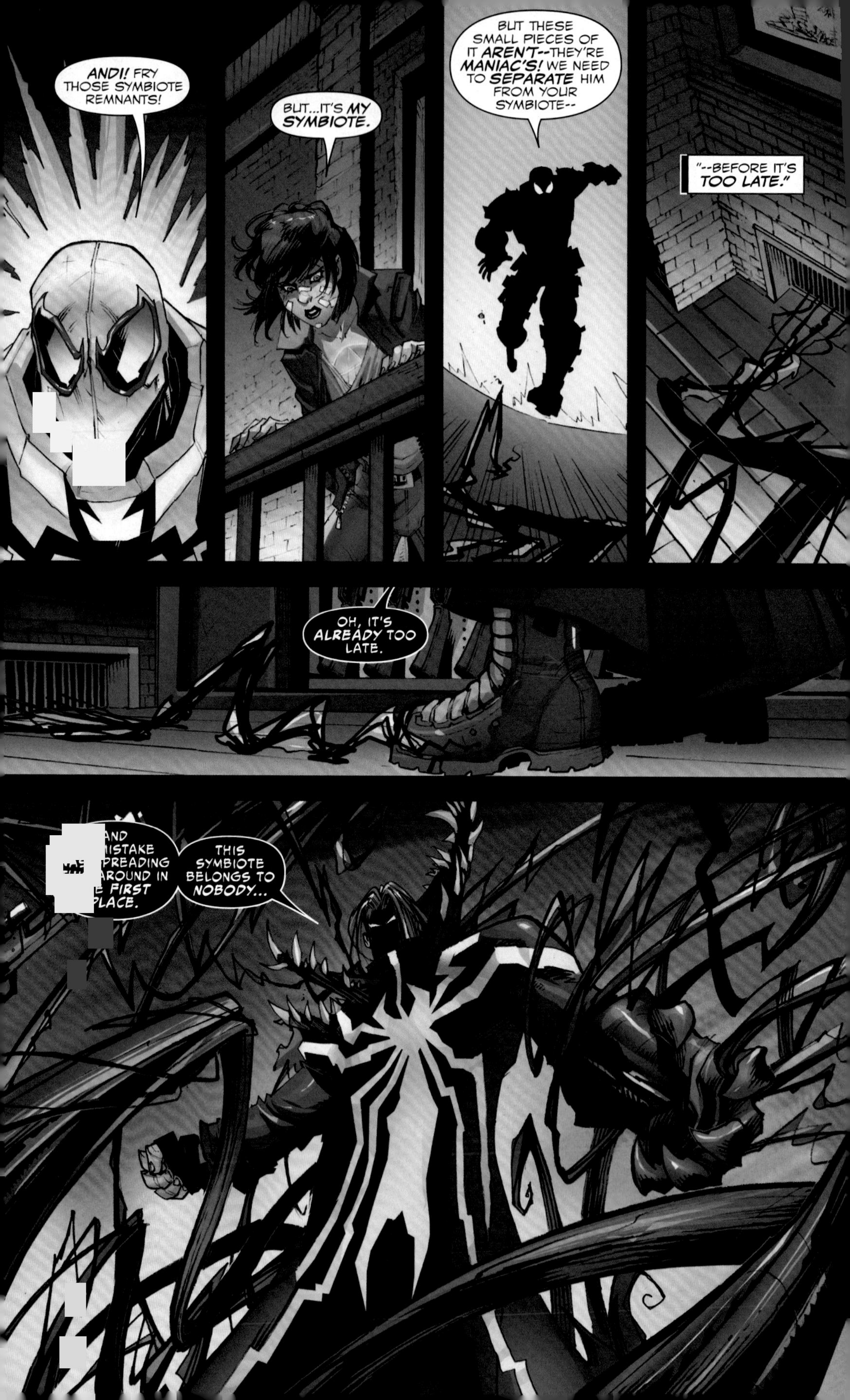
ANDI! FRY THOSE SYMBIOTE REMNANTS!
BUT...IT'S MY SYMBIOTE.
BUT THESE SMALL PIECES OF IT AREN'T--THEY'RE MANIAC'S! WE NEED TO SEPARATE HIM FROM YOUR SYMBIOTE--
"--BEFORE IT'S TOO LATE."
OH, IT'S ALREADY TOO LATE.
AND
MISTAKE
PREADING
AROUND IN
E FIRST
PLACE.
THIS SYMBIOTE BELONGS TO NOBODY...

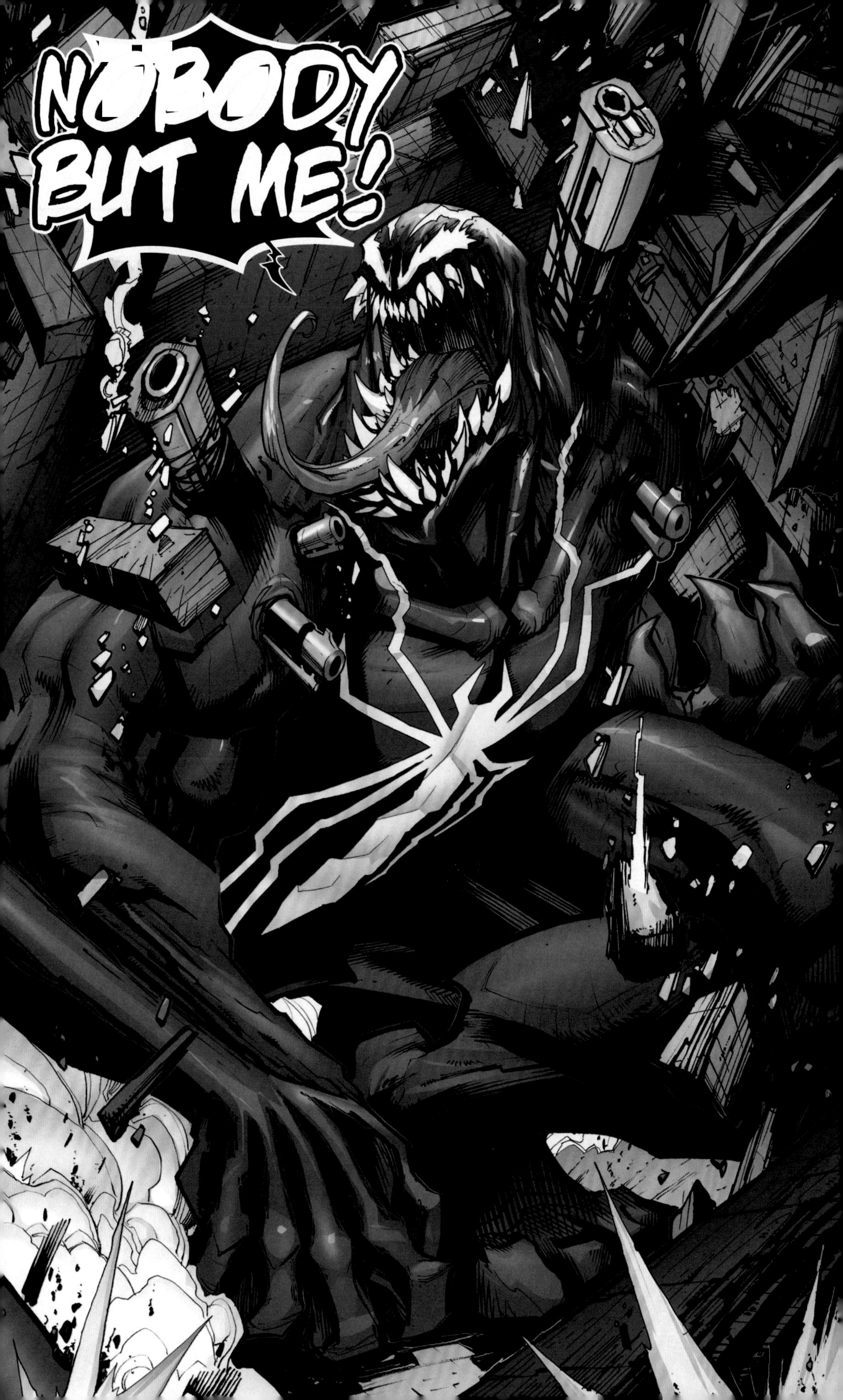
NOBODY BUT ME!

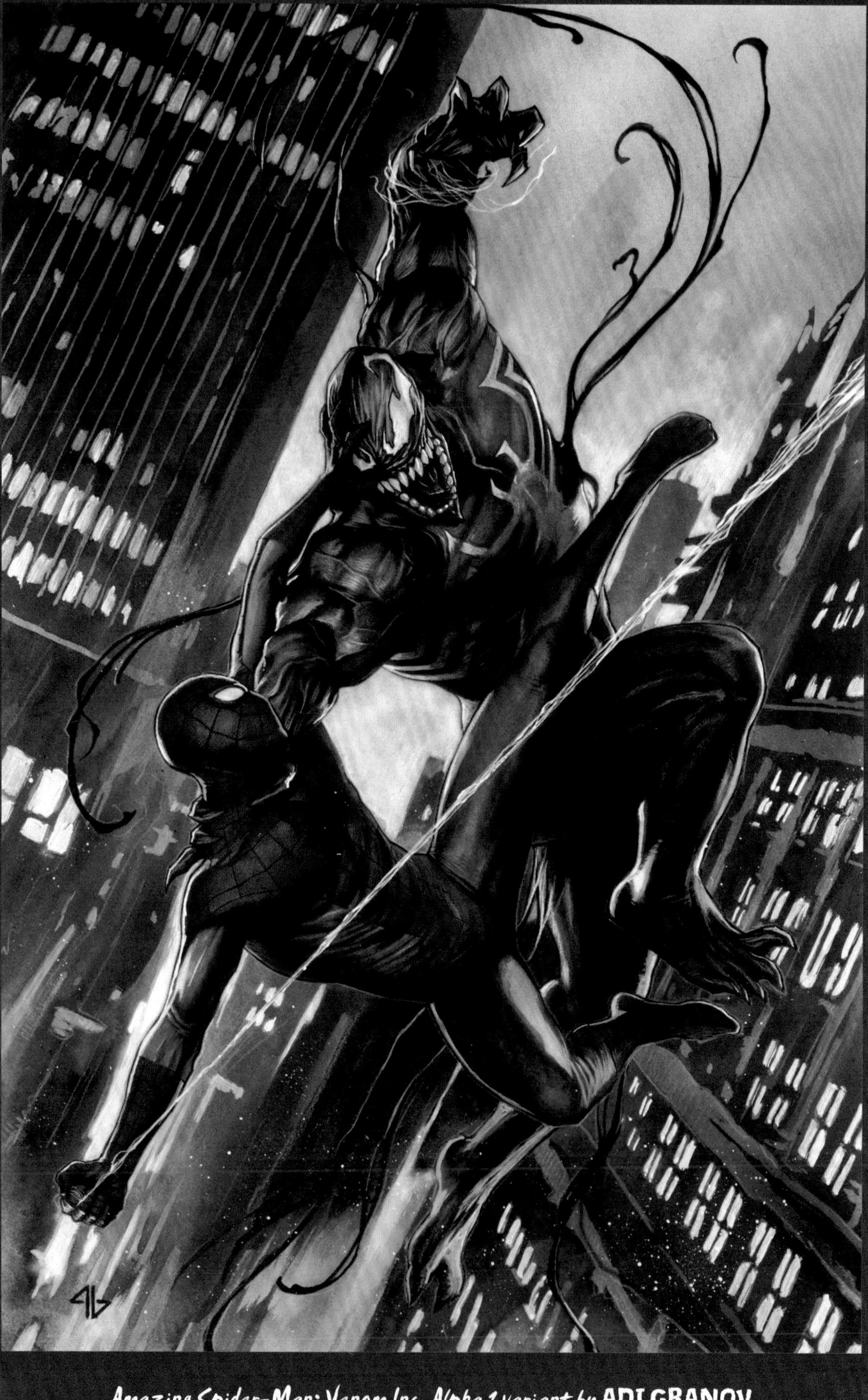

Amazing Spider-Man: Venom Inc. Alpha 1 variant by **ADI GRANOV**

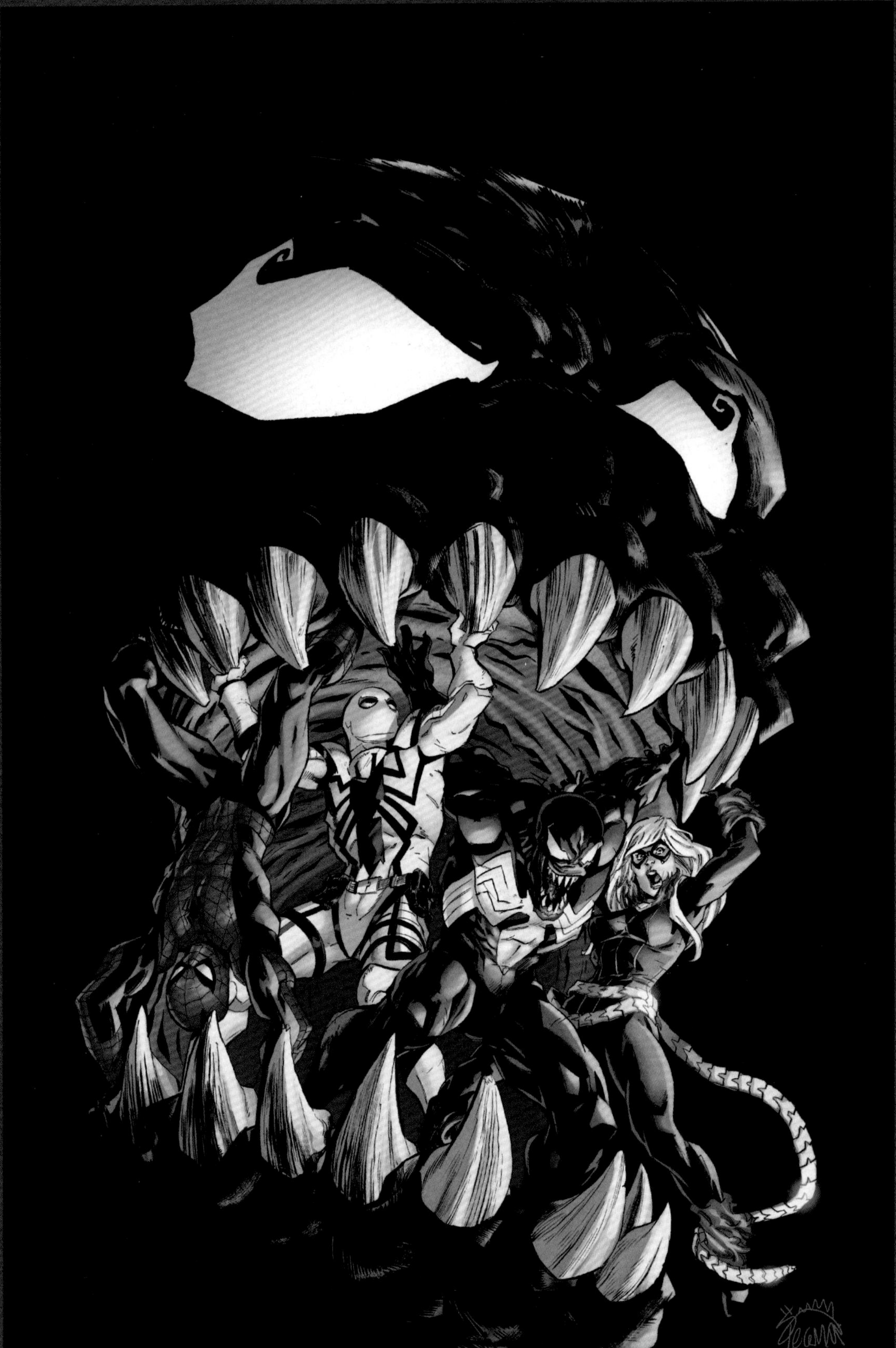

AMAZING SPIDER-MAN: VENOM INC. OMEGA 1

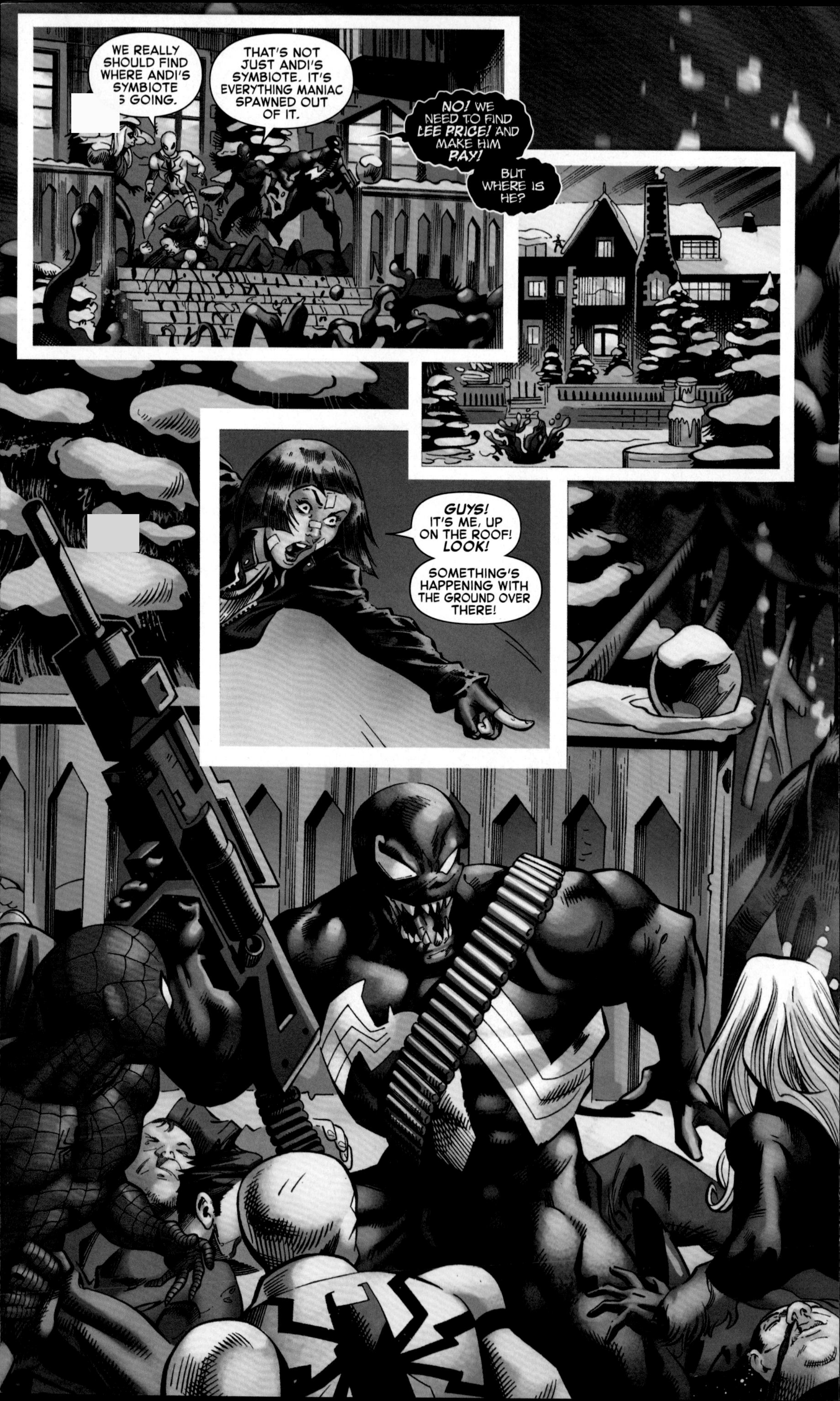
WE REALLY SHOULD FIND WHERE ANDI'S SYMBIOTE S GOING.
THAT'S NOT JUST ANDI'S SYMBIOTE. IT'S EVERYTHING MANIAC SPAWNED OUT OF IT.
NO! WE NEED TO FIND LEE PRICE! AND MAKE HIM PAY!
BUT WHERE IS HE?
GUYS! IT'S ME, UP ON THE ROOF! LOOK!
SOMETHING'S HAPPENING WITH THE GROUND OVER THERE!

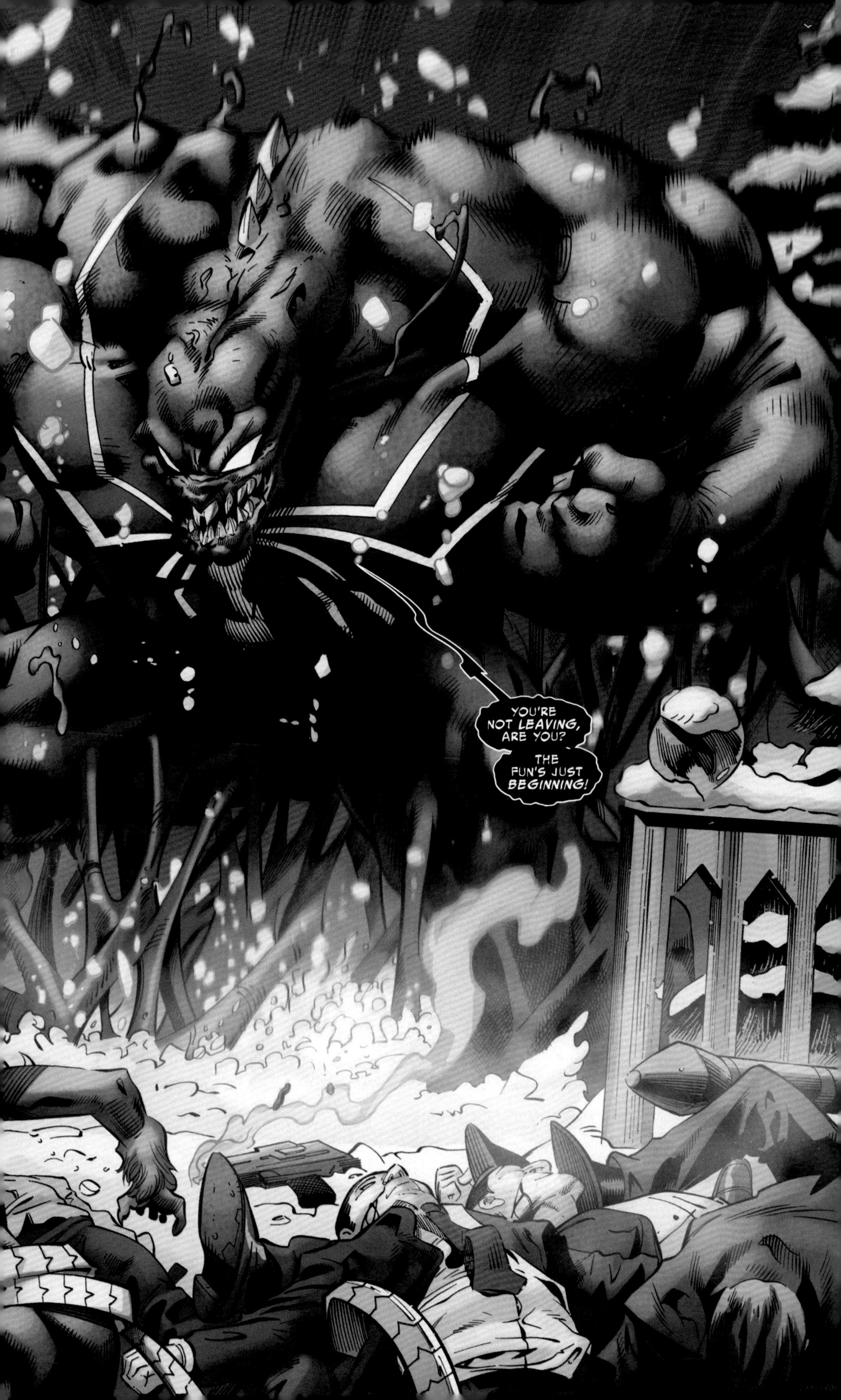
YOU'RE NOT LEAVING, ARE YOU?
THE FUN'S JUST BEGINNING!

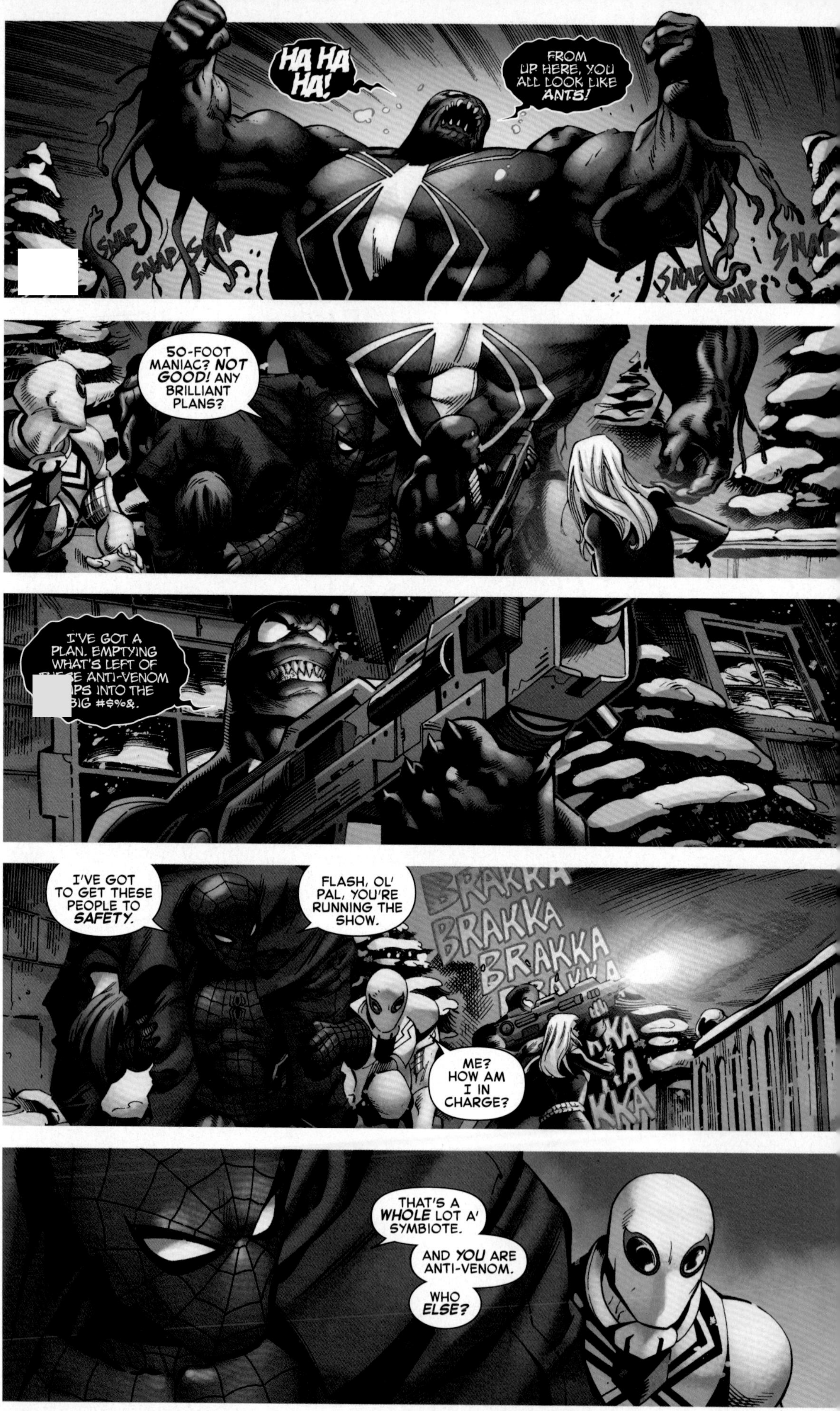
HA HA HA!
FROM UP HERE, YOU ALL LOOK LIKE ANTS!
SNAP SNAP SNAP
SNAP SNAP SNAP
50-FOOT MANIAC? NOT GOOD! ANY BRILLIANT PLANS?
I'VE GOT A PLAN. EMPTYING WHAT'S LEFT OF ANTI-VENOM INTO THE BIG #$%&.
I'VE GOT TO GET THESE PEOPLE TO SAFETY.
FLASH, OL' PAL, YOU'RE RUNNING THE SHOW.
BRAKKA BRAKKA BRAKKA
ME? HOW AM I IN CHARGE?
THAT'S A WHOLE LOT A' SYMBIOTE.
AND YOU ARE ANTI-VENOM.
WHO ELSE?

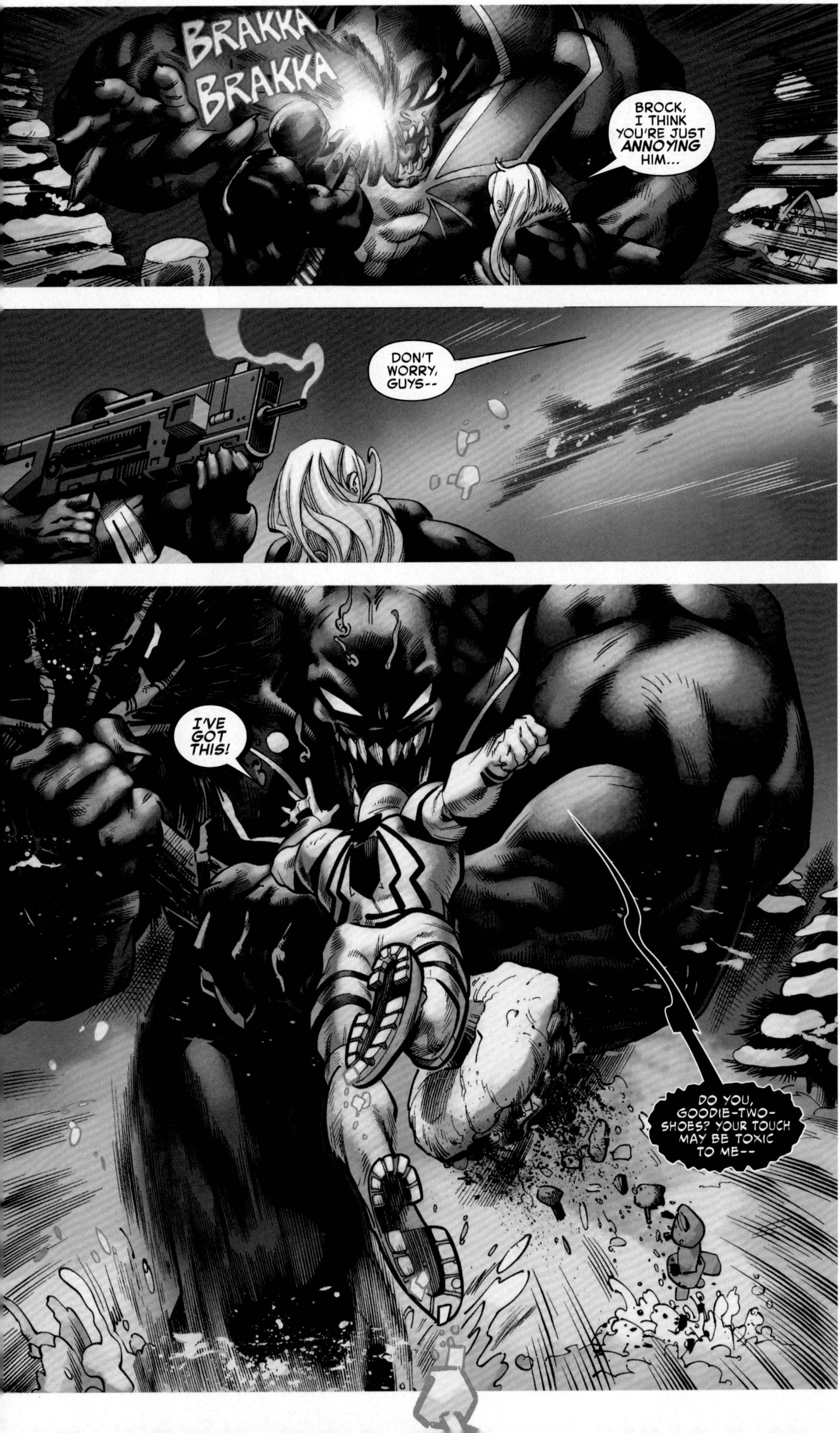
BRAKKA
BRAKKA
BROCK, I THINK YOU'RE JUST ANNOYING HIM...
DON'T WORRY, GUYS--
I'VE GOT THIS!
DO YOU, GOODIE-TWO-SHOES? YOUR TOUCH MAY BE TOXIC TO ME--

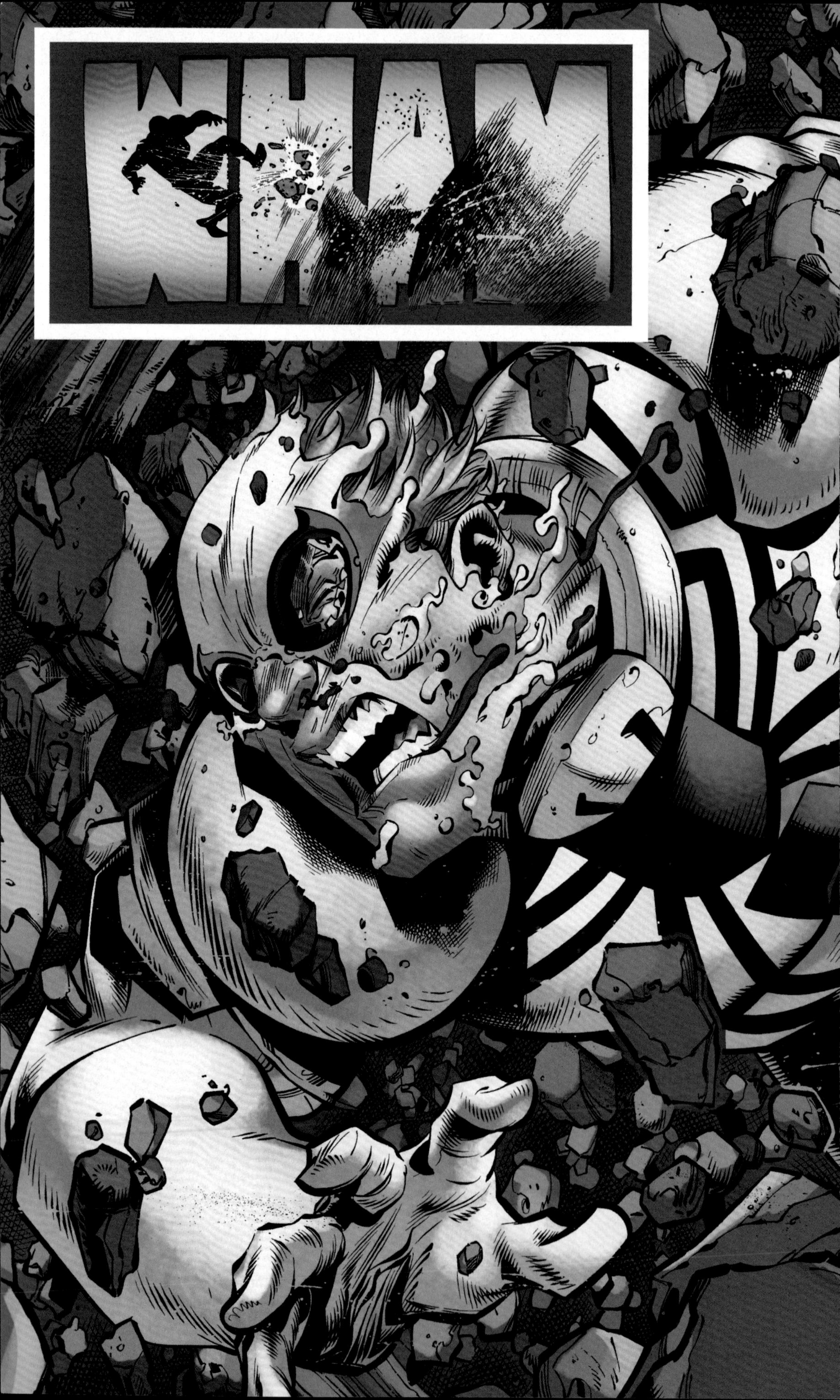
WHAM

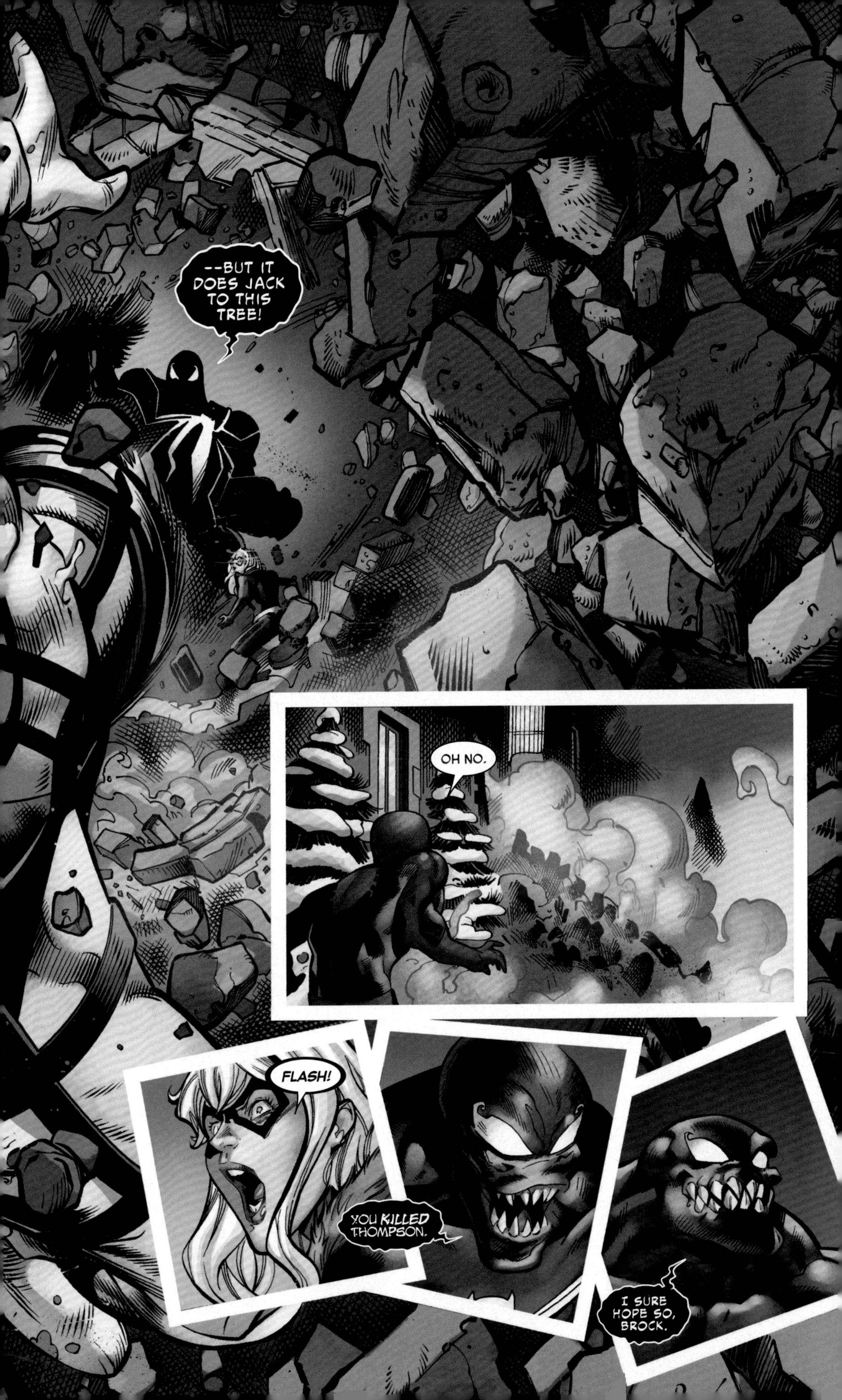
--BUT IT DOES JACK TO THIS TREE!
OH NO.
FLASH!
YOU KILLED THOMPSON.
I SURE HOPE SO, BROCK.

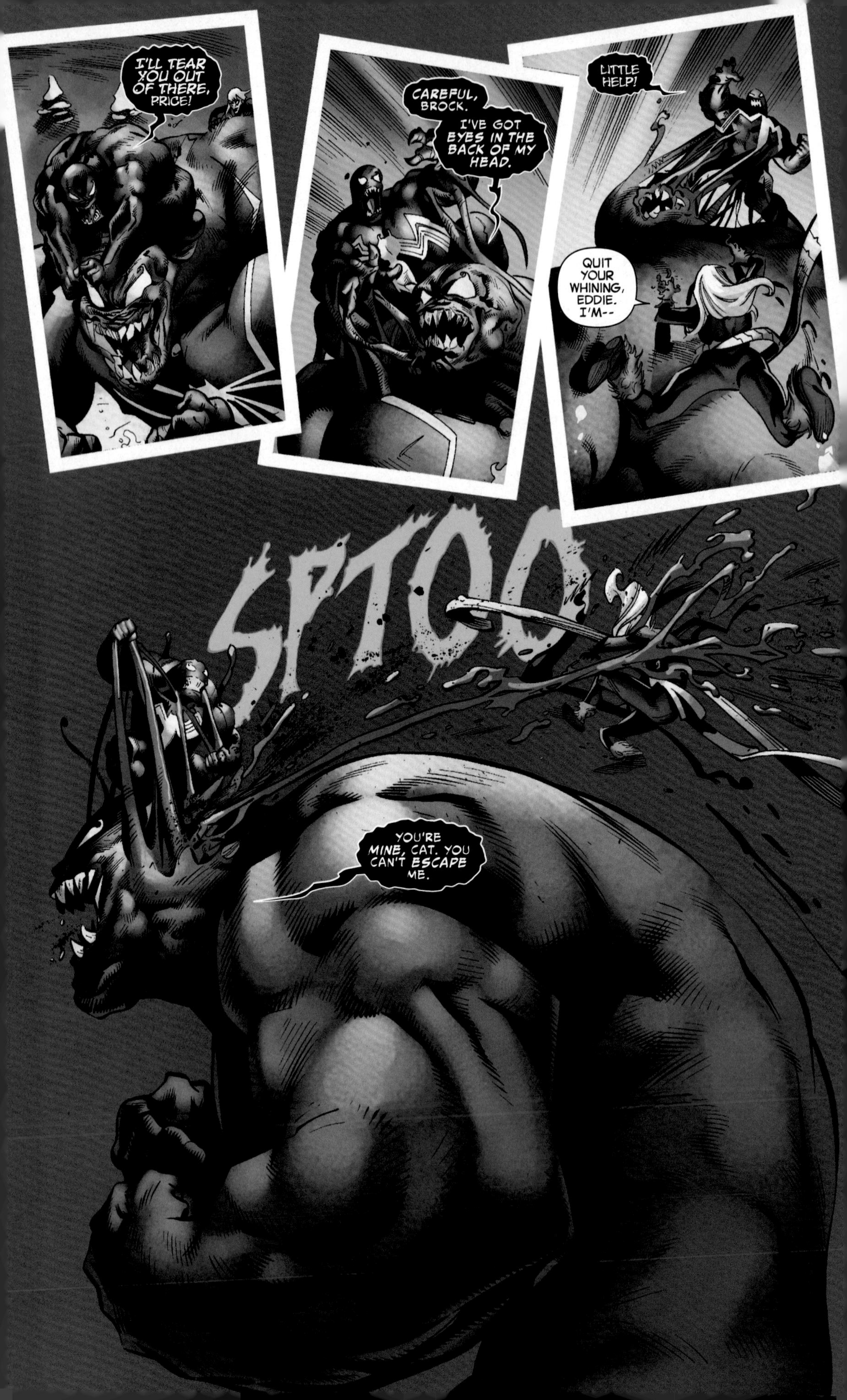
I'LL TEAR YOU OUT OF THERE, PRICE!
CAREFUL, BROCK.
I'VE GOT EYES IN THE BACK OF MY HEAD.
LITTLE HELP!
QUIT YOUR WHINING, EDDIE. I'M--
SPTOO
YOU'RE MINE, CAT. YOU CAN'T ESCAPE ME.

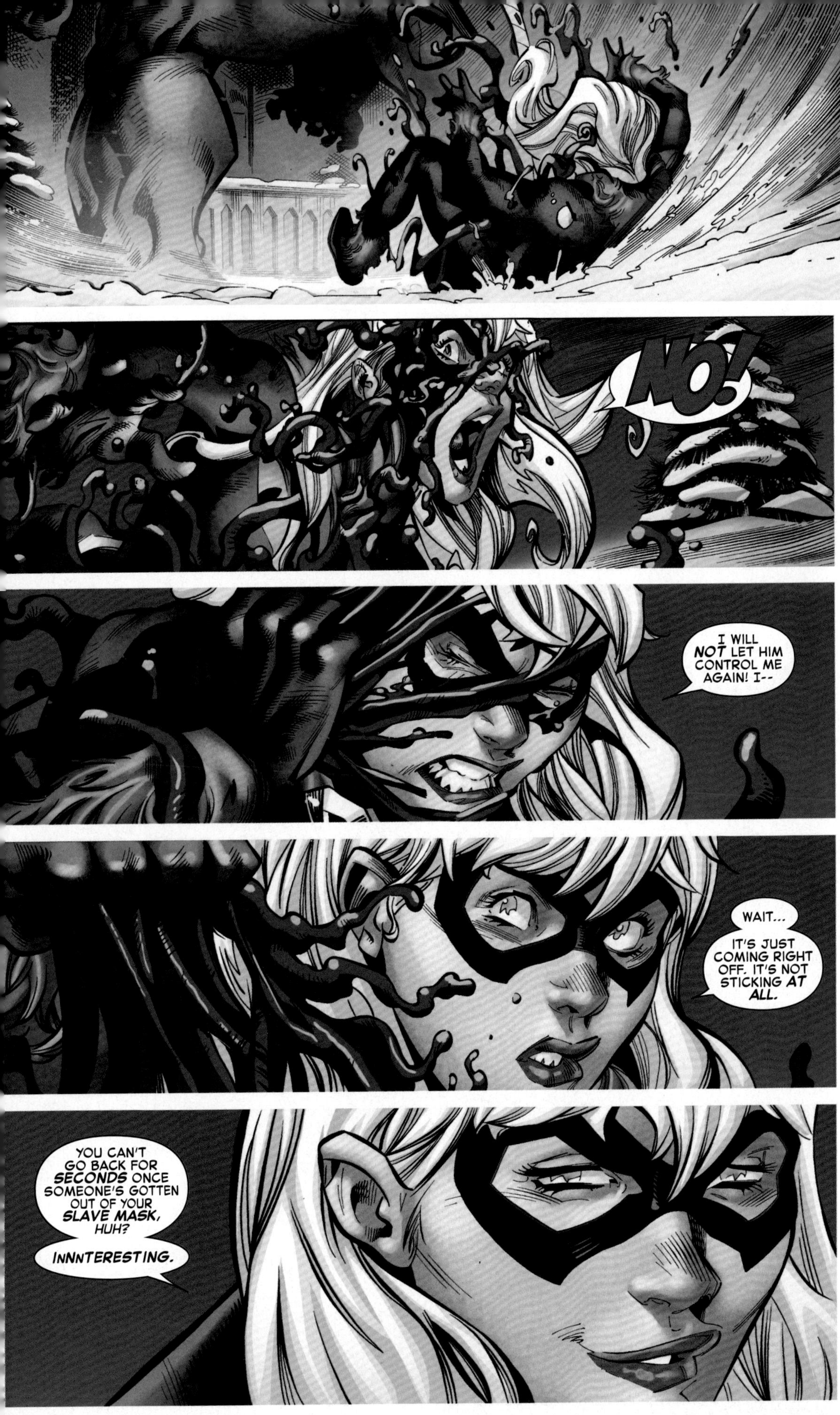
NO!
I WILL NOT LET HIM CONTROL ME AGAIN! I--
WAIT...
IT'S JUST COMING RIGHT OFF. IT'S NOT STICKING AT ALL.
YOU CAN'T GO BACK FOR SECONDS ONCE SOMEONE'S GOTTEN OUT OF YOUR SLAVE MASK, HUH?
INNNTERESTING.

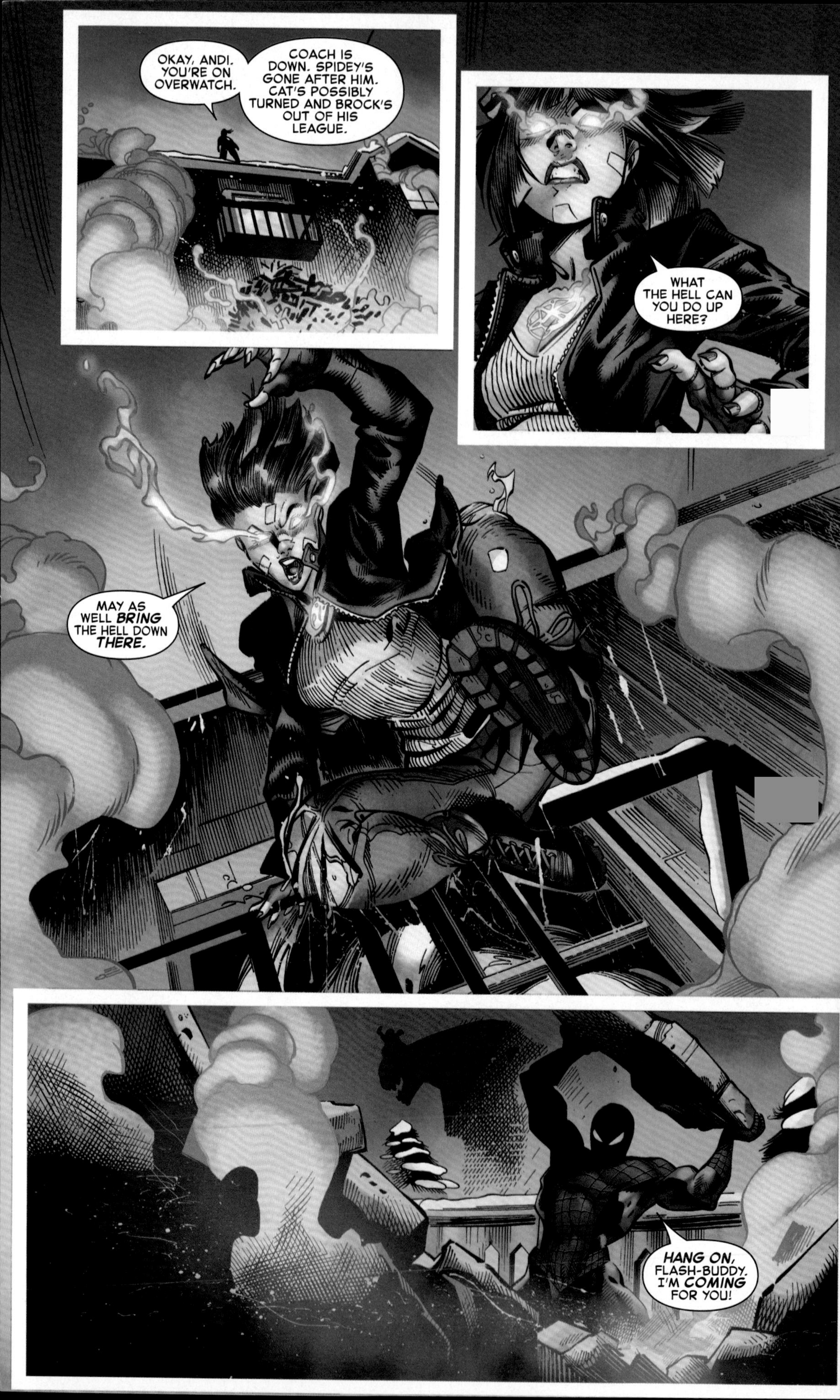
OKAY, ANDI. YOU'RE ON OVERWATCH.
COACH IS DOWN. SPIDEY'S GONE AFTER HIM. CAT'S POSSIBLY TURNED AND BROCK'S OUT OF HIS LEAGUE.
WHAT THE HELL CAN YOU DO UP HERE?
MAY AS WELL BRING THE HELL DOWN THERE.
HANG ON, FLASH-BUDDY. I'M COMING FOR YOU!

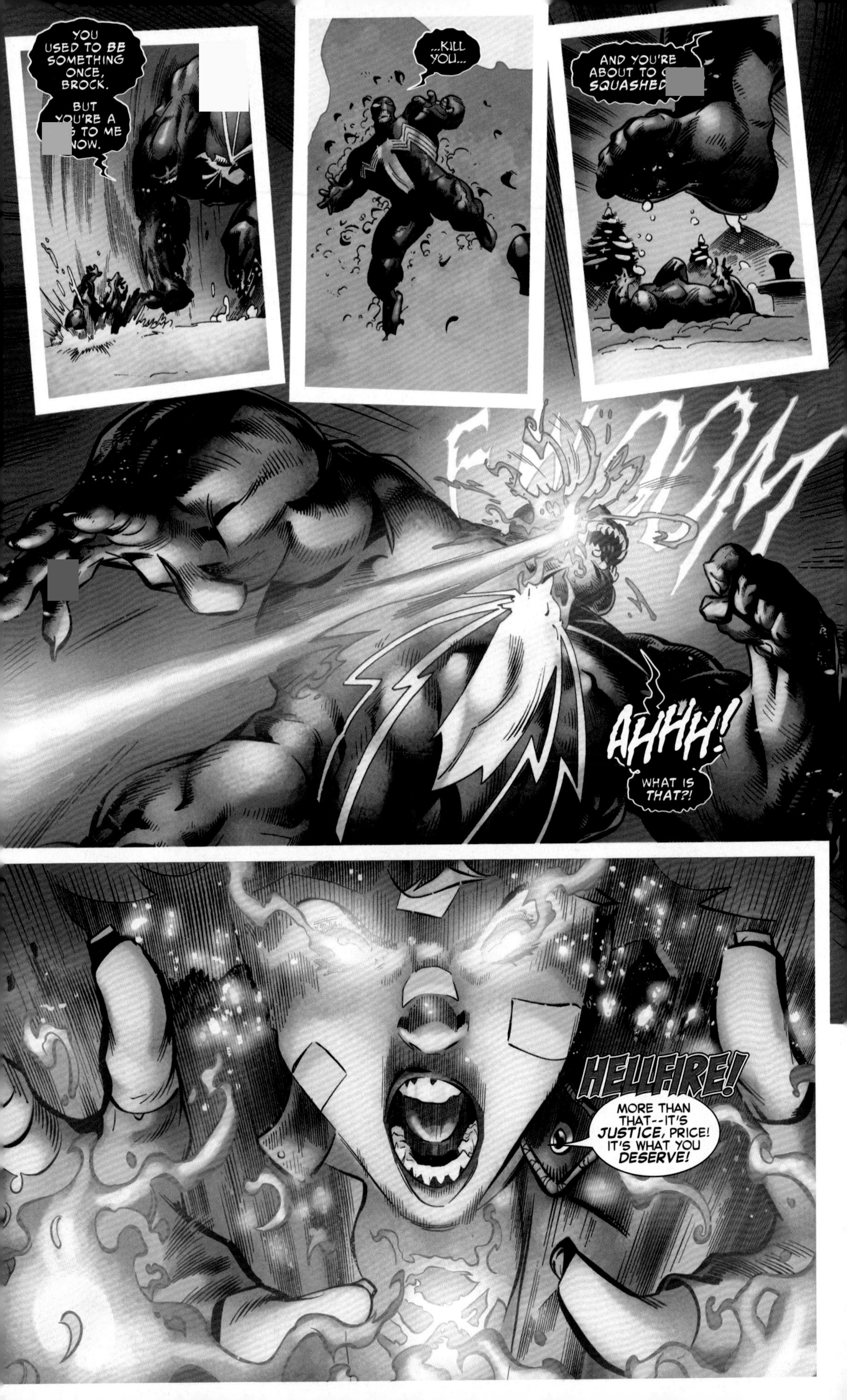

YOU USED TO BE SOMETHING ONCE, BROCK.
BUT YOU'RE A TO ME NOW.
...KILL YOU...
AND YOU'RE ABOUT TO SQUASHED
AHHH!
WHAT IS THAT?!
HELLFIRE!
MORE THAN THAT--IT'S JUSTICE, PRICE! IT'S WHAT YOU DESERVE!

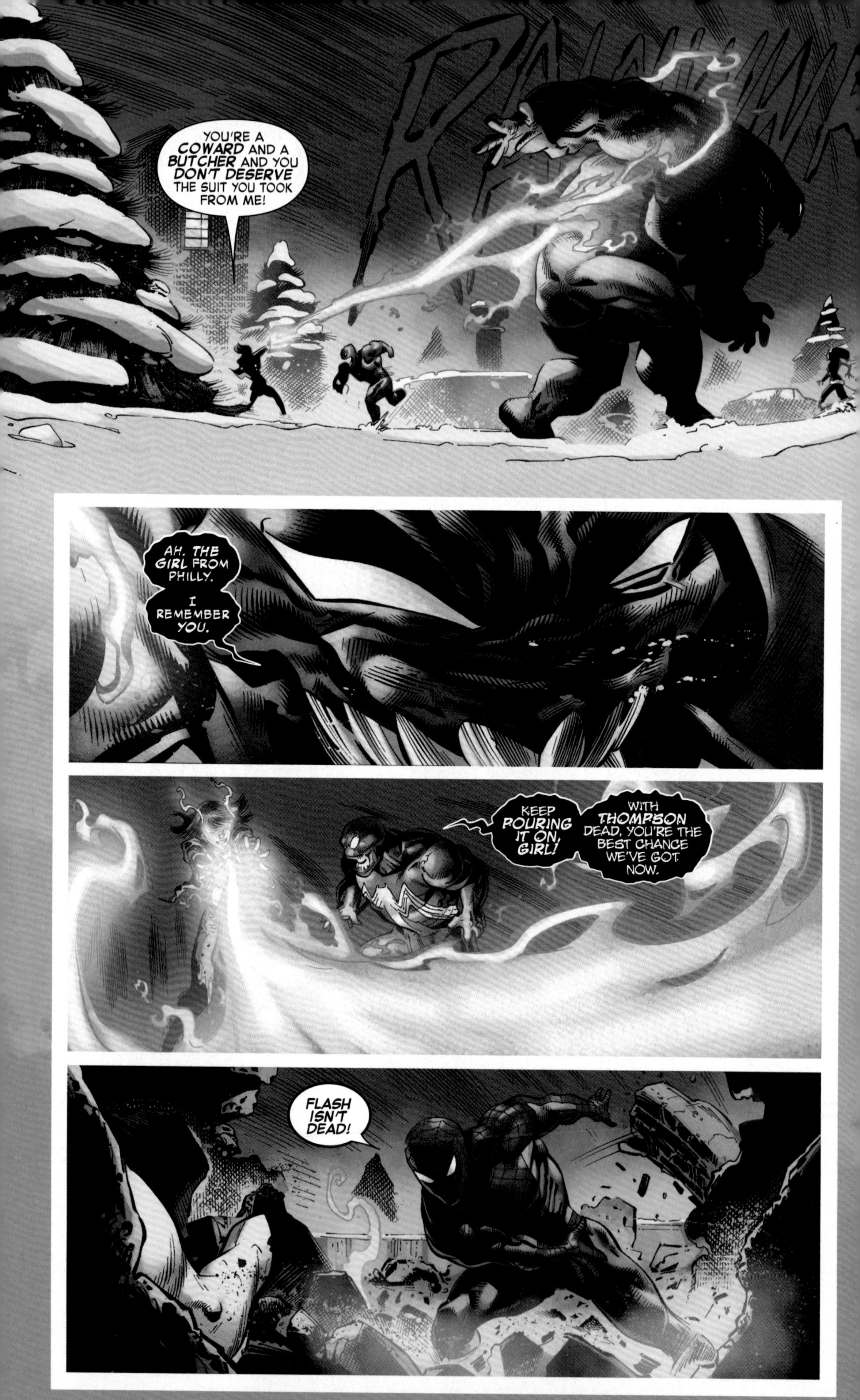
YOU'RE A COWARD AND A BUTCHER AND YOU DON'T DESERVE THE SUIT YOU TOOK FROM ME!
AH. THE GIRL FROM PHILLY.
I REMEMBER YOU.
KEEP POURING IT ON, GIRL!
WITH THOMPSON DEAD, YOU'RE THE BEST CHANCE WE'VE GOT NOW.
FLASH ISN'T DEAD!

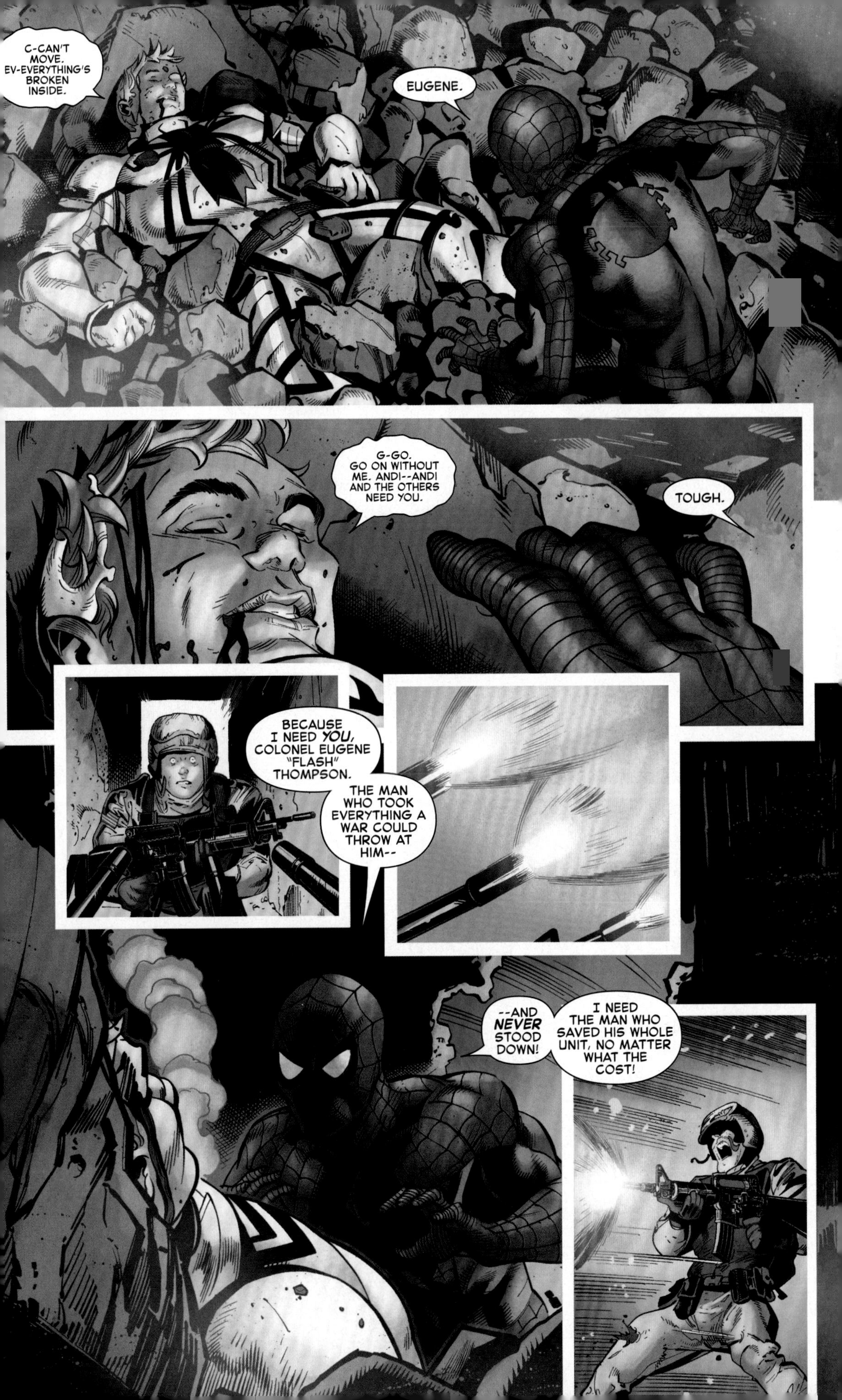
C-CAN'T MOVE. EV-EVERYTHING'S BROKEN INSIDE.
EUGENE.
G-GO. GO ON WITHOUT ME. ANDI--ANDI AND THE OTHERS NEED YOU.
TOUGH.
BECAUSE I NEED YOU, COLONEL EUGENE "FLASH" THOMPSON.
THE MAN WHO TOOK EVERYTHING A WAR COULD THROW AT HIM--
--AND NEVER STOOD DOWN!
I NEED THE MAN WHO SAVED HIS WHOLE UNIT, NO MATTER WHAT THE COST!

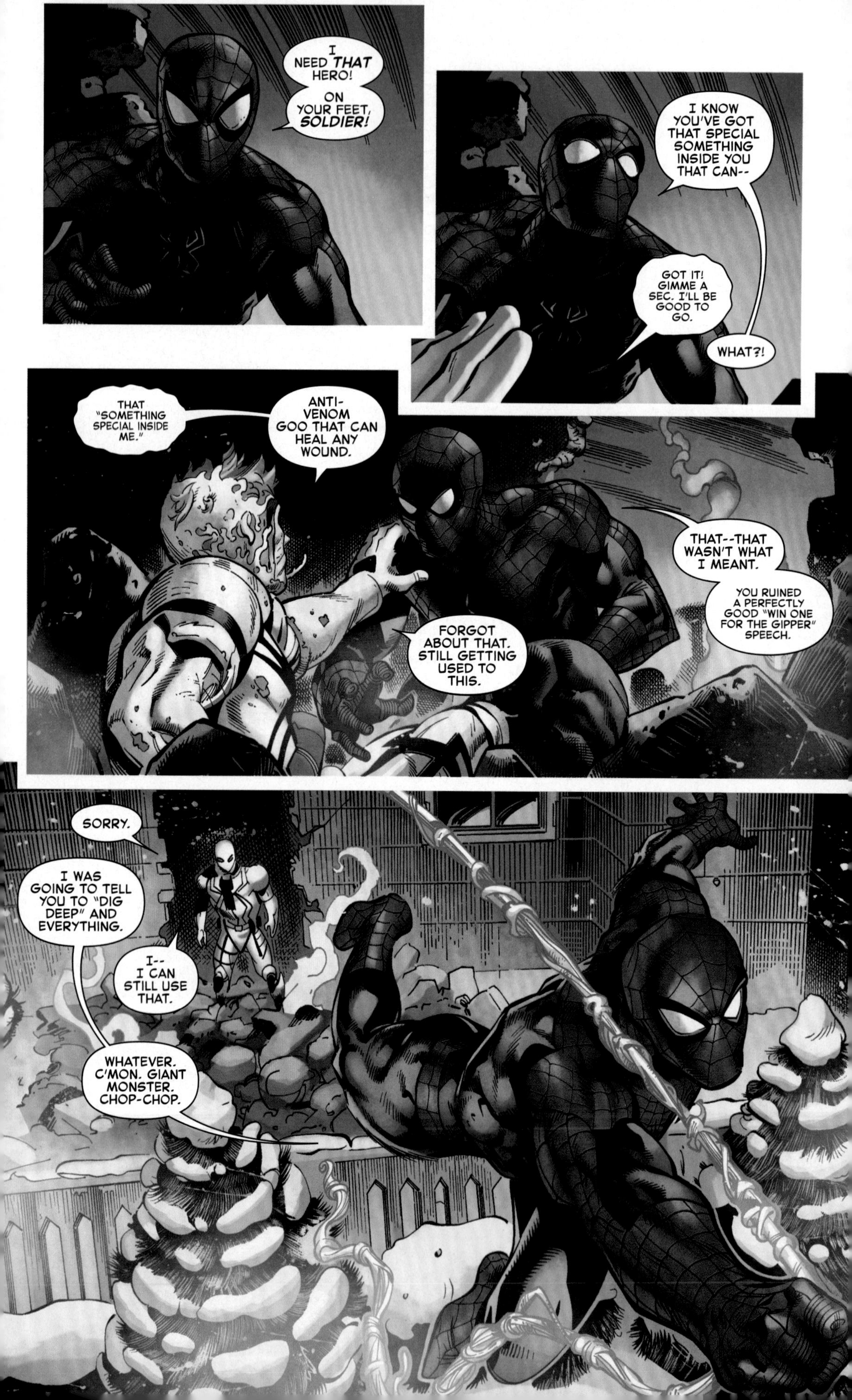

I NEED THAT HERO!
ON YOUR FEET, SOLDIER!
I KNOW YOU'VE GOT THAT SPECIAL SOMETHING INSIDE YOU THAT CAN--
GOT IT! GIMME A SEC. I'LL BE GOOD TO GO.
WHAT?!
THAT "SOMETHING SPECIAL INSIDE ME."
ANTI-VENOM GOO THAT CAN HEAL ANY WOUND.
THAT--THAT WASN'T WHAT I MEANT.
YOU RUINED A PERFECTLY GOOD "WIN ONE FOR THE GIPPER" SPEECH.
FORGOT ABOUT THAT. STILL GETTING USED TO THIS.
SORRY.
I WAS GOING TO TELL YOU TO "DIG DEEP" AND EVERYTHING.
I-- I CAN STILL USE THAT.
WHATEVER. C'MON. GIANT MONSTER. CHOP-CHOP.

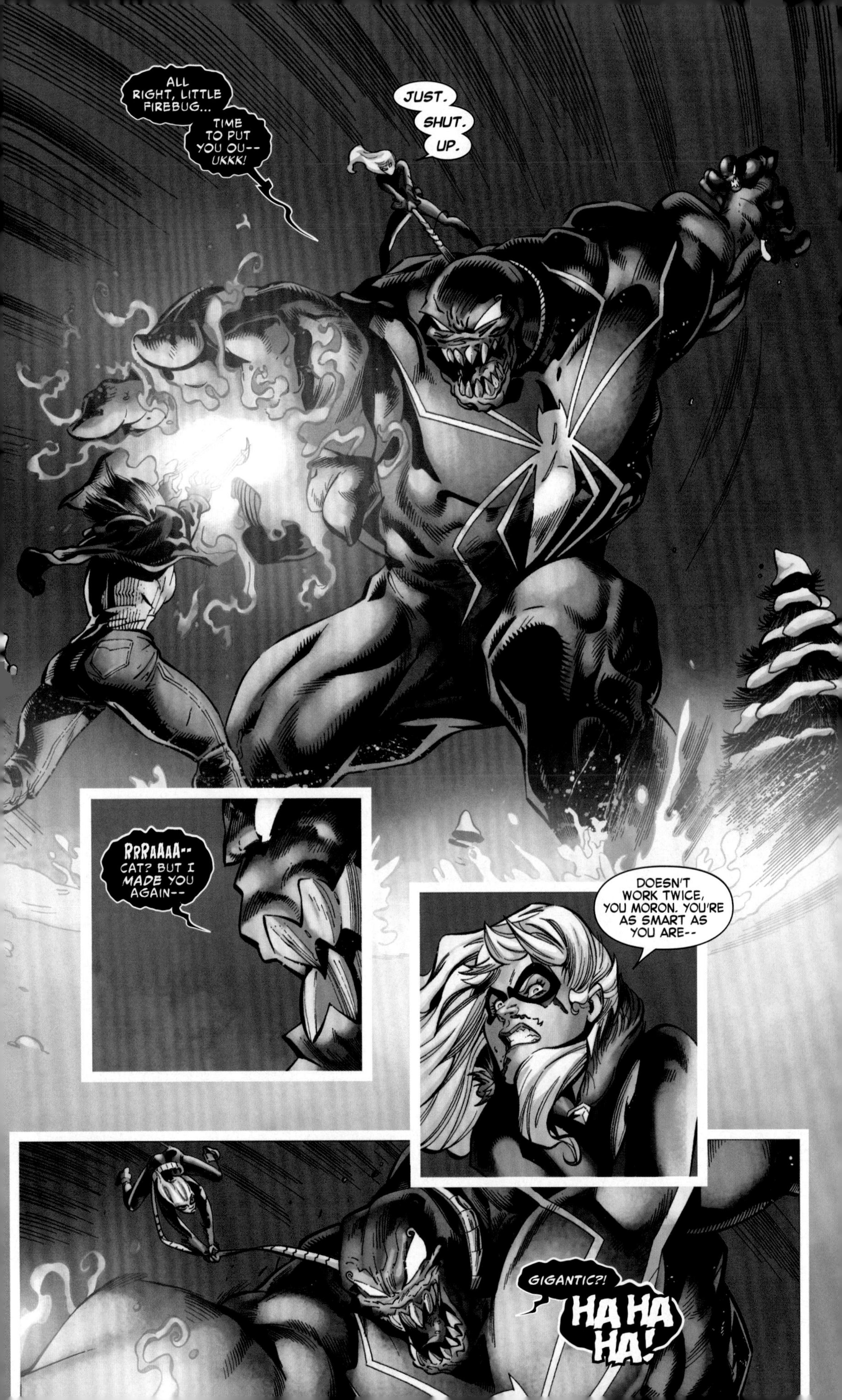
ALL RIGHT, LITTLE FIREBUG...
TIME TO PUT YOU OU-- UKKK!
JUST.
SHUT.
UP.
RRRAAAA-- CAT? BUT I MADE YOU AGAIN--
DOESN'T WORK TWICE, YOU MORON. YOU'RE AS SMART AS YOU ARE--
GIGANTIC?!
HA HA HA!

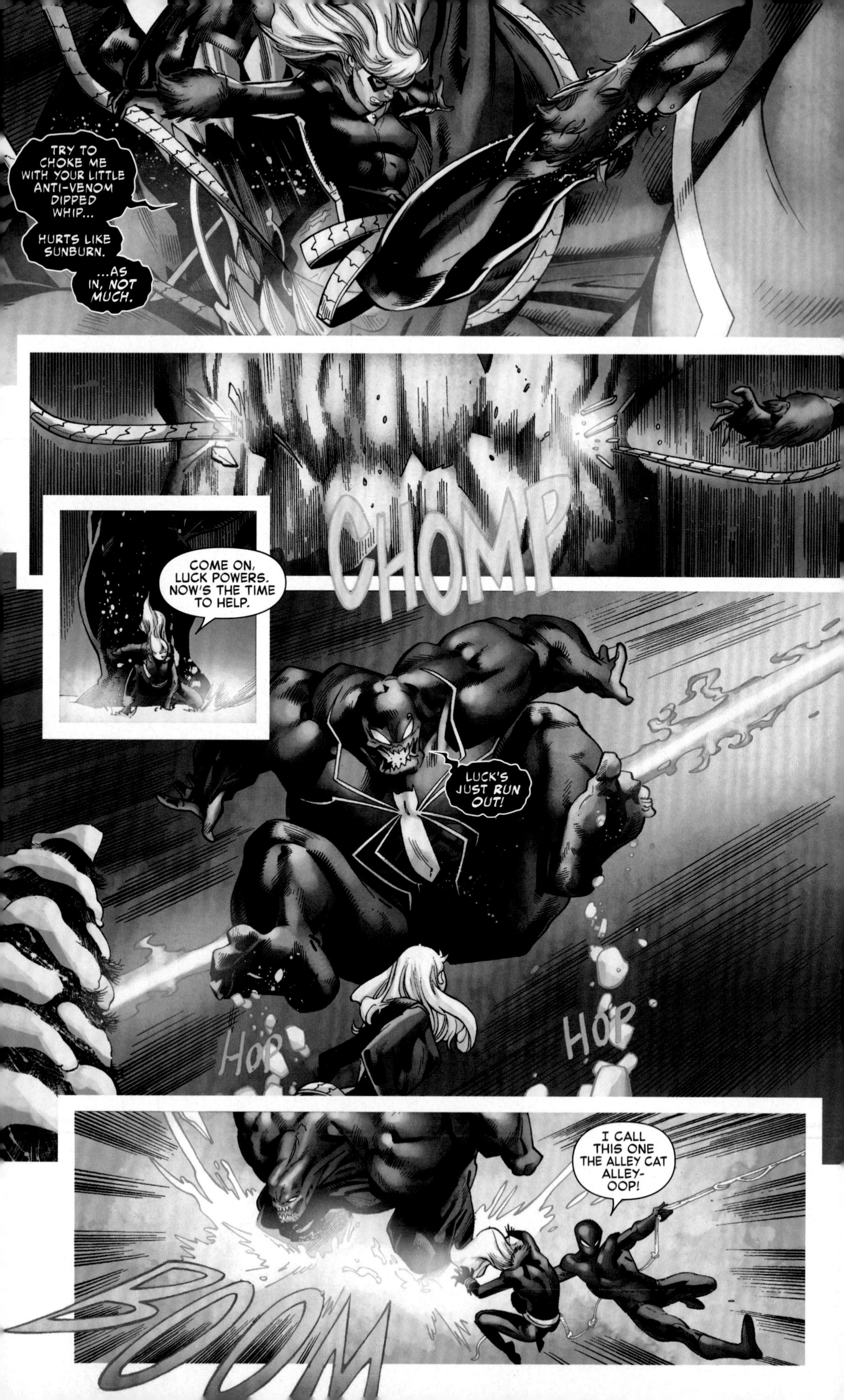
TRY TO CHOKE ME WITH YOUR LITTLE ANTI-VENOM DIPPED WHIP...
HURTS LIKE SUNBURN.
...AS IN, NOT MUCH.
CHOMP
COME ON, LUCK POWERS. NOW'S THE TIME TO HELP.
LUCK'S JUST RUN OUT!
HOP
HOP
I CALL THIS ONE THE ALLEY CAT ALLEY-OOP!
BOOM

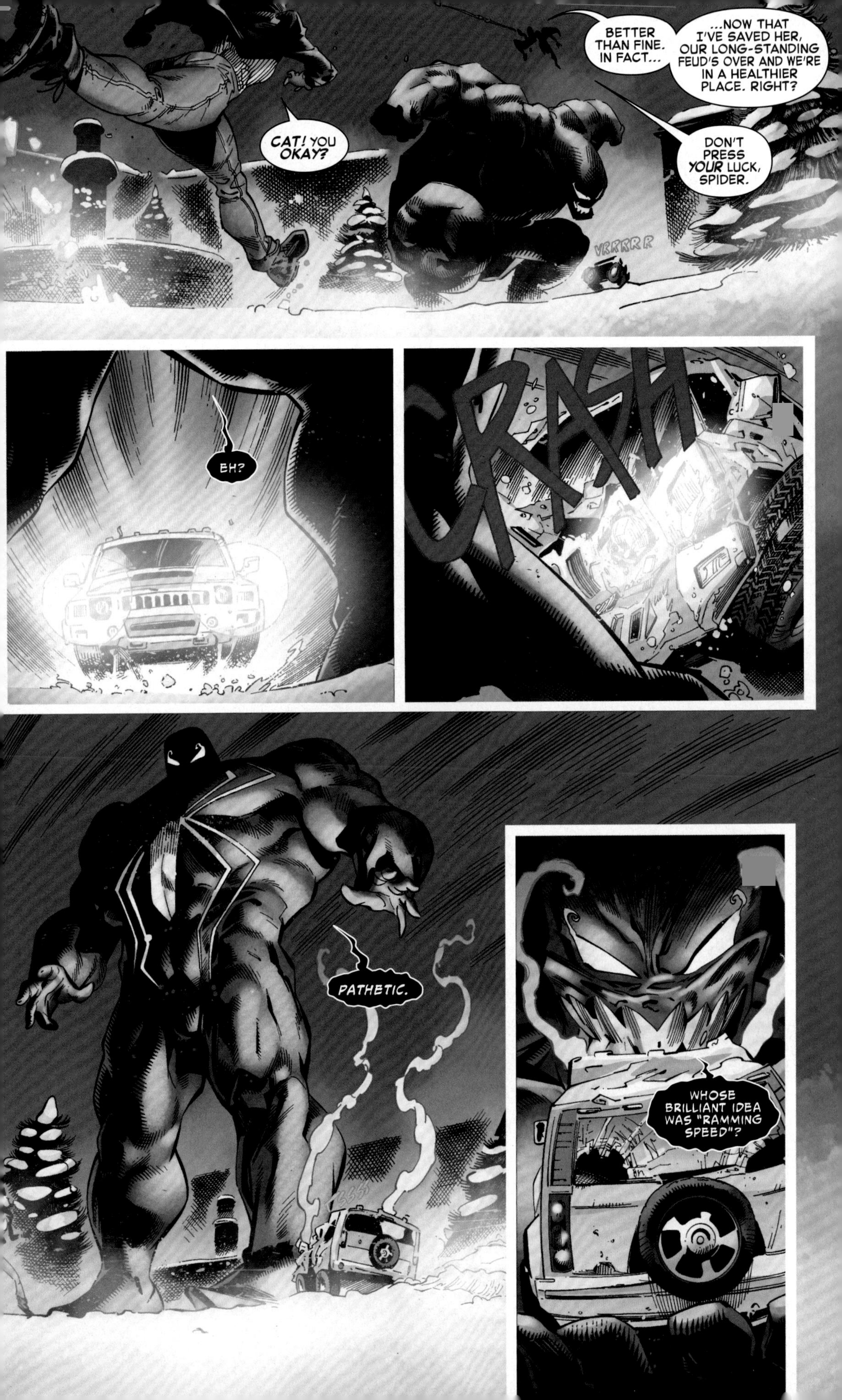
CAT! YOU OKAY?
BETTER THAN FINE. IN FACT...
...NOW THAT I'VE SAVED HER, OUR LONG-STANDING FEUD'S OVER AND WE'RE IN A HEALTHIER PLACE. RIGHT?
DON'T PRESS YOUR LUCK, SPIDER.
VRRRRR
EH?
CRASH
PATHETIC.
WHOSE BRILLIANT IDEA WAS "RAMMING SPEED"?

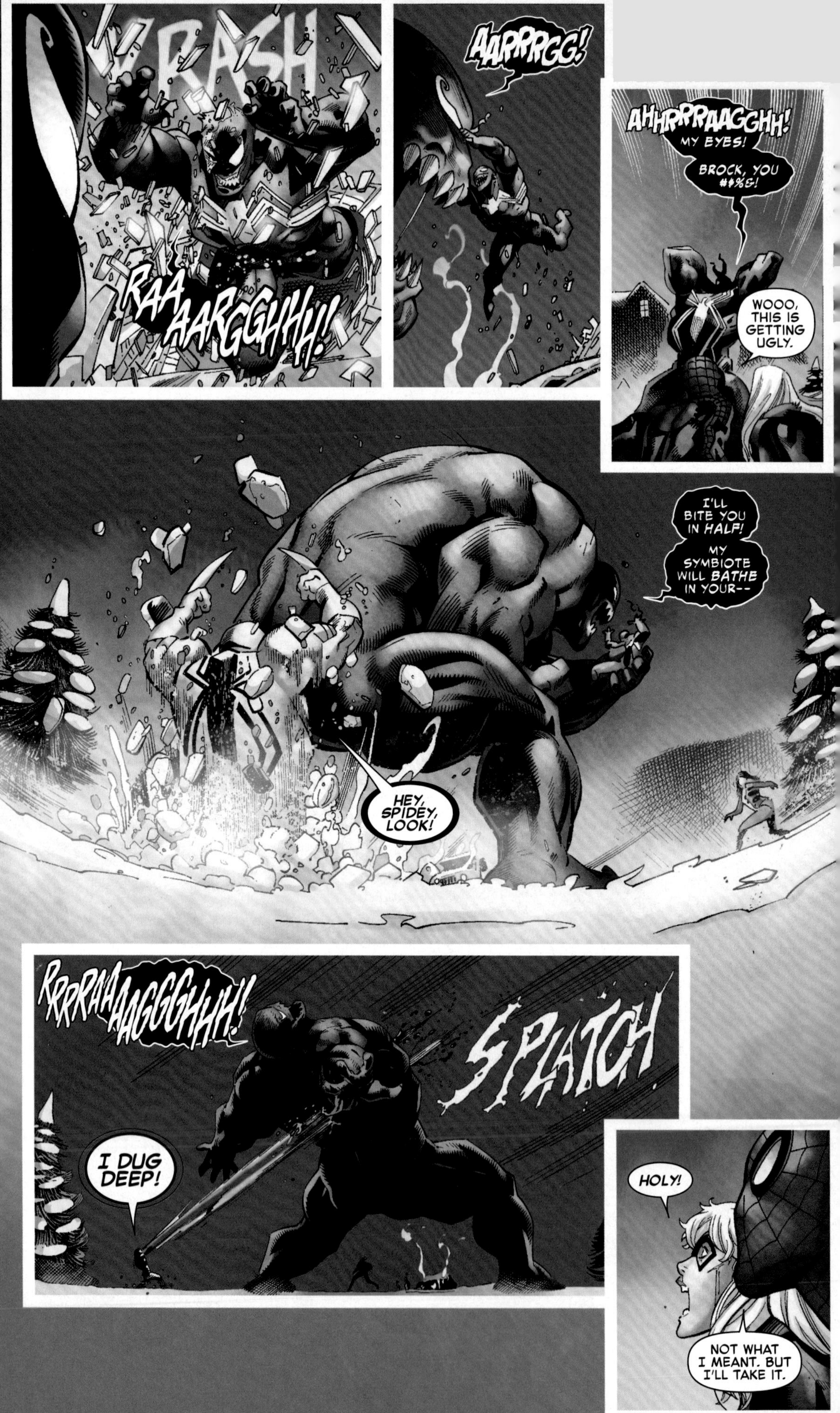
RASH
RAAAARGGHHH!
AARRRGG!
AHHRRRAAGGHH!
MY EYES!
BROCK, YOU #$%&!
WOOO, THIS IS GETTING UGLY.
I'LL BITE YOU IN *HALF!*
MY SYMBIOTE WILL *BATHE* IN YOUR--
HEY, SPIDEY, LOOK!
RRRRAAAAGGGHHH!
SPLATCH
I DUG DEEP!
HOLY!
NOT WHAT I MEANT. BUT I'LL TAKE IT.

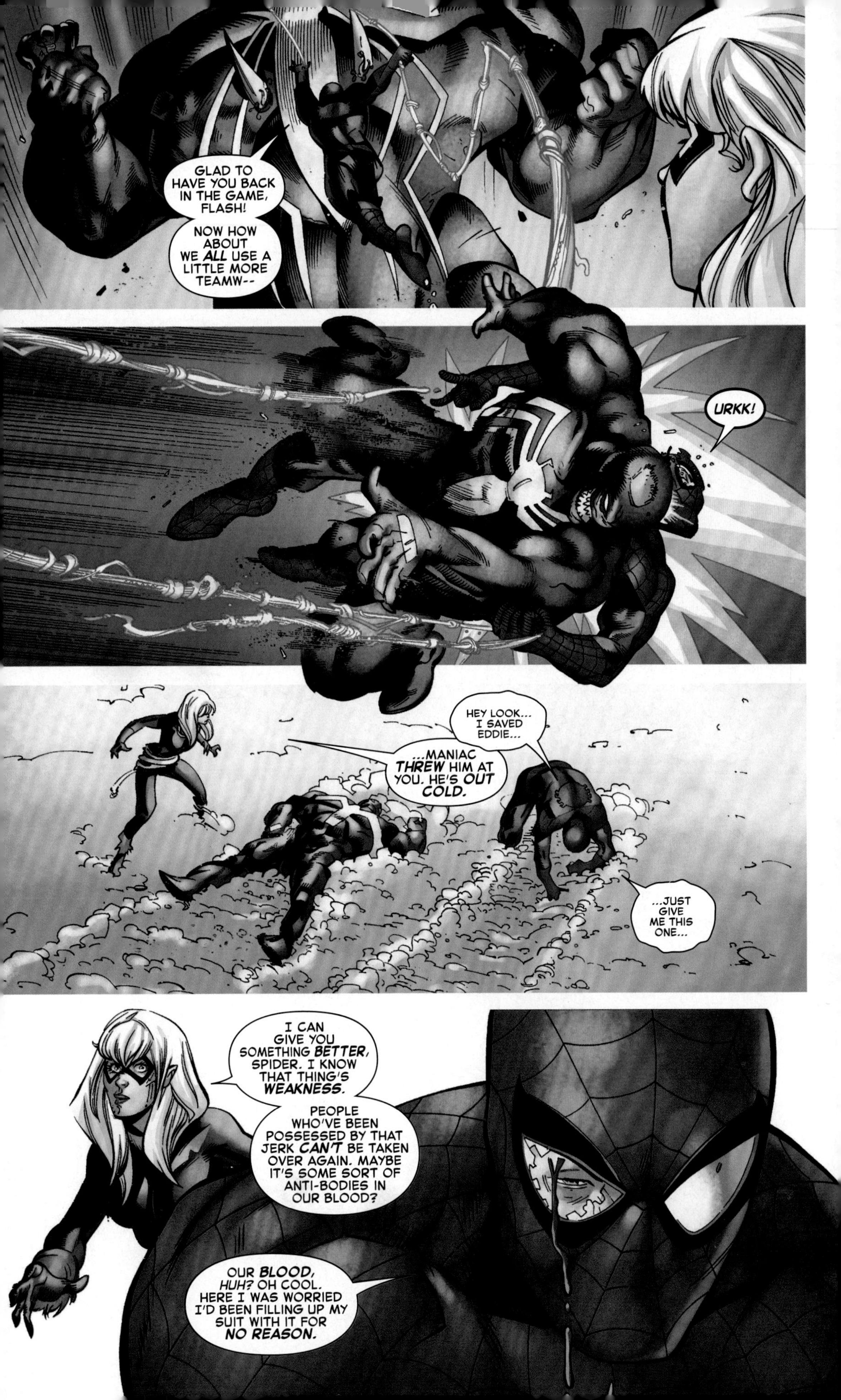
GLAD TO HAVE YOU BACK IN THE GAME, FLASH!
NOW HOW ABOUT WE ALL USE A LITTLE MORE TEAMW--
URKK!
HEY LOOK... I SAVED EDDIE...
...MANIAC THREW HIM AT YOU. HE'S OUT COLD.
...JUST GIVE ME THIS ONE...
I CAN GIVE YOU SOMETHING BETTER, SPIDER. I KNOW THAT THING'S WEAKNESS.
PEOPLE WHO'VE BEEN POSSESSED BY THAT JERK CAN'T BE TAKEN OVER AGAIN. MAYBE IT'S SOME SORT OF ANTI-BODIES IN OUR BLOOD?
OUR BLOOD, HUH? OH COOL. HERE I WAS WORRIED I'D BEEN FILLING UP MY SUIT WITH IT FOR NO REASON.

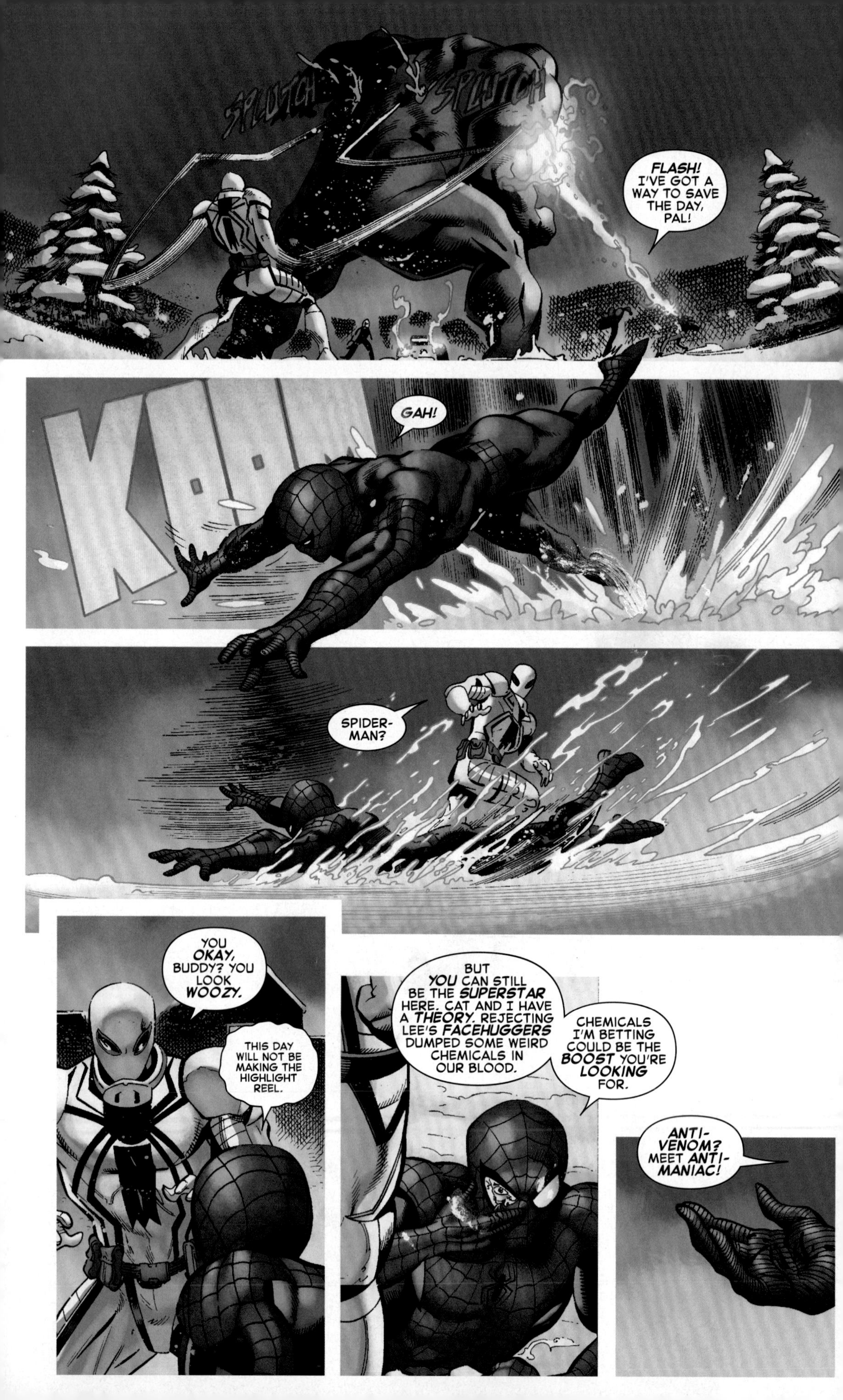
SPLUTCH
SPLUTCH
FLASH! I'VE GOT A WAY TO SAVE THE DAY, PAL!
GAH!
SPIDER-MAN?
YOU OKAY, BUDDY? YOU LOOK WOOZY.
THIS DAY WILL NOT BE MAKING THE HIGHLIGHT REEL.
BUT YOU CAN STILL BE THE SUPERSTAR HERE. CAT AND I HAVE A THEORY. REJECTING LEE'S FACEHUGGERS DUMPED SOME WEIRD CHEMICALS IN OUR BLOOD.
CHEMICALS I'M BETTING COULD BE THE BOOST YOU'RE LOOKING FOR.
ANTI-VENOM? MEET ANTI-MANIAC!

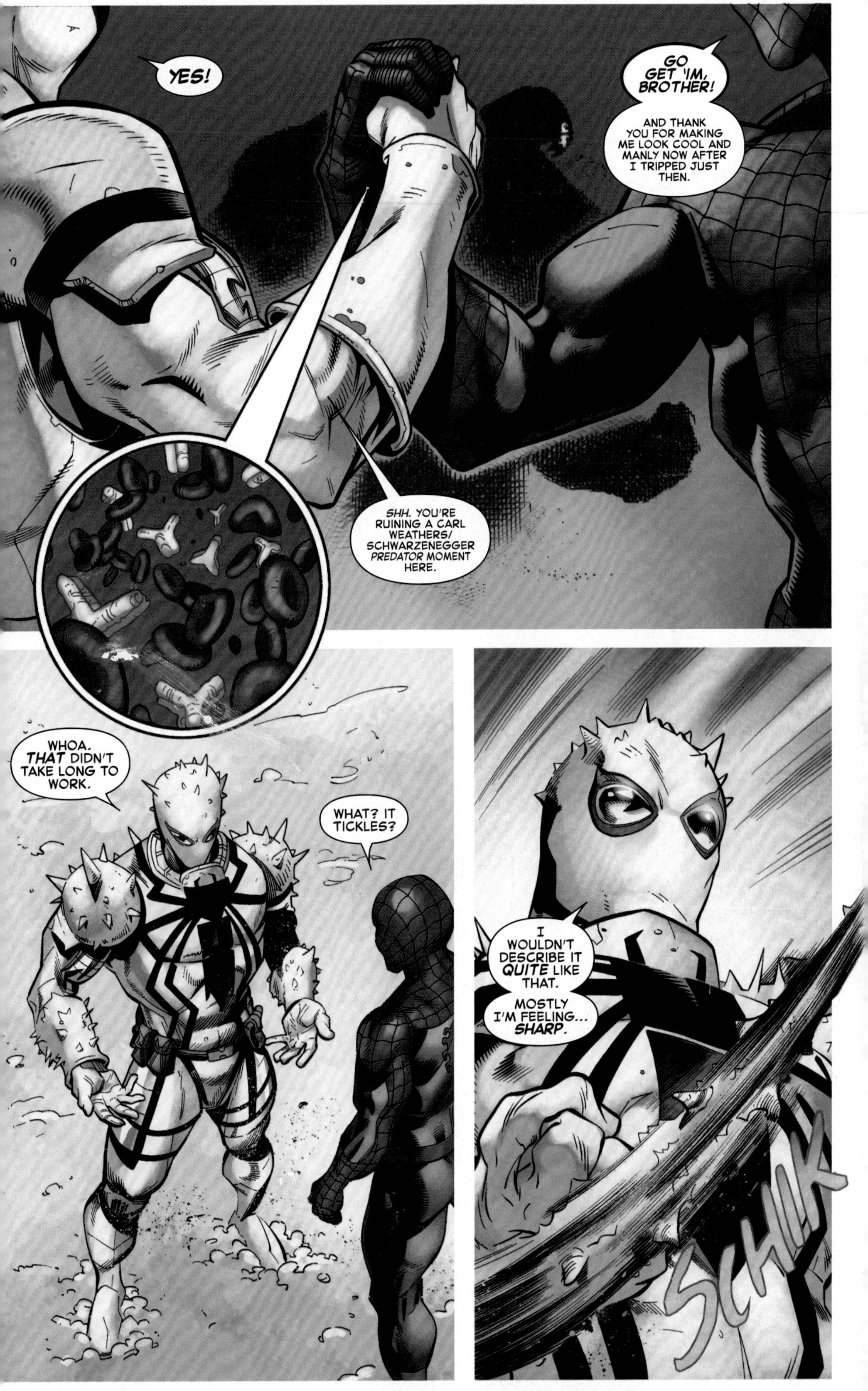
YES!
GO GET 'IM, BROTHER!
AND THANK YOU FOR MAKING ME LOOK COOL AND MANLY NOW AFTER I TRIPPED JUST THEN.
SHH. YOU'RE RUINING A CARL WEATHERS/ SCHWARZENEGGER PREDATOR MOMENT HERE.
WHOA. THAT DIDN'T TAKE LONG TO WORK.
WHAT? IT TICKLES?
I WOULDN'T DESCRIBE IT QUITE LIKE THAT.
MOSTLY I'M FEELING... SHARP.
SCHIK

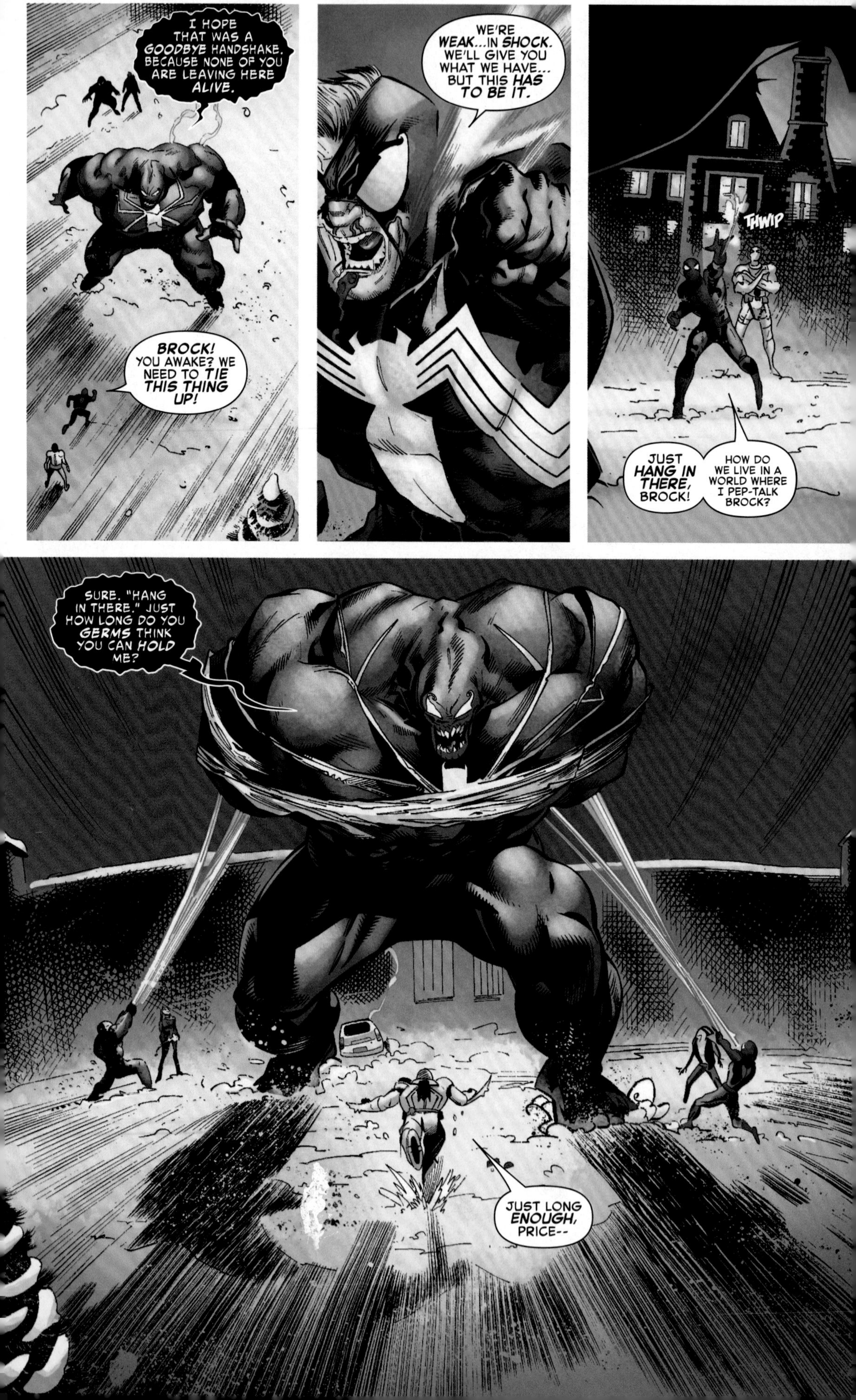
I HOPE THAT WAS A GOODBYE HANDSHAKE. BECAUSE NONE OF YOU ARE LEAVING HERE ALIVE.
BROCK! YOU AWAKE? WE NEED TO TIE THIS THING UP!
WE'RE WEAK...IN SHOCK. WE'LL GIVE YOU WHAT WE HAVE... BUT THIS HAS TO BE IT.
THWIP
JUST HANG IN THERE, BROCK!
HOW DO WE LIVE IN A WORLD WHERE I PEP-TALK BROCK?
SURE. "HANG IN THERE." JUST HOW LONG DO YOU GERMS THINK YOU CAN HOLD ME?
JUST LONG ENOUGH, PRICE--

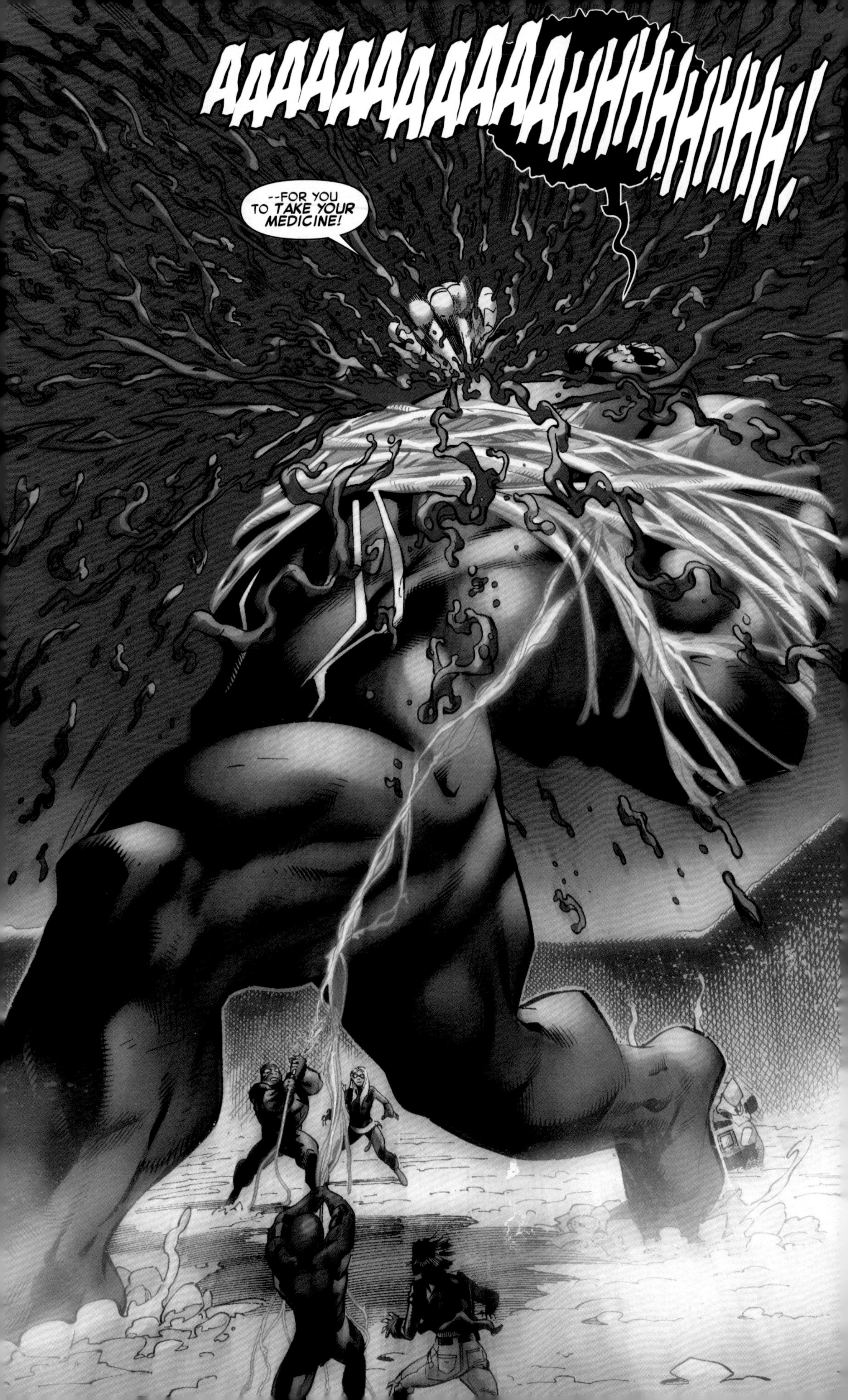
--FOR YOU TO TAKE YOUR MEDICINE!
AAAAAAAAAAAAAHHHHHHHHH!

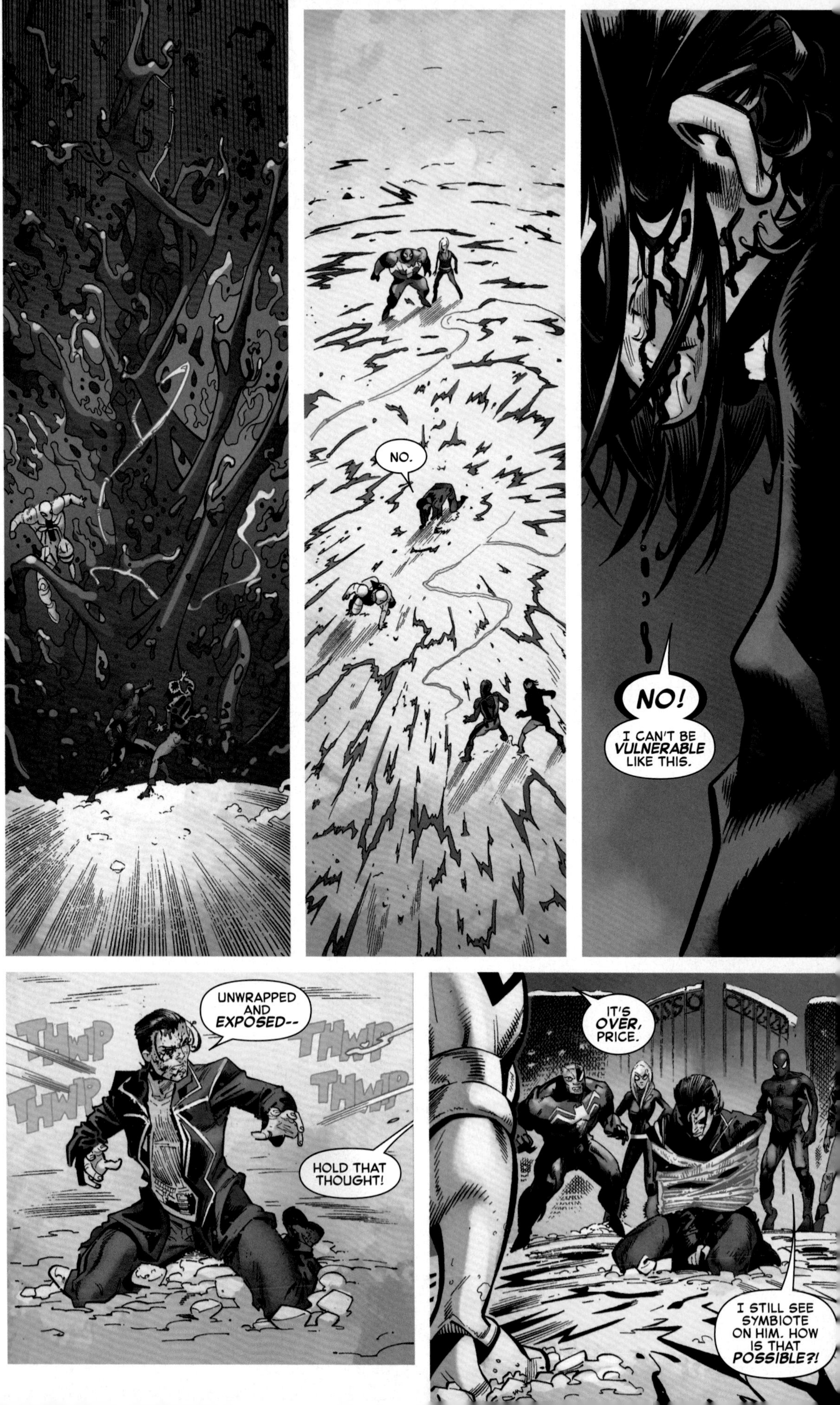
NO.
NO!
I CAN'T BE VULNERABLE LIKE THIS.
UNWRAPPED AND EXPOSED--
THWIP
THWIP
THWIP
THWIP
HOLD THAT THOUGHT!
IT'S OVER, PRICE.
I STILL SEE SYMBIOTE ON HIM. HOW IS THAT POSSIBLE?!

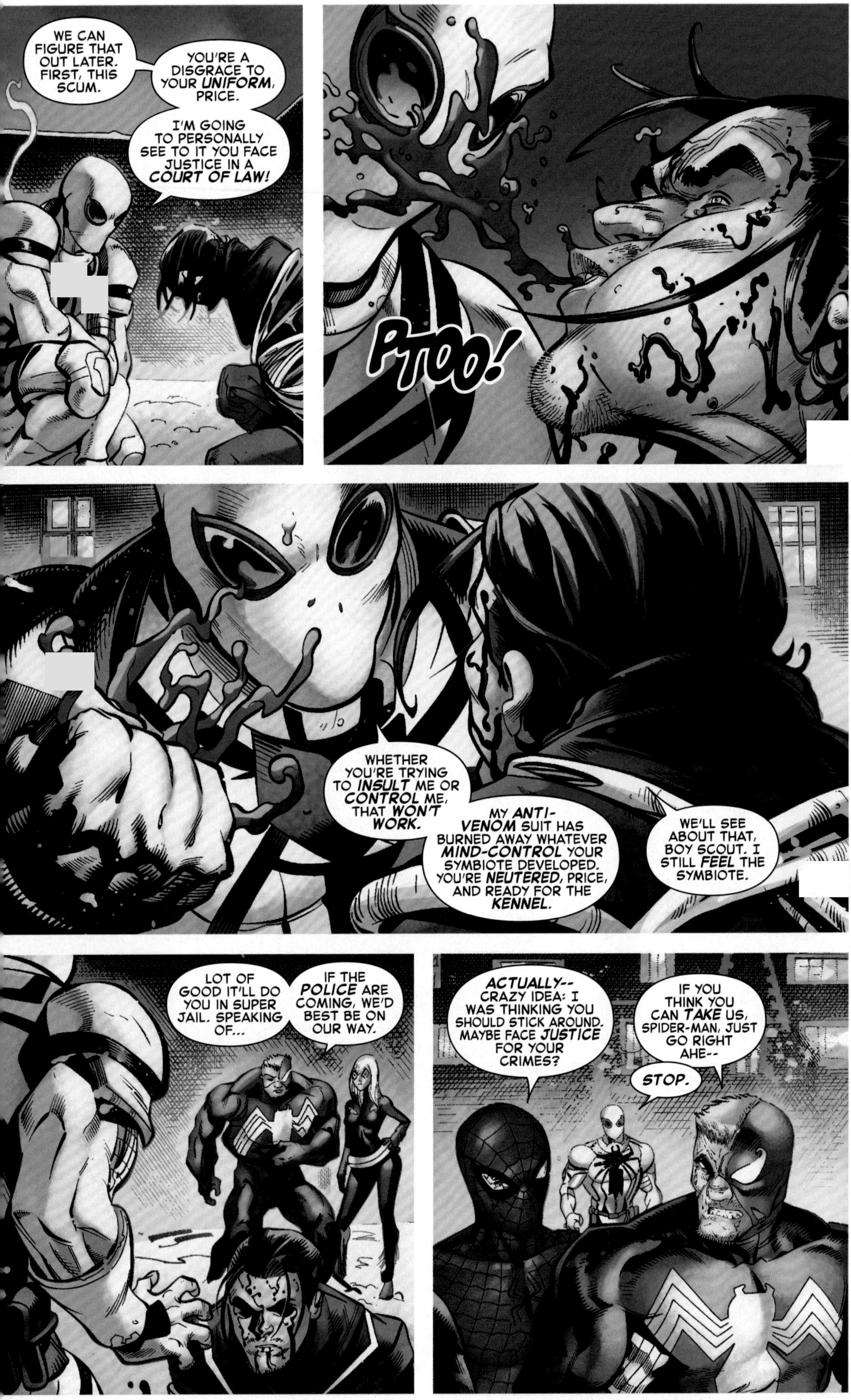
WE CAN FIGURE THAT OUT LATER. FIRST, THIS SCUM.
YOU'RE A DISGRACE TO YOUR UNIFORM, PRICE.
I'M GOING TO PERSONALLY SEE TO IT YOU FACE JUSTICE IN A COURT OF LAW!
PTOO!
WHETHER YOU'RE TRYING TO INSULT ME OR CONTROL ME, THAT WON'T WORK.
MY ANTI-VENOM SUIT HAS BURNED AWAY WHATEVER MIND-CONTROL YOUR SYMBIOTE DEVELOPED. YOU'RE NEUTERED, PRICE, AND READY FOR THE KENNEL.
WE'LL SEE ABOUT THAT, BOY SCOUT. I STILL FEEL THE SYMBIOTE.
LOT OF GOOD IT'LL DO YOU IN SUPER JAIL. SPEAKING OF...
IF THE POLICE ARE COMING, WE'D BEST BE ON OUR WAY.
ACTUALLY-- CRAZY IDEA: I WAS THINKING YOU SHOULD STICK AROUND. MAYBE FACE JUSTICE FOR YOUR CRIMES?
IF YOU THINK YOU CAN TAKE US, SPIDER-MAN, JUST GO RIGHT AHE--
STOP.

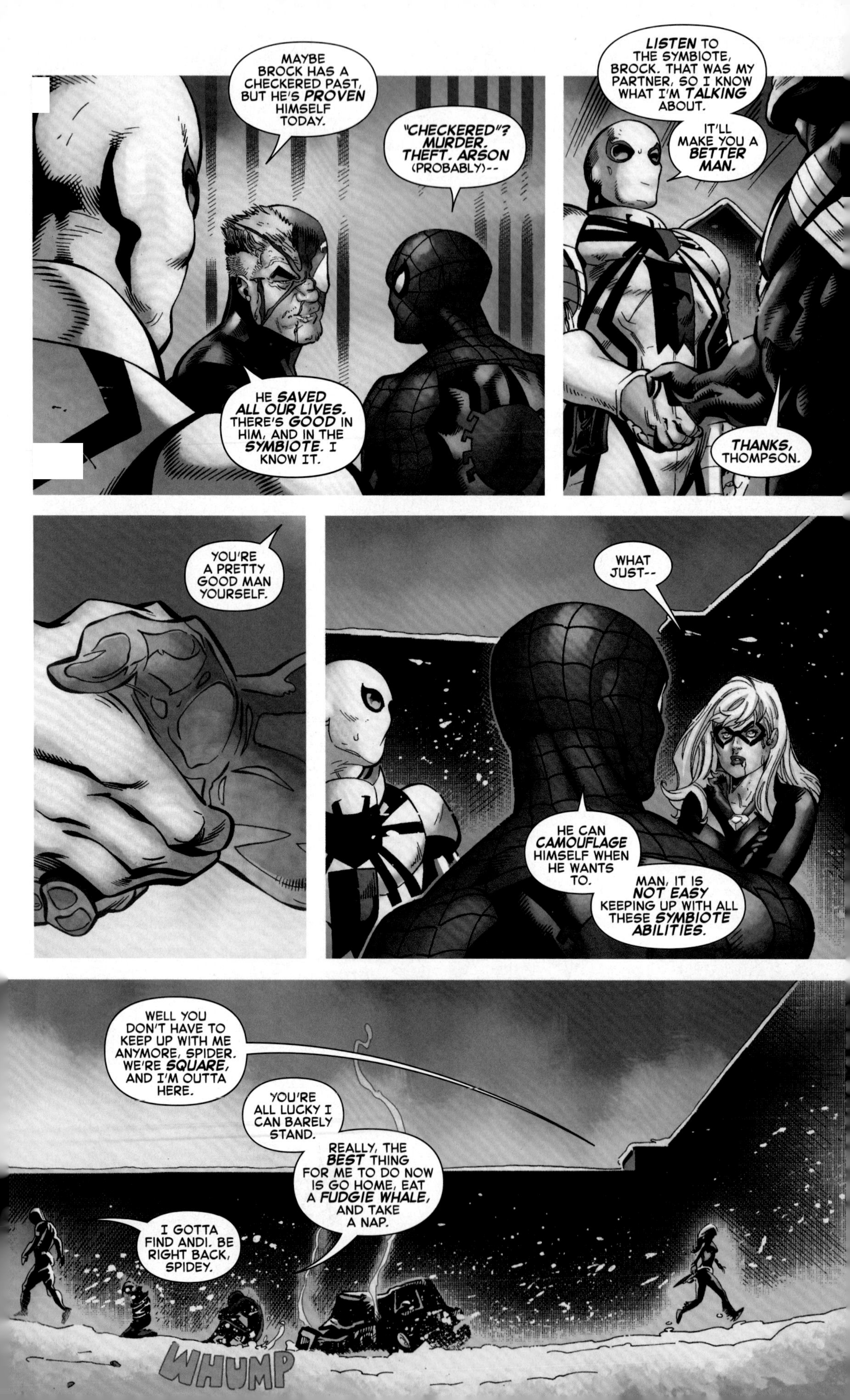
MAYBE BROCK HAS A CHECKERED PAST, BUT HE'S PROVEN HIMSELF TODAY.
"CHECKERED"? MURDER. THEFT. ARSON (PROBABLY)--
HE SAVED ALL OUR LIVES. THERE'S GOOD IN HIM, AND IN THE SYMBIOTE. I KNOW IT.
LISTEN TO THE SYMBIOTE, BROCK. THAT WAS MY PARTNER, SO I KNOW WHAT I'M TALKING ABOUT.
IT'LL MAKE YOU A BETTER MAN.
THANKS, THOMPSON.
YOU'RE A PRETTY GOOD MAN YOURSELF.
WHAT JUST--
HE CAN CAMOUFLAGE HIMSELF WHEN HE WANTS TO.
MAN, IT IS NOT EASY KEEPING UP WITH ALL THESE SYMBIOTE ABILITIES.
WELL YOU DON'T HAVE TO KEEP UP WITH ME ANYMORE, SPIDER. WE'RE SQUARE, AND I'M OUTTA HERE.
YOU'RE ALL LUCKY I CAN BARELY STAND.
REALLY, THE BEST THING FOR ME TO DO NOW IS GO HOME, EAT A FUDGIE WHALE, AND TAKE A NAP.
I GOTTA FIND ANDI. BE RIGHT BACK, SPIDEY.
WHUMP

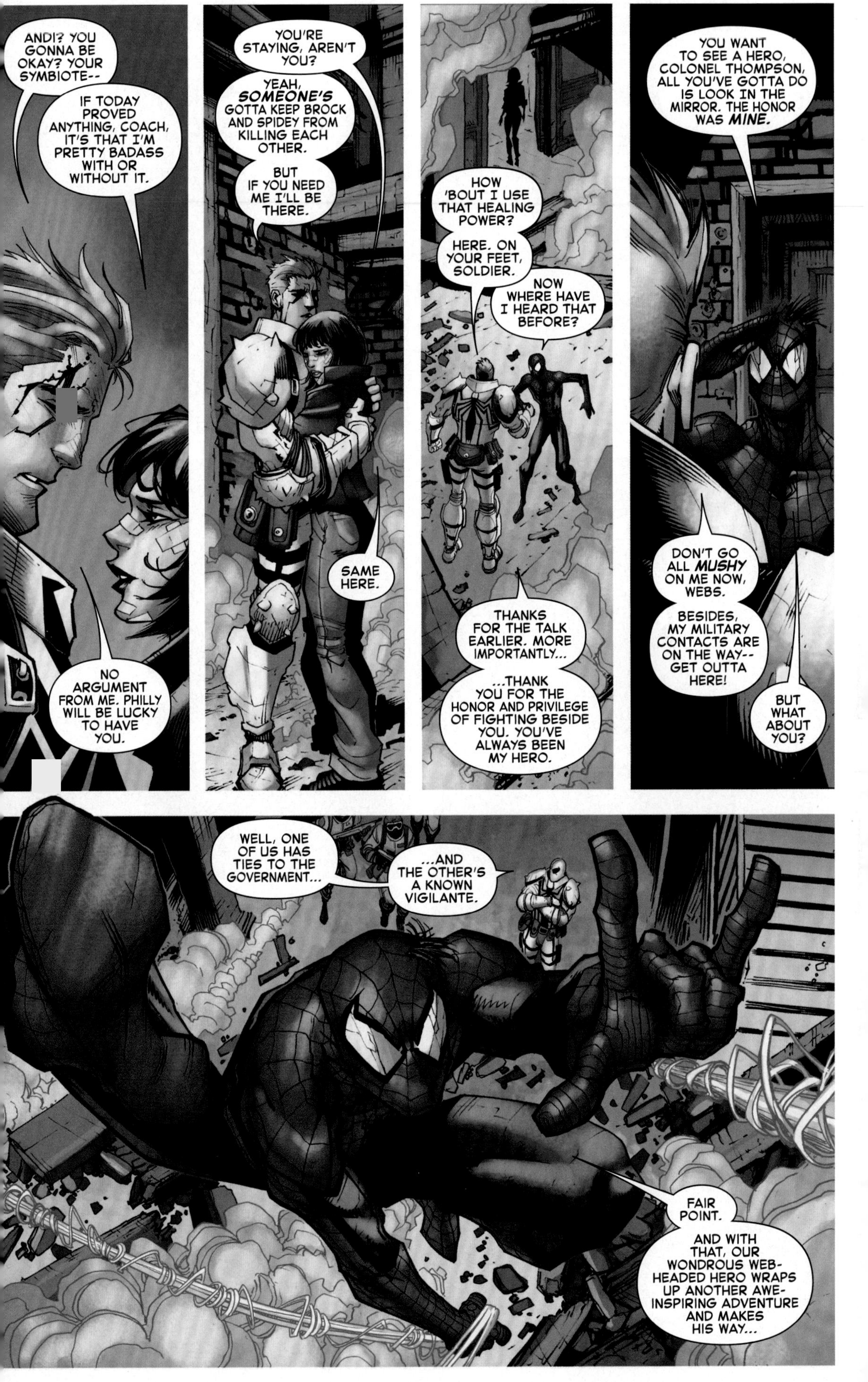
ANDI? YOU GONNA BE OKAY? YOUR SYMBIOTE--
IF TODAY PROVED ANYTHING, COACH, IT'S THAT I'M PRETTY BADASS WITH OR WITHOUT IT.
NO ARGUMENT FROM ME. PHILLY WILL BE LUCKY TO HAVE YOU.
YOU'RE STAYING, AREN'T YOU?
YEAH, SOMEONE'S GOTTA KEEP BROCK AND SPIDEY FROM KILLING EACH OTHER.
BUT IF YOU NEED ME I'LL BE THERE.
SAME HERE.
HOW 'BOUT I USE THAT HEALING POWER?
HERE. ON YOUR FEET, SOLDIER.
NOW WHERE HAVE I HEARD THAT BEFORE?
THANKS FOR THE TALK EARLIER. MORE IMPORTANTLY...
...THANK YOU FOR THE HONOR AND PRIVILEGE OF FIGHTING BESIDE YOU. YOU'VE ALWAYS BEEN MY HERO.
YOU WANT TO SEE A HERO, COLONEL THOMPSON, ALL YOU'VE GOTTA DO IS LOOK IN THE MIRROR. THE HONOR WAS MINE.
DON'T GO ALL MUSHY ON ME NOW, WEBS.
BESIDES, MY MILITARY CONTACTS ARE ON THE WAY--GET OUTTA HERE!
BUT WHAT ABOUT YOU?
WELL, ONE OF US HAS TIES TO THE GOVERNMENT...
...AND THE OTHER'S A KNOWN VIGILANTE.
FAIR POINT.
AND WITH THAT, OUR WONDROUS WEB-HEADED HERO WRAPS UP ANOTHER AWE-INSPIRING ADVENTURE AND MAKES HIS WAY...

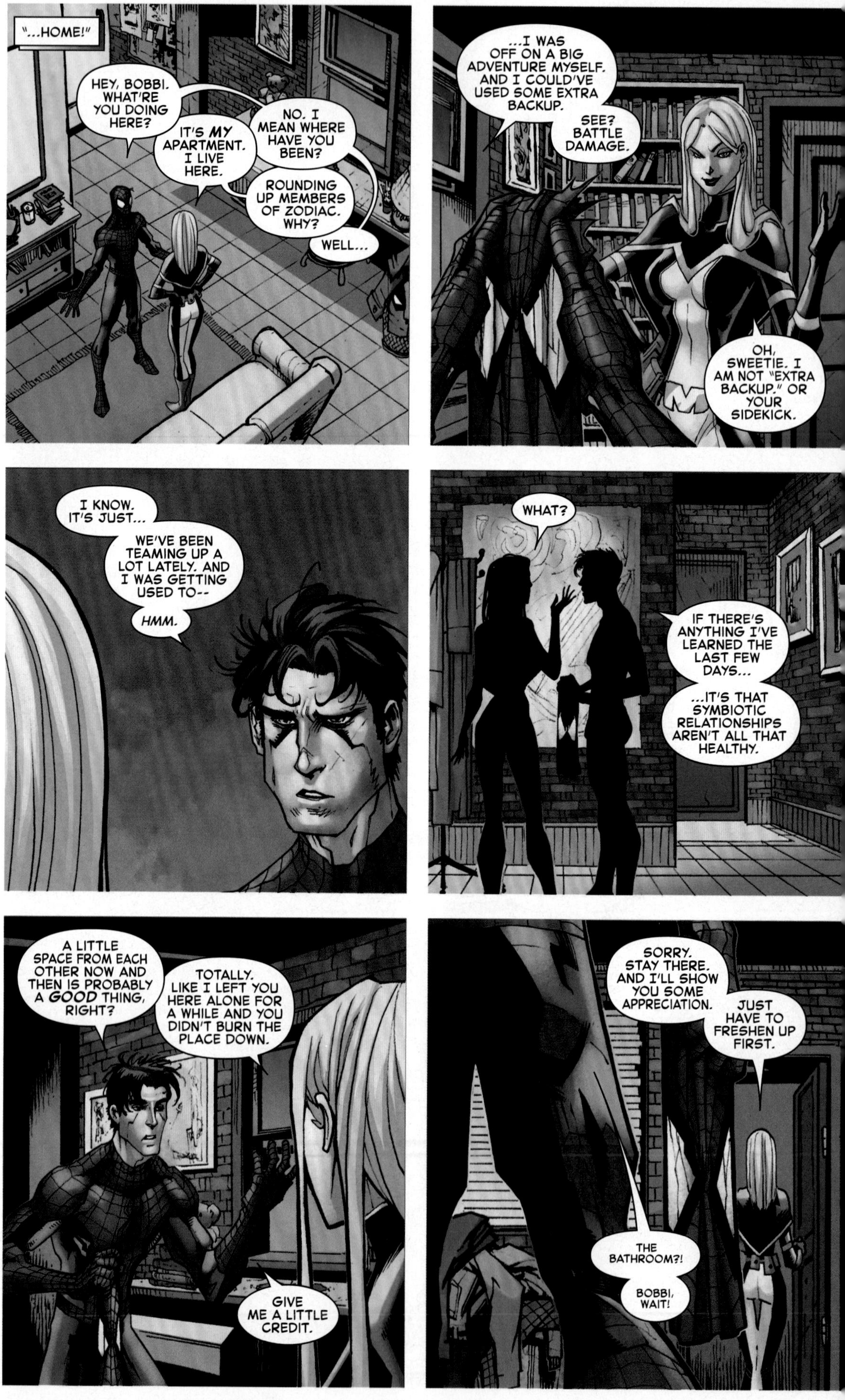

"...HOME!"
HEY, BOBBI. WHAT'RE YOU DOING HERE?
IT'S MY APARTMENT. I LIVE HERE.
NO. I MEAN WHERE HAVE YOU BEEN?
ROUNDING UP MEMBERS OF ZODIAC. WHY?
WELL...
...I WAS OFF ON A BIG ADVENTURE MYSELF. AND I COULD'VE USED SOME EXTRA BACKUP.
SEE? BATTLE DAMAGE.
OH, SWEETIE. I AM NOT "EXTRA BACKUP." OR YOUR SIDEKICK.
I KNOW. IT'S JUST...
WE'VE BEEN TEAMING UP A LOT LATELY. AND I WAS GETTING USED TO--
HMM.
WHAT?
IF THERE'S ANYTHING I'VE LEARNED THE LAST FEW DAYS...
...IT'S THAT SYMBIOTIC RELATIONSHIPS AREN'T ALL THAT HEALTHY.
A LITTLE SPACE FROM EACH OTHER NOW AND THEN IS PROBABLY A GOOD THING, RIGHT?
TOTALLY. LIKE I LEFT YOU HERE ALONE FOR A WHILE AND YOU DIDN'T BURN THE PLACE DOWN.
GIVE ME A LITTLE CREDIT.
SORRY. STAY THERE. AND I'LL SHOW YOU SOME APPRECIATION.
JUST HAVE TO FRESHEN UP FIRST.
THE BATHROOM?!
BOBBI, WAIT!

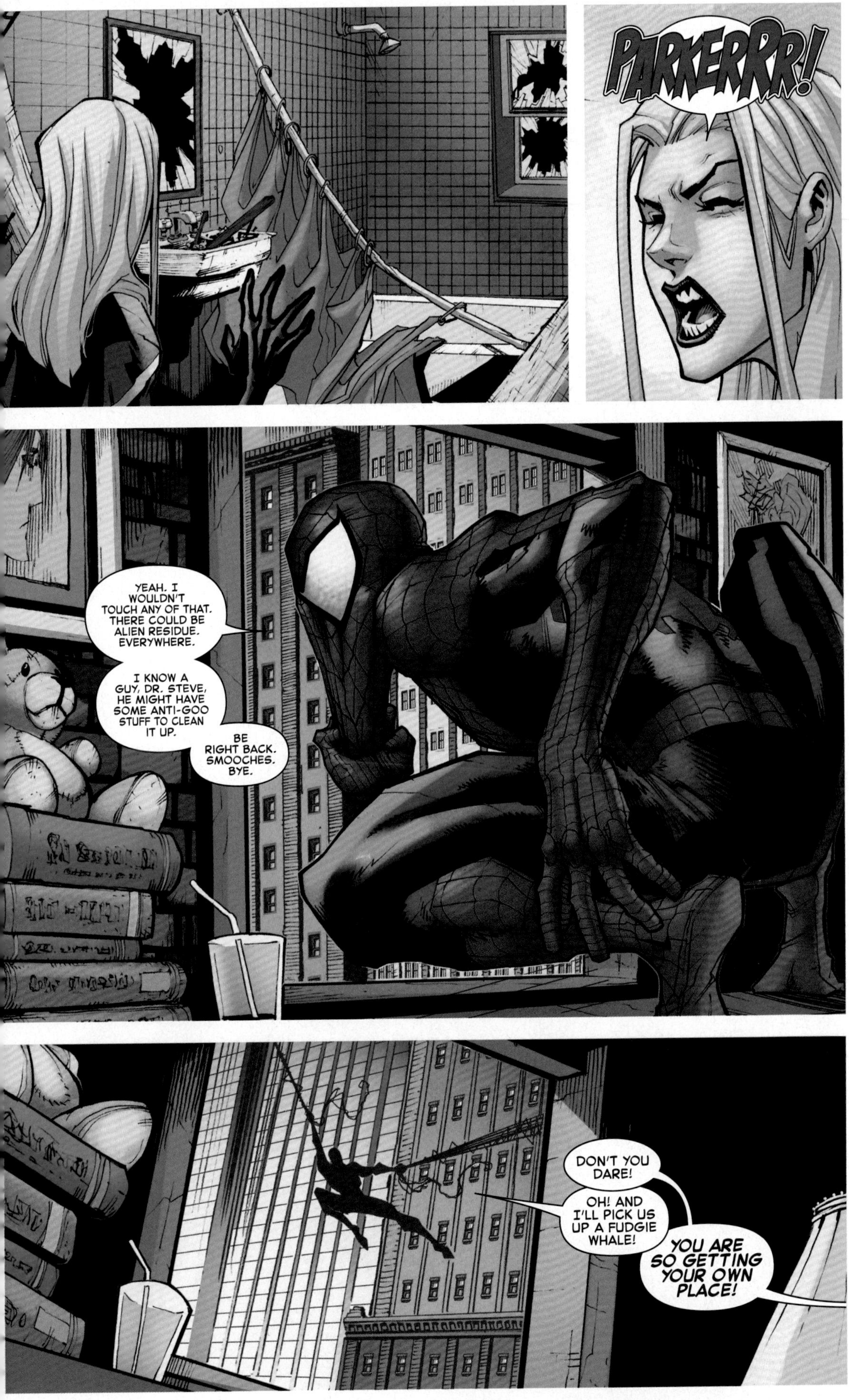
PARKERRR!
YEAH. I WOULDN'T TOUCH ANY OF THAT. THERE COULD BE ALIEN RESIDUE. EVERYWHERE.
I KNOW A GUY, DR. STEVE, HE MIGHT HAVE SOME ANTI-GOO STUFF TO CLEAN IT UP.
BE RIGHT BACK. SMOOCHES. BYE.
DON'T YOU DARE!
OH! AND I'LL PICK US UP A FUDGIE WHALE!
YOU ARE SO GETTING YOUR OWN PLACE!

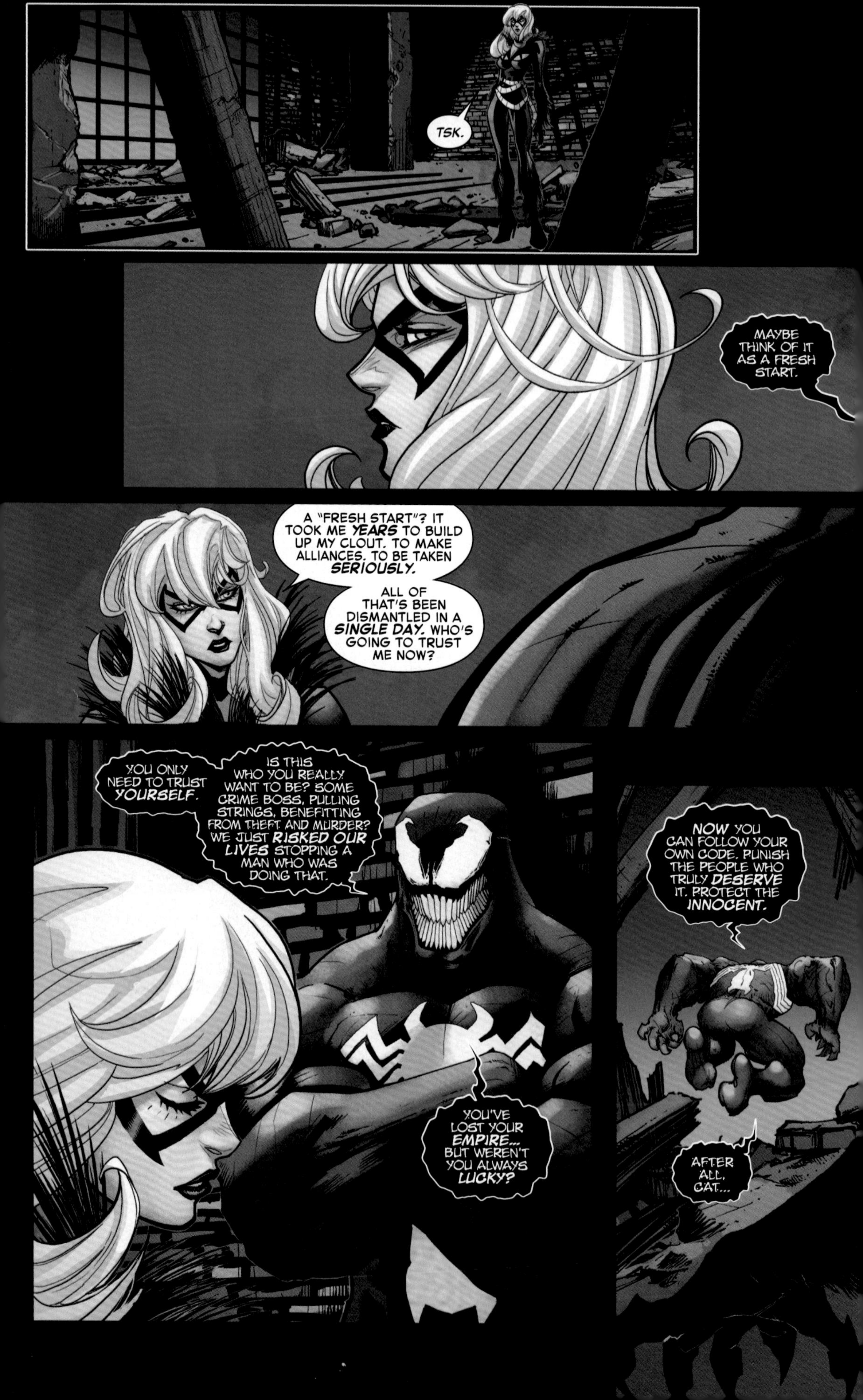
TSK.
MAYBE THINK OF IT AS A FRESH START.
A "FRESH START"? IT TOOK ME YEARS TO BUILD UP MY CLOUT. TO MAKE ALLIANCES. TO BE TAKEN SERIOUSLY.
ALL OF THAT'S BEEN DISMANTLED IN A SINGLE DAY. WHO'S GOING TO TRUST ME NOW?
YOU ONLY NEED TO TRUST YOURSELF.
IS THIS WHO YOU REALLY WANT TO BE? SOME CRIME BOSS, PULLING STRINGS, BENEFITTING FROM THEFT AND MURDER? WE JUST RISKED OUR LIVES STOPPING A MAN WHO WAS DOING THAT.
YOU'VE LOST YOUR EMPIRE... BUT WEREN'T YOU ALWAYS LUCKY?
NOW YOU CAN FOLLOW YOUR OWN CODE. PUNISH THE PEOPLE WHO TRULY DESERVE IT. PROTECT THE INNOCENT.
AFTER ALL, CAT...

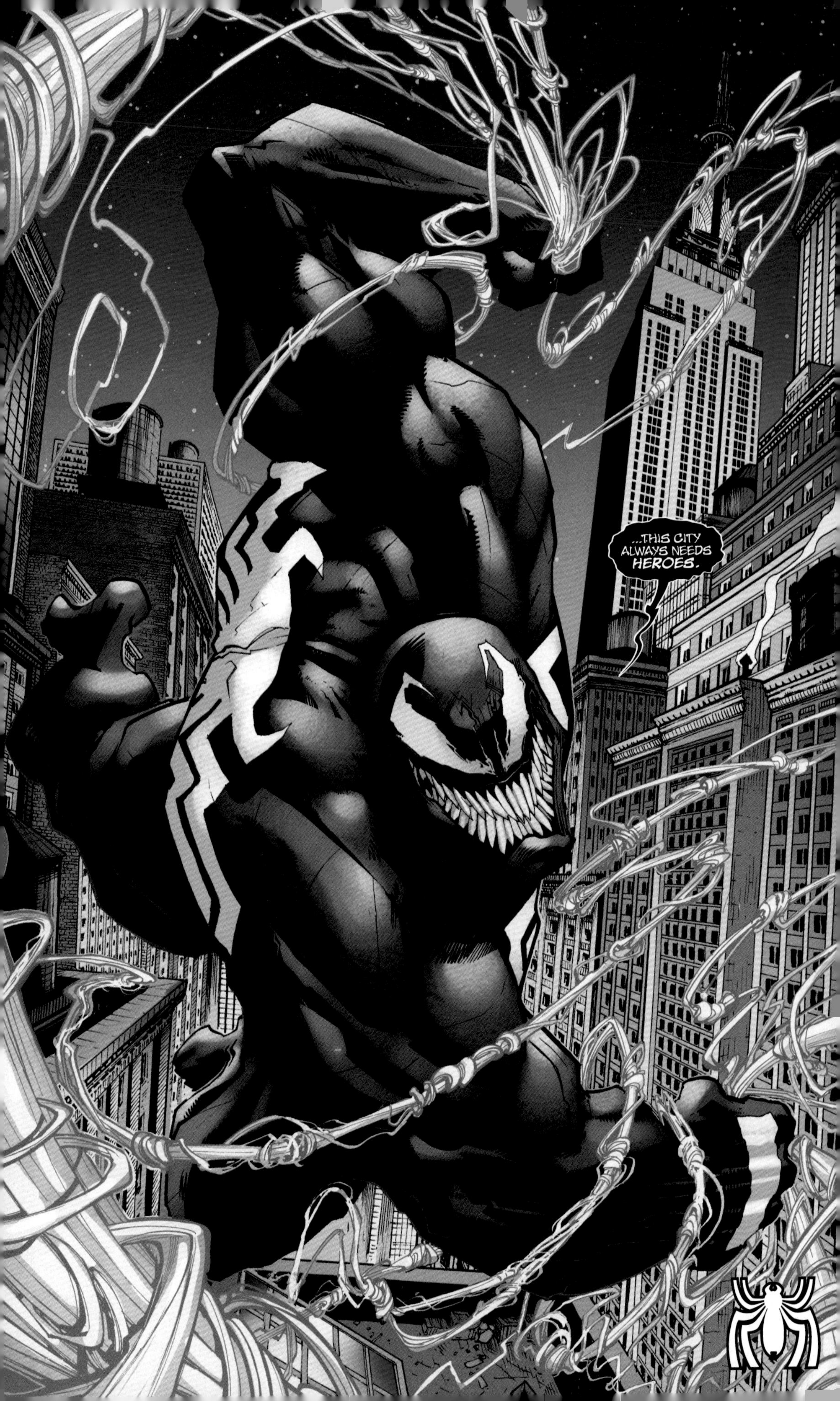
...THIS CITY ALWAYS NEEDS HEROES.

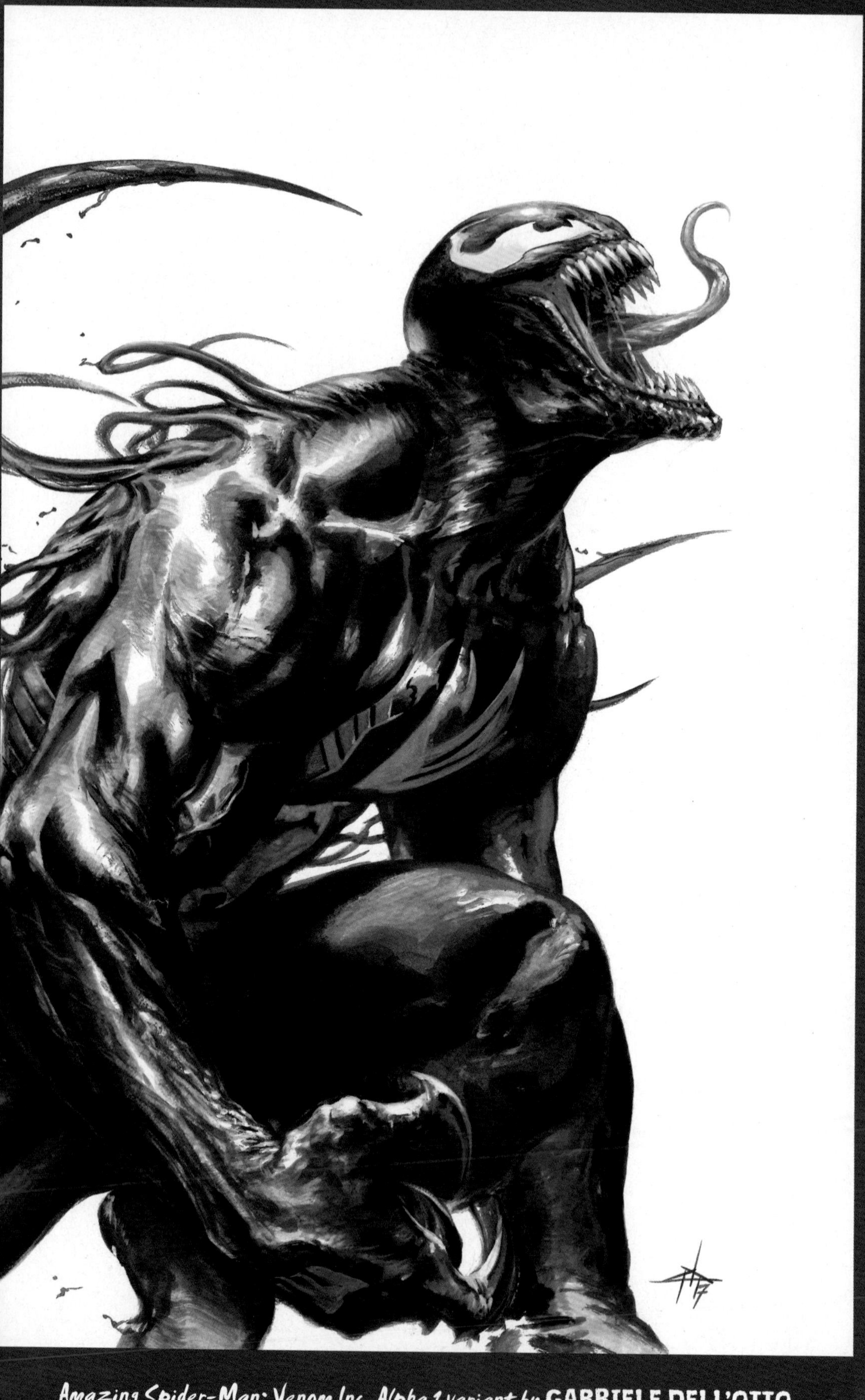

Amazing Spider-Man: Venom Inc. Alpha 1 variant by **GABRIELE DELL'OTTO**

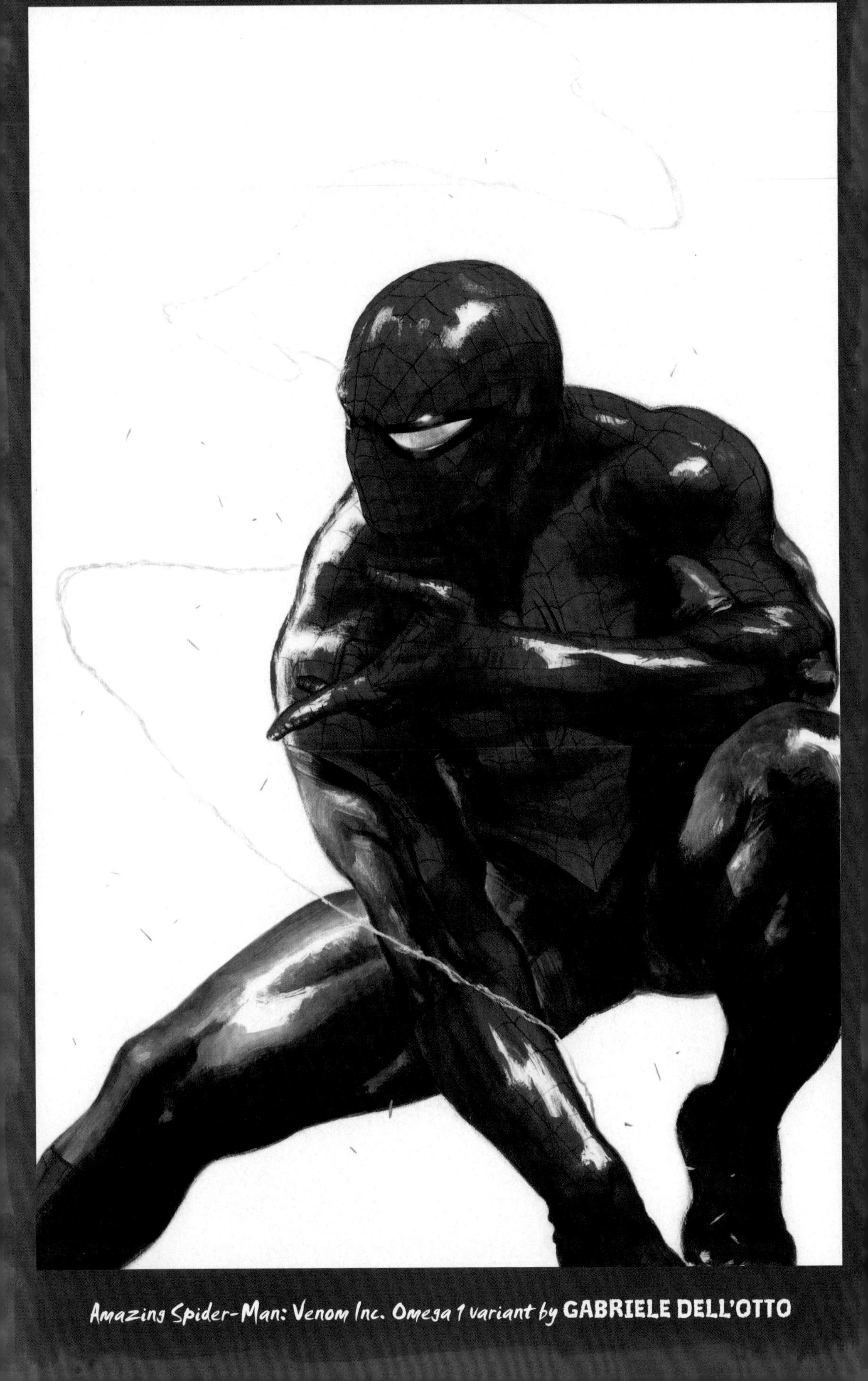

Amazing Spider-Man: Venom Inc. Omega 1 variant by **GABRIELE DELL'OTTO**

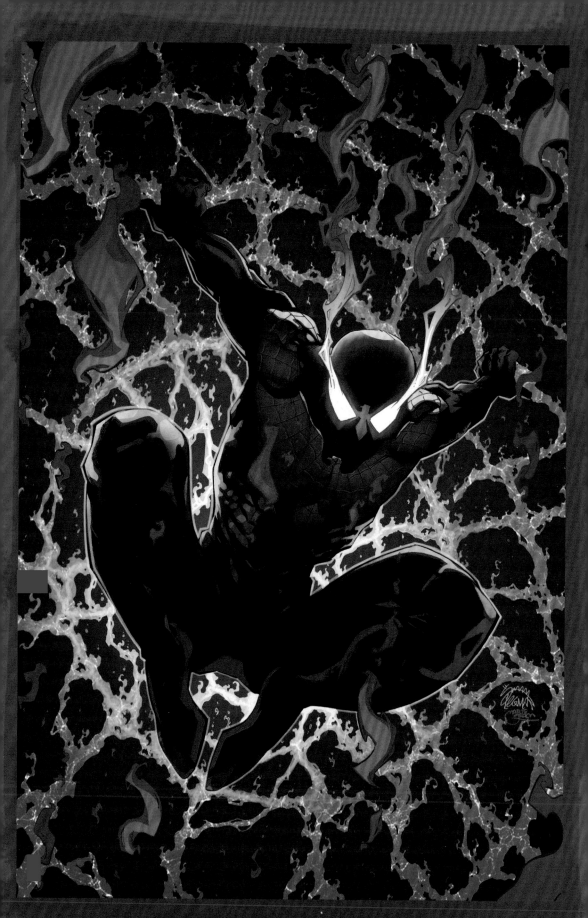

Amazing Spider-Man 792 variant by **RYAN STEGMAN** & **MARTE GRACIA**

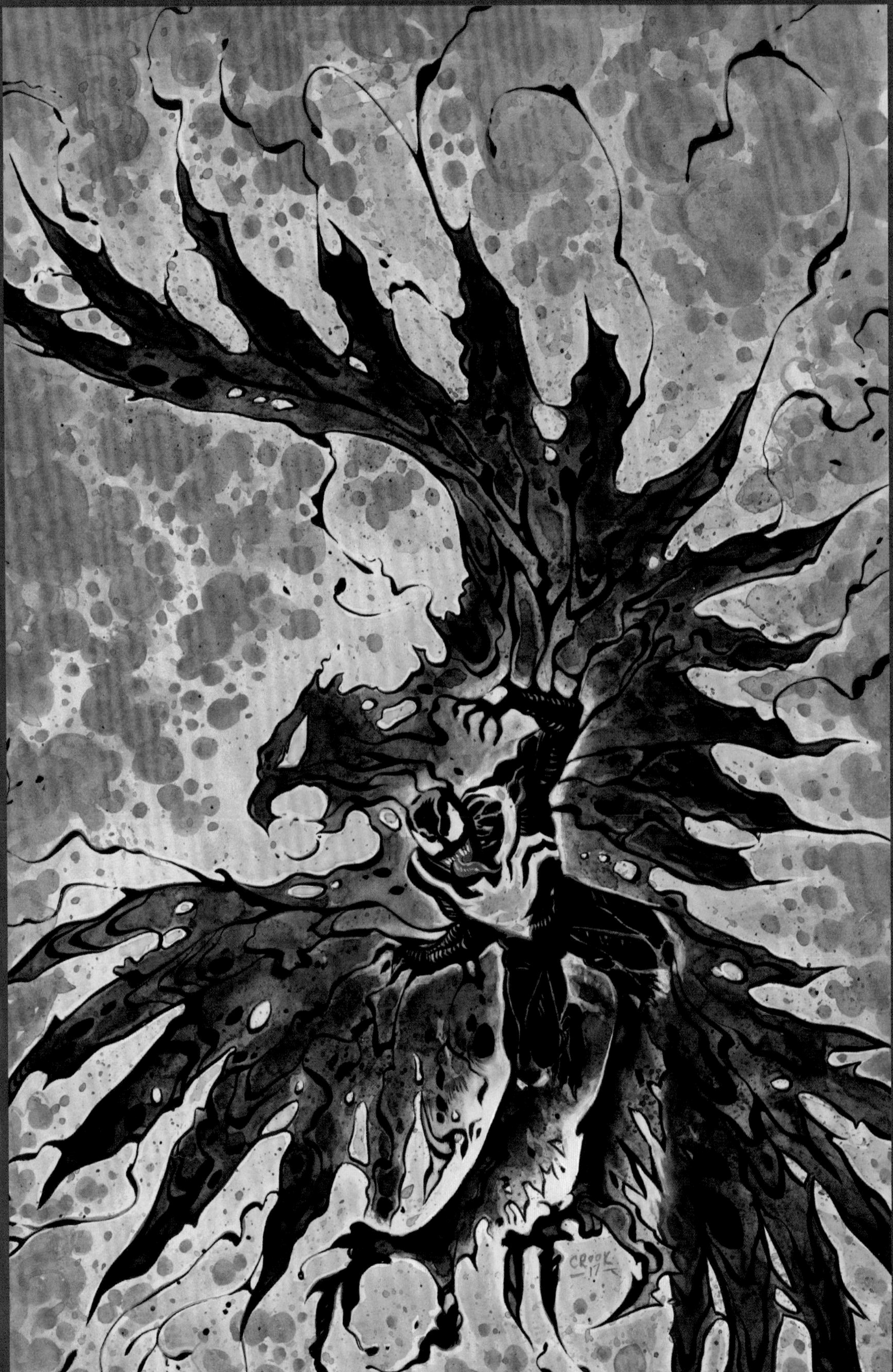
CROOK
'17

Venom 159 variant by **TYLER CROOK**

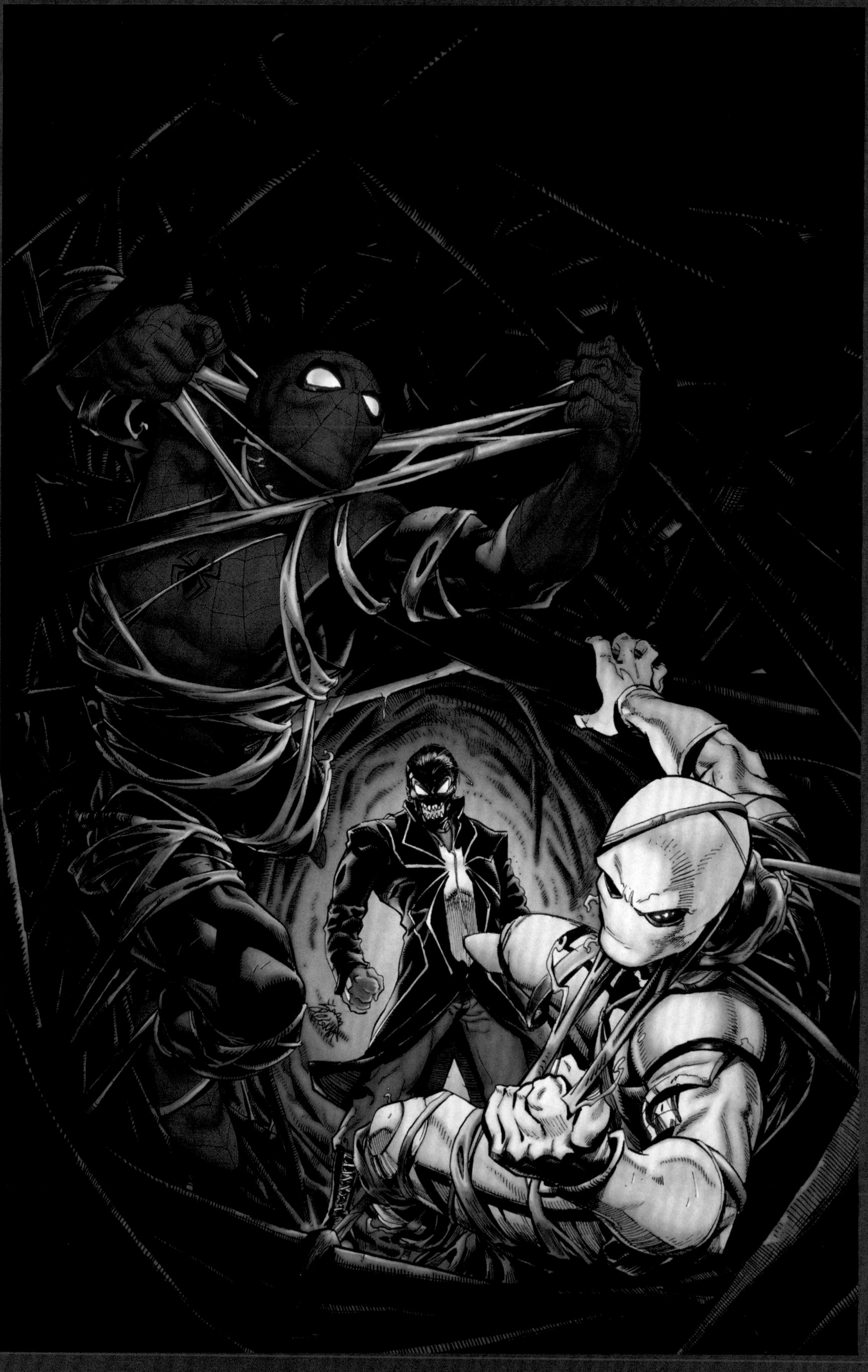

Amazing Spider-Man 792 variant by **RYAN STEGMAN & MORRY HOLLOWELL**

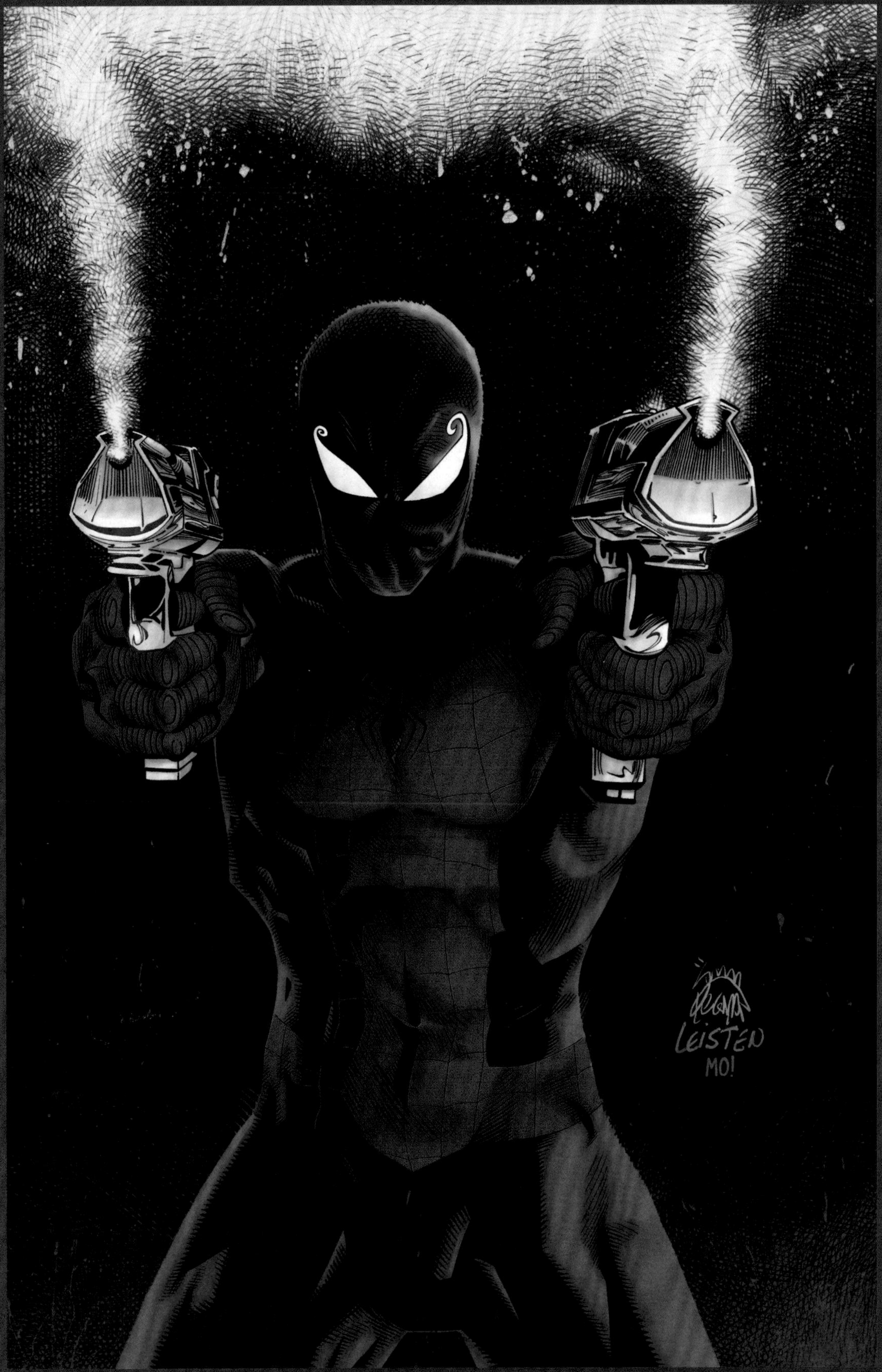
LEISTEN
MO!

Amazing Spider-Man 792 variant
by **RYAN STEGMAN, JAY LEISTEN & MORRY HOLLOWELL**

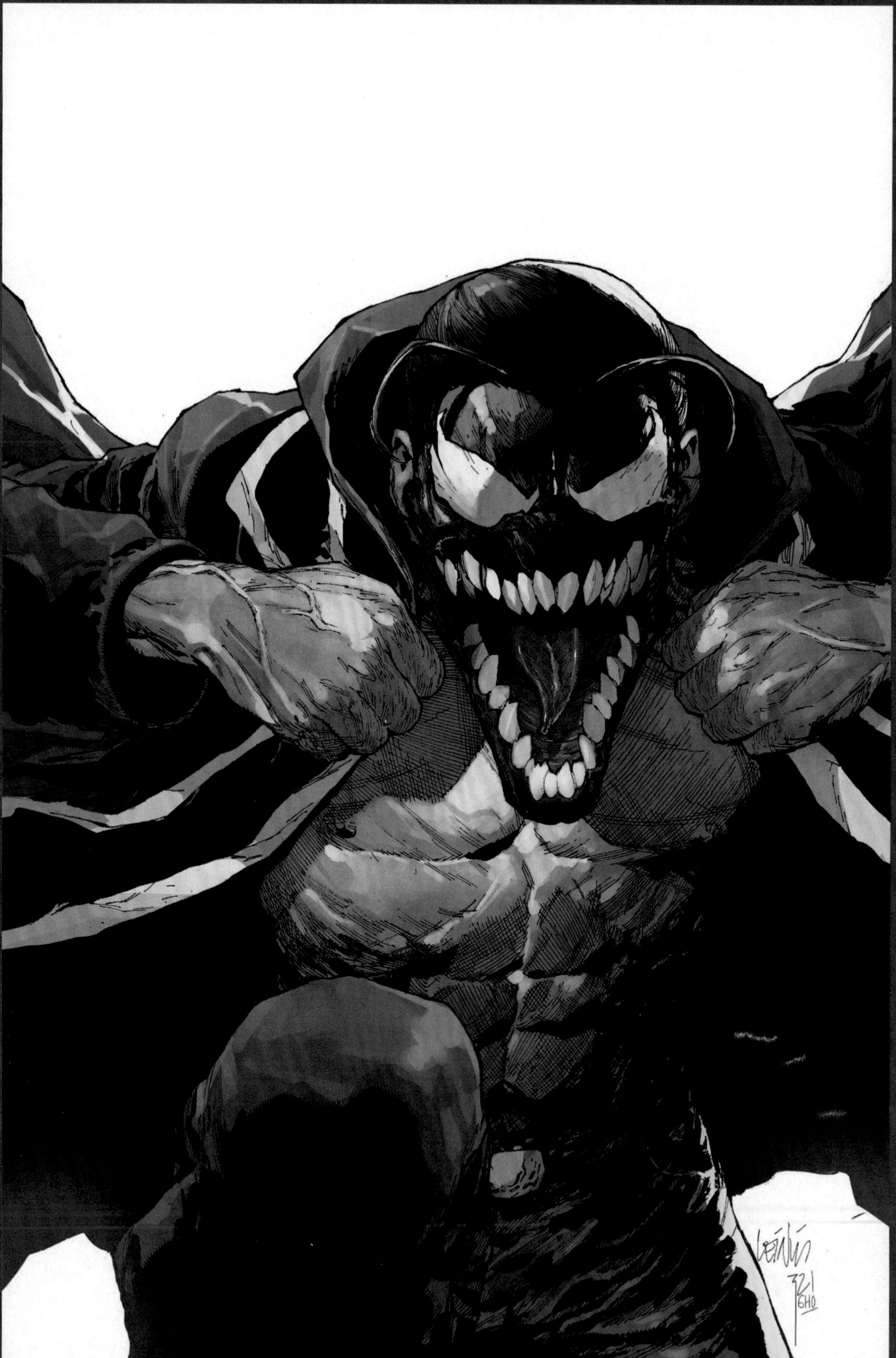

Amazing Spider-Man 792 variant by **LEINIL FRANCIS YU & SUNNY GHO**

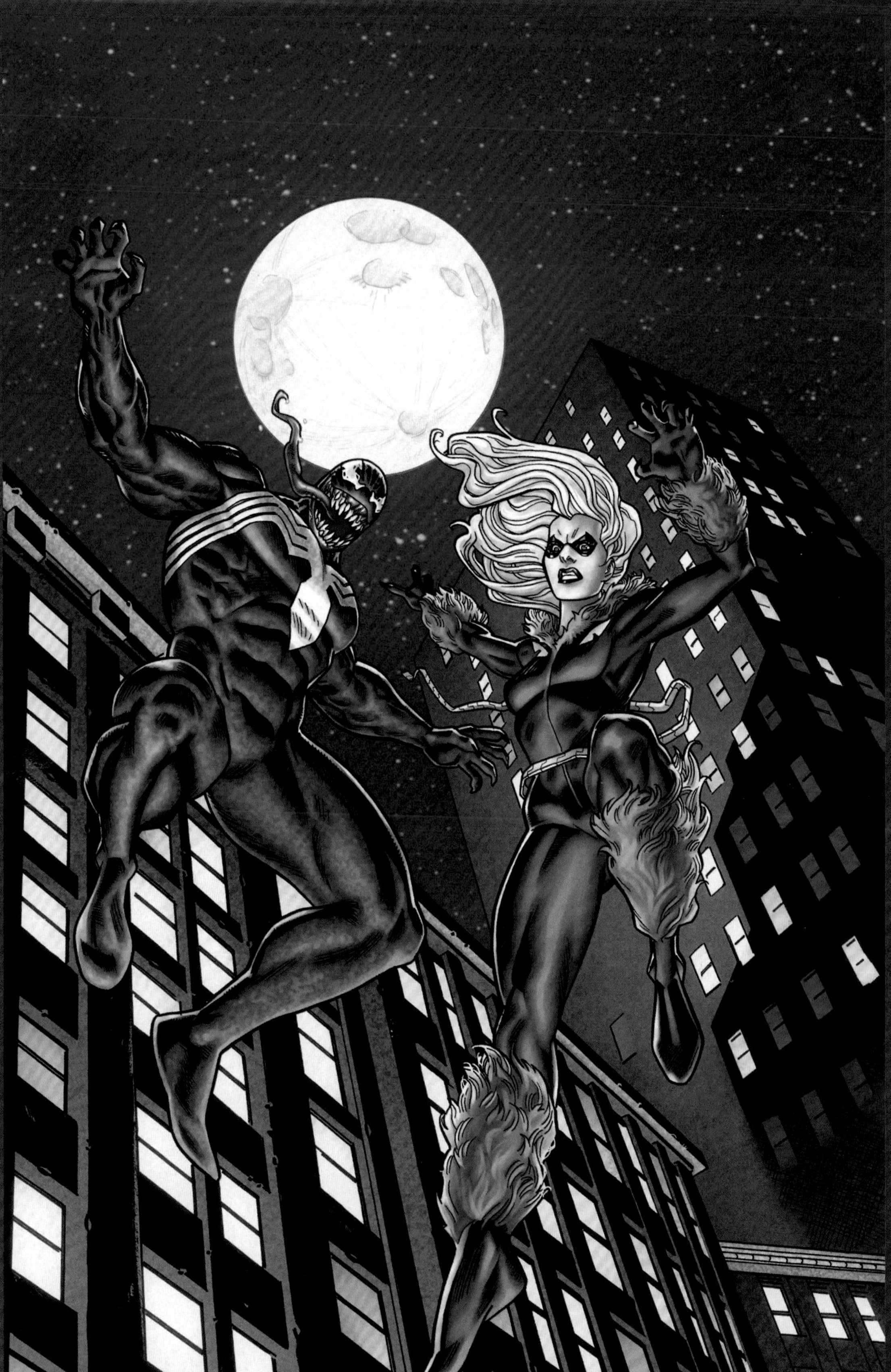

Venom 159 variant
by **MIKE HAWTHORNE & MORRY HOLLOWELL**

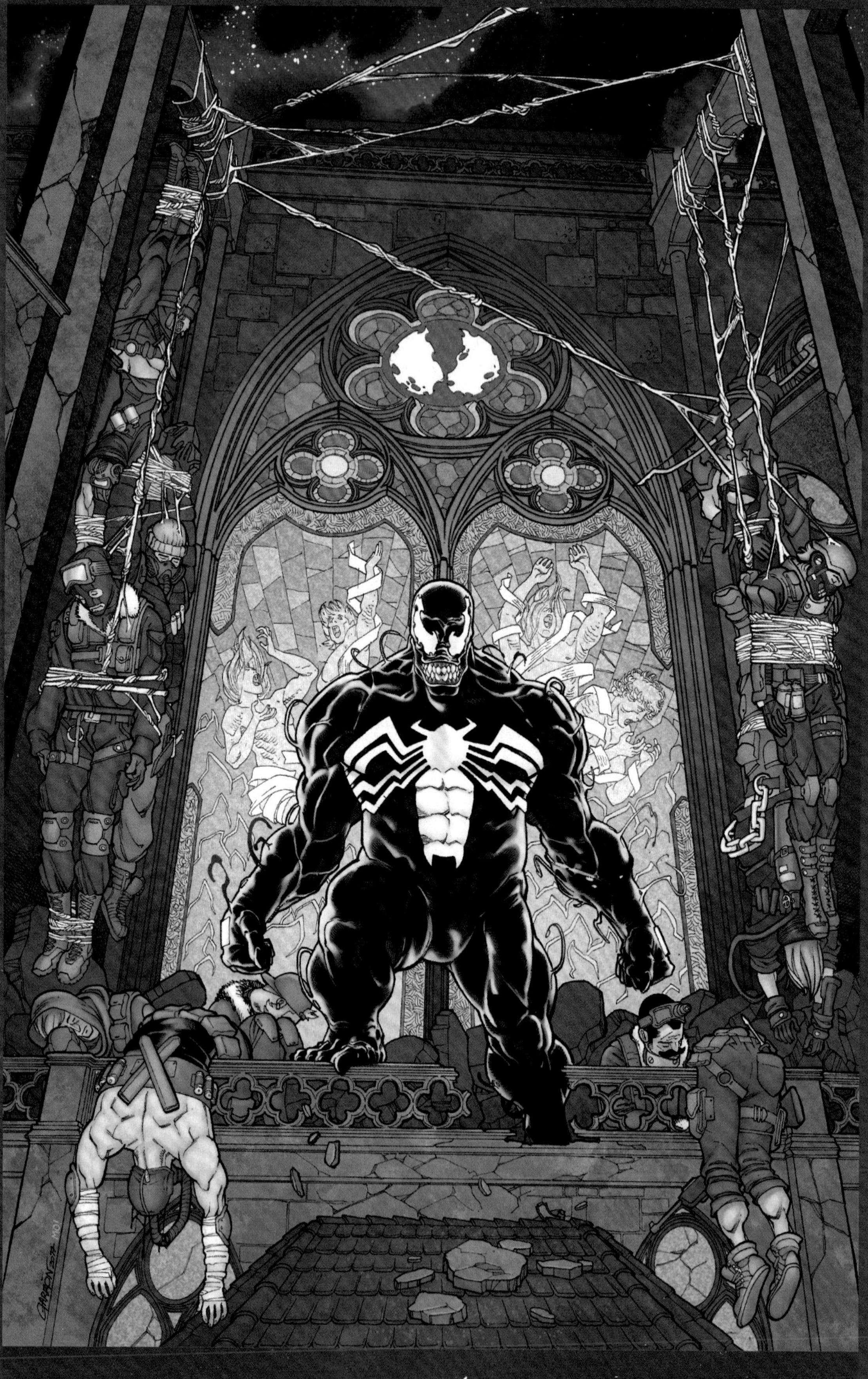

Venom 160 variant by JAVIER GARRÓN & MORRY HOLLOWELL